D1257941

PACE COLLEGE
OPPORTVNITAS
ARS COMMERCIVM CIVITAS
MCMVI
NEW YORK

THE GOLDEN HAZE

RODERICK CAMERON

THE GOLDEN HAZE

with Captain Cook in the South Pacific

THE WORLD PUBLISHING COMPANY
CLEVELAND AND NEW YORK

Published by The World Publishing Company
2231 West 110th Street, Cleveland 2, Ohio

Library of Congress Catalog Card Number: 64-12055

FIRST EDITION

GBWP

Printed in Great Britain.

To

Peggy Bernier and Michael Mahoney

with gratitude for their

sharp pencils

Contents

Illustrations

Illustrations

[*between pages 102 and 103*]

[*between pages 150 and 151*]

[*between pages 166 and 167*]

[*between pages 182 and 183*]

Illustrations

Illustrations

[*between pages 262 and 263*]

[*between pages 278 and 279*]

Illustrations numbers 2, 13, 21, 38, 39, 57, 68, 70, 79 and 82 were photographed by John R. Freeman & Co. Number 16 by the Parker Gallery, number 20 by the National Maritime Museum, numbers 23, 28, 29 by A. Sylvain, Papeete, number 65 by the Zoological Society of London, number 69 by the National Portrait Gallery, number 76 by the Hawaii Visitors' Bureau, numbers 77 and 79 by Fritz Henle and number 83 by Ansel Adams. All other photographs were taken by the author.

The author would also like to express his gratitude to the National History Museum, London, for allowing him to reproduce their engraving of Carl Daniel Solander, also the drawing of a breadfruit by Sydney Parkinson and the colour wash of the sea bird by George Forster, both plates having been taken from originals, hitherto unpublished. His thanks are also due to the National Portrait Gallery for allowing him to photograph their engravings of James King and John Webber. Fritz Henle's photographs appear in an album of his entitled Hawaii, *published by Hasting House, New York in 1948 and Ansel Adams' photograph was expressly taken for a commemorative album celebrating the one-hundredth anniversary of the Bishop National Bank of Hawaii.*

Maps

Acknowledgements

I would like to express my indebtedness to the many people who helped me while on my travels in the South Pacific. It is thanks to their guidance that I was able to glimpse a side of life not always apparent to the stranger. I cannot sufficiently express my gratitude to Bengt Danielsson and his wife in Tahiti and the charming Etienne and Pauline Schyle, also the intuitive Madame Natua, who told me so much about the Pomarés, to whom she is related. In New Caledonia Luc Chevalier the curator of the Bernheim Museum at Noumea proved an excellent and ever-willing guide, so also did the British Resident of the New Hebrides. The Bishop Museum of Honolulu was also most co-operative and thanks to their librarians I was able to sift through much valuable material, some of it not yet available in print. Among their published works I would like to make particular mention of *Ancient Tahiti* by Teuira Henry based on notes recorded by Rev. J. M. Orsmond, Miss Henry's grandfather, and collected by him during the early years of the preceding century. This book is of primary importance to anyone making a study of Polynesian history.

On this side of the ocean I would like to express my thanks to the British Museum of Natural History and to the ever resourceful Mrs St George Saunders, director of the invaluable *Writers and Readers Research*, but above all others it is Dr Beaglehole I would single out. I cannot praise sufficiently the splendid service he has rendered the English-speaking public in editing *Cook's Voyages*, a task undertaken for the Hakluyt Society. His edition of the famous voyages must be regarded as the definitive work as far as this particular subject is concerned and no serious study of Pacific discoveries can be undertaken without reference to these volumes. His notes and wise assessments were of inestimable help to the author who has quoted from them liberally.

Last but not least is the energetic Miss Molesworth of International Services Limited, a travel agency capable of such personal service that they even supply letters of introduction for their clients from members of the Foreign Office to people in the most improbable places.

LA FIORENTINA
ST JEAN CAP FERRAT A.M.
JUNE 1963

Track of Endeavour 1768, 1769, 1770 and 1771.

Tracks of Reso

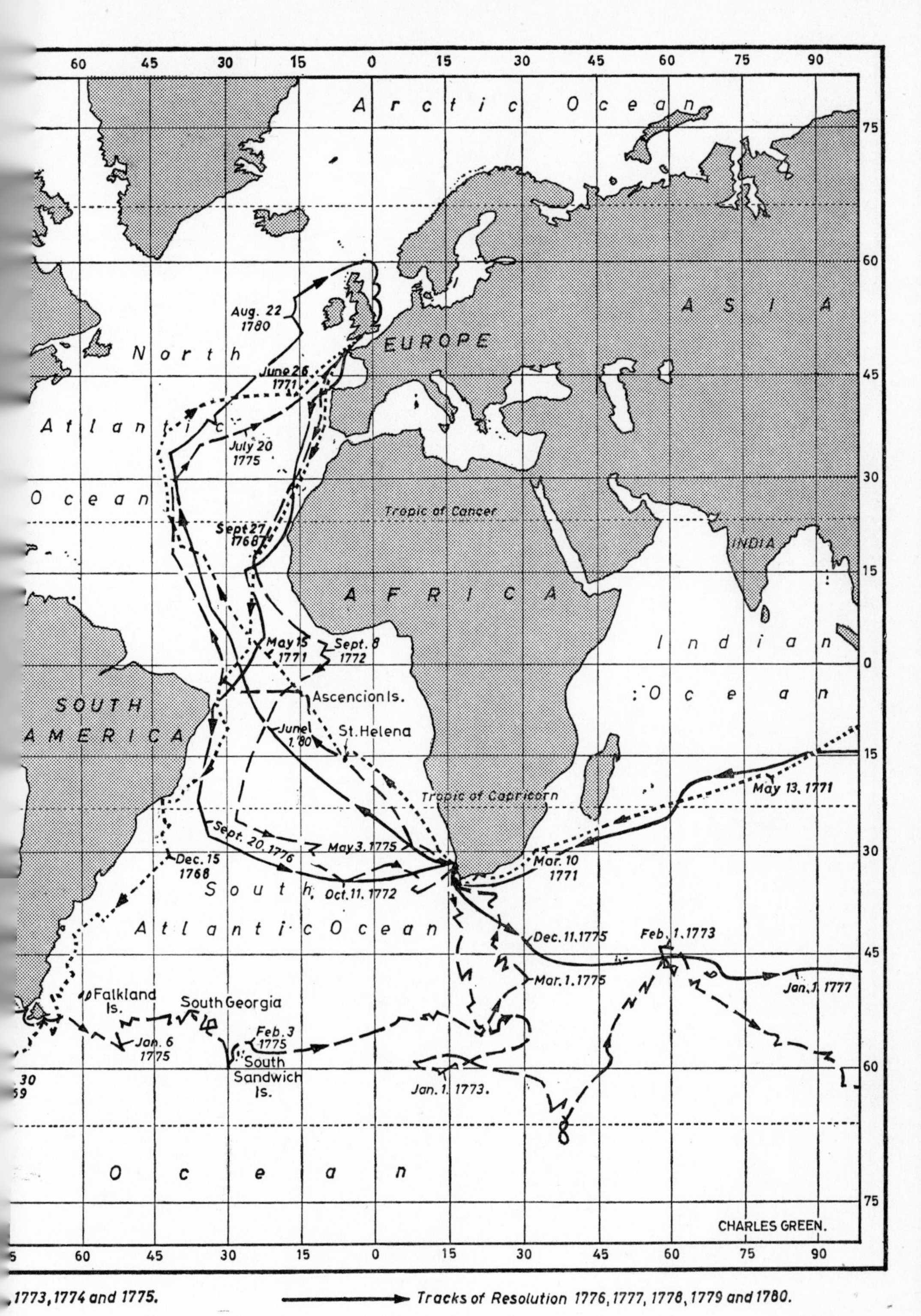

, 1773, 1774 and 1775. Tracks of Resolution 1776, 1777, 1778, 1779 and 1780.

B

[Chapter 1]

Preliminaries

A COUPLE of years ago, when I was suddenly asked if I had a subject for a new book, I heard myself answering, much to my own surprise, that I should like to write about the South Pacific. Why I made this announcement, I am still not quite sure. Perhaps because, apart from a visit to the Australian Great Barrier Reef, I had seen so little of that region of the world. But, once I had announced my plan, I felt obliged to go ahead, and bought a map, which made my temerity appear even more astonishing: for there, scattered across an endless stretch of waters, I saw an irregular galaxy of small islands, an expanse that at its broadest point – between Panama and Mindanas in the Philippines – measures over 10,000 miles, an area greater than the whole land surface of the globe.

Its population, I discovered, fell roughly into three main ethnic groups, and the islands and islets, geologically speaking, into three completely different classes. Some are large land masses, cut off during the remote past from a nearby continent; some are isolated islands, or clusters of islands, thrown up from the ocean depths; some extend in crescent-shaped formations, often a thousand miles long, the last being coral atolls, built by busy insect colonies.

As for the historical background of the regions I hoped to describe, I learned that they had probably been settled about five hundred years after the birth of Christ, when adventurers, coming from Asia by way of Micronesia, crossed the ocean from island to island, with Tahiti as their central base. No one can tell us what impelled this invasion, but clearly it was led by brave and capable navigators, who understood the currents and the winds. We also hear of inspired prophets, seers who pointed towards the rising sun and spoke of a promised land just beyond the eastern skyline. There must have been many disasters before the goal was reached: many expeditions must have vanished without a trace. The distances they sailed were gigantic; and the ablest primitive seamen would sometimes have committed fatal errors.

As I read, I was dismayed by the prospect of attempting to cover this enormous territory – and then, I was reluctant to destroy an illusion. So little in the world today remains mysterious. Why forfeit another imaginary paradise? I had already admired and enjoyed the Tropics. I remembered the coasts of Ceylon, half-obscured by the waves' mist-like spume; nights on the beaches of Zanzibar, the land-crabs clattering home over heaps of dry weed; Mombasa, and another type of crab, tiny, ethereal pink-and-white crustacea, that dance in their thousands amid the breaking surf. The Tropics, I knew, were full of enchantment; but, for the European traveller, now and then they are entirely tedious.

Nevertheless, having embarked on my plan, I decided I must persevere. I do not regret my decision. Besides enlarging my knowledge of the world, I collected a series of extraordinarily vivid pictures. For example, a glimpse of a native bar at Papeete. A couple – not fat, but solidly built, as Polynesians almost always are – were performing the *tamure*, the local erotic dance. They wore loose-brimmed pandanas hats, tilted back, turned up on one side, and encircled with wreaths of big flowers. The girl reminded me of the portrait of a beauty at the court of Ludwig I, hung in the Schönheits Galerie in Munich. Her long black hair flowed down her spine, and she scarcely moved her straight shoulders. The befuddled crowd wore wreaths of fern. It was a scene that recalled a tavern in Imperial Rome.

Next, my search for the site of Gauguin's house, when a native boy, who might have emerged from one of the master's most romantic and exotic pictures, came galloping down the beach on an unsaddled white pony. Rupert Brooke's was another ghost I followed. A Frenchman at Mataiea showed me the stream by which he used to sit. He spent several months in Tahiti, wore a *pareu* like the natives – who called him Pupure, which means 'fair' – seldom went into the town and wrote, among others, his lovely poem *Retrospect*. The building where he lodged has vanished; and so has the wooden pier, 'with deep clear water for diving', mentioned in a letter to his mother. But the stream still flows into the Pacific, past the Frenchman's new square, ugly house. I doubt if he has ever heard of Brooke, but he is a professional *yaourt* culturist, and gave me some interesting advice about his trade.

Not all the pictures I gathered were derived from Tahiti. Once, stranded at Noumea, the sad capital of New Caledonia, in a hideous bungalow-hotel which, French though it was, did not include a kitchen or a dining-room, I was advised to visit the private aquarium kept by a Monsieur and Madame Catala-Stucky. There I saw clumps of phosphorescent corals, lit by ultra-violet rays and glowing through the artificial dusk in tones of vivid red, mauve, green and electric blue. But best of all was the only *Nautilus Pompilus* in captivity, its heavy reddish-brown porcelain shell striped like the fur of a tortoise-shell cat. That shell I had seen often enough; but the nautilus itself, a member of the octopus family, is very seldom caught alive. A creature of the depths, if it is too rapidly brought to the surface it suffers from 'bends', as do unwary human divers. But Madame Catala-Stucky's specimen appeared to be in perfect health. Obediently, with the help of its siphon, it moved up to her submerged hand, extended its tentacles, accepted a lump of fish, packed the gift into its mouth and then retired to a corner of the tank, where it gradually absorbed its meal.

From New Caledonia, my recollections take me on to Tonga, Hawaii and the New Hebrides. In Tonga, Ve'ehala, the keeper of the Royal Records, gave me a recital on his nose-flute. We were sitting in his office at Nuku'alofa, the capital of the island, preparatory to visiting Queen Salote's palace, when, unexpectedly, he put his flute to his nose, blocked one nostril with a thumb and breathed gently down the instrument. The subject of his tune was the sorrow of a seagull who, at the hour of dawn, discovers she has lost a feather.

On Tonga, the Beach House is the only boarding-house or hotel. It included some curious human beings – a young Australian tattooed from head to foot, with a butterfly on his private parts and a little blue daisy inscribed on each toe, who assured me that he had sold his epidermis to a Sydney museum for two thousand pounds; and a frail, deaf old man, shunned by his fellow-boarders, who was hard at work compiling a Tongan grammar for the Oxford University Press. An ordained minister, he had been asked to officiate on Sundays at the Chapel Royal. The service was conducted in English, but the hymns were sung in Tongan. My new friend was, of course, bilingual, and once, as he was energetically bawling out a hymn, I noticed that he abruptly paused. In the Tongan version of 'From Greenland's Icy Mountains', he had just become aware of an egregious mistake!

Finally, amid a very different archipelago, lying some thirteen hundred miles to the north-east, I visited the delightfully unpretentious little Kona Hulikee Palace, on the western shore of the main island of Hawaii, once the favourite summer residence of the Hawaiian royal family. There had been a storm, and from behind a huge slate-blue cloud escaped a golden shaft of sunlight. I climbed to the upper floor, and entered a bedroom with pointed Gothic windows, containing a large four-poster bed. Its feet were carved in the semblance of pine-apples, and surmounting the bedposts were small tasselled cushions supporting royal crowns.

But I must return to the primary purpose of my journey. At the onset, it occurred to me that Captain Cook's three famous voyages across the Pacific might provide the connecting thread I needed. What better guide could I hope to find? I could concentrate on his Pacific travels, thus restricting myself to the so-called 'South Seas', an area that stretched from tropic to tropic, from about 160° West to 130° East, a parallelogram of 70° by 47°; and I would describe only the islands that Cook had visited on his two ships, the *Endeavour* and the *Resolution*.

Except for Easter Island and the Marquesas, all these islands or island-groups – New Caledonia, the New Hebrides, Tonga, Tahiti, Hawaii – are now accessible by plane. It is a question of reaching the main island of each archipelago, then arranging one's own itinerary. For instance, to visit Tana, Eromanga and Malekula in the New Hebrides, I was obliged to charter a fifty-foot launch, the *Trudy*, which belonged to a young Australian shell-diver.

In New Caledonia, on the other hand, to visit the Isle of Pines, I bumped through the clouds with the Curator of the Noumea Museum aboard a hired Puss Moth. My most primitive means of transport was the local yawl that took me to the islands of Lifuka and Nomuka in the Tongan group, under the command of a youthful navigator from Nuku'alofa, whose uniform was a string of pearls and a large straw hat. Less primitive, but even more uncomfortable, was the converted Thames steamer on which I travelled to Eua, some fifty miles south-west of Tonga. She had changed her name, but kept her flat keel, and pitched like a barge as soon as she had left behind the protective reefs of Tongatapu, often plunging down into the hollow of the waves until only sea and sky were visible; and I began to remember how many craft had vanished mysteriously in the Pacific.

Thus, sometimes on sea, sometimes in the air, I did my best to follow Cook's three voyages. His Journals are everywhere my main source, but, now and then, I have included material drawn from the travel literature of other periods – from Orsmond and Ellis, missionaries who devoted their lives to exploring and describing Polynesia: and from travellers and writers as diverse as Bougainville, Kotzebüe, Krusenstern, Langsdorff, Melville, Keable and Calderon. My personal impressions I have employed chiefly to supplement the accounts given by Cook and his associates, and to answer the queries that their accounts raise: Is the Bay of Moorea still as beautiful as when the *Endeavour* anchored there? Does Tana's volcano still spew forth 'prodigious clouds of smoke', succeeded by 'loud bellowings'?

Cook's Tahiti had already vanished a hundred years after he discovered it. 'Tahiti,' writes Chateaubriand in 1826, 'a perdu ses danses, ses choeurs, ses moeurs voluptueuses. Les belles habitantes de la Nouvelle Cythère expient dans un grand ennui la trop grande gaité de leur mère' – and this surely is the nostalgia that we find in all of Gauguin's Tahitian paintings. And we are indebted to Cook for the diligence and accuracy with which he noted down his observations. He prided himself, above all, upon his love of truth, and was not ashamed to confess the limitations of his own knowledge. 'I have learned so little,' he admits when discussing Polynesian religious faiths, 'that I hardly dare to talk upon it.'

His Journal, nevertheless, is an extraordinarily interesting and informative document. But, having studied his narrative and the narratives of his companions, I wished to know more of the circumstances that led up to the voyages, of the personalities of the men who had sailed with him, and of the life they had shared aboard the *Endeavour* and the *Resolution.* These details I found particularly attractive; for, as Hawkesworth remarks, 'the participants in such expeditions have generally looked only upon the great outlines of nature, without attending to the variety of shades within'. It was the shades that I hoped to supply. At the same time, I must not lose sight of the grand purpose of Cook's journey. He had been commissioned to observe an important astronomical event – the transit of the planet Venus.

[Chapter 2]

The Transit of Venus

THE TRANSIT of Venus is not a particularly spectacular occurrence: revolving round the sun inside the earth's orbit, Venus sometimes transits the face of the sun and is seen as a small black dot stealing its way across the gassy flames. Important deductions can be made from its passage – the scale of the solar system and the distance of the earth from the sun.

This transit is a rare occurrence, for Venus does not pass directly between the earth and the sun at every revolution. Venus and the sun do not lie quite in the same plane, hence the planet usually passes just over, or just under, the sun. The few occasions that the earth, Venus and the sun all lie in a straight line happen only four times in 243 years, and to complicate matters further, the intervals between the transits are irregular, being from eight to over a hundred years apart. The first transit to be actually observed was in 1639, seen by Jeremiah Horrox, a young clergyman. It was a Sunday morning and his clerical duties interfered considerably with his observations, 'but in the afternoon he saw the phenomenon plain'. Little, however, of much importance was learned from his zeal. It was only forty years later that Edmond Halley, the Astronomer-Royal, suggested that the transit of Venus be utilized for the determination of the solar parallax. He foresaw the re-occurrence in 1761 and again in 1769 and gave a lecture to the Royal Society on the subject. Not expecting to be present himself – he was born in 1656 – he laid down instructions for young astronomers 'who may, perhaps, live to observe these things'.

As it happened, the observation of 1761 proved unsuccessful, so that of June 3rd 1769 became of singular importance, for there would not be another transit until 1874. The Royal Society, whose concern was that of improving natural knowledge, took a lively interest in the occurrence and after several meetings eventually petitioned the King, urging him not to neglect this chance of furthering the fame 'in the learned world' of British astronomy, 'a science', they pointed out, 'on which navigation so much depends'. Several European nations, notably Russia, were interested in establishing points of observation, and England, they argued, should certainly do the same.

The Royal Society, chartered by Charles II in 1662, was considered the world's most distinguished scientific body and their memorial carried some weight with the King. George III, anyway, was interested in science and exploration and the idea of sending an expedition to the great South Sea to observe the transit of Venus appealed to him. He immediately agreed to defray the expenses of the undertaking, granting £4,000 and a ship belonging to the Navy.

The Royal Society's memorial was dated February 15th 1768 and already by March 5th the Admiralty wrote to the Navy Board instructing them that 'it was His Majesty's pleasure that a proper vessel be prepared to sail early in spring'. It was essential that the observers, who were to pass the equinoctial line, should leave early in spring 'because it might be some time before they could fix upon a proper place for making the observations within the limits required'.

The Marquesas, discovered by Mendana in 1595, or the then islands of Rotterdam and Amsterdam (now called Nomuka and Tongatapu) discovered by Tasman in 1643, were first considered as the best places then known for making such observations. It was the return of Captain Wallis in the *Dolphin* in May 1768 with the news of the discovery of a paradise inhabited by friendly natives, christened by him George's Island (now known exclusively as Tahiti), that finally decided the matter. Still more important than the charm of the island was the fact that its position had been firmly fixed and would therefore not have to be 'rediscovered' as would probably have been the case with the other islands. When one considers the vastness of the Pacific, being almost twice the size of the Atlantic and three times the size of the Indian Ocean, the idea of navigating its unknown spaces appals one. Indeed, the Marquesas and the Tongatapu group would have been fatally easy to miss, particularly as their discovery had been made before scientific methods of fixing the positions had been worked out with any accuracy. Their 'rediscovery' would have been largely a matter of chance.

But we are jumping ahead and must return to the vital question of the ship. The Navy Board immediately made several suggestions, but the ships mentioned either would take too long to refurbish or were too small. Eventually the Deptford yard proposed a coaling ship called the *Earl of Pembroke*. By the 29th of March she had been purchased for the sum of £2,307 and renamed the *Endeavour* – or to be more precise Bark *Endeavour* to distinguish her from another vessel in the Royal Navy of the same name. There seems to be no record of who actually christened her, presumably the Admiralty. In any event it was a suitable name.

A Whitby collier does not sound very appropriate for a voyage of discovery over largely uncharted seas. But her peculiar characteristics were precisely her chief recommendations: she was very stoutly built, had a bluff wide bow, a wide, deep waist and a flat keel. The wide waist meant that she was capable of stowing away a large quantity of provisions. The flat keel enabled her to take the ground with less damage than most types of vessels, and meant too that her own crew could beach her and effect repairs, which later they were obliged to do when she ran foul of a reef on the North Queensland coast. That she was a little over three years old was also an advantage, for it is well known that ships are easier to handle and navigate when they are what might be termed loosened in the joints. The life of a ship in those days was about eight or nine years, which meant that the *Endeavour* was in her prime. She was not a very handsome ship but entirely suitable for the job.

It was natural that the Royal Society, responsible for the expedition, should propose its commander, and their choice quite understandably was Alexander Dalrymple, author of a recently published work dealing with discoveries in the South Pacific.* The book had been an immediate success and had put him, as the *Dictionary of National Biography* tells us, in contact 'with persons interested in the progress of discovery'. Dalrymple, unfortunately or fortunately as far as history is concerned, had far too high an opinion of himself. When the appointment was offered to him, he would only accept if given a commission as Captain in the Navy, which meant that he would actually command the ship as well as the expedition. The Admiralty immediately replied that such a suggestion was 'entirely repugnant to them and against all the regulations of the Navy', nobody but a king's officer being allowed to command one of His Majesty's ships.

It is at this point that we find the first mention of Cook, then commanding the *Grenville*, a schooner that had been engaged for the past few years in surveying the coast of Newfoundland for the Admiralty. Cook had proved himself intelligent, capable and remarkably efficient. While on one of the surveys he had taken an accurate observation of an eclipse of the sun and on his return to England at the end of the year, had handed the results of his observations to Doctor Bevis, a prominent Fellow of the Royal Society.

It has never been quite clear how it came about that Cook was selected for the command of the expedition. The Admiralty correspondence, usually so detailed, reveals nothing on the subject. Several letters appear to be missing. Had the Royal Society made inquiries regarding the Master of the *Grenville* or was it Sir Hugh Palliser, then captain in the Navy and lately governor and commander-in-chief of Newfoundland, who suggested him? He knew Cook, indeed must have known him

* *Account of Discoveries in the South Pacific Ocean before 1764*, published in 1767.

intimately. We know also that Philip Stephens, Secretary to the Admiralty, was impressed with Cook's performance as surveyor in Newfoundland. Perhaps it was a happy combination of events, anyhow his name was certainly familiar to the people responsible for the choice. Disappointed in Dalrymple, it is not surprising, as Beaglehole points out, 'that the Council for the Royal Society should have accepted Cook as the solution to their problems'.*

On May the 5th Cook was summoned to a meeting of the Royal Society, then at Crane Court, and while waiting for his audience met Charles Green, who was there hoping to be appointed the Society's observer on the *Endeavour*. Green, aged thirty-three, had been assistant to Maskelyne, Astronomer-Royal at Greenwich, and had sailed with him to the Barbados where the latter had been testing Harrison's chronometer as an aid to checking precise positions at sea. He seems to have quarrelled with Maskelyne and entered the Navy, and at the time of the interview he was serving as purser on the *Aurora*. The two men had very similar backgrounds for Green, like Cook, was the son of a Yorkshire farmer. They had spent their youth in the same countryside and both were sailors. We have no record, however, of this meeting beyond dry minutes. One would like to know Cook's reactions to his interviewers; this august body of learned nobles and 'country parsons with an interest in local archaeology' who occupied themselves, among other things, with the ventilation of prisons, the protection of buildings and ships from lightning and in the problem of frogs, which, frozen to a flint-like hardness in the winter, could be thawed out and brought to life again. He was certainly politely received by Lord Morton, the president, for wherever he went Cook was treated with respect, and he already had an impressive record behind him – particularly so for a self-made man. The outcome of the interview was that Cook, already elected to be in command of the ship, was also appointed one of the Royal Society's observers. The second observer, after the interview, being Green.

Little is known of Cook's life prior to his accepting the command of *Endeavour*, but he was of Scots extraction, his grandfather being among those who flocked across the border into the north of Yorkshire to follow the alum trade. His father became a labourer in the small village of Marton in North Riding and his mother was a Yorkshire girl from the Cleveland Hills. Cook left no personal record of his boyhood but a vicar from a nearby parish, George Young, interested himself in the recently dead hero and wrote a life of Cook, published in 1836, based, he claimed, on information gathered from relatives, friends and even one or two surviving school companions.

* *The Journals of Captain James Cook*, edited by J. C. Beaglehole, Cambridge, published for the Hakluyt Society at the University Press, 1955.

From Young we know that Cook was one of several children and that he spent his first years at Marton helping his father in the fields. A Mistress Mary Walker, struck by the boy's intelligence, 'taught him his letters and a little reading'. At the age of eight he attended school at Ayton, and at seventeen he was working in a grocer's shop at Staithes. The shop where Cook worked was so close to the sea that it had to be pulled down before it was totally engulfed by the waves. It was Saunderson, his employer, who took him to Whitby and introduced him to John Walker, a member of a reputable shipping firm. Whitby was then an important centre of the coaling trade and it was easy enough to find young James a job. By 1750 Cook was in the Baltic trade. Two years later he was appointed mate on one of Walker's new vessels – rapid promotion for a youth with nothing but ability.

With the threatened outbreak of war with France, young Cook volunteered for the Royal Navy. Men of experience were needed, and the North Sea coaling trade was considered the best kind of training. He signed on as an able seaman but was immediately rated master's mate on H.M.S. *Eagle*, a sixty-gun ship with a complement of four hundred men and fifty-six marines.

Cook saw service in a variety of ships, eventually transferring to a large man-of-war engaged in the campaign that was to wrest Canada from France. We hear of him being employed in surveying the St Lawrence River, a task he accomplished with such efficiency that the charts he produced remained standard for a century.

More surveys follow and we are told that he employed his spare time in solid reading of mathematics and improving his knowledge in astronomy.

In December 1762 he was married to Elizabeth Batts, a girl of twenty, the daughter of a fairly well-to-do carrier from Wapping. Cook was thirty-four. The young married couple went first to Shadwell to live in what is now London's Whitechapel district, moving later to Mile End where Cook bought a house. He was married seventeen years but was away on duty for most of the time. His home life, if one adds up his different leaves and the months he spent between voyages, makes a tally of some four years. Sometimes poor Elizabeth had no news of him for months, even years. Very little is known of his private life for Mrs Cook seems to have destroyed all his letters before she died, a lonely old lady of ninety-three. She had been widowed at thirty-seven, and lost her three sons within a period of a few years.

From Kitson's *Life** we learn that Mrs Cook always wore a ring containing a lock of his hair, 'and measured everything by his standard of morality and honour. The greatest disapprobation she could express was

* *The Life of Captain James Cook* by Arthur Kitson, John Murray, London, 1911.

"Mr Cook would never have done so". He was always Mr Cook to her'.

Four months after his marriage Cook went to Newfoundland for the Admiralty, making charts and maps to be used by the fishing fleets and the Navy. He was under contract from 1763 to 1767. The charts for which he was responsible were admirably executed. It was no easy job to survey six thousand miles of practically unknown coast, a veritable fretwork of indentations, bays, creeks and great headlands thrusting out into the Atlantic. His survey work lasted from early spring to late autumn, the chronic winter storms allowing Cook to winter at home with his wife and work on his charts. These were published in 1766 and 1768 and the last printing marks the end of his work in Newfoundland. It is interesting to note that his charts are not yet wholly superseded by the more detailed surveys of modern times.

On one of these surveys he had a nasty accident: a powder horn exploded in his hand, marking him for life. He seems to have been holding the large powder horn which ignited by mistake and suddenly exploded. 'His hand,' writes Kitson, 'was shattered in a terrible manner.' There happened to be a French ship nearby which had a doctor on board where he was able to secure some sort of medical assistance, though, as Kitson points out, 'of an exceedingly rough nature'. At that time surgery, especially on board ships, was very primitive; 'a glass of spirits the only anodine, and boiling pitch the most reliable styptic'.

It was this scar that enabled the crew of his ship to identify his body when he was murdered in Hawaii years later. Doctor Samwell, surgeon on the *Discovery*, described it as 'dividing the thumb from the finger the whole length of the metacarpal bone'.

This brings us now to the spring of 1769: the *Endeavour* is being fitted out and Cook has just received his commission as First Lieutenant. We still know very little of him as a person, for the facts noted above are mostly gleaned from official reports. It is obvious from his journals that he was a reserved character, and there is little to be learned about him from contemporary diaries. Even after his return from his first voyage when he was fêted by the *beau monde* he is seldom mentioned. James King, second lieutenant on board the *Resolution* when Cook was killed, gives us the best summing up of his character. 'Temperance in him,' King writes, 'was scarcely a virtue; so great was the indifference with which he submitted to every kind of self-denial.' King had the greatest affection for Cook and admired him enormously, as did all his men. 'The qualities of his mind were of the same hardy, vigorous kind with those of his body while his manners were plain and unaffected.' King admits that Cook's one failing was his temper, but hastens to add that this was counter-balanced by a most benevolent and humane disposition.

For his appearance we turn again to Dr Samwell. We know already that he was tall, 'his person was about six feet high, and though a good-looking man he was plain both in address and appearance. His head was small, his hair, which was dark brown, he wore tied behind. His face was full of expression, his nose exceedingly well-shaped, his eyes, which were small and of a brown cast, were quick and piercing; his eyebrows prominent, which gave his countenance all together an air of austerity'. Samwell also informs us that the best likeness of him was unquestionably the portrait by Nathaniel Dance painted in 1776 after his return from the second voyage. 'It is a most excellent likeness – and more to be valued, as it is the only one I have seen that bears any resemblance to him.' Remember, however, that on this first voyage we are dealing with a man eight years younger and with perhaps less authority.

The first entry in Cook's journal is dated Friday, May the 27th: 'moderate and fair weather, at 11 am hoisted the pendant and took charge of the ship.' The *Endeavour* was lying in the basin of London's docks at Deptford.

For the next two months the ship was provisioned, and the crew drafted. It was clear that the sailing dates would have to be postponed, but now that the final destination had been fixed, that Tahiti had been singled out as an appropriate place from which to observe the transit, there was no particular hurry. Tahiti's position, accurately marked on a map, should be easy to find. Cook, the experienced navigator, could reasonably guarantee to disembark the expedition six weeks before the transit as the Royal Society wished, 'in order that the instruments they were sending out could be got into proper working order'.

[Chapter 3]

His Majesty's Bark *Endeavour*

FROM THE VERY beginning this expedition, the first of Cook's three voyages, was conceived with a specific scientific purpose rather than with the more general aims of exploration or expanding trade. No efforts were spared to make it a success. Arrangements went forward smoothly with a remarkable lack of the usual red tape. The dockyards gave the *Endeavour* preferential treatment until she was got under way.

By following the numerous letters and minutes that passed between Cook and the Admiralty, and between the Admiralty and the Navy Board, we can get a general idea of the atmosphere of the preparations and also a fairly accurate picture of the ship. We shall examine these preparations and the ship in some detail here, for they were to be similar on Cook's other two voyages in the *Resolution* – again a ship originally designed for the collier trade.

The *Endeavour* was three-masted and, of course, square rigged, sixty feet long overall, and her greatest width being just over twenty-nine feet. Her complement was originally to have been seventy-strong but this was soon swelled to a total of eighty-five, including twelve marines. The marines were to join the ship at Plymouth and proved a necessary and wise addition.

Two officers were appointed with Cook: twenty-nine-year-old Zachariah Hicks, who was later to die of consumption (in fact he must have been consumptive when he boarded the ship) and John Gore, aged thirty-eight. Gore had already been to Tahiti with Wallis in the *Dolphin* and was undoubtedly very useful. Three others of the crew had also sailed with Wallis. Cook does not seem to have had a special hand in picking the crew. We know, however, that five of the men who had been with him in the *Grenville* on the Newfoundland survey transferred with him; one of them, Isaac Smith, a sixteen-year-old cousin of Mrs Cook's, and a very expert surveyor.

Servants were appointed, one to each of the lieutenants. The master, the boatswain, the gunner, carpenter, surgeon and cook were also entitled to servants: young boys generally in training for midshipmen.

Looking through the list of the crew one is struck by their youth. Cook was forty and there were only three men older than he. On an average, few of the men were over thirty. John Ravenhill, the sailmaker, was the old man of the party, and he was only forty-nine, and apparently the only one of the crew not to fall sick at Batavia on the way home. The surgeon attributed this to the fact that he spent the major part of every day happily besotted – pickled in rum.

It is amusing to note that Cook had two namesakes on board, one of them even bearing his Christian name. Both were servants, one being allotted to Hicks and the other to the carpenter. In the entire complement there were only two foreigners, one a young man from Venice and the other a boy from 'the Brazils'. There was also an American – James Magra from New York – a good-for-nothing, says Cook – who afterwards became British Consul at Teneriffe, then Secretary to the British Embassy at Constantinople, eventually ending up as Consul in Tangier. It was unusual for Cook to come out with a derogatory statement on his men, so one presumes the criticism was merited.

The voluminous correspondence reveals that Cook did, in fact, pick out three of the crew: Mr Forwood, a gunner; John Gathrey, the boatswain; and Taylor, the armourer. He had trouble later on with Forwood who drank too much, and Gathrey died of dysentery. Cook also had something to say about another proposed member of the crew. On June 13th we find him writing to the Navy Board – not without a certain hint of sarcasm, one feels – 'the man you have been pleased to appoint cook of H.M. Bark *Endeavour*, is a lame infirm man, and incapable of doing his duty without the assistance of others, and he doth not seem to like his appointment. I beg you will be pleased to appoint another'. Another was forthwith appointed, but this time a man with only one hand, and to make matters worse it was his right hand that he had lost. Immediately another letter from Cook follows, stating that he was 'very desirous of having no one on board but what is fully able to do their duty'.* This time the Navy Board would do nothing about it, answering rather lamely, that no other opening could be found for John Thompson, implying that the *Endeavour* would have to make the best of it. As J. C. Beaglehole† points out in his excellent introduction to the Hakluyt Society's edition of Cook's first voyage: 'the one-handed John Thompson does not seem to have been unsuccessful in his profession, whether he was dealing with the salt beef of convention or the gannet-pie, the kangaroo, the buzzards, shags and sharks with which

* This is a good example of Cook's occasional lapses in English, but considering his education one marvels that he wrote as well as he did.

† *The Journals of Captain James Cook*, edited by J. C. Beaglehole, Cambridge, published for the Hakluyt Society at the University Press, 1955.

diet was diversified'. No complaints were registered in any of the numerous journals.

We learn also that the *Endeavour* needed more iron ballast aft; she was too light in the bow. The painting was already finished, but we do not know the colour. There was no uniformity of colour in the Navy until the end of the century. Up till Nelson's time the captains used their own discretion as regards the exterior of a ship. Internally it was the practice to paint the sides vermilion, in an attempt to hide the blood with which they were so often and so liberally bespattered. Cook, considering the nature of the ship, would most probably have dispensed with this gruesome precaution. A green baize floor cloth was ordered for the great cabin. There is a water colour of the *Resolution* in the Mitchell Library in Sydney which shows her white-keeled with a black water line. Above this the sides appear to be brown. The stern windows of the great cabin were gilded and it is more than probable that the *Endeavour* was treated the same way. Certainly her keel would have been painted with white lead as a protection against the destructive *Teredo navalis*, or large ship worm of tropical seas.

The question of supplies was very important. An almost perpetual correspondence passed between the Victualling Board and Cook, and between Cook and the so-called 'Sick and Hurt Board'. Cook, like any seaman of the period, had had personal experience of scurvy, a disease caused as we now know by a dietary deficiency of vitamin C. But the eighteenth century was an age ignorant of vitamins or calories, and scurvy was a common complaint among soldiers on campaign, beleaguered cities and sailors at sea. Mortality rates, for instance, on a voyage from Europe to the Indies were apt to run as high as twenty per cent. During the Seven Years War more men died of scurvy than were killed in all the engagements.

The first symptoms were influenza, lassitude, aching of the limbs, terrible mental depression, and a general loss of strength. Then followed sunken eyes and livid blotches on the skin that, as the disease progressed, became black and putrid. Troubled vision was another symptom, also a swelling of the gums. These became so spongy as to almost cover the teeth which in their turn became so loose that they sometimes fell out. An Elizabethan surgeon, describing the disease, says that the victims were of so filthy a savour, and so odious 'that I was scarce able to wash and dress their mouths'. The unfortunate patient suffered agony: he was prone to faint and the least motion and any violent, unexpected noise, such as the firing of cannons, frequently occasioned syncope and even sometimes instant death. During the final stages foul ulcers formed in different parts, particularly on the legs. Internal haemorrhages, followed by pneumonia or kidney disease or some other complaint, heralded the end. However, if the patient was given any fresh food such as potatoes, cabbages, onions or carrots, he recovered almost immediately, however bad his case.

Attempts had been made to control the disease. The Dutch East India Company, alarmed by the unusually heavy death rates on board their ships to Batavia, asked the medical faculty of the famous University of Leyden for advice. Reports were drawn up but none of them based upon personal observations. No doctor had thought to make the voyage himself to observe the disease at close quarters. James Lind, a surgeon in the Navy, was the first practitioner to consider the matter seriously. He wrote a treatise, published in Edinburgh in 1754, in which he recommends oranges and lemons and plenty of green food, or where these were not obtainable, lemon juice. But it was not until fourteen years later, when another naval surgeon, David MacBride, published his report on the subject, that the Admiralty took any notice. What was needed was somebody with enough will to carry out these men's theories. Backed by the Admiralty Cook was this man. The attention he gave to his crew's health won him the Copley Gold Medal awarded by the Royal Society on his return from the second voyage. Only three slight cases of scorbutic disorders occurred before the *Endeavour* reached Tahiti, and none at all on the two subsequent voyages in the *Resolution*. A very remarkable achievement for the period.

MacBride had recommended malt as the great cure for scorbutic disorders and it was this commodity, more than any other, that Cook used. Reports on the treatment were favourable, but Cook, in spite of his faith in malt, had not limited himself to this panacea exclusively. He tried everything and it was therefore hard for him to tell which of the precautions was the most successful. In any event lime juice and not malt finally proved to be the actual preventative, but this was not before 1795. Only then was the regular administration of lime juice begun in the British Navy. Meanwhile intelligence and perseverance were needed to fight the dreaded scourge.

Cook had his own theories, cleanliness being one of them. He inspected the men at least once a week and saw to it that they took baths and changed their clothing. Their bedding was aired and the whole ship was stove dried and fumigated even in the hottest weather. The ordinary sailor was intensely conservative and was suspicious of changes. It needed constant supervision to enforce these odd customs and strange diet. Cook set great store on different greens which he had collected at every land they visited. Sauerkraut was also another of his favourites. 'The men would not at first eat it,' writes Cook, 'until I put in practice a method I never once knew to fail with seamen, and this was to have some of it dressed every day for the cabin table, and permitted all the officers without exception to make use of it and left it to the option of the men either to take as much as they please or none at all.' Within a week's time Cook was obliged to put every one on rations, it became so popular.

In another place Cook writes that 'Nothing contributed more to the health of the seamen, than having plenty of water'; and this was always one of his major concerns on all the three voyages. It had not been discovered yet that water kept fresh much longer in iron drums than in wooden kegs.

What was called portable broth was given to the men three times a week. This consisted of a square brick made of dry essence of meat which could be melted down in boiling water thus making a kind of bouillon. There was sassafras, obtained from an aromatic lauraceous tree and saloop made from the dried tubers of some orchidaceous plant, both of them used as hot infusions. A gentleman named Baron Storsch of Berlin had recommended marmalade of carrots obtained from the juice of carrots condensed till it is the thickness of fluid honey.

Mr Perry, the surgeon's mate, tells us that 'the allowances of salt beef and pork were abridged from nearly the beginning of the voyage, and the sailors' usual custom of mixing the salt beef fat with the flour was strictly forbidden'. Cheeses and butter were also ruled out as soon as they became rancid. Thompson, the one-handed cook, was formally enjoined not to give his slush to the men, slush being melted salt fat obtained from boiled beef or pork, in other words dripping. The men used it for making their own duffs or puddings and scarcely anything more unwholesome can be imagined. The men, however, had a craving for it and when the ship's copper was tallowed, or when the topmen were greasing down the rigging they had to be watched to stop them swallowing the stuff.

As a solid backing to these precautions there was MacBride's malt served as a regular diet if there was the slightest trace of scurvy. The Admiralty's secretary writes to Cook telling him how it should be prepared. The malt was to be kept in the bread room, or some very dry part of the ship and it should be ground fresh every day, under the direction of the surgeon. One quart of malt and three quarts of boiling water stirred for three or four hours, then the malt to be boiled into a panda (bread boiled to pulp) and flavoured with sea biscuits or dried fruits. The patient was to make at least two meals a day on the said panda and drink a quart or more of the fresh infusion every twenty-four hours. It is quite obvious that it was useless being squeamish on board the *Endeavour*.

On July the 21st the *Endeavour* left Deptford and called at Gallion's Reach to take in her guns: ten carriage guns and eight swivels. At

Plymouth four more swivels were added for use in the boats. She had three boats: the largest, the longboat, used for carrying water and stores; the pinnace, for the captain's use; and the yawl, for all kinds of odd jobs.

Then among the Admiralty minutes describing these preparations the name of Joseph Banks appears. It seems strange that there had been no official notice of his existence before this. The Royal Society, who sponsored him, must have decided, long ago, that this rich young man, one of England's foremost naturalists, was to be attached to the expedition. Along with him were included Solander, a Swedish botanist, the favourite pupil of the renowned Linnaeus; Hermann Spöring, another Swede, acting as an assistant naturalist; two painters: Buchan and Parkinson. These two young men had been engaged by Banks: Buchan to paint figures and landscapes, and Parkinson to draw plants, fishes and insects. With them came Banks' two retainers from his estates in Lincolnshire and two negro servants, and, of course, as he was an English squire, two dogs, one of them a greyhound. Negroes, we know, were a fashionable conceit of the times, but surely they could have been dispensed with on this particular occasion considering the cramped space. In any case they met with an untimely death and so are not in the picture for long. It is difficult to understand that those responsible for fitting out the *Endeavour* should have been advised at so late a date of this sudden invasion, comprising in all nine people, five of them gentlemen who had to be lodged in their own cabins, for there was no question of stowing them away in hammocks below decks. Green, the official observer, was expected but it was only on July 22nd that Cook was informed by the Admiralty about Banks. No documents exist which intimate that Cook knew anything about him. One wonders what Cook's reactions were when he opened the dispatch. We can be pretty sure that the shipwrights must have been irritated when they heard the news. It meant refitting the cabins, or rather adding further subdivisions. It was thought to be advisable to add a platform over the tiller – 'apparently,' as Beaglehole points out, 'to keep the gentlemen from tripping over in their promenades.' Originally the tiller swept the quarterdeck abaft the mizzen-mast, making it very cramped for exercise. All those alterations had to be carried out at Plymouth for the *Endeavour* had already left Deptford when news reached Cook of Banks' 'descent'. The work must have been superficial for it only took four days to accomplish. The divisions between the cabins were probably little better than plywood, or its equivalent in those times. There could not have been much privacy.

The National Maritime Museum at Greenwich has all the deck plans of the *Endeavour* and we can see exactly how the cabin space was divided.

The great cabin, running across the stern, was just over fourteen feet long by twenty-three feet at the widest. There were five large glazed windows facing aft over the stern, the windows probably being about two feet broad, just wide enough for a man's shoulders. Cook's sleeping quarters were to the left of the great cabin and measured about ten feet by eight. They had two doors, one opening into the great cabin and the other on to a small lobby through which passed the mizzen-mast. There were three masts: the fore, the main and the mizzen-masts. The mizzen (middle) mast was of course originally midships but it had become the last of the three masts on a full-rigged ship, keeping its former name according to the tradition of the sea. Banks' quarters lay directly opposite to Cook's and were smaller, an exact square measuring eight feet by eight. Taking the bunk into consideration there was not much room in which to turn around. Green's cabin was somewhat larger than Banks'. There remained three cabins of the same size to be divided up between Solander, Parkinson, Buchan and Spöring. There is no record as to which two shared a cabin, perhaps the two artists Buchan and Parkinson. We have no record either as to what the cabins looked like. They were usually very bare, furnished with a fixed table, a fixed sleeping cot and a wooden wash-stand with a basin. There are three cubicles left blank on the plan. These probably served as lavatories; one might possibly have been a washroom but no mention of this is made. Two serving pantries and a stairway down to the lower deck made up the quarters.

Pacing out the measurements one can see that the space was constricted, almost claustrophobic. All but the shortest must have been aware of the singularly hard oak beams for the ceiling was excessively low. They must, in fact, have almost crouched as they walked. One door had to be closed before another could be opened. There were no complaints but, on the second voyage, Banks refused to accept the accommodation offered to him, perhaps a hint of the first journey's discomfort.

It is strange that with all the details we have concerning the voyage not one of such a visually sophisticated party described their living quarters or for that matter the mechanics of their daily life. Landscapes, the flora and fauna, and the inhabitants of the islands they visited are described with the minutest details, but not once in all three voyages does anyone give us a picture of the great cabin, beyond Banks' fleeting glimpse when he writes: 'Now do I wish that our friends in England could by the assistance of some magical spying glass take a peep at our situation: Dr Solander sits at the cabin table describing, myself at my bureau journalising, between us hangs a large bunch of sea weed and upon the table lays a piece of wood covered with barnacles' pulled up out of the sea that afternoon. But we have no description of the furnishings.

There was a long table obviously, or perhaps two oval tables, for thirteen of them had their meals served to them there. Was it panelled in oak or pine, or perhaps painted? There are several representations of such cabins to guide us. For instance, Hogarth's scene in the National Maritime Museum at Greenwich of Lord George Graham on board ship. His lordship is taking his ease smoking a clay pipe, a great coat lined with fur falls from his shoulders, and he is attended by the purser, the chaplain, the cook and a black servant and, of course, his dogs. The floor is carpeted and the furniture is of walnut. Gilded capitals top the decorative pilasters on the panelling and the windows incline elegantly outwards over the stern. But Hogarth's mid-eighteenth-century cabin is certainly far too splendid for the *Endeavour*. So also are the descriptions of silk-clad worthies luxuriating in cabins hung with Italian pictures – men with such delicate sensibilities, that they kept perfume burning in silver censers to destroy the odour of bilge. Nearer the mark is a painting in the same museum by Mason Chamberlin showing Captain Bentick and his son, dated 1775. On hurried inspection Bentick could easily be mistaken for Cook, his is almost the same uniform: a long-tailed coat of bright blue with white lapels and gold anchor buttons worn over a white cloth waistcoat with white knee breeches and stockings. Black shoes with large silver buckles complete the outfit. The cabin, what one sees of it, must also resemble quite closely that of the *Endeavour*: the walls are of plain wooden panelling with little decoration. A green baize cloth covers a heavy-legged table, and the captain is seated on a sturdy leather-upholstered chair.

Let us now take a quick look at the lower deck. The first and second lieutenants were lodged aft, also the surgeon, the gunner, the master and the captain's clerk. The carpenter and boatswain had cabins forward with the stores and sailrooms. The rest of the crew slept in hammocks swung closely together in the forecastle.

The atmosphere below decks was apt to be noxious, even in the best regulated ships. Those with experience tell us that the reek of the seepage that stagnated in the keel – the bilge – was unlike any smell in the world for its foulness, especially in bad weather, when the ship was sometimes battened down for days. Without any fresh air the humidity was appalling. Every inch of timber dripped with salt water, and to make matters worse, oak had a tendency to sweat more than other woods. To overcome this dampness, captains had portable fires carried about between decks. Fumigation was also used to try to drown the fusty smells, the most common means being to burn a preparation of gunpowder soaked in vinegar in iron pans. The powder spattered, sending out a quantity of acrid smoke, which was also reckoned a powerful disinfectant. But in spite of fumigation, no ship was ever free from unpleasant smells. Certainly the *Endeavour* was better than most, no captain worked more diligently for his crew's well-being than Cook. The men's health was of primary importance to the success of the voyage, and however obvious this would seem, it had, strangely enough, seldom guided other naval commanders.

One could imagine Cook to have been on fairly intimate terms with his men. There was, however, a very strict division between the quarter and lower decks. In fact, they were two worlds apart. As John Masefield tells us,* the captain in a man-of-war lived alone 'like a little god in heaven, shrouded from view by the cabin bulkheads and guarded always by a red coated sentry armed with a drawn sword. If he came on deck, the lieutenants at once shifted to the side out of respect to the great man. No man on board dared to address him, save on some question relating to the duty of the day. Nor would a sailor dream of speaking to him with his hat upon his head. He lived alone in his cabin, eating in solitude, save when he desired his lieutenants and midshipmen to dine with him'.

This we know was not Cook's case. Crowded as he was with 'scientific gentlemen', he can seldom have been alone except in his narrow cabin. But there must have been a certain formality. The doings of the men forward were, in spite of the short length of the ship, quite apart from the officers 'aft'. The Navy was still in the process of transition from a haphazard collection of armed merchant vessels to a highly organized fleet.

Discipline in the eighteenth century was unequal; in one ship it was preposterously lax, in another it was brutally severe. Life in the *Endeavour*, an armed ship on a scientific mission, rather than a man-of-war, must have fallen somewhere between the two. The seamen anyhow seemed to have treated the scientists as a special group, with respect.

* *Sea Life in Nelson's Time*, John Masefield, Methuen & Co., London, 1905.

[Chapter 4]

The Gentlemen

FROM THE SHIP and her captain let us now turn to the scientific gentlemen, or simply 'the gentlemen', as Cook always referred to Banks and members of his party in his journal.

It was August and the *Endeavour* had had a rough passage down the Channel. It had taken her a week to reach Plymouth. On the 14th Cook sent word to Banks and Solander, who were still in London, that he was ready for sea, and was only waiting for a fair wind to sail. Banks' luggage was already on board.

We know a great deal more about Banks than we do about his captain. The Admiralty, when writing to Cook, make mention of him as being 'a gentleman of large fortune'. John Ellis, corresponding with Linnaeus, is less discreet and tells us his income exactly – £6,000 – which in the eighteenth century had about four times the value it has today. In the same letter we learn that 'no people ever went to sea better fitted out. They have got a fine library of natural history; they have all sorts of machines for catching and preserving insects; all kinds of nets, trawls, drags and hooks for coral fishing. They have even a curious contrivance of a telescope, by which, put into the water, you can see the bottom at a great depth, when it is clear. They have many cases of bottles with ground stoppers of several sizes to preserve animals in spirits'. They also had salts and wax in which to keep seeds. Ellis informs Linnaeus that the expedition would cost Banks £10,000. 'All this is owing to you and your writings.' Linnaeus had written several books on botany, the best known of which was his *Systema Naturae*; in it he works out a system to classify plants. Roughly speaking, it was a question of the number of stamens and pistils in a flower and the way the different sections were joined together. Until then flora had been catalogued in a very haphazard way.

Banks had the conventional upbringing of a country squire's son: Eton and Christ Church College, Oxford. As a child he was described as being well disposed and good tempered, but so immoderately fond of play that his attention wandered from his studies – in short, the ordinary little boy. One hot summer evening when he was fourteen a change

1. Captain Cook's Portrait by Sir Nathaniel Dance.
It was painted in 1776 after his return from the second voyage, and according to Samwell is by far the best likeness. (*page 12*)

3. Sydney Parkinson.
A very poor portrait,
the frontispiece to his own journal. (*page 27*)

2. Portrait of Joseph Banks by Benjamin West,
engraved by J. R. Smith, 1771.
(Painting has disappeared) (*page 24*)

4. Carl Daniel Solander. Artist unknown—from an oil painting in the possession of the Linnean Society of London.

occurred; overnight, as it were, he became a botanist. It was to be the ruling passion of his life. When he was an old man, a gouty cripple in a bath chair, he described how it happened – a form of conversion, as if he had seen a vision. Hector Cameron tells us about it in his book on Banks* and it is a charming story.

He had been bathing in a river with some friends and had lingered behind so that he found himself wandering home alone through lanes banked with masses of wild flowers. The sun was setting and the hedgerows were bathed in a copper light so sharp that it picked out every detail in the flowers. The columbines and the arbutulum, sprigged over with Queen Anne's lace, were as vivid as the meticulous borders in an early missal. The young boy was overcome by their beauty; on the spot he resolved to become a botanist. His first teachers were the garrulous old crones that he found down the lane culling simples to be sold to the druggist of the town. For a few pennies they agreed to spend their summer evenings teaching him what they knew.

Up at Oxford the youthful enthusiast found himself saddled with a professor of botany who did not teach botany. The best he could do for Banks was to give him a letter of introduction to his counterpart at Cambridge. Through him Banks found a young Jew called Israel Lyons, who had distinguished himself in botany and astronomy and who, for a consideration, returned with Banks to Oxford as his instructor.

When Banks was eighteen, during his first year at Oxford, his father died. He left Oxford in December 1763 and coming of age two months later took possession of his fortune. One would have expected Banks to embark on the Grand Tour, to wander along the banks of the Rhine and cross the Alps, perhaps visiting the new excavations at Pompeii – but not he. John Hawkesworth, the official recorder of the first voyage, pays him a fine compliment. He places him as a young man meant for the enjoyments rather than the labours of life: 'yet an ardent desire to know more of nature than could be learned from books determined him, at a very early age, to forgo what are generally thought to be the principal advantages of a liberal fortune and to apply the revenue, not in procuring the pleasures of leisure and ease, but in the pursuit of his favourite study, through a series of fatigues and dangers which, in such circumstances, have very seldom been voluntarily incurred, except to gratify the restless and insatiable desires of avarice and ambition'. It is strong language but not exaggerated.

In 1766 the Government had sent H.M.S. *Niger* to survey the British fisheries off the Newfoundland coasts. It was a precautionary measure to see that the British fishermen kept within bounds and did not poach on French interests. On board the *Niger* was young Banks, there to visit

* *Sir Joseph Banks* by Hector Charles Cameron, The Batchworth Press, London, 1952.

the Esquimaux and collect plants. Weather conditions prevented him from visiting the Esquimaux but he found many plants and much to note in his journal. It was while on board the *Niger* that he learned of his nomination to a fellowship of the Royal Society. To quote Beaglehole 'he had made no single contribution to any department of learning whatsoever; but that, at the time, was no disqualification whatsoever; he was an excellent young man, energetic and interested, quite devoted to botany; a learned gentleman with a really enviable income; it would have been an insult to keep him out'.* This august body did not regret their new recruit.

Banks was in his twenty-fifth year when he sailed in the *Endeavour*, a pleasant-looking, dark-haired young man. Sir Joshua Reynolds, who painted him on his return from the first voyage, shows him sitting at a desk dressed in a red velvet coat lined with sable. A terrestrial globe stands at his elbow while his left hand lies clenched on some papers, no doubt pages of his journal. His right hand presses against the arm of his chair as if he were about to get up. The whole posture expresses energy. The eyes are intelligent and lively and a faint smile plays around the mouth, a rather sensual mouth.

There are various likenesses of him; a shadow silhouette in profile by James Lind, accentuates his long, rounded nose and receding chin; and a lost Benjamin West painting known from a mezzotint by J. R. Smith where he is standing against a column conventionally draped in brocaded hangings, looped with a cord of plaited silk. It is a dull composition but the exotic paraphernalia is interesting. Banks has an elaborate Maori cloak thrown over his own clothes. He points out the dog's hair fringe to the spectator. A large Polynesian adze, or axe, lies at his feet; there are also lances and the paddles of a canoe. These were strange, unfamiliar objects, for Europeans had not yet started to make Pacific ethnographical collections.

All Banks' portraits reflect the cheerfulness of his nature. Even in Thomas Phillips' painting of him as the august Sir Joseph, President of the Royal Society, a smile seems to hover round the heavy jaws. He must have been a pleasant companion, especially when a young man.

Another sympathetic trait was his shyness, or awkwardness in society. That voluble Fanny Burney, when she met him in 1788, writes in her diary 'Sir Joseph Banks was so exceedingly shy that we made no acquaintance at all. If instead of going round the world, he had fallen from the moon he could not appear less versed in the usual modes of a tea-drinking party. But what, you will say, has a tea-party to do with a

* *The Endeavour Journals of Joseph Banks*, edited by J. C. Beaglehole, Angus and Robertson, in association with the Trustees of the Public Library of New South Wales, Sydney, 1962.

botanist, a man of science and a President of the Royal Society?' We know, however, that he talked well when discussing the subjects that interested him, for even Sir Humphrey Davy, who succeeded Banks as President of the Royal Society and never liked him, bears this out.

So much for Banks, who emerges as a more definite character as the voyage progresses. What of the other members of this party: Solander, Spöring, Parkinson and Buchan?

Doctor Carl Daniel Solander, thirty-five at the time, Fellow of the Royal Society, was a Swede by origin and Linnaeus' favourite pupil. He had come to England when he was twenty-six as Linnaeus' protégé and speedily made a reputation for himself, eventually being considered the ablest botanist in the country. From Boswell we know that his English was excellent; he spoke it, in fact, 'with more propriety than most natives'. One must suppose, however, that he had a slight accent. He had been in England two years when on Linnaeus' suggestion he was appointed professor of botany at the Academy of Science at St Petersburg. He declined the offer and instead became adviser to the Duchess of Portland, helping her to arrange her famous collection. We next hear of him cataloguing the natural history collection in the British Museum. It was at about this time, during a dinner given by a mutual friend, that Solander suggested himself as a travelling companion to Banks for the forthcoming year. Banks, of course, accepted immediately. Solander, as well as being an extremely gifted botanist, was also a great charmer. If Fanny Burney had found Banks a bore this was certainly not the case with Solander. It has even been suggested that his social gifts were a hindrance to his work. He was too popular and so taken up with the pleasures of life that he sometimes forgot his duties. Linnaeus, writing from Sweden, implores a friend to intervene on his behalf. 'Pray persuade Solander to write to his excellent mother who has not received a letter from her beloved son for several years.' After his death it was said that many of his mother's letters to him were found unopened. This, however, is the only shadow on an otherwise very sympathetic character.

On their return from the Pacific in 1771 Banks established him in his house at Soho Square as his secretary and librarian. He visited Iceland with Banks and in 1773 was made keeper of the Natural History Department at the British Museum. Nine years later he had a severe stroke which killed him. His untimely death prevented the publication of what would have been his most important work: the twenty manuscript volumes, still preserved in the Botanical Department of the British Museum, containing the description of plants collected during the voyage of the *Endeavour*.

Banks and Solander were of the same calibre, sophisticated men moving in the same circles, and sharing similar interests. They were close companions during the voyage. The remaining three were conscious, no doubt, of their position in regard to their rich employer.

We know very little about the other scientist in the party, Hermann Dietrich Spöring. He was the son of a professor of medicine at the University of Abo in Finland and was in his late thirties when he sailed in the *Endeavour*. Banks seems to have employed him as a secretary. He was also an excellent draughtsman (some of his drawings were recently identified in the Natural History Department of the British Museum). He also appears to have been adept with his hands, for after he had mended a quadrant Cook referred to him as 'one of Mr Banks' ingenious gentlemen'. We know nothing, however, of his character or appearance. He remains just a name, a shadowy ghost, one of the many who died of dysentery at Batavia.

We know a little more about Banks' two artists, Sydney Parkinson and Alexander Buchan. Both were young men, Parkinson a Quaker from Edinburgh, and Buchan another Scot though we know nothing of his background.

Buchan had been engaged by Banks as a figure and landscape painter and Parkinson as his botanical draughtsman. Cook refers to Buchan as a sober, diligent and ingenious young man, but unfortunately he proved to be an epileptic and probably should never have joined the voyage.

After a series of bilious disorders he died of a fit three days after the *Endeavour* reached Tahiti. 'I sincerely regret him,' mourns Banks in his journal. 'His loss to me is irretrievable, my airy dreams of entertaining my friends in England with the scenes that I am to see here are vanished. No account of the figures and dresses of men can be satisfactory unless illustrated with drawings; had providence spared him a month longer what an advantage would it have been to my undertaking – but I must submit.'

Indeed Banks lost a very valuable ethnographical assistant as can be seen from his wash drawings in the British Museum. One of them shows us the interior of a native hut in Tierra del Fuego, a drawing that unfortunately was very much romanticized when Cipriani (the best known painter of historical scenes at the time) redesigned it for Bartolozzi's plate illustrating Hawkesworth's edition of the first voyage.

Buchan's death meant also that Parkinson had double the amount of work to do. Poor Parkinson made over six hundred sketches during the voyage and frequently worked late into the night. His drawings of plant specimens and fauna collected by the naturalists are excellent, and it is only when he attempts landscapes, Buchan's province, that he is less successful. His views of Matavai Bay or his representations of a funeral rite in Tahiti show how very limited he was. The figures are awkwardly drawn, even the coconut palms, so graceful in reality, look stiff and unnatural, like feather dusters stuck into the sky line. But then one can hardly blame Parkinson for he was, after all, never engaged as a landscape artist. He was so meticulous and accurate in his botanical drawings that the young man himself must have been critical of his own landscape efforts. He was not to know that one day they would appear without his name – but this is another story and will come in a later chapter.

Although we have no idea of Buchan's appearance, we know more or less what Parkinson looked like from an anonymous portrait in the British Museum. There is also a poor engraving, by James Newton, used as frontispiece for his own journal, representing him as a long-nosed, straight-backed youth surrounded with drawing materials and specimens. He was twenty-three when he embarked in the *Endeavour* and had already been working for Banks a year before he sailed, copying on vellum a collection of drawings brought back from Ceylon by a retired governor.

One would like to have many more details about Banks and his suite; for instance, what kind of clothes did they have? We know that a friend advised Banks to take 'a sufficiency of umbrellas both of the silk, French kind and the strong oil skin ones'. We know also, from Parkinson, that Banks was apt to dress elegantly, having many embroidered waistcoats. It is fairly certain that they were most inappropriately clad in heavy broadcloth breeches, laced jackets, and gallant headgears; finery, however, that served its purpose when they arrived in the islands – the natives were thoroughly impressed.

There remains only to mention Green, who was presumably already on board with Captain Cook. He was thirty-three when the voyage started, energetic, capable, very conscientious and drastically untidy. Yet he remains little more than a name in the ship's company. He tried to initiate his shipmates into the mysteries of scientific navigation, not always successfully, it must be admitted. He also appears to have been adventuresome and possessed of extraordinary *sang froid*. Whenever any exploration was afoot on a new island, he was generally to be found amongst those who made up the expedition. Once, on the Great Barrier Reef when the *Endeavour* had got caught in a current and was drifting rapidly towards the breakers, what Cook, generally so reserved, termed 'a truly terrible situation', Green calmly went ahead with the business in hand, 'taking a lunar to obtain the correct longitude'. The horizon was clear and the conditions were excellent, he could not let the opportunity escape. It was only afterwards that he noticed that 'we were about a hundred yards from the reef where we expected the ship to strike every minute. . . .' Green was amongst those unfortunates destined never to see their native shores again. He died soon after the ship left Batavia but not, it would seem, of the dreaded dysentery. A newspaper of the period, reporting his death, said that he had been ill for some time and had been directed by the surgeon to keep himself warm, 'but, in a fit of frenzy he got up in the night and put his legs out of the porthole which was the occasion of his death'. Cook describes the causes differently, saying that he had long been in a bad state of health 'which he took no care to repare but on the contrary lived in such a manner as greatly promoted the disorders he had long upon him. This brought on the flux which put a period to his life'.

Cook certainly missed him, for his accurate readings had been an inestimable help in the difficult job of charting thousands of miles of unknown coasts.

This brings us back to the auspicious day of departure. Banks and his suite had arrived in Plymouth on August 20th, but contrary winds prevented the *Endeavour* from sailing. Not till the 25th did Cook hoist the Jack at the foremast as a sign for Mr Banks to come on board. On the 26th they finally sailed.

At six in the morning they were off the Lizard and sounding at noon they had 'fifty fathoms, grey sand with small stones and broken shells' – the last they were to see of English soil for nearly three years. There must have been doubt in everyone's mind as Cornwall's shores disappeared into the blue August morning: for how many on board would it be for ever?

Ninety-six persons left in the *Endeavour* and only fifty-five returned, a low mortality rate for those days. Forty-one died on the voyage, thirty-three at Batavia either of dysentery or fever, and Hicks who died of consumption. The eight other deaths were lives no commander could have saved: two drownings, one suicide, two frozen to death, tuberculosis, drink, and poor Buchan's epilepsy. Cook lost not one man from scurvy. Had he been less energetic in combating this ill the results would have been crippling. It was a remarkable record.

[Chapter 5]

Plymouth to the Horn

How much one would have enjoyed being a witness to the first meeting between Cook and his scientific companions. Cook, the experienced sailor, must surely have had certain misgivings about embarking with so varied a company of landsmen. It was to be a long and dangerous voyage and he could not have welcomed the idea of being confined in so small a space with men he had never met. There would, also, have been a hesitation on both sides arising from the delicate question of birth, for the eighteenth century was not a democratic age. Cook, of humble beginnings, had risen from the ranks, and while now an officer, would not thus automatically be considered a 'gentleman'. Although John Masefield tells us 'that he who rose to be an officer might consider himself, were he not one before, to have risen also to be a gentleman; and his claim was often accepted by public opinion and sometimes even by society,' he continues that such a rise was remarkably rare, the great majority of officers being 'gentlemen born'. To us this may be a ridiculously snobbish consideration, but it cannot be ignored for it must certainly have been in the minds of both Cook and Banks. Cook also could well have entertained doubts of another nature. There had been a good deal of conversation regarding wealth where our young botanist was concerned. Now, here he was in person, just twenty-four years old, arriving amidst a bustle of coaches, attended by four servants, two of them negroes. He was an ardent naturalist, but certainly not a professional. Might not Cook quite legitimately have suspected him of being, what nowadays, one would call a rather pretentious amateur? Luckily for all concerned, both men were above the effects of such futile considerations.

Reading Cook's journal of the first voyage – his own account and not Hawkesworth's polished arrangement of it – one quickly realizes that he was indeed one of nature's gentlemen. We know his superb qualities as a seaman, but here, through the plain, straightforward sentences emerges something else; an instinctive intelligence and an enormous amount of good Scottish commonsense; added to which one remarks an ever-growing sensitiveness to his surroundings. His descriptions of place and people are often excellent, especially during the second and third voyages. His powers of observation had undoubtedly been sharpened by contact with men such as Banks and Solander, and afterwards, tiresome though one of them proved to be, with his intellectual naturalists of the second voyage, Forster and his son, George. There is not a reaction, nor a reflection in the journals to which one could take exception. He was understanding and fair with his men who were 'attached to him from affection and obedient from confidence' as one of his officers wrote. In the words of the same officer, he was always attentive 'and full of tender compassion for the savages'. He was for ever trying 'by kind treatment to dissipate their fear and court their friendship'. It is true that the Royal Society had sent him admirably humane directives on the subject, but it was Cook's own interpretation of them that counted in the end.

Dance's portrait of Cook gives an indication of what a likeable human being he must have been: straightforward, firm, direct, probably with no small talk; in fact with the traits one looks for in a commander.

As for Banks, here also was an exceptional person, not cast, perhaps, in so noble a mould as his captain but of considerable stature. They seem to have taken an immediate liking to each other, setting the climate for the rest of the company. There were to be no trivial controversies. Life aboard was harmonious. Banks must also be given some credit for having had the perspicacity to appreciate Cook's qualities long before he became England's famous circumnavigator. Actually, for the first few years after their return, the polite world had a tendency to regard the voyage as Banks' and Solander's rather than Cook's. As Beaglehole points out, Banks and Solander were the first to see the King.

Let us imagine their initial dinner together in the great cabin. Eight bells had just been struck and it was midday. This meal must have been set for ten people, more than likely around a table laid with a mixture of pewter and china plates which, in rough weather, would be buttressed with sand-filled baize cushions. Having just left port, the food would certainly have been fresh meat and vegetables rather than the salt pork that was soon enough to become their monotonous fare, except when varied with exotic and not always palatable titbits, such as grilled shark or a stewed albatross served up with sauerkraut to help combat scurvy.

Cook must have had the place of honour, possibly with Banks opposite him and Solander nearby, but perhaps Green, the official observer, even took precedence over Banks, one does not know. Maybe Gore and Hicks, Cook's two lieutenants and Monkhouse, the surgeon, were interspersed amongst the supernumeraries to even out the conversation, or perhaps the officers ate at a separate table. Anyhow, on this occasion, if they were at Cook's table, one can be fairly certain that wherever they sat, they were on the silent side; lieutenants, according to the etiquette of the Navy, only spoke when spoken to by their superiors. Parkinson, Buchan, and Spöring no doubt followed suit unless they had their own little clique at the end of the table, but on this first meal attention would certainly have been on what their captain had to say.

Probably the conversation was between Banks, Cook, Solander and Green. Both Banks and Cook had been to Newfoundland and both of them knew Palliser, at that time commanding the Newfoundland Squadron. Banks had dined with him at St John's to celebrate the Coronation of George III, and afterwards attended a ball where, owing to the shortage of women, the host had been obliged to extend invitations to Banks' washerwoman and her daughter.

Cook, when he wanted to, could talk well and, once started on a familiar topic, undoubtedly had anecdotes enough to amuse the company. At one point during the siege of Quebec Cook had narrowly missed being captured by a band of Iroquois Indians who were allied with the French. He could also have given them his impressions of Wolfe and details of his death, for Cook knew him personally. We know this for the General mentions him in a dispatch.

There must have been days of tedium, as indeed there are on board any ship, days when all Cook could note in his journal were the variable winds, the clouds and showers, the fresh breezes and seaweed – days on end when all they saw were the taut sails outlined against the sharp blue sky, the only noise the lapping of the water as it slapped by the swollen hull.

The *Endeavour* was not speedy and at her fastest only managed seven or eight knots. The average progress of a ship in the eighteenth century being not more than fifty miles a day.

A brief stay of five days was made at Madeira and on the 19th of September they weighed anchor, and on the 23rd sighted Teneriffe. On the morning of October 21st, the Line was crossed. On November the 6th, we get Cook writing in his journal that he was determined to put into Rio de Janeiro in preference to any other port in Brazil or in the Falkland Islands. He knew he could stock necessary provisions there, 'and I doubt not but we should be well received'. Cook had certainly heard of Commodore Byron's reception there four years previously when he had been met at the top of the stairs of the Viceroy's palace by His Excellency in person and, with much ceremony, been conducted to the rooms of state. It was impossible for him to foresee how very different his own reception would be. For the eighteen days they were in port they were to be under close arrest. The officer Cook sent ashore to arrange for a pilot – and one presumes to negotiate an audience with Don Antonio Rolim de Moura – was detained until Cook himself appeared. The meeting must have been short and to the point, just long enough for Cook to obtain leave to purchase provisions and refreshments for the ship. One can sense Cook's indignation. 'He certainly did not believe a word about our being bound southward to observe the transit of Venus, but looked upon it only as an invented story to cover some other design we must be upon, for he could form no other idea of that phenomenon (after I had explained to him) than the North Sea passing through the South Pole (these were his own words).' Cook was to be the only member of the party allowed to land and then only under escort, with the result that, after one or two more attempts, he refused to go at all.

The real trouble was Don Antonio's grave doubts about the *Endeavour*. The strange appearance of a converted collier manned by officers and men of the Royal Navy with carriage guns and a file of marines aroused his worst suspicions, and after ten days of altercation, he finally admitted to Cook that he quite frankly did not believe that the *Endeavour* was in the service of His Majesty. He must have been a singularly unimaginative man, for one of the details he found the most suspicious was the fact that the ship had no figure-head.

Hardly able to appreciate the Viceroy's misgivings, Cook and his party had to accept a situation galling in the extreme for everybody, but especially for the naturalists. As Banks explained, no one had attempted to describe the country since Willem Piso, a Dutch naturalist and George Marcgrave, a German scholar, published their discoveries made in Brazil in 1636 when travelling with Prince Maurice of Nassau. 'It is easy to guess the state in which the natural history of such a country must be.'

In addition to the annoyance of not being able to land, they had to bear the discomfort of remaining on board while the ship was being keeled down for cleaning which meant that it was impossible to walk about the decks. The cabins, stuffy even at sea, became unbearable in the hot, land-locked harbour where sometimes there was hardly a breath of air. It must have been with relief that Cook gave orders to weigh anchor and stand south.

The run from Rio de Janeiro to Cape Horn was roughly 2,270 miles and the *Endeavour*, leaving Rio on December the 7th, had passed the Horn by January the 27th.

Cook was avoiding the strait discovered by Magellan with its contrary winds and currents. It had taken Byron seven weeks to negotiate the passage, and Wallis even longer. Wallis had little good to say of it:

'the country had the most dreary and fearsome appearance'. Bleak mountains rose up on both sides sparsely covered with stunted and withered trees. Above the snow line were piled fragments of broken rocks; and above this again 'rude and naked summits, towering above the clouds in vast crags rising one upon another'.

On the morning of the 11th Tierra del Fuego, south of Magellan's straits, was sighted; great high mountains wreathed in clouds and patched with snow. Magellan had found it a forbidding land, 'stark with eternal cold', and had named it Tierra del Fuego from the natives' many fires he observed burning on the shores.

It was Magellan who also named the natives 'Patagonians', meaning 'big footed'. They were very primitive and were reputed to be giants. Byron describes them as enormous goblins measuring hardly less than seven feet. He saw some of them eating the pouch of an ostrich 'quite raw without any other preparation or cleaning than just turning it inside out and shaking it'.

The natives were indeed primitive, their colour resembled 'that of the rust of iron mixed with oil'. They were daubed with streaks of red and black paint and were scantily clothed in llama or seal skins; 'the men taking no care to hide their privy parts'. Their huts were mostly crude shelters built to the windward of a small fire. 'In a word,' writes Cook, 'they are perhaps as miserable a set of people as are this day upon earth.' There was no question of their being giants. Cook finds them 'something above the middle size', but nothing more.

Instead of the Straits of Magellan, Cook was bound for the Straits of Le Maire, named after the Dutch navigator who discovered them late in the seventeenth century. Though difficult and not without danger they were far less hazardous. They run between the southernmost tip of Tierra del Fuego and Staten Island, and it is through them that Cook sailed, anchoring in the Bay of Success.

Early in the morning of the 16th an ill-fated expedition set out. Here in this hostile land, Banks lost his two negro servants. It could, indeed, have proved disastrous, for, included in the party, were all of Cook's scientific staff with the exception of Parkinson and Spöring: Green, Banks, Solander, Buchan and Monkhouse the surgeon, plus two seamen and Banks' four servants.

It was a bright sunny day when they left to climb the high hill above the bay. It looked easy enough from the ship, but once some way up, the going proved unexpectedly difficult and progress was slow. They got caught in a tangle of low-growing bushes rooted in a swamp. Buchan, it must be remembered, was an epileptic, and the exertion of struggling with the unyielding branches, while wading ankle-deep in a bog, was too much for him. Three-quarters way through he fell into a fit. Meanwhile the weather had changed and had become bitterly cold, developing into a blizzard. Solander, a Scandinavian, warned of the dangers of giving way to the irresistible desire to sleep induced by great cold. Ironically Solander himself was the first victim. Only thanks to Banks' energy did they manage to drag him up from the ground when he had slumped, an inert weight.

There was no question now of getting back to the ship and the night was spent on stony ground hunched round a fire – their only food a vulture they shot. Then it was noticed that the two negro servants were missing. Feeling the cold more than the others they had lagged behind. A seaman was sent back immediately to hurry them on. When he found them they were already lying down and refused to move. Told they would freeze to death unless they joined the others, they replied that all they wanted was to die. Unfortunately they had been given the expedition's supply of rum to look after, and the combination of the alcohol and the cold was too much for them. They were found in the morning, beyond help.

It was the afternoon of the following day before the party got back to the beach. Reviewing their tracks from the ship, they found that they had not gone very far, having made a half circle round the hills.

As Le Maire's Straits had not yet been charted, it was not till January 27th that the *Endeavour* rounded Cape Horn. They were in the Pacific.

[Chapter 6]

The Pacific

WHAT WERE the reactions of the men of the *Endeavour* when faced with the vast reaches of this little-explored ocean?

Sailing for interminable days across a flat sea Magellan had called Balboa's *Mar del Zur*, the Pacific. Little did he realize how seldom it was to live up to its name. His Pacific was not long in acquiring a bad reputation. It was swept by typhoons of such ferocity that coconuts were wrenched off trees and sent shooting like cannon balls across the sky. As the ferocity increased, the trees themselves would be torn loose from the soil to disappear like darts into the leaden clouds. Even worse than this were the reefs. Only too often the indigo depths shallowed to aquamarine revealing knife-edged corals. The Pacific stood and stands, in fact, for the most extreme rigours that sailors have ever known. Its inhabitants were an unknown quantity, and had been responsible for the death of Magellan, and were eventually to kill Cook too. But this is jumping years ahead. Oddly not one member of the *Endeavour*'s crew pauses in his notes to reflect on the situation. The fact that they were on the confines of a vaguely outlined, watery world appears to have left them quite unmoved.

Parkinson writes home to a friend that they 'went round Cape Horn as easy as if it had been the North-Foreland, and so through the South Seas to George's Island', as Tahiti was then called. Cook, in a note to the Admiralty explains, how in their passage to Tahiti 'they had made a far more westerly trail than any ship had ever done before'. He makes no comments other than ordinary observations on the weather. Cape Horn itself was rather obscured by fog and there were a great many albatross about the ship. Banks, the sportsman, rows out in a boat and shoots one, probably the Royal Albatross or *Diomedea epomophora*. No mention is made of the bad luck it was supposed to bring. This, no doubt, is a superstition of a later age. Banks, ever enthusiastic, always interested, has nothing to say about the Pacific, but does give us a recipe for cooking albatross. They must be skinned and soaked overnight in salt water. They are then parboiled – always in salt water – and finally stewed in a little fresh water, and when sufficiently tender, served up with a savoury sauce. What ingredients could have gone into the sauce? Anyway, it proved to be a very popular dish, even when there was fresh pork on the table. Equally appreciated was a large, sepia cuttlefish found floating on top of the water, just dead, but so pulled to pieces by birds that his species was unrecognizable. 'Only this I know, that of him was made one of the best soups I ever ate.'

The naturalists were absorbed in their own world and far too occupied to worry about supposed dangers. 'Sailed this morning,' writes Banks, 'the wind foul, but our keeping boxes being full of new plants we little regarded any wind providing it was but moderate enough to let the draftsmen work, who, to do them justice, are now so used to the sea that it must blow a gale of wind before they leave off.' Cook and Green spent their time surveying, fixing the correct position of capes, bays, and mountains and taking observations between the sun and the moon to find the longitude. Reefing the sails and taking soundings were all part of Cook's responsibilities. Ever watchfully analysing the character of the sea he was struck by the complete absence of currents during his ten-week run to Tahiti, thereby correctly inferring that there was no large land mass in the vicinity, because near land, as he notes, 'are generally found currents'. This strengthened his doubts of the existence of a Great Southern Continent.

Cook was not yet continent-hunting, but the transit of Venus observed and Tahiti and any other new islands surveyed, his main task on this first voyage was to investigate a fabled land, known until then as the *Terra Australis Incognita*, a shadowy area 'sketched in on many an old chart with a free and uncontrolled hand, around the South Pole'.

Geographers were struck by the fact that unlike the northern hemisphere, the southern Pacific had no large land masses. Having accepted the spherical nature of the earth, they came to the nearly logical conclusion – considering the limited knowledge of their time – that, in order to keep its stability, the amount of solid land in the two hemispheres must balance: hence there must be a great unknown continent in the southern part of the Pacific. Tasman was supposed to have touched it when he sailed along the western shores of New Zealand. Many believed that Quiros had seen yet another part of it when he landed on Espirito Santo in the New Hebrides. But no one was quite certain and it was to be one of Cook's major discoveries to prove that such a continent existed only in fertile imaginations.

The story of all previous expeditions had been much the same. During the first weeks out of port there was fresh meat and even milk from cattle embarked for the purpose, but by the time they had fought their way through the Straits of Magellan and round the Horn, conditions had deteriorated; fresh food had given out and rations were salt beef and hard ship's biscuits. Meat had frequently been several years in salt before it came to the cook 'by which time it needed rather a magician than a cook to make it edible'.* It was of stony hardness, fibrous, shrunken, dark, gristly, glistened with salt crystals and looked like mahogany. Strange tales were told about it. Old, pigtailed seamen would allude to horseshoes found in the meat casks; of curious barkings and neighings heard in the slaughterhouses; and of negroes who disappeared near the victualling yards, to be seen no more. Whatever meat it may have been, it was certainly abominable.

The ship's biscuits, made of mixed wheat and pea-flour with sometimes a base addition of bone-dust, were so hard that they have been likened to paving stones and were impossible to chew with bleeding gums and teeth affected, as they often were, by malaria or tropical fevers.

This ship's 'bread' was kept in tin-lined bread rooms. After a long passage in a hot climate it became unspeakably bad and full of weevils and maggots. Rebaking in the ship's ovens sometimes remedied this evil, but the most common custom was to leave the creatures and eat the biscuits at night, 'when the eye saw not, and the tender heart was spared'.†

Water was another problem. Iron was not yet used for kegs and water kept in wooden casks became a miniature aquarium ten days out of port. 'No matter what substitutes were added to keep the water fresh, sooner or later a greenish or brownish slime began to ooze from the spigots of the water barrels that stood near the forecastle and which contained the only supply of drinking water for the lower grades.'‡

Sometimes when ships were caught in the doldrums between the belts of trade winds, whole crews were reduced to such straits that they ate the leather which was fastened around the masts and the yard-arms as a protection against friction of the ropes. The leather, impregnated with salt and burned dry by the sun, was softened in salt water, cut up, and rationed to the famished crew; a crew that in such circumstances found roasted rat the greatest delicacy. Mercifully the ships were nearly always plagued with the creatures.

Added to these already appalling conditions was the dreaded scourge, scurvy. Every expedition hoped they would be exempt from it, but each was reduced to impotence by its effects. Small wonder, then, that captains were loath to leave the beaten tracks where winds were known to blow in fixed directions, and where 'places of refreshment' were certain.

* Masefield.
† Banks.
‡ Hendrik Willem Van Loon, *Ships and How They Sail*, Harrap & Co., London, 1935.

Back to the *Endeavour*, like a gull on taut wings we wheel down through the blue-washed landscape of the Pacific; great banks of clouds are tucked in behind the horizon. The ship presents a squat, compact silhouette but is not without a certain elegance, her masts and yards describing black nervous lines as they swing against the sky, her sails white on white against the clouds. Over the stern we can distinguish the heavy lantern in its ponderous case.

If the trails of previous explorations were to be visible lines drawn on a map they would appear as thin threads twined together, almost plaited in their criss-crossing over the immensity of the ocean. Pick out now, in red ink, Cook's first voyage, see how it detaches itself in dips and loops, completely individual and quite separate from the rest. From Tahiti he plunges down to 40° longitude south of the Equator; no navigator had dared this before. From here the line rises north again and circles New Zealand. Tasman must still have the credit for having first seen New Zealand, but to Cook alone belongs the honour of having explored it. He determined that there were two islands and discovered the straits separating them and named after him. He also made a complete survey. Striking west he then winds his way slowly up two thousand miles of Australia's eastern seaboard; straight through the dangerous channel separating the mainland from the reef. 'Let no man enter the uncharted intricacies of the Great Barrier Reef,' writes Flinders long after, 'whose nerves were not strong enough to thread the needle through its maze.'

It is when studying the timid lines drawn by the expeditions immediately preceding the voyage of the *Endeavour* that one realizes Cook's greatness as an explorer. His dogged determination and the extraordinary resourcefulness he exhibited in dangerous situations, and, of course, a thorough and accurate knowledge of his business contributed to his success. But above all what singled him out as a born leader for such an expedition was his ability to maintain the crew's health and morale on this and the two other voyages to follow.

When we left the *Endeavour*, the great cabin had been regaling itself on albatross stew. It is now March the 1st, fine weather and very pleasant. 'Began a new month,' writes Banks, 'by pulling off an under waistcoat.'

On the 25th a young marine called William Greenslade jumped overboard and was not missed until it was too late. This poignant incident illustrates an unpleasant side of ship-board psychology, when pent-up men's nerves led them to thoughtless brutality.

Greenslade, a remarkably quiet and industrious boy in his teens, was on sentry duty outside the cabin door. With him was one of Cook's servants busy cutting up a sealskin, the small pieces he was preparing

5. Bumping my way over a sandy trail leading out to the point I suddenly saw a ship. (*page 45*)

6. Point Venus Fort and observatory, engraved by S. Middiman after S. Parkinson. (*page 46*)

7. The black beach of Matavai Bay. A view taken from the spot where Cook's fort must have stood. The trees in the near foreground are the oft-mentioned *aito* or ironwoods. (*page 46*)

8. Parts of Tahiti have changed but little
during the intervening years of its discovery. (*page 56*)

9. The affluent sometimes manage two-storied houses, tenebrous retreats faced with cornices, banisters and screens of perforated lattice work. (*page 56*)

11. Pomaré IV's palace. (*page* 63)

10. Patterned with the pinnated leaves of the bread-fruit. (*page* 56)

12. Queen Pomaré Vahiné from a portrait, hanging in the Papeete museum, by an unknown artist. (*page 63*)

destined to become tobacco pouches. It seems that he had promised a patch to several of the men, but for some reason had refused one to this young fellow. When the servant was called away for a moment Greenslade, more as a joke than anything else, snatched the piece he wanted. On returning the servant immediately saw what had happened and protested vehemently, threatening to report the boy if the object in question was not returned.

It would all have ended here but unfortunately a fellow marine happened to overhear the conversation and repeated it to the others. They decided that Greenslade's act cast dishonour on the entire corps. It was inexcusable, they argued, for a sentry on duty to commit a theft. The Captain himself must be told about it.

Meanwhile poor Greenslade, 'a raw fellow' according to Cook, took to his bunk in an agony of shame and confusion, his companions' accusations 'driving him almost mad'. When the sergeant of the marines summoned him on deck to be reported to the Captain, Greenslade followed without a word but once above, slipped forward through the gathering dusk, never to be seen again. Cook undoubtedly felt very badly about it for he notes that he 'was neither made acquainted with the theft or the circumstances attending it until the man was gone'.

In April the *Endeavour* experienced strange weathers: calms succeeded by bad squalls – what the seamen called the trolly-lollys. On the morning of the 4th Peter Briscoe, one of Banks' servants, posted in the crow's nest, sighted land; a low-lying island tufted with coconut palms. The first things observed on sighting such atolls are always the coconut palms, which show up as a line of green appearing to grow out of the sea. On approaching, huts could be discerned under the palms, with people running along the beach making signals. One cannot imagine what a relief it must have been after ten solid weeks of only sky and water to smell land, an indescribable wonder, impossible to convey to those who have not experienced it. Softly the scent of these Pacific islands comes to one across the reefs, borne out by a land breeze. One is engulfed in warm clouds of sweetness, the odour of growing things spiked with a heavy scent of tropical flowers and the fragrance of sandalwood. Sometimes the island from which the scent comes is too far off even to be seen.

Welcome now, what must these sweet breezes have represented in the days of sailing-ships with cramped quarters crowded with unwashed men. One can of course wash in sea-water, but it never really cleans. It leaves the skin sticky and adds greatly to the miseries of those afflicted with prickly heat, an affection from which most sailors seemed to have suffered from the day they entered the tropics until the day they left them.

For the next ten days they sailed slowly by a succession of islands: Aki-Aki – which Cook called Thrum Cap – then Marokau and Ravahére, all part of what is now known as the Tuamotu archipelago. Cook did not attempt to land because of the reefs.

One evening a halo was observed round the moon and a very disagreeable night followed, 'the wind being all round the compass with lightning and heavy rain'. On the 10th, Osnaburg, or Méhétia, the easternmost of the Society Isles discovered by the *Dolphin* on its last voyage, was sighted and some hours later George III Land, or Tahiti, appeared on the horizon, 'but so faint that very few could see it'. The men had a dispute as to whether what they saw was really land or only vapours. It is very easy in the Pacific to be deceived by cloud banks. In the ensuing excitement the future Sir Joseph clambered up the masthead, 'but the sunset was cloudy and we could see nothing of the island'. Next morning, however, it appeared clearly, for the clouds had rolled away from off the green hills. A gentle breeze carried the *Endeavour* lazily round the north-east point of the island. Canoes paddled out to meet her and finally on the morning of the 13th she came to anchor in Port Royal Bay. They had arrived.

Chapter 7

First Days in Tahiti

ON ALL of Cook's charts and views and in the different journals one finds Tahiti referred to as King George III Island, while Matavai Bay is generally, to begin with anyway, Port Royal Harbour. It was Captain Wallis who discovered the island in June 1767 who named them thus. Too weak to leave the ship himself, Wallis delegated one of his officers, Lieutenant Furneaux, to represent him. An official landing was made and planting the British flag, formal possession of the island was taken in the name of His Majesty. The natives, not yet entirely amicably disposed, but subjugated nevertheless by a recent salute of the *Dolphin*'s guns, watched the white man's antics in silence from the far banks of the river. They had pennants of their own on their great war canoes and must have conceived a fairly accurate idea of the implications of the ceremony. Their prompt reaction would certainly suggest it. That same night, assembling all the people in the district, 'they formed a large, torch-light procession, and went heralded with drums and conch trumpets and other instruments of noise to bear away the flag on its staff'.* Tahiti was to be claimed quite independently by three different nations, and all within a period of five years.

The form of the island has been compared to an hour glass but, perhaps, the figure eight, set on its side with one of its loops slightly distended, would be a more accurate image. It consists of two peninsulas joined by a narrow two-mile-wide isthmus across which the Tahitians used to draw their canoes to save the journey round the smaller of the two islands, Taiarapu (lesser Tahiti). I explain this to make the various landings clear, for the expeditions anchored at different points. Wallis and Cook sheltered in Port Royal, or Matavai Bay, situated on the north coast of the larger island, Tahiti-nui (greater Tahiti). Bougainville, arriving before Cook, but only ten months after Wallis in April 1768, landed also on the main peninsula at a break in the reefs known as Hitiaa. He only learned of the previous occupancy of the island on his way home, and quite legitimately, as far as he was concerned,

* *Ancient Tahiti* by Miss Teuira Henry. Based on Material Recorded by J. M. Orsmond and published by the Benrice P. Bishop Museum, Honolulu, Hawaii, 1928.

claimed his beautiful 'Nouvelle Cythère' for France which, with its neighbours, he called the Archipel de Bourbon.

Spain made the third claim four years later when officials in Peru, resuming their country's traditional interest in the Pacific, sent out an expedition under the command of Don Domingo Boenechea. Sailing from Callao in the *Aguila* he arrived at Tahiti on November the 8th, 1772, and anchored off the northern coast of Tairapu, where he stayed for ten days. Like Wallis and Bougainville before him, he claimed the island for his country, naming it Ile d'Amat after the Viceroy of Peru.

The natives completely disregarded these repeated christenings. As for the Europeans, there was as yet no advantage in pressing rival claims for these small groups of Pacific islands. Tahiti remained independent, she even established a dynasty of kings who ruled until she became the first victim of nineteenth-century European imperialism in the Pacific with the French annexation of 1843.

Such was the order in which Tahiti was first visited. Let me briefly mention the problem of nomenclature. Cook's charts and journals show that whenever possible he reverted to the native names. Port Royal Harbour became Matavai Bay, Matavai being its native appellation and meaning 'face of the water'. Similarly, King George Island became Tahiti, or rather Otahiti. Here Cook made a mistake in adding an extra vowel, 'O', but it is easy to understand how this happened. O'Tahiti signifies 'it is Tahiti', the answer a native would have given had he been asked what land it was. Henceforth, I think it much simpler to adopt either ancient native or current western nomenclature, for I have wasted hours myself tracing place names in the journals, some of them having no connection whatever with present-day usage.

Point Venus, forming the eastern extremity of Matavai Bay, is one of the few places to retain its anglicized name. In Tahitian it is appropriately called Te-auroa (meaning long arm) as it is a long spit of black sand. Here Cook erected his observatory incorporated in a small fort. It was also my first place of pilgrimage. I drove over one evening from Papeete, the road climbing the famous 'One Tree Hill'.

Matavai Bay is not the best anchorage on the island. Papeete harbour is more protected from the wind, as Bligh discovered when he was driven there by a gale. However, Wallis and Cook had set the fashion for Matavai Bay, and One Tree Hill was a convenient landmark, easily recognized by an approaching vessel. Nowadays a whole group of trees fringe its summit; a species of *casuarina*, known in the islands as 'ironwood' or *aito*. It is a sad tree, rather primitive in its construction; its plumed foliage made up of dusty green, tubular needles that come away in segments like certain bog plants. The Tahitian will tell you that the wind moaning through its branches represents the

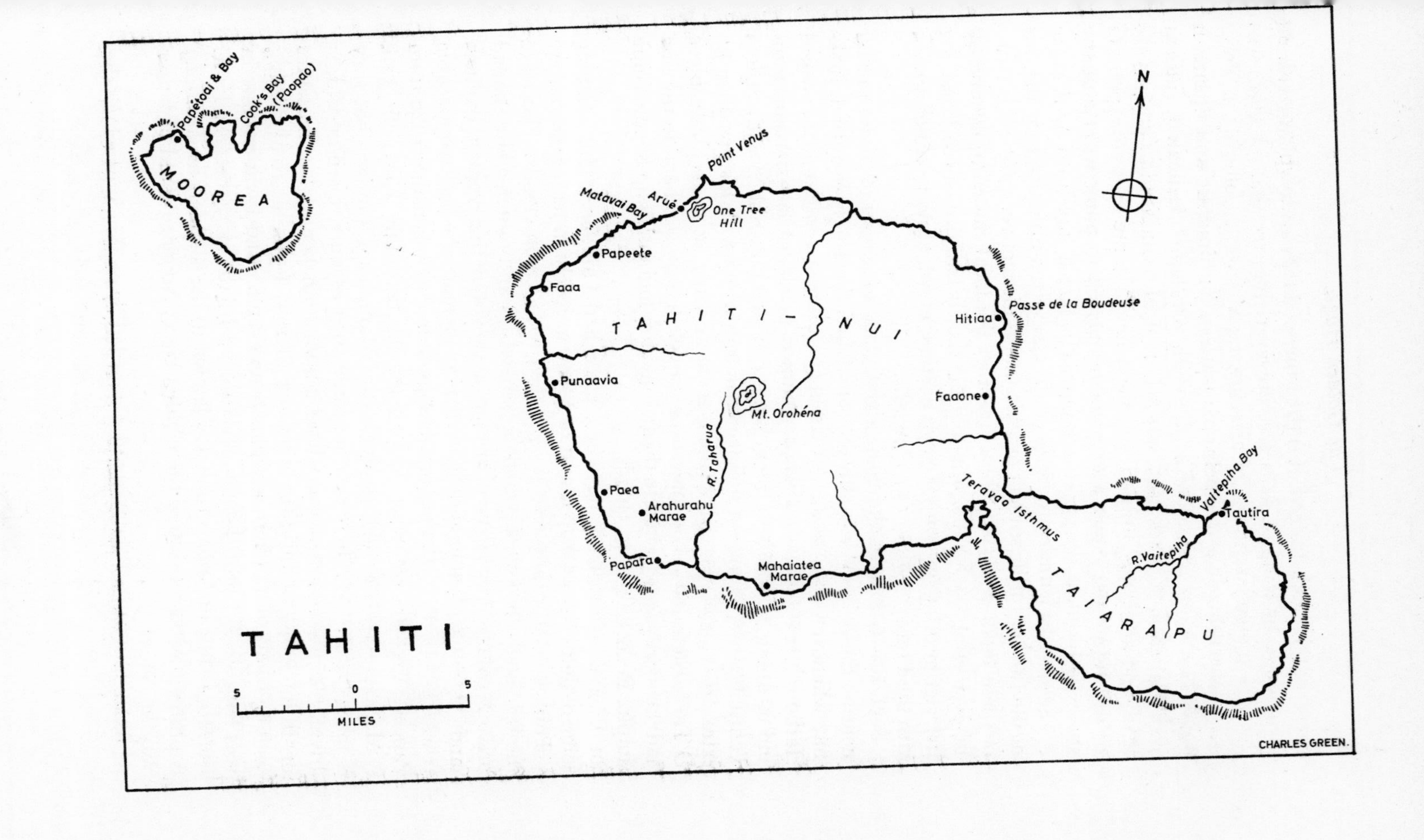
TAHITI
MOOREA
Papetoai & Bay
Cook's Bay
(Paopao)
Point Venus
Matavai Bay
Arué
One Tree
Hill
Papeete
Faaa
TAHITI-NUI
Punaavia
Mt. Orohéna
R. Taharua
Paea
Arahurahu
Marae
Papara
Mahaiatea
Marae
Hitiaa
Passe de la Boudeuse
Faaone
Teravao Isthmus
TAIARAPU
R. Vaitepiha
Vaitepiha Bay
Tautira
N
5
0
5
MILES
CHARLES GREEN.

voices of the dead. Indeed, it is the ironwood they always planted round their *marais* or temples. It is not, however, the tree that for years was the well-known landmark for arriving ships.

Parkinson made a monochrome wash of it; romantic and blasted it stands in the foreground while the *Endeavour*, faintly indicated, rides at anchor far below. Parkinson was a botanical draughtsman and, as we have seen, had only limited abilities when it came to landscapes. He was, anyhow, too much a child of his period to paint what actually confronted him in the great outdoors. His sketch mixed up by mistake in a folder of Flemish drawings could easily pass unnoticed for there is nothing either in the subject or style that is distinctive.

A charming Tahitian, the curator of the local museum, eventually identified the tree for me. She told me that it had been a red-flowering *Erythrina indica*, commonly known as 'tiger claw', almost extinct now in Tahiti, but still common in Hawaii.

The tree may have changed, given place to several of a more usual species, but the view was still the same; breathtakingly beautiful, looking right out across Tahiti's indented coast line, a verdant coast packed tight with coconut palms whose plumed heads feather the slopes inclining gently upwards to the great, green clad hills ribbed with valleys and glens that Parkinson delineates more vividly with his pen than he could with his brushes, describing them as being 'as uneven as a piece of crumpled paper'. The majestic sweep of the bay is echoed in the line of the hills; there is no end to them, fold after fold piling up to culminate in lofty peaks hidden in clouds.

The sun was just setting when I reached One Tree Hill, dipping down behind the nearby island of Moorea, lovely in its jagged outline thrown against a turquoise sky streaked with lemon clouds. There are always clouds in Tahiti, whether banked up and oyster-white shaded with a leaden promise of rain, or then, as they were this evening, banners of joyful orange, lemon and flame. In my memory the only comparable sunsets are those of Egypt, miraculous moments when the Mokattam hills are washed an intense copper, the sky becoming a metallic-pink pricked by the crescented domes of the Mamalukes' tombs – but they are in a different key, here every evening one's eyes are rinsed in gold.

The circumference of the whole island, both peninsulas, measures about one hundred and fifty miles and there is a possible road skirting the major part of it. There was hardly an evening that I was not out on the road, driving into the sun, hypnotized by the extraordinary light. Indeed, Tahiti in Cook's time was known to the islanders as *Tahiti-nui mare'are'a* or Great Tahiti of the Golden Haze. No place could be better named.

The shoreline of a Pacific island is guarded by reefs against which the sea breaks in a whirl of snowy foam. The reefs are a mile or so off-shore and the noise of the crashing waves remains almost inaudible, reduced by the distance to the faintest murmur, no louder than the echo in a shell. Between the reefs and the shore the water takes on the limpid quality of glass and only a storm can curl the mirror-like surface of these lagoons. The colours of Tahiti's lagoons are not the apple-green and aquamarine stains found in most of the other islands for here the sands are black. It is misleading, however, to paint them in quite so inky a hue for if one looks carefully, runs the fine sand through one's fingers, one will soon see that it is not blacker than a black pearl is black. Rather is it gold overlaid with charcoal, darkening only when it is wetted by the gentle lapping of lagoon waves. Over these sands the coconuts curl their long slender trunks, elegant, hardly anchored, it would seem, to the tumble of rocks from which they miraculously draw their sustenance. Brown and green are their colours over which the sinking sun throws a liquid varnish of yellow, yellowing also the oil-cloth leaves of the banana. The red ginger flowers stand out even redder than they are, afire in the golden light that falls in shafts through the big trees.

This then was my first impression of the island. I had been told that MGM were on location at Point Venus, shooting another version of the *Mutiny on the 'Bounty'* and I expected the worst, and had even been advised to postpone my visit altogether. But I am glad now that I went. Bumping my way over the sandy trail leading out to the Point, I suddenly saw a ship riding at anchor some way out on the lagoon. Time was playing me a trick. I knew it to be a faithful reproduction of the *Bounty*, but at first sight it could certainly have been the *Endeavour*. Her sails were furled and from her flagstaff flew the Jack, freed in all its great size, 'as large as a mizzen top gallant sail'. Flung out into the breeze it floated majestically: the Union Flag of Great Britain, the joined crosses of St George and St Andrew upon the enormous banner of blue. Round the ship bobbed a fleet of outrigger canoes, looking like ants. The beach, when I eventually reached it, was crowded. It is unimportant at this point to describe it more fully, but the details were amusing, even down to young bread-fruit trees in their small, flat-sided wooden tubs with rope handles; Bligh's cargo and the reason for his presence in Tahiti.

How many times was I to see this same beach empty, with not a soul on it. I was familiar enough with Cook's plans to find my way about, and one would have to know them, for the local authorities are not much assistance. They have recently restored a whitewashed column supposedly erected by Cook on the spot where the observatory stood. It has no connection whatever with our captain, except in the minds of unsuspecting tourists. The fort had never stood out on the point, but quite a way up the beach, on a narrow spit of sand between the lagoon and the Vaipopoo River, a river that no longer exists since it has long ago changed its course and flows now into a neighbouring bay lying to the east. All that is left of Cook's 'broad sweet river' where he watered is a stagnant pool that loses itself in a swamp.

However, following the plans, the former site is found, near enough to the water's edge to be 'under command of the ship's guns'. The natives had not been at all disturbed at the proceedings and even helped in the work. 'The ground we had fixed upon was of no use to them being part of the sandy beach upon the shore of the bay and not near to any of their habitations.' Cook with his usual tact had been very careful about invading their property. They 'purchased every stick of wood which was used upon the occasion, and cut down no trees till we had first obtained their consent'. They threw up banks of turf and mud four and a half feet high topped with palisades; while on the river side, the direction from which the attack would have come had there been any, they made a bastion of water casks mounted with swivel guns off the ship. Within the walls there was a marquee for Banks and Solander, a tent for the ship's company, a pen for the sheep, and the armourer's forge. There was also a cookhouse complete with oven and, of course, the *pièce de résistance*, the portable observatory; a wooden frame covered with canvas, said to have been designed by Smeaton, the civil engineer, builder of the Eddystone lighthouse.

Parkinson tells us that 'the sandy ground on which the fort stood was very troublesome when the wind was high'. He also made a drawing of the place, for Buchan had died almost immediately on arrival, never recovering from an ultimate epileptic coma. Judging from the very competent watercolour Buchan did of Tierra del Fuego his rendering would certainly have been more sophisticated than Parkinson's, which looks exactly like a schoolboy's scribble of something inspired by Henty. But to do Parkinson justice, the naïve effect must have reflected the fort's actual character. Banks' marquee is made up of three separate units joined, it would seem, with canvas corridors. A flag flies bravely from the central pavilion. Considering the circumstances, it is almost viceregal in its splendour.

Cook gives us an amusing glimpse of their first hours ashore while the building was in progress. 'It being too late in the day to do anything more, a party with a petty officer was left to guard the tents, while we with another party took a walk into the woods and with us most of the natives. We had just crossed the river when Mr Banks shot three ducks at one shot which surprised them so much that most of them fell down as though they had been shot likewise.' Banks has no comment to make on his own marksmanship, rather his attention centred elsewhere – on the ladies. They showed the Englishmen all kinds of civilities, 'but,' adds Banks, 'there were no places of retirement. The houses being entirely without walls we had not an opportunity of putting their politeness to every test that maybe some of us would not have failed to have done had circumstances been more favourable. Indeed we had no reason to doubt any part of their politeness, as by their frequently pointing to the mats on the ground and sometimes by force seating themselves and us upon them they plainly showed that they were much less jealous of observation than we were.'

Bougainville reports very similar episodes. His sailors working on shore 'were invited to enter the houses, where the people gave them to eat; nor did the civility of their hosts stop at a slight collation, they offered them young girls. The hut was immediately filled with a curious crowd of men and women, who made a circle round the guests and the young victim of hospitality. The ground was spread with leaves and flowers and the musicians sang an hymeneal song to the tune of their flutes. Here Venus is the goddess of hospitality, her worship does not admit of any mysteries, and every tribute paid to her is a feat for the whole nation. They were surprised at the confusion which our people appeared to be in, as our customs did not admit of their public proceedings. However,' ends Bougainville, 'every one of our men found it possible to conquer his repugnance, and conform to the customs of the country.'

The chevalier also tells us of a young girl who managed to clamber on board. Making for the quarterdeck, she stood over one of the hatchways which was open, and dropping the *pareu* which covered her, 'appeared to the eye of all beholders, such as Venus showed herself to the Phrygian shepherd, having, indeed the celestial form of that goddess'.

Bougainville admits it was as difficult to keep command of the officers as of the sailors.

There were moments when shore leave had to be cancelled. The cook, however, managed to escape, but he bitterly regretted his disobedience. He was brought back on board more dead than alive. He had hardly set foot on the land with his girl 'when he was immediately surrounded by a crowd who undressed him from head to toe'. More details follow and, adds Bougainville, 'the poor lad told me that I might reprimand him as much as I pleased, but that I could never frighten him so much, as he had just now been frightened on shore'.

These were Bougainville's problems. We revert to Cook who suffered a similar episode a few days later.

It was Sunday and Cook had divine service performed in one of the tents in the fort. Several natives attended. Cook in his journal makes no mention of having coerced them. Hawkesworth however, tells us that 'the party was desirous of having some of the principal natives attend', but one suspects that he inserted this detail to please the pious at home. Cook was remarkably broad-minded and never gives one the impression of wishing to proselytize. The idea of human sacrifice shocked him, but otherwise he showed a perfectly unbiased interest in all that touched on Tahitian religious beliefs. The natives on this particular occasion behaved 'with great decency' but showed absolutely no curiosity about the service and asked no questions, 'nor would they attend at all to any explanations we attempted to give them'. Hawkesworth in his version of Cook's voyages deals with the service and ends up 'such, anyhow were our matins', and then, good editor that he was, could not resist taking advantage of events, running them together, making one episode out of two separate events. 'Our Indians,' he quips, 'thought fit to perform vespers of a very different kind.' Cook words it quite differently and tells us soberly that the day closed with an odd scene at the gate of the fort 'when a young fellow about six feet high lay with a little girl about ten or twelve years of age publicly before several of our people and a number of natives'. Nobody exhibited any sense of shame and among the spectators were several women of superior rank, among them Obarea (Wallis's Queen Purea), who may properly be said to have assisted, for she gave instructions to the girl how to perform her part, 'who, young as she was, did not seem much to want it'.

The days pass on and the next attention-commanding episode was a dinner Cook and Banks attended, given by a local chief. They ate heartily of raw fish and bread-fruit with plantains, but it is not their menu so much as Banks' uncharacteristically tactless behaviour that surprises us. He was seated in a place of honour next to the chief's wife, who unfortunately was very ugly. Glancing at the watching crowd he suddenly saw a pretty girl and taken 'by the fire in her eyes' beckons her over. After much argument he eventually persuaded her to sit next to him, the other side from the chief's wife. This clearly was a serious breach of etiquette for his noble companion remonstrated furiously. Taking no notice of her, Banks proceeded to load his pretty girl 'with beads and every present I could think pleasing to her' while the chief's wife continued to feed him sulkily with fish and coconut milk. Fortunately the embarrassing situation was interrupted by the appearance of a flustered Solander who had just had his pockets picked, because, as Banks pointed out, he had not been in as good company as himself.

Constant pilfering was to try the explorers' patience and prove their most aggravating problem. Indeed, in the end, it was indirectly to be the cause of Cook's death. However, the islanders were very honest among themselves. Their houses, Parkinson tells us, are without any fastenings. 'Locks, bolts and bars,' he continues, 'are peculiar to civilized countries, where their moral theory is the best, and their moral practice too generally of the worst.' On the second voyage Forster knew of the natives' disposition to theft, but never lost anything of value. 'Our handkerchiefs which were the easiest to come at, were made of their own cloth (the thinnest variety of *tapa*) so that they found themselves disappointed as often as they had dexterously picked our pockets, and with great good humour returned them to us.' The Polynesian regarded stealing from strangers as a challenge to ingenuity and a game of skill, and not at all a matter of moral obliquity. One has to appreciate also that a great ship full of dazzling objects, particularly firearms, was sore temptation to a primitive people who knew only fibre rope, basalt axes and wooden spears.

Cook proposed to stop these losses by seizing either a chief or their canoes as hostages. The thefts were generally committed by the ordinary people, the chiefs seldom stooping to demean themselves, but sometimes their servants were directed to steal some particular object. This is certainly what happened to Banks' pistols, stolen from him while he slept, at the instigation of Wallis's Queen Purea. Of course, when the natives realized Cook's methods of obtaining restitution, they took their own measure of combating them. Cook explains how 'the moment a theft of importance is committed it spreads like the wind over the whole neighbourhood and everyone takes the alarm and begins to move off with their possessions in all haste'. The chief of the district 'gives orders to bring us no supplies and flies to some distant part; all this is sometimes done in so short a time that we have obtained by this means the first knowledge of our being robbed. Whether we oblige them to make restitutions or no, the chief must be reconciled before any of the people are permitted to bring any refreshments – they know very well we cannot do without them, therefore never fail of strictly observing this rule, without ever considering that all their war canoes on which the strength of their nation depends, their houses, and even the very fruit they refuse to supply us with are entirely in our power'.

The disappearance of the astronomical quadrant proved to be the most serious theft. 'Without this,' writes Cook, 'we could not perform the service for which our voyage was principally undertaken.' Green and Cook had landed early one morning and going to the fort had found the quadrant missing. It had never been unpacked and had lain all night on Captain Cook's bed where no one slept. The quadrant was a heavy object, seemingly impossible to carry off without being noticed, especially as a sentry had been posted all night within five yards of the tent. Cook first supposed that some sailor, imagining the case to contain nails or some other object or traffic, had absconded with it, and offered a large reward for the instrument's return. However, it was found that a native had made off with it in the night. A chief identified the culprit and they set out immediately to the westward in pursuit. The people along the way readily told them in which direction the thief had gone and how long it was since he had passed. They pressed forward, walking and running alternately in stifling heat, climbing a hill. After about seven miles a man was found with part of the quadrant in his hand. Menaced by Banks, he produced all the missing pieces.

Cook was to return to Tahiti several times, and on his last visit in 1777, Tu, or Otoo as Cook called him, took every precaution to prevent Cook and his party from being robbed. Tu was the famous chief who eventually proclaimed himself king of the island, styling himself Pomaré I. Sentinels from the royal entourage were posted behind the tents, some across the river and others close to. 'We were,' as Cook puts it, 'surrounded by them. From their stations, they not only guarded us in the night from thieves, but could observe everything that passed in the day,' and as Cook adds wryly, 'the measure adopted by Tu to secure their safety also swelled his treasury, for his guards collected contributions from such girls as had private connection with our people; which was generally done every morning.'

Apart from the constant irritation of having to guard against theft, the explorers' relationship with the Tahitians was excellent. Cook outlined a procedure for trading with them 'that such merchandise as we had on board for the purpose might continue to bear a proper value and not leave it to everyone's own particular fancy which could not fail to bring on confusion and quarrels between us and the natives'. 'Three things,' he went on to say, 'make them our friends; their own good natured and benevolent disposition, gentle treatment on our part, and the dread of our fire arms.'

Lord Morton, President of the Royal Society, made 'a list of hints offered to the consideration of Captain Cook and other gentlemen' in the *Endeavour*; and I quote them here in some detail for it gives us an insight into the most enlightened of eighteenth-century attitudes. Morton enjoins 'the utmost patience and forbearance with respect to the natives of the several lands where the ship may touch'. He asks Cook 'to check the petulance of the sailors and restrain the wanton use of fire arms'. He should 'have it in view that the shedding of blood of these people is a crime of the highest nature. They are human creatures, the work of the same omnipotent author, equally under his care with the most polished Europeans; perhaps being less offensive, more entitled to his favour'. He continues, stating that 'no European nation has a right to occupy any part of their country, or settle among them without their voluntary consent. Conquest over such people can give no just title; because they could never be the aggressors'. Should they attempt to repel intruders and kill some men in the attempt 'even this would hardly justify firing among them till every other gentle method has been tried'. Morton then enumerates several ways by which the explorers could convince the natives of European superiority of arms 'without slaying any of these poor people'. He suggests their shooting 'some of the birds or other animals that are near them; showing them that a bird upon a wing may be brought down by a shot – such an appearance would strike them with amazement and awe'. As we have seen this was precisely what happened.

Fortunately Morton's advice did not fall on deaf ears. Often in the past the discovery of a new country had meant massacre for the natives as in the conquests of Mexico or Peru. But one can hardly compare Cook with Pisarro or Cortes. He openly doubted the beneficial effects of our civilization upon the Tahitians, or indeed any of the Pacific islands. 'Our occasional visits,' writes Cook on his third voyage, 'may in some respects have benefited its inhabitants but a permanent establishment amongst them, conducted as most European establishments amongst the Indian nations have unfortunately been, would I fear, give them just cause to lament that our ships had ever found them out . . . it is my real opinion that it would have been far better for these people, never to have known our superiority in the accommodations and arts that make life comfortable, than, after once knowing it to be left again, and abandoned to their original incapacity of improvement. Indeed, they cannot be restored to that happy mediocrity in which they lived before we discovered them, if the intercourse between us be discontinued. It seems to me, that it has become, in a measure, incumbent on the Europeans to visit them once in three or four years in order to supply them with those conveniences which we have introduced among them. The want of such occasioned supplies will, probably, be felt very heavily by them, when it may be too late to go back to their own less perfect contrivances, which they now despise and have discontinued since the introduction of ours. For by the time that the iron tools of which they are now possessed, are worn out, they will have almost lost the knowledge of their own. A stone hatchet is, at present, as rare a thing amongst them, as an iron one was eight years ago; and a chisel of bone, or stone, is not to be seen.'

How right also Morton proved to be when he warned Cook of 'petulance of the sailors'. A midshipman had been put in command of the fort, and one of the sentinels he had posted being taken unawares, a native had snatched a musket out of his hand. Immediately the midshipman gave orders to shoot. 'The men obeyed,' writes Parkinson, 'with the greatest glee imaginable, as if they had been shooting at wild duck. They killed one man and wounded many others.'

Banks shared the same views as the Captain, for when he heard of the fray, he was highly displeased. 'If we quarrel with these Indians,' he snapped, 'we should not agree with angels.'

It is not our intention here to follow the explorers day by day, anyone can do this by reading the different logs, but rather to give a general impression of the island as it was when Cook first was there, comparing it to the picture it presents in our time. There is, nevertheless, one more thing I would mention before passing on to a description of the island, the flies. Besides the constant thieving, the flies were the only drawback to an otherwise ideal existence.

'The flies,' writes Banks, 'have been so troublesome ever since we have been ashore that we can scarce get any business done from them.' They made it almost impossible for Parkinson to work; they swarmed over his drawing board and even ate the colour off the surface of his drawings as fast as he could lay it on. A kind of mosquito net was improvised under which Parkinson sat as if in a small tent. This helped make the inconveniences tolerable, but did not remove it. Nor did a home-made fly trap of tar and molasses succeed any better. The plate in which they mixed the glutinous concoction was left outside the mosquito net every day for the servant to change. One morning Banks saw a native who thought he was unobserved scoop it up in his hand. Curious to know what he would do with it, Banks watched him. 'The gentleman had a large sore upon his backside to which this clammy liniment was applied, but with what success I never took the pain to enquire.'

[Chapter 8]

Tahiti Today

MOST WRITERS say that the ancient Tahiti disappeared a hundred years after its first contact with Europeans. In a sense this is true; there was the usual breakdown of old customs. It was the familiar pattern of a primitive people who, relinquishing their old traditions, gained but little in return. They had already believed in a supreme deity long before the advent of missionaries – Taaroa, the unique one, the ancestor of all the gods, the creator of all things. For a long period Taaroa dwelt in a shell. It was round like an egg, and revolved in space in continual darkness. There was no sun, no moon, no land, no mountains, all was in a confluent state until, breaking open his protective covering, Taaroa created the earth, using one half of the shell as the dome of the sky. Numerous gods were always found carved on his image, indicating they were all part of him. As their religion entered into everything they did, the introduction of the new faith of the missionaries was made to destroy every old practice of their society. They were persuaded to abandon idolatry and conform with outward observances without understanding them. Otto von Kotzebüe, the early nineteenth-century navigator and explorer, sums up the situation very concisely in his book of voyages;* 'the religion of the missionaries has, with a great deal of evil, effected some good. It has retained the vices of theft and incontinence; but it has given birth to ignorance, hypocrisy, and a hatred of all other modes of faith which was once foreign to the open and benevolent character of the Tahitians'. Even worse than this, it has left them quite defenceless, incapable of combating the most insidious of all emotions – boredom, a profound boredom bred of the congenital indolence of the South Seas. One can read it in their faces and see it in the enigmatic stares of Gauguin's heavy-lidded, broad-nosed *vahinés*. So definite a part of their character has it become that it veils the blue-gold air of their island; a definite substance that cloys, a net of spider webs that could be brushed aside with a stick.

Before the coming of the white man this boredom was kept at bay by

* Otto von Kotzebüe. *A New Voyage Round the World in the Year 1823*, Colbrun & Bentley, London, 1830.

endless pagan ceremonies involving songs and dances, elaborate taboos, superstitions and internecine wars, almost Homeric in character, consisting chiefly of personal combat.

So lazy are they by nature that many of the islanders still do not talk French, and who can blame them really for preferring their own soft and musical tongue? Their words mainly end with a vowel and they do violence to our proper names if these grate too harshly. Cook thus became Toote; Solander, Tolano, and Banks, Opane. Green was Treene.

Banks recalls that he saw only one sick person the whole time he was in Tahiti. This not including those skin eruptions and ulcers caused by coral poisonings. It is well known that cuts sustained fishing on coral reefs nearly always become infected. But in general these islanders, isolated in a natural quarantine for centuries, eating simple food, and hardened by wearing few clothes were remarkably healthy. The diseases endemic to Tahiti were scrofula, tuberculosis, asthma, elephantiasis and the yaws. Venereal diseases and a number of other infectious complaints were unknown, and therefore they had no resistance when exposed to epidemics. As Dr Danielsson, the anthropologist of the Kon-Tiki expedition, wrote:* 'Even such mild diseases as influenza and measles caused innumerable deaths and spread as swiftly as a forest fire. The result was an astounding decrease of the population. According to careful computations the population was reduced in half a century to scarcely one-tenth of what it had originally been.'

Alcohol was another disruptive element. Teaching the art of distillation to the Tahitian brought with it violence and misery. The terrible effects of the use of gunpowder which Pomaré I first obtained from the mutineers of the *Bounty* contributed to the general disintegration of the old society.

The usual controversy arose as to which expedition was responsible for introducing venereal disease. Cook took what precautions he could and had the surgeon examine every man of the ship's company 'to discover if any had the disorder upon him for above a month before our arrival'. Only one man in the ship was infected and he was put in quarantine as far as women were concerned. Cook was naturally worried when eventually more than thirty of his men became affected with the disease. 'No such thing,' he writes, 'happened to any of the *Dolphin*'s people while she was here, that I ever heard of. I had reason (notwithstanding the improbability of the thing) to think that we had brought it along with us, which gave me no small uneasiness.' He was much relieved when the natives assured him that the ships which had visited the island a month previously had been responsible for its propagation. Bougainville, on reading Cook's report, denied it. It is even

* Bengt Danielsson, *Love in The South Seas*, George Allen & Unwin, London, 1956.

13. Bread-fruit from an unpublished drawing by Sydney Parkinson. (*page 68*)

14. The famous *tiara* or *Gardenia tahitiensis*. (*page 70*)

15. The large crinums, or spider lilies, growing as high as a man's shoulder, down by the water's edge. (*page 70*)

16. Tahitian mourning costume. Engraved by W. Woollett after W. Hodges. (*page 73*)

17. The embalmed body of Ti'i. 'The only remarkable alteration,' writes Cook 'that had happened, was a shrinking of the muscular parts at the eye.' Engraved by W. Byrne after J. Webber. (*page 75*)

18. Pomaré V's tomb, a strange mausoleum, its sloping coral walls overgrown with fern, its corrugated roof topped with what looks like a large bottle of Benedictine. (*page 78*)

19. Ladies of rank performing a dance. Engraved by J. K. Sherwin after J. Webber. (*page 91*)

20. A view taken in
Tautira Bay
by William Hodges.
Lent by the Admiralty
to the National Maritime
Museum, Greenwich. (*page 101*)

quite possible that the disease was introduced at a much later date than has been supposed. Modern medicine suggests that what the early explorers took to be syphilis was in fact yaws, a contagious disease endemic to the Pacific, displaying very similar symptoms and responding to the same treatment.

What of the present-day physical aspect of the island? Parts of Tahiti and of the outlying islands have changed but little. Much of Cook's own description still applies. 'Between the foot of the ridges and the sea is a border of low land surrounding the whole island, except in a few places where the ridges rise directly from the sea, this low land is of various breadths but nowhere exceeds a mile and a half; the soil is rich and fertile being for the most part well stocked with fruit trees and small plantations and well watered by a number of small rivulets of excellent water which comes from the adjacent hills. It is upon this low land that the greatest part of the inhabitants live, not in towns or villages but dispersed everywhere around the whole island.' Parkinson tells us that the island looks like one continual village 'the houses being built about fifty yards from each other, under the shade of trees and surrounded by various odoriferous shrubs'.

'No country,' says Cook, 'can boast of more delightful walks than this; the plains where the natives reside are covered with groves of bread fruit and cocoanuts.' Only grass grows under the trees and the houses are reached by a criss-crossing of paths. The houses themselves were 'admirably calculated for the continual warmth of the climate', always in the woods and without walls, 'so that the air cooled by the shade of the trees has free access in whatever direction it happens to blow'. They were generally oblong in form with neatly thatched roofs made from coconuts or pandanus supported on posts. Inside there was little or no furniture, a stool perhaps for the master of the house and blocks of wood to serve as pillows. The floor was covered with freshly cut hay over which mats were spread. The poorer houses seldom had any partitions. 'They all huddle and sleep together, yet in this they generally observe some order, the married people laying by themselves and the unmarried each sex by themselves at some small distance from each other.' The better houses, however, all had walls, a kind of wicker woven from narrow slats of bamboo 'but not so close but to admit a free circulation of air'. The chiefs enjoyed more privacy 'having small moveable houses like a tent, so constructed as to be carried about in their canoes from place to place.

'Besides their common houses there are others much larger, two hundred feet long and upwards thirty broad and twenty in height. There are generally two or three of them in every district.' In these they held their entertainments.

Cook mentions the natives' excellent workmanship. 'One cannot help but admire it, especially when one considers the tools they have.' These consisted of adzes, chisels and gouges made of human bones, generally the bones of the forearm. 'With these ordinary tools that a European would expect to break at the first stroke I have seen them work surprisingly fast.' They smooth the beams of the houses with shells and then polish them, Parkinson adds, 'with a species of coral, or sea mushroom'.

The landscape is not so very much changed. Every day I would leave my ramshackle bungalow in Papeete and take a drive round the island. The road runs within a few feet of the shore, the dead shore line of a lagoon, nibbled at by the same insipid ripples that one finds on lakes. It makes a complete tour of the main island and is dusty and filled with potholes, but it is nevertheless a road. Before, everyone travelled by canoe. From Pirae, the district in which Papeete is situated, I would bump my way down to Faaa, down the coast to the fashionable residential district of Punaavia, on to Paea and Papara, once the most populous and powerful part of the island and where Purea built her great temple on its relatively wide flat plain. The boundary lines of the different districts are always the same, rivulets or low hills. 'Private properties,' writes Cook on his third voyage, 'are marked by large stones which have remained from one generation to another and long custom seems to secure the ownership here as effectively as the most severe laws in other countries.' These in many cases are still in place and denote the boundaries of a local chief, who now more often than not, is mayor of his district.

The buildings have changed in style but their character remains much the same. The open-sided hut with the pandanus thatch has become a corrugated iron roofed bungalow with a deep veranda, and where once could be found the large, many-columned hall where the *arioi* religious society danced and acted their erotic mimes now stands an austere, thinly steepled church dedicated to one of the apostles. The affluent sometimes manage two-storied houses, tenebrous retreats faced with cornices, banisters and screens of perforated lattice-work as fragile-looking as the paper lace found in a chocolate box. But whether bungalow, church or house, they are situated very much as the old dwelling used to be, carpeted around with green lawns, separated only by footpaths, the only dividing lines between the properties. High above the roofs curve the graceful trunks of the palms. It is like walking in a continual park with a delicious impression of light and shade, a dappling of broad, tropical leaves. One moves against a subaqueous light, patterned with the pinnated leaves of the bread-fruit trees. Small wonder that Bougainville found Tahiti the realizition of a Rousseauesque dream and that he named it *la Nouvelle Cythère*. 'Often,' he writes, 'I thought I was walking in the garden of Eden.' Often have I remembered his words.

In Moorea I stayed at Taero Mataitai's house. His was the largest bungalow in the district as he was the son of a chief. It was the kind of house that Mrs Robert Louis Stevenson in her letters would describe as 'a bird cage of a house, a house in a fairy tale with all the doors and windows open'. As a great favour the hospitable Pauline Schyle, one of the leading figures on the island, arranged for me to live there and I was attended by an enchanting brown-skinned princess, very suitable for a house of a fairy tale. Her fleeting shadow was the only sign of life I observed the whole time I was there. Never have I seen a more polished, immaculate household. The floors were highly waxed squares of flowered linoleum and heavy crochet work curtains hung at the windows which opened on to a solid wall of great, luminous, yellow-green leaves, belonging to one of the lilies of the *crinium* family. There were several bedrooms, all empty it would seem, for there was never anyone in them. One room led to another with two beds to every room; brass beds covered in great splashes of colour, splendid *ti fai fai*, serving as bedspreads, blankets and sheets all in one.

Ti fai fai, meaning 'cutting', are made by sewing a coloured cut-out design on a white background, or the application of a white design on a coloured background. The designs are apt to be rather stiff and are nearly always composed of floral or leaf motives, blocked out in the corners, and oriented towards the middle. One sees immediately that they are not an indigenous handicraft, for Tahitian women were taught to sew by British or American missionaries' wives and are still rather awkward with their needles.

Weaving was a completely unknown art in the islands of the South Pacific, the only cloth that Polynesians had being pieced sections of beaten or hammered vegetable matter, or *tapa*. Even today with sewing machines and with all the cottons they want, specially printed for them in Lille or Roubaix, they still prefer Mother Hubbards, or then, the classical *pareu* (sarong) to the European mode of dress; a form of apparel that demands a minimum of preparation. The most elaborate sewing they do is on their *ti fai fai*, which through the years have come to replace the *tapa* cloths under which they used to sleep.

It might well have been these *ti fai fais* that inspired Matisse's light-hearted inventions of bright coloured cut-outs on a plain ground, the *papiers découpés*. When he was in Tahiti his delightful egeria, Pauline Schyle, showed him women making these bold appliquéd quilts. Years later, bedridden, unable to work at an easel, he took to the scissors, deftly cutting from sheets of solid colour rhythmical leaf-like shapes, reminiscent of the philodendrons about him in southern France – or even perhaps the distantly remembered bread-fruit leaves of Tahiti.

I went into several houses and they were all much the same. Once at Hitaa, on the other side of the island, I was looking for a guide to take us into the mountains. A woman suggested we take one of her brothers. She indicated a small house on the banks of the river. 'He lives over there with my mother.' She spoke English and was clearly only half Polynesian. Few of the natives on the mainland are of pure blood. They have been intermarrying for years now, first with the English, and later with the French. In Papeete itself there is a fairly strong admixture of Chinese, the first Chinese being imported some ninety years ago by an English planter who despaired of ever making the Tahitians work. A very fortunate mixture it proved to be for it has produced some creatures of great beauty.

We found the woman's mother, a frail old lady sitting on a grass mat, wrapped in a quilt. She also understood only English, speaking it hesitantly. Perhaps her greatgrandfather had been an American sea captain, even a whaler from Nantucket; I did not like to question her but it pleased me to imagine so. The bungalow was typical of its kind; well swept, wooden floors and walls that, some eighty or seventy years ago, might have been painted, though hardly any trace of colour remained today. Again there were several beds to a room, one of them with its wooden headboard stencilled with a small wreath of flowers. In a corner I noticed a mahogany sea chest with brass handles.

In front of these houses is a straight walk bordered with lilies. Wooden steps lead on to a veranda, where there are canvas chairs, a table spread with an embroidered cloth and on it some shells. The inevitable crochet work hangs on the door; a door that is always wide open, as are the windows likewise. One wonders, in fact, if they are able to be closed. With such an open-air effect it needs little effort of the imagination to picture the houses as they were a hundred and ninety-two years ago.

Following the road you cross a stream every few hundred yards, and every mile or so a stream big enough to be called a river. It is by these river-valleys that the interior can be reached. There are no roads; only small paths run up towards the mountains, or one takes the water courses. Sometimes, from the top of a ridge or at the head of a valley, one can get a glimpse of the great serrated peaks of the interior. Jagged and sharp they tear at the sky, their steep sides wreathed in scarves of clouds. Clouds in Tahiti are either boiling, volatile mists or great static cumuli. It rains frequently but they are quick showers that, after ten minutes of clattering noisily on banana, *taro* and palm, end in a rainbow.

These valleys are extraordinarily beautiful and, more often than not, lead up to great waterfalls reduced in the distance to long plumes of water flashing out in the sunshine as they twist and cascade down over solid walls of green.

Out of so many astonishing views, I remember one in particular seen from an outrigger canoe while rounding the southern tip of Taiarapu, the smaller of the two peninsulas where there are no roads. A pass cuts deep into the hills exposing a fantastic landscape of what looked like giant obelisks, needles of sheer rock. It reminded one of the ephemeral scenes viewed on a Chinese scroll painting, scenes interpreting the upper reaches of the Yangtse Kiang in a gauzy poetry. Here it was reality and almost impossible to believe. It was overcast when we first took to the canoe, clouds still clothed the dense clumps of verdure that clung to even the most precipitous of the obelisks that rose a thousand feet or more into the sky.

Near to the palm fringed shore there were clearings of grass, sites of the old cultivations, for these valleys were inhabited at one time when the population of the island was more than double what it is now. There used to be roads across the island in the old days; now few people ever penetrate into the hinterland. The Tahitians do not climb mountains as we do to admire the views, it means nothing to them. They climb them to gather yams or wild oranges, or to trail a pig.

How many newcomers to the island has one seen setting out enthusiastically on an expedition into the hills? The inviting waterfalls are only a few miles away, but in point of fact to reach them entails long hours of marching with a guide. The gentlest rise behind one's hut turns out to be a major problem. The first two hundred feet of slope are cultivated with such crops as tapioca by the families who live on the shore. Then, what appears easy going from below is, in reality, a cruel slope of knife-sharp, volcanic rocks tumbled in a loose avalanche hidden by creepers. Whichever way one turns the slope is precipitous. Above this one blunders into a thicket of *ti*, or more correctly, *Cordyline terminalis*, wild hibiscus and a form of reed; a tangle through which one has to hack one's way. However tough the climb, the view beyond is always rewarding. With luck one will catch a glimpse of Tahiti's peaks: Tvirairai, Orophena or Mauru, rising like great rock temples up against the sky, the green foothills twisting and turning towards them, their edges too sharp, it would appear, even to stand on.

I decided to trek inland to a very dramatic fall in the Hitiaa district near the spot where Bougainville anchored. Our guide appeared, straw-hatted, carrying a hatchet with which he hacked away the vines looping across our path. He led us first through a swampy pasture in which grazed sleek Friesians. Then into light thickets of banana beyond which towered some great Tahitian chestnuts or *mape* as they call them.

They were in bloom and the trees were frosted over with fleecy, thick clusters of small white flowers which filled the air with a strong, sweet odour. The *mape* is a very large tree usually attaining a height of about fifty feet. Their trunks are anchored to the damp ground by buttress-like roots. The bark is grey and smooth like the skin of a snake. One expects that the roots will be warm and resilient, instead they emit a dry hollow sound when touched. They are strange, unreal trees. Little black pools of water gather in the hollows at their feet and toadstools grow on the rotting husks of last year's nuts. Suddenly one has the impression of having walked into a Rackham drawing illustrating *Rumpelstiltzchen.*

Further on, among the débris of fallen trees, are remains of a *marai*, or temple, the rounded, cushion-like stones, green under a covering of moss. There are tumbled walls and a stone pavement, all part of the temple, and the remains of an old village. We cross and re-cross the river several times. Here it is only two feet deep, running crystal clear and weedless over dark pebbles. The cascade to which our guide leads us falls about three hundred feet into a black, bottomless pool fringed with ferns. To reach the point where it roared down, dashing its strength against a slippery monolith of rock, we had to strip and swim a narrow chasm of jet black ice – the only noise the falling of the water that spread out in widening circles of cold which took our breath away.

When I think back, now, on the various expeditions, the thing that impresses me most is the almost total lack of animal life. Cook's naturalist on the second voyage attributes this fact to the small size of the island, an island entirely isolated from any possible contact by thousands of miles of ocean. In the pool described, for instance, there were a few small fish and some black snails that I pulled off the rocks, otherwise no sign of any living thing. There is a remarkable dearth of wild life in Tahiti. Pigs, dogs, and a small fruit-eating indigenous rat used to be the island's only quadrupeds. Other livestock, of course, has since been imported. However, the scale seems to have tipped the other way as far as birds are concerned, for there were many more in Cook's day than there are now. Forster tells us that the coconut palms harboured a very small sapphire-blue parakeet 'while another sort of a greenish colour marked with red spots were more common among the bananas'. Rarest of all were the purple parakeets from the island of Bora Bora. Dark green kingfishers with white throats used to flash up the stream, while wood pigeons and small green and maroon doves and long-tailed cuckoos were as common as were the bluish-grey herons that stalked gravely along the shore of the lagoon picking up shellfish and worms. High up in the mountains between the great Orohena's twin peaks, there is a lake in which lived a species of red-feathered duck. Its plumes were once the prerogative of Tahiti's chieftains, or kings. Orohena is the highest mountain on the island, nearly seven thousand feet, and men known as 'rock clingers' were sent up the precipitous sides to snare the duck.

Of all these birds – and others not mentioned – the only ones to have survived our guns and the destructive foreign rat imported by the different trading ships, are the grey herons and some of the sea birds.

The island's greatest pest was also imported, the maina bird, or what the French call *les merles des Moluques*, that cheeky, beady-eyed mimic the size of a large blackbird that can be taught to speak like a parrot. It was introduced to destroy a beetle (also imported) that attacked the sugar cane. They destroyed the beetle but in turn proved far more destructive than their victim. Multiplying out of all bounds, they now gorge themselves on fruit.

Teuira Henry's invaluable *Ancient Tahiti* makes brief mention of butterflies and moths, crickets, dragonflies and lizards, spiders and non-venomous centipedes, one of the two species being long and threadlike and phosphorescent. There are worms and salamanders and coconut crabs that can split open the nuts with their great claws. There used to be no mosquitoes and there are still no snakes. Fleas, like the mosquitoes, were imported. Some historians blame the fleas on the ships' cats, which no vessel ever sailed without. But there is a far more amusing story of their provenance. It takes us back to Don Domingo de Boeneche's second expedition in 1774 to Tahiti. He anchored in Vaitephia Bay, Cook's anchorage of the preceding year, and after officially christening the bay Puerto de Santa Maria Magdalena the unfortunate man contracted a high fever and died. He was buried ashore with full military honours and over his grave was erected a large cross. What interested the Tahitians was the beautiful red blanket covering Don Domingo's coffin. In wondering silence they had watched the crew file past the grave, each man throwing a small green branch on to the blanket. In silence also they watched the men shovel earth over the coffin. Hardly had the Spanish retired from the place than the procedure was reversed. Deftly extracting the coveted treasure, the natives left the grave exactly as they had found it. There was one drawback to an otherwise highly successful venture: their blanket was swarming with fleas, the first seen in Tahiti, and as Miss Henry put it in language worthy of the Bible, 'they soon increased and spread throughout the land'.

This is not modern Papeete with its thatched and beamed hotels hung with *tapa* cloth, its bamboo cinemas, its bars and waterfront cafés, its girls, both available and numerous, its shops selling lais of shells, straw hats, gaily printed cottons, and carved pieces of mother-of-pearl; but the country of the coast, pleasantly colonial and old-fashioned, fretted with Victorianisms but still lived in as centuries of Tahitians had lived before.

For instance, there is Pomaré IV's palace, a large two-storied building with deep columned verandas giving on to the main square of the town. It is built of rather poor material in a homely style. It could be the plantation house of some successful but undemanding settler in the West Indies or, for that matter, any tropical clime. Its purpose was purely one of prestige, for she never had any intention of living in it. Official receptions were to be held there, but Her Majesty lived in her people's traditional surroundings: the usual chief's house, a low, spacious edifice with an exceedingly steep roof of pandanus leaves, situated in the new palace grounds.

Herman Melville, visiting the island in 1847, describes this favoured residence.* By flirting with one of Pomaré's ladies-in-waiting he had managed to gain admittance and even an unanticipated audience with the Queen.

The hall was about a hundred and fifty feet in length, very wide with low eaves. There were neither doors nor windows; nothing along the sides but the slight posts supporting the rafters, and between these posts curtains of fine *tapa* matting. Some of them were partly drawn aside to admit light and air.

As Melville wrote: 'Inside the apartment was an immense hall about forty feet high, a kind of banquette of mats extended along each side, with here and there very slight screens, forming recesses where groups of women were reclining at their evening meal.'

Melville was astonished by the incongruous collection of costly objects from all over the globe. 'Cheek by jowl they lay beside the rudest native articles, without the slightest attempt of order. Superb writing-desks in rose wood, inlaid with silver and mother-of-pearl, decanters and goblets of cut glass; embossed plates, gilded candelabra, sets of globes and mathematical instruments; the finest porcelains; richly mounted sabres and fowling-pieces; laced hats and sumptuous garments of all sorts. All this strewn around among greasy calabashes half filled with *poi* and rolls of old *tapa*, paddles and fish spears – the ordinary furniture of a Tahitian dwelling.'

These were doubtless presents from foreign powers and all in very poor condition, the fowling-pieces rusted and the furniture scratched. Melville noticed a folio volume of Hogarth's *Rake's Progress* lying open with 'a cocoa nut shell of some musty preparation capsized among the miscellaneous furniture of the Rake's apartment where that inconsiderate young gentleman is being measured for a coat'.

* *Omoo* by Herman Melville.

Pomaré Vahiné, as she was called, being the first female of her line, was herself something of a rake and had been excommunicated by her adopted church on account of her conjugal infidelities. She was twice married and seems to have made her unfortunate husbands' lives miserable, spending most of her time sailing about from island to island 'attended by a licentious court and being entertained by all manners of games'. She was fond of display and for several years maintained a regiment of household troops; 'trouserless fellows in a uniform of calico shorts and pasteboard hats, armed with muskets of all shapes and calibres and commanded by a great wiry chief who strutted about in a coat of fiery red.' These heroes escorted their mistress wherever she went and cost the royal exchequer a fortune.

Another charming story is about her crown, a gift from her sister Queen Victoria: a showy piece which she had no intention of hiding away till needed for the rare ceremonies at which she officiated. Melville tells us that she sported it whenever she appeared in public, 'and to show her familiarity with European customs politely touched it to all foreigners of distinction, whaling captains and the like, whom she happened to meet in her evening walk'.

It must have been an awkward moment for Melville during his clandestine visit to the Queen's apartment, when the young lady-in-waiting suddenly plucked his sleeve. Majesty was arriving. Being too late to hide she implored him to bow very low. 'Just then,' wrote Melville, 'a curtain nearby lifted; and from a small building a few yards distant, the queen entered unattended. She wore a loose gown of blue silk, with two rich shawls, one red and the other yellow about her shoulders. Her Royal Majesty was bare footed.'

Melville says 'she was about the ordinary size, rather matronly; her features not very handsome, her mouth voluptuous; but there was a care-worn expression in her face. From her appearance one would judge her about forty, but she is not that old'. She was born in 1813 which would make her thirty-four when Melville saw her.

There are no Pomarés left now; Princess Takau, the last of her line, having died in Nice about four months after my return from Tahiti. She was an old lady of seventy, the daughter of Pomaré V's queen. I tried to visit her house in Papeete where I might have found some of the pieces described by Melville, but the housekeeper, quite understandably, would not allow me in. I had to content myself with photographing her house from the garden.

There is so much that I remember, among other things a hot afternoon spent in Papeete's deserted cemetery. It was like a dream; I was there alone, walking down the paths bordered by blindingly white marble graves. Some of the tombs were set with cast-iron crosses overgrown with asparagus ferns, others decorated with pots of blue geraniums worked in beads. Even in these surroundings the Tahitian flavour was evident: on the grave of a young boy killed in the last war, a hot square of pulverized coral, lay a wreath of white flowers made entirely of small, spiral shells, the leaves thin, oval plaques of tortoise-shell.

I shall always remember the drives around the island. But beautiful as they were there was something almost tedious about them. Where else was one to go except round the island, there were no other roads. It is like being in Venice, try as one will, the inevitable end to any walk is always the Piazza San Marco.

Certain images remain: a young woman seated with her back to the road, her legs straight out in front of her; heavy legs with splayed feet, the result of walking without shoes. She is dressed in a flowered *pareu* with her long, shiny hair falling down her back. She looks round over her shoulder as the car approaches, a sideways look, quizzical, calm. Why is it so familiar? The road darkens, becoming purple while the shadows change to orange, red and yellow; the trunks of the trees becoming almost blue. It is a Gauguin! Over and over one is reminded of this extraordinary painter. The image he has evoked for us in his pictures has fixed for ever our vision of the beauty and seduction of the South Seas. We tend to see that world as Gauguin chose to see it, but the world and the people he depicted are, in fact, reality. Constantly one comes across scenes he might have painted.

The flora as we see it now presents quite a different aspect to what it did in Cook's days. Great changes have taken place within the last hundred and fifty years, particularly in the cultivated strips along the coast. A large proportion of the present plants and trees have been imported, while the indigenous flora which played an important rôle in the Tahitians' economy has almost entirely disappeared.

An example is the *fau*, or *Broussoneta papyfera*, known to the early navigators as the cloth tree or paper mulberry; the bark was used by all Polynesians for making *tapa*. Every house had a patch of it, 'planted very neatly', as Parkinson described it, 'and protected from the pigs by fencing; having ditches cut through the bed to draw off the water; the earth banks neatly built up with stone. In these drains they plant the arum which yields the yam they call *taro*', the *Colocasia antiquorum*, an immense *caladium* which requires very marshy ground to grow in. There are two kinds of *taro*, one with bluish-green leaves and tuberous roots about four feet long and another, much smaller, with velvety leaves and a more palatable root. 'Both,' Forster informs us, 'are excessively pungent and caustic till boiled in several waters.' The leaves of the small variety taste somewhat like spinach when picked young.

It was not until I reached Tonga that I found the paper mulberry in cultivation, trained as it used to be in Tahiti, planted in rows like young osiers, long shoots ten to twelve feet high and about three inches in circumference. It is while the shoots are still young that they should be cut and stripped of their bark.

There is still some *taro* and *Piper methysticum* but certainly not in the quantities that existed in earlier times. The *Piper methysticum* is a plant from which *kava*, the vaguely intoxicating beverage of the South Seas, is extracted. The juice is pressed from the root, which is first reduced to a pulp and kneaded in water. It is opaque and putty-coloured when served and not, to me anyway, particularly pleasant in taste. I am told, however, that the after-effects are soothing and refreshing when taken in moderation. When taken to excess it produces white scaly blotches on the skin, which in former times were regarded as marks of breeding, for *kava* was a prerogative of high chiefs. One learns from various sources that the juice obtained from the fibrous roots was extracted by mastication – generally by young girls. The missionaries, unsuccessful in their attempts to suppress the habit of drinking *kava* were, at least, on the ground of hygiene, able to modify its method of preparation and it is now crushed in stone mortars with pestles cut from lumps of dead coral.

Here again, as with the paper mulberry, I did not find the *kava* plant until I got to Tonga, although I am told that it still grows in Tahiti, in the recesses of unfrequented valleys.

The bread-fruit, the established larder of old Tahiti, has diminished considerably in number while the coconut, on account of the copra trade, has multiplied out of all proportion, invading every inch of spare ground, flourishing, it would seem, in the shallowest soil, even growing on the barren sea beach amid fragments of coral and sand where its roots are actually washed by the tide. Everywhere in the coastal plains there are palms: should there be a pasture, or an occasional clearing, it is only because the coconuts have been felled. Encircling their trunks about three-quarters of the way up are metal shields, shining in the sun like slave bracelets, there to fend off marauding rats or an occasional land crab. The rodents with their soft-padded feet find it easy enough to climb the rough texture of the fibrous wood but slip on the metal surface of the shields.

Often, when lying in bed, I have heard the tearing of large leaves followed by a loud thud, just outside my window – the falling of a coconut. One wonders why there are not more casualties, for a ripe nut is the equivalent of a fair-sized rock falling from the top of a four-storey building.

Copra now heads the list of Tahiti's exports, but the coconut has always played an important rôle in the island's economy. From leaf to root the palm is useful to the Polynesians. The hard wood is used for posts, and the framework of houses, and warriors used it for their lances. The mature fronds are braided into thatch and screens for huts and sheds, while the young leaves are bleached and made into hats, fans and baskets. Teuira Henry tells us of yet another more frivolous use. The very young, tender leaves, not yet exposed to the sun, are covered with a thin, delicate coating which can be drawn off between thumb and fingers. The coating is white, very light, and semi-transparent, and when a great many are attached to the rib of a dry coconut leaf, form a beautiful plume, called *revareva*, which is used as an ornament on the head and sometimes on native capes and dresses. Miss Henry describes receptions given in Papeete just after the French occupation, balls attended by ladies from Paris 'who have not disdained to wear the *revareva* as a headdress or decoration floating gracefully from their dresses'.

The nut, like the leaf, has its different uses according to its maturity. When young, the meat is thin and tender, similar in appearance to the white of a soft-boiled egg and can be eaten out of the nut with a spoon. Now, while the husk is still a tender green, the milk is at its sweetest. The nut takes about a year to mature and the water then has a flat taste. The tree begins to bear five or six years after being planted; then continues for over sixty years, and lives on, bearing less plentifully, through a century. A good bearing tree has more than a hundred nuts at one time, in different stages of development, in addition there are often great sheaths of white, pungent-smelling blossoms. An expert picker, shinnying up the tree, can tell in an instant, by tapping the green husks, how ripe they are. It is when the meat of the nut matures that it is used in Polynesian cuisine. Grating the white meat they press it through a strainer to extract a thick cream-like substance which is called the cream or milk and in fact is a good substitute for milk in strong tea or coffee. The Tahitians use it in a variety of dishes; in puddings, vegetables, and some sea food. There is a delicious recipe for raw fish marinated in lime juice with onions, mixed with coconut cream, but this must be of fairly recent origin for no form of citrus fruit was known on the island before Captain Cook's time.

From the earliest times the Tahitians have extracted oils from the milk of the coconut by a process of evaporation. Placing the milk (not to be confused with the water) in the sun, the heat soon evaporates the liquid, leaving the oil. This they scent with sandalwood shavings and different aromatic flowers. The oil thus treated is known as *paru* and is used on the hair, and is said to be a very soothing liniment for aches and pains. It was not until the arrival of British missionaries, however, that the Tahitians knew that oil from the coconuts would burn. The Rev. Mr Bicknell was the first to use it as lamp oil, and from him they learned to make lamps in coconut cups containing oil and a little sand to hold the wick. Before this the *Aleurites moluccana*, or candlenut, served the islanders as a form of illumination. The nut, about the size of a large chestnut, is rich in oil and many of them threaded together on the rib of a coconut leaf form a kind of taper.

The copra industry is comparatively recent, and now the most important product of the coconut palm. Copra, a Spanish-Portuguese word adapted from the Malayan *kopperah*, is the sun-dried or kiln-baked kernel or meat of the coconut. The oil-bearing meat, once separated from the shell, is packed into sacks and taken by the various small farmers who prepare it to a large central warehouse where it is shipped to a processing centre, Marseilles, in the case of Tahiti. The oil is used largely in the production of soap and margarine. But it has, also, various secondary uses, as an ingredient of synthetic rubber, glycerine and hydraulic brake fluid.

Wherever one goes in the Pacific one is dogged by the smell of copra, a cloying, sweet, curiously pervasive smell, hard to get out of one's nostrils. I can even smell it now, while writing. Some find it nauseating, but I can't say I do, and in fact even remember it with a considerable degree of nostalgia.

Since we have been so thorough in our examination of the coconut, there is one more by-product that should be mentioned; the 'coir' of the husk; a tough, wiry fibre that can be mechanically carded, producing a hardy, water-resistant rope. From time immemorial the islanders have used it in the same manner, twisting it into cords of about the thickness of a thin pencil. To them it is *nape*, in translation sennit. Before nails, timber was joined with sennit, bound in overlapping and interwoven coils, worked with elaborate nicety. The Tahitians also used coir in its crude state for caulking the planks of their canoes. Miss Henry notes another curious use of the nut's shell. She had seen a trepanned human skull where the damaged section was carefully filled in with coconut shell. The bone had knitted itself round the shell.

It is impossible to conceive of Tahiti without the coconut palm. No pictorial representation is ever complete without its cylindrical trunk, tapering gradually to a beautiful crown of graceful plumes. Inevitably it evokes the exotic aspect of the landscape. I, for one, never tired of photographing it.

Quite different in character, but equally seductive, is the bread-fruit tree; the famous *uru*. It used to be as prolific as the coconut. Few trees can claim such fame and it has certainly been the subject of more botanical speculation than most other plants. Quiros makes the first mention of it at the end of the sixteenth century when he discovered it in the Marquesas. It was not until the beginning of the eighteenth century, however, that we find any reference to it in England. William Dampier, the buccaneer navigator, praises it in his *Observations on the Coast of New Holland.* Anson and Cook were equally enthusiastic. 'If a man,' writes Banks, echoing their sentiments, 'should, in the course of his lifetime, plant ten such trees, he would completely fulfil his duty to his own as well as future generations.' So much was said in its favour that many people believed that loaves of bread actually grew on the tree and had only to be gathered and baked.

The tree is large and handsome with heavy, dark green foliage, rather like that of a fig, only shinier, bigger and more dentilated. In Tahiti it bears three crops a year and there is hardly a moment that it is entirely without fruit, which ripens from a light pea-green to a dirty yellow. Cook describes it better than anybody. 'The fruit is about the size and shape of a child's head, and the surface is reticulated not unlike a truffle; it is covered with a thin skin and has a core about as big as the handle of a knife; the edible part lies between the skin and the core; and is as white as snow, and somewhat of the consistency of new bread. It must be roasted before it is eaten. Its taste is insipid, with a slight sweetness somewhat resembling that of crumbs of wheaten-bread eaten with a Jerusalem artichoke.'

Bligh, writing eighteen years later, points out that 'there is neither seeds nor stone in the inside but all is pure substance like bread. It must be eaten new for if it is kept above twenty-four hours it grows hard and choky'.

Cook also mentions the sap which exudes from the bark when punctured; a thin, milky fluid which gradually coagulates, becoming thick and mucilaginous and hard when exposed to the sun. Smeared over the coir-stuffed planks of a canoe it makes an ideal watertight covering.

The bread-fruit most closely resembles bread when the fruit is baked before maturity, while it is still firm, and before the starch is converted into sugar. The Tahitians also make a pudding out of it called *popoi.* The ripe fruit is cooked and then pounded into a batter. Steamed bananas are added to the mixture and the whole folded into banana leaves and rebaked. I ate it with a sauce made from coconut cream, a kind of caramel, and found it delicious.

Great interest was shown when early reports on the bread-fruit were published, particularly among the planters of the British West Indies. If this extraordinary tree could be acclimatized in their country its fruit might well provide a cheap and nourishing food for the African labourer. George III was petitioned and steps were taken to introduce the bread-fruit into the colonies. The first attempt ended in disaster, the mutiny in the *Bounty*.

Bligh had served with Cook in the *Resolution* as ship-master and, seconded by Banks, had been a natural choice for the Admiral to sail from England on his fateful voyage in December 1787. Banks, knighted by then and already President of the Royal Society and manager of the Royal Gardens at Kew, prepared a lengthy memorandum for Bligh on the difficulty of carrying plants at sea. 'A small sprinkling of salt water,' he warns, 'or of salt dew which fills the air, even in a moderate gale, will immediately destroy them if not immediately washed off with fresh water. It is necessary therefore that a cabin be appropriated to the sole purpose of making a kind of greenhouse. The key of it should be given to the custody of the gardener.' Further instructions follow: 'in case of cold weather, in going round the Cape, a stove should be provided by which the cabin may be kept in a temperature equal to that of the inter-tropical countries.'

But the unfortunate Bligh never had to worry about the stove, for after nearly two months of hard work collecting a thousand young plants, all stowed away in wooden tubs, he and they were unceremoniously jettisoned by the mutineers.

From the various descriptions of the men travelling with Cook one gathers that the inhabited areas of Tahiti were fairly intensely cultivated; a kind of diversified park land with neatly worked patches of *taro*; next to them, straight lines of the cloth-mulberry, looking rather like the stripling poplars one sees growing in the plains of Northern Italy. Near every house would stand a handsome cluster of bread-fruit trees, while above them rose the slender grey stems of the coconut, so high some of them, that one was not conscious of their crowns. At the present time the country has an unkempt look; much of it still parkland, but a park with unshaven lawns and overrun with coconut palms. The bread-fruit are there, but in very reduced quantities; the bakers and tinned foods of Europe having thinned their ranks. Instead of them one finds the mango, equal in size but not so distinctive.

Today one finds the houses fenced around with croton, some of them growing as high as fifteen feet. Frangipani bloom on the settlers' lawns and variegated philodendrons are trained up the palms. There are papaws, also introduced at the beginning of the nineteenth century. These different plants have acclimatized themselves so thoroughly that it is difficult not to believe them indigenous. There is also vanilla (the island's fourth most important product after copra, phosphates and pearl shell): sometimes the still evenings reek of the familiar aroma. I always remember the turning one has to take to bump down a sandy road to Point Venus where a Chinese-Tahitian family's store serves as a collecting point for vanilla beans, the whole countryside is impregnated with the smell.

There are other plants I remember, but one cannot enumerate them all; the large crinums, or spider lilies, growing as high as a man's shoulder, that are found on the water's edge where the crabs have their lairs; and then, of course, the famous *tiara* or *Gardenia tahitiensis*, indigenous as its Latin name suggests, to the island. Their shrubs are spangled with snow-white, waxy flowers; nature's stars with which the women used to sprig their hair in the days when it was dressed on top of their heads. Now that it flows down their back they hang them at the neck, strung in lais, or worked into plaited bands like a Plantagenet crown.

The plant grows best in sandy soil, and the largest plants are found on long sand points where the ancient chiefs used to have their dwellings. The flowers intended for wreaths are picked while still in bud and just beginning to unfold. They are gathered before the sun is up and sprinkled with water, and arrive in the market-place of Papeete wrapped up in *taro* leaves secured with raffia. The flowers have varying numbers of petals; one I picked had six, another seven, and yet a third eight.

In passing one might note that Tahiti has about fifteen different kinds of plantains. Strangely, of all the herbs introduced into the island only basil seems to have prospered. On the other hand, the planting of vegetables and fruit by Gore and Cook and his companions provided the basis for a considerable trade as soon as whaling began, the ships loading up with peaches, cabbages, melons and beans, which by the early nineteenth century had become quite common.

One last tree I must mention, and that is the *hutu* or *Barringtonia speciosa*; the most beautiful tree in the world according to Forster. It is not unlike a large deciduous magnolia and bears fragile cup-like flowers, their white petals tipped with magenta. The most interesting thing about these trees is their toxic seeds. Grate some and throw the powder into the lagoon among the fish and immediately it has the most surprising effect: paralysed by the poison, the fish float to the surface, and can be picked out of the water.

21. The great *marae* of Mahaiatea.
From Wilson's *A Missionary Voyage*. (*page 107*)

22. Cook watches the offering up of a human sacrifice.
Engraved by W. Woollett after J. Webber. (*page 114*)

23. 'The top of the *ahu* was spiked with god sticks on which the gods perched when they descended to earth in the guise of white birds.' (*page 111*)

[Chapter 9]

The Past Observed

THE *Endeavour* had been anchored now at Matavai Bay for nearly three weeks. The transit was to occur on June 3rd and Cook was occupying himself with the preparations. It had been decided to split the observers up into three different parties in order to try and eliminate the possibility of obscure vision. Banks, Gore and Monkhouse, the surgeon, along with Spöring, were sent over to Moorea. Hicks, with some of the crew, stationed himself on the peninsula of Taiarapu, the most easterly point of Tahiti, while Cook with Green and Solander remained at the fort, at the other end of the island.

The auspicious day dawned, and Cook tells us that it 'proved as favourable to our purpose as we could wish, not a cloud was to be seen and the air was perfectly clear'. The observation, however, was not a success, but through no fault of the observers. 'We very distinctly saw,' writes Cook, 'an atmosphere or dusky shade round the form of the planet which very much disturbed the times of the contacts.' He differed with Green in observing these times, 'much more than could be expected'.

The 'dusky shade' was the trouble; it was precisely the atmosphere round Venus that obscured its form, rendering it almost impossible to distinguish the vapour from the crust of the planet and to make correct observations. Calculations of the distance between the earth and the sun were bound to be out by some millions of miles. Venus apparently is chronically bemantled, and all the subsequent observations proved equally unsatisfactory, so the distances between the earth and the sun had to be worked out by other means.

One gathers that Banks was sent to Moorea, not for any part he would play in the observation, but because of his tact in handling the natives. Cook had great faith in his ability to make friends. In spite of its proximity, no member of the *Endeavour*'s company had as yet visited the island.

Gore and Monkhouse set up their instruments on an islet just inside the reef, beyond the Taotoi pass at the north-west point of Moorea. 'I then wished success to the observers,' writes Banks, 'and repaired to the island where I could do the double service of examining the natural produce and buying provisions for my companions who were engaged in so useful a work.'

Viewed from Tahiti's shores Moorea is the most dramatic stage setting ever conceived. The sun sets behind its serrated silhouette sending a diadem of pale, amber rays opening like a fan across the azure sky. It used to be said that the noise of the sun could be heard as it sank each night into the sea, a sizzling, one presumes, of molten copper. Anyhow Moorea is an island of extraordinary beauty, and I shall never forget my own first impression of it when flying in through the dawn to make a landing on Papeete's new airstrip. Seen from the air the mountains are paper-thin at the apex, like wedges of hot sealing wax that, plucked upwards, have been left to cool. I am not indulging in flights of poetic fancy; the whole island has the appearance of a piece of nervous sculpture cast by one of the young abstractionists, the knife-edged mountains manipulated by agile fingers, worked up out of a solid mass of what, from a distance, looks like green felt. This, of course, is not the impression Banks could have had of the island, but we will return to that later when the *Endeavour* anchors in its two extraordinary bays.

Back on board the ship, the travellers were greeted with the 'melancholy news that a large part of our stock of nails had been purloined by some of the ship's company during the time of the observation, when everybody was ashore who had any degree of command. One of the thieves was detected but only seven nails were found upon him. This loss is of a very serious nature as these nails, if circulated by the people among the Indians, will much lessen the value of iron, our staple commodity'. Wallis, in his log, had already made it quite clear that the natives had a keen sense of business and very precise ideas regarding the value of nails. The *Dolphin* had only been anchored in Matavai Bay a few weeks when already 'the size of the nail that was demanded for the enjoyment of a lady was always in proportion to her charm'. The *Endeavour*'s nails had been taken for the same purpose – illicit trade with the Tahitian women – and Archibald Wolf, the thief, was given two dozen lashes, double the quantity generally inflicted, which shows the importance Cook gave to the episode.

The civilization of ancient Tahiti, simple in its material equipment, was far more evolved socially, politically and religiously than one would expect of a Stone Age people. There was an ancient aristocracy, a dignified way of life, that was to be entirely overturned by the arrival of a ship. Manners and customs were as much altered as were those of imperial Rome by the onslaught of the Goths, only the change was less brutal and not immediately apparent. Old Tahiti was slow to die; it was the ascendancy of the missionary that eventually killed it. The *Endeavour* was to ring a change in the island's politics but not its manners – for some years still it was to sleep on in its 'golden haze'.

During Banks' absence on Moorea a woman of some consequence had died, 'and was placed not far from the fort to rot above ground as is the custom of the island'. 'I went there to see her,' writes Banks. 'A small square was neatly railed in with bamboo and in the midst of it a canoe awning set up upon two posts. In this the body was laid, covered with fine cloth.'

Banks, always curious about ethnological matters, had asked for permission to attend the mourning ceremonies; it was granted, provided he agreed to take part. This necessitated his stripping to the skin, 'the only garment I was allowed to wear being a small loin cloth'. He was not at all bashful about his nakedness for the two women participating in the ceremony with him were no more covered than he. A young boy and another man, probably a priest, or possibly a relation of the deceased, disguised in a dress 'most fantastical though not unbecoming' made up the cortège. They must have presented a strange sight for all of them, except for the fantastical figure, had been daubed with a thick black paste made from water and charcoal, the boy entirely covered in it and looking like a negro, while Banks and the women had it over their faces and down to their shoulders.

The costume of the priest, or relative, was very extraordinary; both Parkinson and Hodges, on a second voyage, have left us drawings. Cook also tries to describe it, with a warning that he finds his attempt inadequate. He pictures 'a man dressed with plumes of feathers, something in the same manner as those worn by hearses and horses at funerals in London'. The costume 'was very neatly made up of black or brown and white cloth, black and white feathers and pearl oysters' shells. It covered the head, face and body as low as the calf of the leg, or lower, and not only looked grand but awful likewise'.

Forster, on the second voyage, gives very exact details: the whole costume appeared to hang from a flat, semicircular board fixed to the head. On this were threaded large pearl shells, followed by still larger pearl shells, fringed with bluish-green pigeon feathers. In the centre of the board, poised in its hollow, were two halves of shell bound together with sennit. These shells, always polished, were generally of a purplish hue, with, round their edges, a halo of long white feathers plucked from the tails of frigate birds. This represented the head of the figure. The white feathers round it extended at least two feet beyond the natural height of the man, thus completely disguising him. From the convex margin of the board hung a kind of armour plating of polished shell in oblong squares from which hung green and yellow feather tassels.

The British Museum possesses one of these costumes in their ethnological collection, given to them, so Forster tells us, by Cook himself. This 'fantastical' garb must, indeed, have been very impressive when seen in all its pristine splendour, glinting in the sun. Forster thinks the costume was calculated to inspire horror. 'Certainly when this strange figure walked abroad, accompanied by his attendants, the purpose was to harass the people.' The reason for the performance, however, remains somewhat vague. 'Whatever it might be,' writes Forster, 'we never could obtain any intelligence from the natives on the subject.'

Teuira Henry, in her invaluable book, gives further details about the actual performance. It would seem that the chief mourner, this awesome figure, always took the lead, jingling a clapper made of finely polished shell. In his other hand he carried a long scythe armed with shark's teeth, while his attendants flourished spears with which they sometimes wounded and even killed hapless persons who crossed their path. 'The sound of the clappers,' writes Miss Henry, 'and the appearance of their persons as they approached, terrified the community. The priest (or the head mourner) sometimes struck the side of the house menacingly with his scythe, while the inmates remained in breathless silence. Some of the people out of doors had time to flee to the local *marae* where they were secure from molestation; but others, particularly if they were not in favour with the terrible party, were either caught and mercilessly beaten with a club, or in fleeing were liable to be hit by the scythe or wounded with spears. The reign of terror lasted an indefinite period, the moon sometimes coming in, waxing, waning and passing on.' The duration of the mourning period depended, it would appear, on the degree of affection entertained for the deceased.

The amusing thing about Banks' particular performance is that, forming part of the cortège, he was obliged to participate in the prescribed chastisement. Furthermore, Fort Venus was to be included in their itinerary. 'To the fort then,' he writes, 'we went to the surprise of our friends and affright of the Indians who were there.' The natives flew before them 'like sheep before a wolf, hiding under grass or whatever else could conceal them'. One presumes that Cook and his entourage enjoyed diplomatic immunity. The day ended with Banks and 'his sable emmisaries' scrubbing each other in the river. 'It was dark before the blacking would come off.'

According to Tahitian beliefs the spirit of a dead person remains on earth until the body has entirely wasted away by putrefaction. Believing this, the people rather naturally turned to the habit of embalming, but as with the Egyptians, it was only the wealthy who could afford it. The poorer classes had to content themselves with mere relic mementoes, or the easiest preserved members of their departed relatives. Skulls, saturated in sweet scented oils and aired many days in the sun, would be enshrined amongst the household fetishes. Finger-nails also furnished another durable relic and, plucked from the corpses, would be polished, threaded together and worn in the hair by young girls as charms.

The method of embalming was quite elaborate and had the island enjoyed a drier climate its effects would undoubtedly have been more lasting. As it was, the body of a chief or important noble, given the full treatment, endured for about a year.

Cook, on his third voyage, saw the embalmed body of Ti'i, Tu's uncle, at one time a minister of state, a chief he knew well on his previous voyage. Ti'i had been dead for about four months and 'the only remarkable alteration,' writes Cook, 'that had happened, was a shrinking of the muscular parts at the eye; but the hair and nails were in their original state, and still adhered firmly; and the several joints were quite pliable. At first,' Cook adds, 'the body is laid out every day, when it does not rain; afterwards the intervals become greater and greater; and at last, it is seldom to be seen.'

Teuira Henry describes the method used by the embalmers. Once the obsequies were over the body was placed on a portable altar over a small pit, within the precincts of a *marae*. Setting to work, the embalmers used the classic means, drawing out the viscera through the anus, and sucking the brain through the nostrils. This accomplished, the body was left to drain, the skin being saturated in oil scented with sandalwood. Every precaution was taken to retain the body's natural form; *tapa*, soaked in oil, was carefully inserted into the emptied stomach, while the limbs were constantly worked to keep them pliant. They detached the skin from the flesh by pinching, the flesh being squeezed out through perforations made under the joints. Afterwards, the body was exposed to the sun and turned frequently until well dried, 'when it was placed,' writes Miss Henry, 'in a house made for it and enclosed in a fence of reeds. There it was adjusted in a sitting posture upon a litter and dressed in choice *tapa*, with a cape over the shoulders and a turban upon the head. When the hair chanced to fall off, it was carefully placed back with gum.' Cook describes the pleasing effect of the draped cloths and mats decorating the bier. We can see how successful the arrangements were in Webber's engraving of the subject.

When not on view, the body was covered by a white pall. There was always an older member of the family, or a priest, in attendance. The dead person was addressed as a living being and every day a member of the family brought the deceased some form of food from which it was supposed to absorb the substance. Only the family or intimate friends were admitted inside the enclosure, though occasionally the body was exhibited to the public outside the palisade.

Miss Henry adds an interesting detail: the embalmers were subject to severe cases of blood poisoning, 'in consequence of following their vocation'. So also were their Egyptian *confrères*.

One day Banks came across a badly preserved body, probably a mummy of more modest origin which had not been elaborately embalmed. 'It was already dropping to pieces with putrefaction and alive with maggots,' and, good naturalist that he was, Banks' attention was held by the maggots. They were the larvae 'of a species of beetle very common here'. Probably some of the maggots found their way into one of those glass-topped bottles of his to be preserved in spirits.

When a mummified body disintegrated, it was given a second burial. The body, wrapped in scented *tapa*, was placed in a canoe-shaped coffin, hewn from the trunk of a tree. Secretly, under cover of darkness, the funeral cortège would wind its way up into the mountains to the final resting place, a cave. Many such caves can still be seen honeycombing the precipitous wall of certain valleys. Some of them, I am told, still contain bones.

Mention has been made in these pages of an aristocracy, ruled by either chieftains or kings. Judging from early reports, it is not clear whether power was delegated to one man, that man a king, or whether it rested in the hands of several leading chiefs. When the English, accustomed to monarchy, arrived, they invested too much power in one single person, elevating him to a rank which did not exist before. But, as Beaglehole points out, 'once treated as a king by influencial outsiders, the new dignitary would begin to consider himself as one.' This is what eventually happened with Tu who, towards the end of his life, styled himself Pomaré I of the ruling house of Tahiti.

When Wallis first discovered the island it was divided into nineteen districts, each one governed by an *arii* or feudal lord. These *arii* in turn were subject to three *arii nuis*, or overlords: Teriirere of Papara on the southern shores of the main peninsula; Vehiatua of Taiarapu, a district of Tahiti-iti, the smaller of the two peninsulas; and Tu of Pare, the northern section of Tahiti proper where Matavai Bay is situated. Tu was still an insecure young man dominated by Tateha, his uncle. Even in his own district he had not yet gained the ascendancy that he was later to achieve. Young as he was, however, his birth gave him considerable social distinction.

These *arii nuis* were treated with great respect, each one keeping a kind of court, having, according to Banks, 'a large attendance of younger brothers and other nobles'. They also enjoyed extraordinary privileges and were surrounded by elaborate ceremony. There was even a special court language, and, according to one report, any unfortunate subject who happened to use the wrong word in conversation with the *arii nui* had his head smashed in. Like the Dalai Lamas of Tibet, they were considered reincarnations of their God, or, more accurately, as descendants of the great Ta'aroa; their persons were holy. Special houses were built for them, because if the *arii nui* entered an ordinary dwelling, even for the shortest stay, it was immediately dismantled when he left, 'no common mortal being thought worthy to inhabit it afterwards'.

Several journals refer to the *arii nui*'s mode of displacement. 'He travels most through his dominion on the shoulders of his subjects,' as Melville put it. On Cook's first meeting with Tu as a young man, the interview took place across a brook, the chief mounted on the back of an attendant. Some years later Tu's son was to boast to missionaries that he was 'a greater man than King George. He rides a horse,' he exclaimed, 'and I on a man!'

Another mark of respect that was practised by both men and women was the lowering of clothes to the waist while in the 'presence'. Cook and his party arranged to doff their hats but, apart from the strangers, the only person exempted from the obeisance was the *arii nui*'s *bòa* or attendant, a kind of lord-in-waiting. Twelve *bòas* in all were appointed to the court, each one officiating in turn.

Forster, on the second voyage, describes the manner in which the *arii nui*'s approach was heralded in public. 'If the King happened to pass by while we sat in a house at Tahiti, the natives who surrounded us were warned to uncover their shoulders, by someone who spied him at a distance simply saying "the lord comes hither" or else they only said "*aree*" which on such occasions always denoted one of the royal family.'

There were strict laws governing eating, but this applies to all the chiefs and not just the *arii nui*. Cook tells us that 'one of the natives who appeared to be a chief dined with us, as he had done some days before; but then there were always some women present; and one or other of them put the victuals into his mouth. One day there happened to be none to perform the office. When he was helped to victuals and desired to eat, he sat in the chair like a statue without once attempting to put a morsel to his mouth, and would certainly have gone without his dinner if one of the servants had not fed him'.

The fact is that few people in the history of the world have had so rigid a social organization as the Polynesians, akin almost to the caste system of the Hindus in India. The chiefs were autocrats who looked down contemptuously on all those less well born than they. Cook informs us that there were three social orders: 'First the *arii* (which he spells *eares*), secondly the *manahoonas*, or middling sort and lastly, the *toutous* which comprehend all the lower class and are by far the most numerous. These seem to live in some sort dependent on the *eares* who together with the *manahoonas* own most, if not all, the lands. This is hereditary in their families and the moment the heir is born he succeeds the father both in the title and estate. At least to the name, for it is most likely the latter must have the power during his son's or daughter's minority.'

It is a wonder he understood the situation as clearly as he did. Boswell, who sat next to Cook one night at dinner shortly after his return from the first voyage, reports on an interesting conversation between them. 'He candidly confessed to me that he and his companions who visited the south sea islands could not be certain of any information they got, or supposed they got, except as to objects falling under the observation of the senses; their knowledge of the language was so imperfect they required the aid of their senses, and anything which they learned about religion, government or tradition might be quite erroneous.'

There were, indeed, three classes and the *arii*, or nobles, headed the list. Next came the *raatira*, landed proprietors not of noble or chiefly blood, and thirdly the *manahune* or commoners. The *manahune*, of course, were Cook's *manahoonas* and it was from amongst their ranks that the *toutou*, or more correctly the *teuteu*, were taken. They were hereditary retainers to the *arii* and formed a group and not a social class. It was also from amongst the *manahune* that the *titi* were drawn, the lowest class or group, the Polynesian untouchables, who were used for human sacrifice.

Considering the 'pomp and circumstances' surrounding the *arii nui* it is not surprising that the British – first Wallis and afterwards Cook – mistook him, or his close relations, for rulers of the island. Anchoring always at Matavai Bay (in the Pare, Arue, Haapape districts) they were always in contact with the same local chiefs. Although the explorers heard vague rumours of other important personages, they did not understand the language sufficiently to take in all the niceties of their hierarchy. It so happened that when Wallis discovered the island in 1767 the famous Oberea, married to the *arii nui* of Papara – better known as Amo '*the winker*' (a name he conferred on himself in honour of some boyish habit of his son) – was on a visit to the district of her birth, being the daughter of the *arii* of Haapape. Of high rank in her own right, married to an *arii nui*, she was a person of consequence. Probably for these reasons she was delegated by her people to welcome the strangers, not before, however, the proud Tahitians had tried to chase them off. She seems to have been a woman of considerable character and it is possible that she acted as a self-appointed ambassadress. In any event, the British were only too willing to accept her as a Queen. It must have simplified matters.

Eighteenth-century England knew her exclusively as Oberea but her real name was Purea, meaning 'Wished for'. Cook was introduced to her by young Robert Molyneux who had met her before, when he sailed with Wallis in the *Dolphin* as master's mate. Molyneux came across her one day sitting, surrounded by female relatives, in one of the tents up at the fort. Again she was visiting the district of her birth, under the protection of her brother-in-law, the powerful chief or *arii* Tuteha (Banks' Hercules). She had not made an official appearance because of her changed circumstances. Like many forceful, intelligent women of history, she had planned a great future for her son. Alarmed at her ambitions, the other chiefs, mostly her relatives, had leagued against her and civil war had broken out. As a result, she and her husband, Amo, had been completely routed and forced to flee Papara, taking refuge in the mountains. The battle had occurred in December 1768, after the departure of the *Dolphin*, and nearly eight months before the arrival of the *Endeavour*.

The idea of conquering a neighbouring realm or district and definitely incorporating it into one's own was entirely foreign to the Polynesians: they contented themselves, as a rule, with putting the enemy to flight and stripping them of the greatest part of their wealth. This is precisely what had happened to Purea. The battle now almost forgotten, she had been allowed down from her mountain retreat and we find her visiting Tuteha, her brother-in-law and one of her antagonists, perfectly at liberty but reduced to the rôle of a poor relative.

This, then, roughly speaking, was the political situation at the time of Cook's arrival. Being quite ignorant of it, however, and having been assured of Purea's importance by those who had known her, Cook, very naturally, had invited her on board. 'I received her,' writes Cook, 'with such marks of distinction as I thought would gratify her most, and was not sparing of my presents, among which this august personage seemed particularly delighted with a child's doll.' Cook, in a draft version of his journal writes that he made her understand that the doll 'was the picture of my wife'. 'Such drollery,' Beaglehole remarks in his notes, 'is unusual in Cook,' and probably Cook omitted this detail from the official journal as frivolous. The rough draft enlarges on the episode. 'As soon as we came ashore she fastened the doll to her breast, took me by her hand and dragged me first this way and then that. The people all the while crowding about us to get sight of the doll.' Then feeling that he had given a poor impression of Purea, Cook adds, 'I have here mentioned the pleasure Oberea took in the doll I gave her, but it must not be understood from thence that these people are fond of trifles, the contrary generally takes place.'

Tuteha happened to be sitting in Banks' tent when Purea and Cook landed, and observing the commotion over the doll 'seemed not to be well pleased with the distinction that was being showed this lady'. Cook, although unfamiliar with the situation, admits that Tuteha was 'to all appearance the chief man of the island' and concludes that he was jealous of Purea. Wishing to rectify the situation Cook immediately asked the old chief on board 'who would not be easy until I gave him such things as he most desired'. One of the things, surely, being another doll, similar to the one exhibited so proudly by Purea.

Purea, Banks tells us, was about forty, 'tall and very lusty, her skin white and her eyes full of meaning. She might have been handsome when young but now few or no traces of it were left'. Parkinson adds a detail regarding her clothes, describing the quantity of different coloured *tapas* she wore. Cook found her 'like most of the other women, very masculine'. Forster, meeting her four years later, on the second voyage, agrees with Cook about her masculinity, adding at the same time that 'something of her former greatness remained'.

Purea seems to have been a lady of strong appetites for we know that she had had her eye on Wallis; now, here she was offering the young, attractive Banks the chance of becoming her paramour; an offer, however, that was declined, Banks intimating that he was otherwise engaged. He did not reveal the identity of the object of his attentions for she happened to be one of 'the queen's' ladies-in-waiting. As it turned out later it was not Banks' charm alone that had seduced Purea, but partly his sartorial elegance. His person she never obtained, but she did manage to spirit away a white jacket and waistcoat with silver froggings.

Little is known about Amo, Purea's husband. It was alleged that she beat him. We know that she had a 'troublesome disposition' for Cook remarks on it later, saying that her husband could not abide it. Purea, anyhow, had been separated from Amo for quite some time previous to the arrival of the *Endeavour*. She had been living openly with Tupaia, a remarkably intelligent man, a distinguished refugee from the island of Raiatea who had been depossessed of his chieftainship and property by an invasion of warriors from the neighbouring island of Bora Bora. When he had arrived at Tahiti, Purea had appointed him her adviser and made him chief priest of her famous *marae* at Papara, the largest ever built in Tahiti, erected at her command to commemorate the birth of her son. Tupaia had actively intrigued against Tuteha and, fearing his power, had tried to persuade Purea to poison him. Purea had not followed this advice with the result that she now found herself 'deprived of her greatness' and in very reduced circumstances.

When Cook met Tupaia he was certainly out of favour with the great Hercules who, however, chose not to persecute him. Probably this ambiguous situation led Tupaia to offer his services to Cook. 'For some time before we left this island,' writes Cook, 'several of the natives were daily offering themselves to go away with us, and as it was thought they must be of use to us in our future discoveries, we resolved to bring away one whose name is Tupaia, a chief and a priest. This man had been with us most of the time we had been upon the island which gave us an opportunity to know something of him. We found him to be a very intelligent person, and to know more of the geography of the islands situated in these seas, their produce and their religious laws and customs of the inhabitants than anyone we had met with, and was the likeliest person to answer our purpose. For these reasons and at the request of Mr Banks I received him on board together with a young boy, his servant.'

'The captain,' Banks writes in his journal, 'refuses to take him on his own account, in my opinion sensibly enough, the government will never in all human probability take any notice of him. I therefore have resolved to take him.' Banks is grateful for the fortune which allows him to indulge in Tupaia's upkeep. In his eyes 'the amusement I shall have in his conversation and the benefit he will be to us on the ship' warranted any expenses he would have to defray. He argues that Tupaia would cost him no more than it did his neighbours to keep lions and tigers. Being a typical son of the eighteenth century, Banks, apart from admiring his qualities, did also have a tendency to regard him as a curiosity, an amusement, much the same way as ladies of fashion would consider a blackamoor. Had Tupaia ever reached England, he would nevertheless have been much appreciated for he was a man of remarkable attainments.

There seems to have been no end to his talents. With the assistance of Pickersgill, a surveyor and maker of charts, he drew a map for Cook of the Pacific (now in the British Museum) on which he recorded many of the island groups, some of which he had visited by canoe. He was also credited with having second sight. Tupaia readily adopted English dress and was quick to pick up his new companion's manners. Banks tells us that before the new recruit finally decided to join the ship he slept on Purea's large double canoe, covered from end to end with an awning, 'not without a bed fellow, though the gentleman cannot be less than forty-five'. Strange that Banks with so lusty an appetite himself in such matters should show surprise. But then, once past the age of forty, one was already considered an old man during the eighteenth century. Purea was no longer his paramour, for in a rough draft of Cook's log we find that 'she keeps a young fellow to lay with her'.

Everything one reads about Tupaia suggests a person of great charm. When on the point of sailing, he made every effort not to show his emotions but 'could not conceal a few heartfelt tears'. Here he exhibited more character than most of his fellow countrymen who invariably dissolved into floods of tears on the slightest provocation. Mastering his grief he had enough presence of mind to send a shirt as a parting gift to Tuteha's favourite mistress. Can one suppose a sentimental attachment? Had Tuteha's mistress, perhaps, been instrumental in saving his life? But this is pure supposition for neither Banks nor Cook makes any mention of it. Banks tells us that he and Tupaia climbed up the topmast as the *Endeavour* made her way out through the passage in the reef 'where we stood a long time waving to the canoes as they went off'.

As had been expected Tupaia proved to be of the utmost service to Cook, and when they reached New Zealand they found to their 'astonishment and delight', that the language was almost identical to his own, enabling him to interpret most efficiently. The languages of the different Polynesian areas are very similar and might even be called dialects. It is quite evident from Tupaia's case that a Maori from New Zealand, a Hawaiian, and a native from the Cook Islands could learn to understand each other quite easily. Tupaia had no difficulty in conversing with the Maoris about the origins of their religion 'and was listened to most attentively'.

But poor Tupaia, his days were numbered. We hear of him taking part in the famous landing at Botany Bay and later, putting on his Tahitian finery, he walked up and down the streets of Batavia in company with Tayeto, his young servant, who 'danced about the place almost mad with the numberless novelties'. Alas, a prolonged stay in Batavia during the eighteenth century was almost tantamount to a death sentence. The dreadful 'Batavia sickness' – what we now know as dysentery – took a shocking yearly toll, as also did the various fevers including malaria. The year of Cook's visit appears to have been an exceptionally bad one, the *Endeavour* lost thirty-three men in all from the result of her stay there. Tayeto was dead within a week of landing, to be followed very shortly by his master. Parkinson, himself one of the victims, tells us that when 'Tupaia heard of Tayeto's death he was quite inconsolable, crying out frequently, "Tayeto! Tayeto!" ' They were both buried on the island of Edam off the shores of the city.

Tu, the future Pomaré I, is the next character to engage our attention. Until quite recently, before Mr Beaglehole with his usual thoroughness proved it to be quite erroneous, many supposed him to have been the son of Amo and Purea. He was actually the offspring of one Hapai and a chiefess from the island of Raiatea. Of noble birth, he was treated with all the respect due to an *arii nui*.

At the time of Cook's first visit we hear very little of Tu, he was overshadowed by the strong personality of Tuteha who purposely kept him in the background. This changed, however, during the four intervening years separating Cook's landings. When Cook returned in the *Resolution* in 1774 he found Tuteha dead, killed the previous year in another of the civil wars that were almost seasonal on the island, and Tu, backed up by the wise Ti'i, his uncle, had come into power. We are told that Ti'i was an able adviser and 'exercised an influence for the good over his nephew and the people making peace between them and the British visitors whenever friction arose, as it did occasionally, chiefly on account of thefts'.

According to Forster, Tu seemed to be twenty-four or twenty-five years old, 'the tallest man we saw on the whole island, measuring six feet, three inches in height. His whole body was proportionally strong, well made, without any tendency to corpulence. His head, notwithstanding a certain gloominess, which seemed to express a fearful disposition, had a majestic and an intelligent air, and there was great expression in his full, black eyes'. Cook bears out his timorous nature, for he tells us that it proved a difficult task luring him on to the *Resolution.* The young chief surrounded by a crowd of natives had stood watching the ships anchor, and then as soon as the British made to land, had fled over One Tree Hill to the adjoining district where he lived, and where Cook went the following day to visit him. He confessed to Cook that he was fearful of the guns.

Tu seems to have been very democratic. In spite of his kingly establishment 'there is very little about Tu's person or court,' writes Cook, 'by which a stranger could distinguish the king from his subjects. I have seldom seen him dressed in anything but a common piece of cloth wrapped round his loins,' and then again 'he seems to avoid all unnecessary pomp and show and even to demean himself, more than any other of the *ariis*. I have seen him at work at the paddles – and even when some of his *toutous* were looking on. Everyone has a free access to him and they speak to him whenever they see him without the least ceremony.' Cook ends his description of Tu with a generality: 'I have observed,' he remarks, 'that the chiefs of these isles are more beloved by the bulk of the people than feared, may we not conclude from this that the government is mild and equitable?'

Another three years were to pass before we get a further glimpse of Tu: Prince Tu by now with his star very much in the ascendant. Cook is back again in the *Resolution* on the third and last of his voyages. This time Cook has brought the young chief a whole menagerie. Lord Bessborough, a staunch Whig and a close friend of the Prince of Wales, had sent him a peacock and a hen. A more sensible choice made up the rest of the list; ducks, geese and turkeys; the cattle consisting of some cows, a bull, a horse and mare, and some sheep. 'The trouble and vexation,' remarks Cook, 'that attended the bringing of this living cargo thus far is hardly to be conceived,' but apparently it had been Farmer George's particular wish and had therefore to be attempted. The horses were a great success and we get an amusing description of the two Captains, Cook and Clerke, mounted on horseback, galloping along the black sand of Matavai Bay. The people were flabbergasted 'and gazed upon us with as much astonishment as if we had been centaurs'. This was the first time they had seen anyone ride. These rides were repeated every day by one member or another of the ship's company and Cook says that the horses, after they had learned the use of them, impressed the people tremendously, 'and conveyed to them a better idea of the greatness of another nation, than all the other novelties put together'.

Tu had already been married but his first wife bore him no children, so that when Cook returned in 1777 he found he had taken a second wife, a chiefess of a high degree from Moorea with the grandiloquent title of Great Princess Roaming in Expansive Palaces. She was an intelligent and able consort and helped her husband considerably in his fight for political domination of the island.

Captain Bligh of the *Bounty* gives further details about Tu. The date is October 1788, exactly ten years after Cook's last visit. During the long absence of Europeans from Tahiti, Tu had greatly extended his dominion and was gaining a firm footing in Taiarapu, until then the main peninsula's sworn enemy. On the other hand, there was trouble with Moorea in spite of his wife's close connection with the island. On several occasions marauding parties from Moorea had laid waste the Pare-Hapape districts. Tu spoke of the matter to Bligh 'and showed a strong desire to avenge himself of his opponents'. Tu had been so helpful in furnishing the young bread-fruit trees requested that Bligh felt obliged to assist him, and gave him a present 'of two muskets, a pair of pistols and a goodly supply of ammunition'. We are informed that in their use 'his wife, who was an exceptionally courageous woman, became expert rather than Tu himself'.

Bligh also met Tu's three children, a daughter and two sons. The heir apparent was about six years old and upon him, as Bligh tells us 'all his father's regal dignity was being concentrated'. By the laws of inheritance the infant automatically assumed Tu's rank and title, and in a few years would be king, although Tu would act as regent until the child came of age. As we have seen, these strange laws of inheritance were peculiar to Tahiti and applied to all classes.

Captain Bligh and some of his officers went to pay their respects to the young prince at Pare. They were given an audience across a river, 'he and his sister and brother standing on one bank with their attendants and we on the other, for he had not yet been brought into contact with the public'.

Tu eventually became King of Tahiti and Moorea in 1793, annexing the Tuamotu, a group of islands lying to the west of Tahiti, a few years later. It was not with the two muskets given to him by Bligh however that Tu eventually subjected Moorea, but with a larger quantity he obtained from the mutineers on their return to Tahiti two months after the *Bounty* had sailed away.

On ascending the throne Tu adopted the name of Pomaré. As Newton Rowe explains: 'it is not unusual for Tahitians to change their names as a result of any incident or phenomenon which catches their fancy, a habit according with the peculiar, sardonic self-depreciatory humour of the Polynesians. Thus the most famous of the future kings took the name of Pomaré which means Night-Cough. Having spent a night sleeping out upon the mountain, he developed a cough which one of his attendants referred to as a night-cough. The assonance and the combination of words took the king's fancy and he adopted it as the name by which he and his descendants are known'.*

Tu, or Pomaré I, died in 1803 and instead of being carried up to some secret mountain cave was buried in the Pomaré ground at Arue. The exact position of his grave is not known today. It should, however, be easy enough to locate if archaeologists cared to dig for it. There are references enough indicating the manner of his burial, the body having been wrapped in a length of red cloth given to him by Cook.

One last detail about Tu: he owned a portrait of Cook painted for him by John Webber, the official artist attached to Cook's last voyage. Bligh mentions it but does not say whether it was a good likeness. The frame was broken and Tu had asked Bligh to have it mended for him. Bligh hung the portrait in his cabin for the duration of the *Bounty*'s stay at Matavai Bay and then, on leaving, signed his name and the date upon the back of the canvas; a practice, Teuira Henry writes, that succeeding commanders of British ships visiting Tahiti kept up until the picture disappeared. What eventually became of it no one knows.

Tahiti had actually been visited by one other ship five months prior to the *Bounty*'s arrival in December, the *Lady Penrhyn*, commanded by Lieutenant Watts on his way to New South Wales. Watts, like Bligh, had served with Cook in the *Resolution*, yet neither of them had thought it prudent to inform the Tahitians of Cook's death. (Cook had been killed in Hawaii ten years before.) The natives had been particularly

* *Voyage to the Amorous Islands*, by Newton Rowe, André Deutsch, London, 1955.

attached to the great captain and the British felt that the good treatment they received from the Tahitians depended, in part, on the respect these entertained for Cook. They feared, perhaps rightly, that knowledge of the manner of his death might have an unfortunate effect. When Fletcher Christian – leader of the *Bounty* mutiny – and his men returned to Tahiti they took advantage of Cook's popularity and told the natives that they had met Captain Cook who had sent the ship back for all the livestock that could be spared to propagate upon an island that Captain Bligh had discovered on his way to Tonga. Christian, by this time, had decided that it was running too great a risk to attempt settling in Tahiti and was preparing to stock up for his run eastward which, as everyone knows, was to end two months later on the shores of a small island which he named Pitcairn. The natives, believing his story, vied with each other to furnish everything they could for the Captain, so that by the 10th of June they had collected four hundred and fifty hogs, fifty goats and many fowls, dogs and cats. The bull and cow which Bligh had committed to the care of Tu were also given to them, but the bull died on the passage.

To return to the Pomarés, the next reference we have to the family comes from the missionary ship *Duff*, commanded by Captain Wilson. She was sent out to Tahiti in 1796, the year following the establishment of the Missionary Society in London, and strange to relate, the favourable manner in which the men of God were received depended, in part, on a manifestation of nature. The day before the arrival of the *Duff* Tahiti had been badly shaken by an earthquake, the first in its history. As is usual in such cases, the tremors had been accompanied by a high sea and a terrible storm. The first shock occurred early in the morning, the second followed at noon, and, already driven out of their houses, the people were prostrate with fear at a third shock that evening. They kept watch all night, expecting some awful calamity; instead, to their surprise, the white sails of a ship appeared over the black horizon. It is not surprising that her arrival should have been taken as a portent. The natives immediately christened the *Duff* the Polynesian equivalent of the *Stirrer*, and treated its passengers with great respect. Pomaré even went so far as to cede them the district of Matavai Bay to be used as they saw fit. This Pomaré was not Tu, but his son, Pomaré II, who in accordance with the habits of the island, had taken on his royal duties.

Pomaré II was still more of an opportunist than his father; seeing he had everything to gain by welcoming the whites, he set about it in no uncertain manner, even becoming one of their first proselytes. Herman Melville, almost an eye-witness – he arrived in Tahiti twenty years after Pomaré II's death – recorded that the king was a debauchee and a drunkard, and hints at unnatural vices. Pomaré was, nevertheless, a good friend of the missionaries, even overdoing his enthusiasm; his zeal for the new faith hurried him into the religious wars whereupon he was defeated and expelled to Moorea. His 'zeal' in fact, had nearly cost him this throne but 'after a short exile,' writes Melville, 'he returned with an army of eight hundred warriors and in the battle of Narii routed the rebellious pagans with great slaughter and re-established himself on the throne.' It was not in vain that the ambitious Pomaré's blood animated his royal person.

Pomaré died in 1821, a recluse on the small island of Motuvta in the middle of Papeete harbour. He had withdrawn here to meditate, his last hours passed, so the story goes, with the Bible in one hand and a bottle in the other.

One would like to know more of the saintly debauchee but until now few facts are available. He was succeeded by his infant son under the title of Pomaré III. The young prince survived his father by only six years, ruling power then passing to his eldest sister Aimata, commonly called Pomaré Vahiné I, or the first female Pomaré. Miss Henry informs us that the name Aimata means 'eye-eater' and was derived from the former custom of presenting the eye of a human victim to a sovereign during the religious rites performed at the national *marae*.

As we already know, Pomaré IV seems to have been somewhat of a Jezebel in private life, but as a monarch she was lenient. The truth is that the missionaries had robbed the regal office in Tahiti of much of its dignity and influence. Melville laments the change: 'How transient human greatness!' – then he describes Pomaré IV, granddaughter of the proud Tu 'who went into laundry business, publicly soliciting, by her agents, the washing of the linen belonging to the officers of ships touching in her harbours'.

Pomaré reigned for half a century enjoying two husbands and innumerable lovers. Her first three children died in infancy to be followed by six others, born apparently out of wedlock. One of them became Pomaré V. This debonair giant succeeded his mother in 1877 but was invested with only the vaguest shadow of sovereignty; bored by the lack of responsibilities he abdicated in 1880 in favour of France. He died in June 1891 – lay dying, in fact, when Gauguin in yellow shoes, red cravat and immense green hat first walked the streets of Papeete. With him ended the history of ancient Tahiti. The palace immediately became government offices, his widow moving to a small villa opposite, hidden from the road by some trees. Her eventual death hardly aroused a comment.

Pomaré V's tomb, like the lost grave of his great-grandfather, is situated on the Pomaré ground at Arue, on the point where the family *marae* once stood. It is a strange little mausoleum with sloping coral walls overgrown with fern and a corrugated roof topped with what looks like a large bottle of Benedictine. No one quite knows the significance of the bottle, or is it perhaps a Tahitian idea of an urn? Above the entrance one finds a large 'P' cut in relief on a cement shield with, capping it, a stylized crown cast in the same material. A semicircle of ironwood trees protects the mausoleum from the sea. It is a species of pine and every smallest breeze sighs in its branches, stirring the long, grey-green needles like an echo.

[Chapter 10]

Great Tahiti of the Golden Haze

It is never easy for a newcomer to detect class distinctions in an unfamiliar country. What is obvious to the natives is sometimes far too subtle for the stranger to grasp. This certainly applies to the Tahitians of today. The short flat noses and thick lips of the Polynesians are still apparent in varying degrees, but these features are less pronounced than they used to be before inter-marriage with the English and the French, not to mention the recent influx of Chinese. Dressed also, for the most part, in a fashion that is foreign to them, it is almost impossible to differentiate social distinctions. The cotton *pareu* now worn by the women (above the breasts instead of under them) has, of course, nothing to do with the way they used to dress.

In Cook's time he had a definite yardstick by which the quality of the visitors rowing out to the *Endeavour* could be gauged. It was a question of pigmentation and clothes. He notes that the working man is of a very dark brown from constant exposure to the sun, while his superior, who spends most of his time in the shadow of his house, is much paler, sometimes not browner than the white people born in the West Indies. Their complexion is described as a clear olive. They are tall by nature, 'the women of superior rank are also in general above our middle stature, but those of an inferior class are rather below it, and some of them are very small. This defect in size probably proceeds from their early commerce with man, the only thing in which they differ from their superiors that could possibly affect their growth'.

Parkinson finds the people well made but 'with prominent bellies'. In the eyes of the Tahitian stoutness was a mark of beauty and characteristic of royal personages. As thin people were thought to be sick, a business was made of fattening children by stuffing them with the best food, mostly preparations of fruit and vegetables. They were also shut up in the dark and made to steam, closely covered by sheets. After two or three months of this treatment, patients became both stout and fair, hence objects of much admiration. Women and sometimes men took this treatment to beautify themselves.

As for clothes, Banks tells us that the rich and well-born 'enjoy wearing as much cloth as possible' and that the men's dress is little different from that of the women. 'The gentry,' he says, 'would come to visit Cook with most of their body exposed but with a large quantity of cloth rolled round their loins – sufficient to clothe a dozen people.' As we have already seen, the exposed shoulder was a sign of respect. 'It is no shame,' writes Cook, 'for any part of the body to be exposed, except those which all mankind hide. The men wear a piece of cloth which goes between their thighs, brought up before and behind, and then wrapped round their waist.' This kind of breech cloth, however, seldom constituted a man's only covering except amongst the working classes. The general form of dress favoured by the gentry seems to have been fairly standard. First came the *pareu*, a piece of cloth about two yards long, which was drawn round the waist and fastened jauntily on one side, falling to the calf of the leg, which was beautifully tattooed. On top of this would come another square of cloth, sometimes two or three, worn like a Mexican poncho with a hole in the middle for the head, hanging to the knees. A wide sash fastened it at the waist, 'it being open at the sides gives free liberty to their arms'. Over this again came a fine white cloth like a muslin 'given various elegant turns round the body'.

Their hair was almost universally black, thick and rather wiry. Men were apt to favour beards but never moustaches, they shaved with a shark's tooth fitted to a thick piece of shell. 'Both sexes eradicate every hair from under their arms and look upon it as a mark of uncleanliness in us that we do not do the same.' Fish scales or shells formed their tweezers, and a black coconut shell filled with water served as a looking-glass. The women as a rule wore their hair short, cropped round their ears. The men, on the other hand, arranged it in different ways; 'the better sort let it grow long, sometimes tying it up on top of their heads, or letting it hang loose over their shoulders but many of the inferiors and those who exercise professions, such as fishing are obliged to wear it cropped short like the women.' Banks tells us that the men wore feathers, the long plumes found in the tropic birds' tails were especially prized. These were stuck perfectly upright on top of the head. 'They also have wigs made of human hair or dog hair which they tie on under their own hair at the back of their head.' Sometimes a single scented flower would be placed in the lobe of the ear as an ear-ring. The nobles often wore turbans and the working classes 'whimsical garlands made of a variety of flowers', or sweet-scented seeds and ferns. Women of rank decked themselves with beautiful wreaths of red, yellow or green *ura* feathers, sometimes twined with strings of pearls, also loops or eardrops of lightly braided hair ornamented with pearls. Both men and women wore ear-rings, but only in one ear. Cook describes them as being made of 'shells, stones, berries, red pease and some small pearls which they wear three tied together; but our beads and buttons very soon supplied their place'. Wallis managed to purchase about a dozen of these pearls. 'They were of good colour but all spoilt by boring,' probably executed with a shark's tooth. Banks says they set a great value on their pearls. The large ones of about twenty-three grains (the size of a large pea) were of good clear water as well as shape. 'For these I offered at different times any price the owner would have, but they would not hear of parting with them. They value them as much as we do ourselves.'

What impressed the travellers most were the elaborate headdresses of some of the nobles' wives – or they were, perhaps, young votresses of the *Arioi Society*. Opinions seemed to differ. Webber, anyhow, made some excellent drawings of them. They were built up with plaits of human hair, 'scarce thicker than common thread'. Banks saw a piece over a mile long worked from end to end without a knot, 'and I have seen five or six such pieces wound round the head of one woman, the effect of which, if done with taste, was most becoming'. These elaborate coiffures were dressed rather wider at the top than at the bottom, giving the effect of a crown, similar to the kind worn by the beautiful Nefret-iti in the well-known bust of her in the Berlin Museum. In between the plaits they used to stick *Gardenia tahitiensis* flowers, or single-petalled gardenias indigenous to the island. Webber shows them as white stars against the black hair. Cook's description gives the impression that these high-dressed heads were worn by any lady of rank providing her birth entitled her to it, nor does he specify any special occasion. On the other hand Banks, and Forster after him, quite definitely state that they were only the appanage of members of the *Arioi Society* and worn while performing their dances. Both gave details of the remarkable *Arioi* costume. It consisted of a tight corsage of black cloth upon which two bunches of black feathers were pinned 'resembling', adds Banks, 'our ladies' nosegays. On their hips rested a quantity of cloth pleated very full which reached almost up to their arms and fell down below into long petticoats reaching below their feet, which they managed with as much dexterity as our opera dancers would have done. These pleats were brown and white alternately but the petticoats were all white.' Forster described the ruffs as red and white, but probably there were a variety of colour schemes. Both men agree more or less as to the dance itself. The women moved sideways, keeping excellent time with the rapid, loud drum-beats, their bare arms waving gracefully, their fingers moving with 'a quickness scarce to be imagined'. 'Their attitude and gestures,' Forster says, 'were much varied, and sometimes might admit of being constructed into wantonness; but they were entirely free from that positive degree of gross indecency which the chaste eyes of English ladies of fashion are forced to behold at the opera.' (One wonders to what performance he refers!) 'The only action which gives offence to all our ideas of gracefulness and harmony, is the frightful custom of writhing their mouths into the strangest distortion which was impossible for any one of us to imitate.'

Forster adds a charming detail about their hair. Being dressed high in an outward sloping crown 'there was a deep hollow left in the middle, which they had filled up with a great quantity of sweet smelling flowers'.

It was the habit of all the women to scent their hair. 'The only disagreeable thing about them,' notes Cook, 'is the oil with which they anoint their heads. *Monoe*, as they call it, is made of coconut oil in which some sweet herbs or flowers are infused. The oil is generally very rancid which makes the wearer of it smell not very agreeable.' Others have described the odour as very pleasant, certainly I found it so. Omai* told Forster that there were no less than fourteen different sorts of plants employed for perfuming, which shows how remarkably fastidious these people were. They still are scrupulously clean, washing in running water several times a day. Bathing in the sea is not considered washing, so if they have no running water at home they will go to the nearest stream or pool, and will travel a good way to find it. 'Their clothes as well as their persons,' remarks Banks, 'are kept almost without spot or stain.'

Like many other travellers, Banks was very impressed with the natural elegance of the women. He describes the grace with which the daughter of a noble received some beads he gave her: she was leaning on the arm of an attendant and stretched out her hand to accept the gift. 'Had she been a princess royal of England giving her hand to be kissed no instruction could have taught her to have done it with a better grace.' Banks went so far as to proclaim the Tahitian women the most elegant in the world. 'Their clothes,' rhapsodizes Bernard Smith, 'were natural and beautiful, such as were found in Europe only upon statues or antique gems, or in the paintings of the great Italians who knew how to clothe their angels and goddesses in loose, natural folds just as worn by the Tahitians.* Such clothing followed Nature, and so grateful Nature had endowed the Tahitians with beautiful bodies.'† 'Their bodies were so beautiful,' says Banks, 'that they might defy the imitation of the chisel of a Phidias or the pencil of an Apelles.'

There are many intriguing details about Tahitian dress such as

* A Tahitian taken back to England on the second voyage.

† Bernard Smith, *European Vision and The South Pacific*, Oxford at The Clarendon Press.

Bougainville's 'little hats made of cane and adorned with flowers'; and the two types of turbans, one very bulky and closely bound for the warriors, as a protection against spears, and the other 'light and tastefully made, being worn as a hat to protect the head from the sun, or as a wig in case of baldness'.

The panoply of war must have been equally decorative. Wars in these islands generally consisted of naval battles and entailed expeditions in their great, double canoes. Cook reports having seen a fleet numbering about two hundred and fourteen of them preparing for an invasion of Moorea. The canoes were usually over a hundred feet long, and had a platform lashed across them for a fighting stage. Forster tells us that they generally had a piece of white cloth running between the prows of the canoes in lieu of an ensign, the wind swelling it like a sail. 'Some likewise had a striped cloth, with various red chequers which were the marks of the divisions under the different commanders.' Hodges made a painting of these war galleys in which the warriors are depicted crowding on to the fighting stages, an area about forty feet square raised on carved posts. They are dressed in the usual ample pieces of cloth worn over an armour of closely braided sennit. Topping their finery come the bulky turbans, above which towers their naval chieftain's headdress, somewhat similar to the high headdress already mentioned as worn in the funeral procession. Forster describes 'a prodigious number of long tail feathers from the tropic bird diverged from its edge, proscribing a radiant line, resembling that glory of light with which our painters commonly ornamented the heads of angels and saints'. A large turban of cloth was required for this huge, unwieldy machine to rest upon; but as it is intended merely to strike the beholder with admiration (and fear, one presumes) it can be of no service and the admiral soon takes it off and places it on the platform near to him.

Fifteen hundred warriors in full regalia were surely an impressive sight. The upward curving prows of these great canoes would cleave the smooth waters of the lagoon as four thousand naked paddlers bent to their oars, their rhythm marked for them, as it would have been on board a Roman trireme, by the beating of deep-toned drums. There would be a moment's hesitation as each canoe reached the narrow reef passage: could the cumbersome canoe really pass through? It was a question of timing. With a cry from the leader, and further shouts from the rowers, they would dig their paddles savagely into the sea and thrust the canoe through the passage, with water roaring and racing on either side. A minute, two minutes' frantic effort, and then the gentle calm of the lagoon would give way to the restless heaving of the ocean. Once out at sea, lost to each other in the haze, they would keep in touch by blowing on large conch trumpets.

It was during the second voyage that Cook entertained the 'admiral' of the fleet at dinner, a man called Towha. 'His hair was a fine silver gray, and his countenance was the most engaging and truly good natured which I ever saw in these islands.' Tu was also of the party and it was then that Cook learned that the fleet intended 'to reduce the rebellious people of York Island (Moorea) to obedience'. Forster tells us that Cook, half in jest, proposed to accompany them with his ships 'and to fire upon the enemy of Tu, which at first they smiled at and approved of'. Discussing the matter later on between themselves they wisely changed their minds, explaining that should they accept Cook's kind offer, it would give too much importance to the enemy. They also pointed out that Tahiti's eventual victory would always be ascribed to the help of the foreigners, and in the long run would cause them additional trouble.

The Polynesians, on the whole were, and still are, a very handsome nation, their one defect being a slight heaviness of leg. To make up for this, however, their arms and hands are remarkably well formed, particularly in the women. Max Radiguet,* a French naval officer, admires their soft hands and finds them astonishingly beautiful, the fingers are gracefully curved; the nails, long and almond-shaped, are well cared for and shine like agates. The texture of the skin is also extremely delicate. Forster remarks on the nails of one of the chiefs, they were very long 'upon which he valued himself not a little and which I imagine were a mark of distinction since only such persons as had no occasion to work could suffer them to grow that length'.

There is no trace of tattooing these days, but Banks says he never saw 'one single person of mature years without it'.

Teuira Henry writes that men were generally tattooed on the limbs and on the body as far as the back of the neck and even to the ears and the roots of the hair. Every variety of motif was to be seen; sometimes whole battles were depicted down to the smallest detail. Ellis, the clerical authority on Polynesia, states that he often admired the taste displayed in the marking of a chief's legs. 'I saw a cocoanut tree correctly and distinctly drawn, its root spreading out at the heel, its elastic stalk pencilled as it were along the tendon, and its waving plume gracefully spread out on the broad part of the calf.'† The Tahitians, unlike their cousins, the Maoris of New Zealand, seldom tattooed their throats or faces. Women had their hands marked as though covered with mittens of fine string, with circles around the wrists and fingers like bracelets or rings. They also had sandal-like prints upon the feet, terminating in an elegantly traced circle round the ankle. Their proud-

* *Les Derniers Sauvages*, Max Radiguet, Paris, 1860.

† *Polynesian Researches*, William Ellis, Fisher & Son, London, 1832.

est exhibit, however, proved to be the tattooing on a more roomy part of their person. Bougainville comments amusingly on the habit, he even finds it attractive; 'the women in Europe,' he writes, 'paint their cheeks red while those in Tahiti dye their loins and buttocks a deep blue, which showed very prettily against their clear brown skin.'

Tattooing was a very painful process and was performed gradually. The victim had to be more or less adult before the first patterns were incised, further growth would obviously have distorted the lines. It took several months, and sometimes years, to complete the tattooing of a chief. If too much was attempted at one time, it could quite easily endanger the patient's life. An authority on the custom informs us that the process was one of intense pain, 'the recumbent figures of the victims wincing and writhing at every stroke of the operation and grieving under the torments inflicted'. Banks saw the operation being performed upon the backside of a girl about thirteen years old. She bore it very stoically for about a quarter of an hour, but eventually the pain became intolerable. 'She first complained in murmurs, then wept, and at last burst out into loud lamentations.' When she began to struggle she was held down by two women, 'who sometimes soothed and sometimes chid her, and now and then, when she was most unruly, gave her a smart blow'. The girl Banks reports on may have writhed, but it was considered very unmanly for a male to shrink from the treatment or to show any sign of suffering.

Tattooing was performed by professional artists and an expert was held in high esteem. In New Zealand, where the art reached its highest attainment, we hear of a man called Aranghie who was considered the greatest master. Men of the highest rank travelled long distances to put their skins under his skilled hands. 'Indeed,' writes a government surveyor, in the nineteenth century, 'so highly was his work esteemed that I have seen many of his drawings exhibited even after his death. A neighbour of mine very lately killed a chief who had been tattooed by Aranghie, and appreciating the artist's work, he skinned the chieftain's thighs and covered his cartouche-box with it. I am astonished to see with what boldness and precision Aranghie drew his designs on the skin and what beautiful ornaments he produced. No rule and compasses could be more exact than the lines and circles he formed. So unrivalled was he in his profession that a highly finished face of a chief from the hands of this artist is as greatly prized in New Zealand as a head from the hands of Sir Thomas Lawrence is amongst us.'* Cook, when he eventually reaches New Zealand, bears out Mr Earle about the precision of the tattooing. 'The spirals,' he writes, 'are drawn with great nicety and even elegance. One side corresponds with the other and they

* *Moko or Maori Tattooing*, Major-General Robley, Chapman & Hall, London, 1896.

appear at first sight to be exactly the same, but on close examination no two were formed alike.' We know, in fact, that the chiefs would draw the markings of one of their cheeks in place of a signature.

The artist tattooer began by tracing the line of the intended incisions with charcoal, but as the operation progressed, blood running from the cuts effaced the marks and he was forced to outline his pattern with a sharper instrument. The implement used for making the incisions in the flesh was like a small chisel usually made from a sea-bird's wing or a shark's tooth, ingeniously bound with fine sennit to a slender stick. The blade was about a quarter of an inch thick and on being applied to the skin was driven in by a smart tap from a small mallet. One can imagine just how painful this procedure must have been.

The dyeing of the tattooing went simultaneously with the cutting, the blade of the chisel being immersed in the pigment, a blue-black paste obtained from the sooty dripping of oil extracted from a burnt candle-nut. When first applied to the skin this inky substance produced a bluish tint, tending to fade with time, but remaining always indelible.

Several of the men on board the *Endeavour* had themselves tattooed, Parkinson being one of them. They limited themselves, however, to the arms, and only chose the simpler motifs.

When describing the various costumes I have, until now, always referred to their being made of cloth. The different journals all did so too, but as we have already seen, the Polynesians knew nothing of weaving, and the 'cloth' was what we call *tapa*. The ancient *tapa*, however, has little in common with the rather coarse, stiff, vegetable fibre which is made now. Constantly one finds Cook and his companions admiring the elegant manner in which the Tahitians draped their 'cloth' around them, 'turning it a hundred different ways, according to the caprice and talents of the wearer'. This 'cloth' was spotlessly white and muslin-thin and cannot be compared to the cardboard-like *tapa* of today, which, even when softened by use, does not lend itself to soft folds.

The Tahitians had various qualities of *tapa*, the best 'cloth' being made from the bark of the bread-fruit tree. The more ordinary form of *tapa* was brown and came from the paper-mulberry, correctly known as *Broussonetta papyriafera*. The *tapa* we see now is exclusively brown and white with, sometimes, an addition of black. It is no longer even made in Tahiti and the pieces one finds in Papeete shops come from other islands, such as the Tongan group or the Wallis Islands. In Cook's time *tapa* was stained a variety of colours. We read of Forster receiving presents of large pieces of fine cloth, 'dyed scarlet, rose or straw-coloured and perfumed with the choicest oils'. 'Cloth' would be stained black or yellow, grey or brown, or many different shades of crimson. Banks particularly admired the wonderful brightness of the crimson. He showed Sir Joshua Reynolds a piece who told him 'the nearest imitation of the colours that he could make would be by mixing vermilion and carmine'. The red *tapa* was highly valued by the Tahitians and was only worn by nobles and chiefs. Newton Rowe writes that the black dye was obtained from the sap of the mountain-plantain or from 'under the roots of such coconut palms as grew in wet and swampy ground, where the cloth was alternately soaked and dried several times in succession until it became a deep black and was then washed in salt water to be fixed. The brown was tanned with the bark of several trees, especially ironwood, which gave a fine bright colour, heightened by the sun. The yellow was extracted from turmeric; the gray was the *tapa*'s natural colour when unbleached; after being half worn it might be dyed brown, and lined with white by pasting two cloths together'.

Sometimes the *tapa* was decorated with fine geometrical drawings; they also had a system of stencilling with leaves and delicate ferns. A leaf was soaked in one of the dyes, then pressed on to the fibre and left to dry; in falling off, its imprint remained. Several such *tapas* can be seen in the Musée de l'Homme in Paris.

The *arii nuis* or chiefs of the island were splendidly dressed when they made an official appearance. During public festivities the nobles wore *pareus* of flexible mats woven with a faint pattern and edged with a fringe. A fringe of red *ura* feathers also bordered their fine, white *tapa* shawls in much the same way as ermine is used on the coronation robes of British peers. As ornaments they wore broad seed necklaces and capes and headdresses of young coconut leaves. On very special occasions the king or high chief wore a very showy headdress, not unlike the headpieces of Aztec and Mayan kings. It consisted of a superb helmet made up of clusters of crimson feathers set on a high framework with, behind it, bursts of outspreading red, black and white feathers. The helmet stood up from a closely fitted headband and being so high seemed to yield with every movement, which must have added considerably to the majesty of its wearer.

When the *arii nui*, and later the kings, were invested, a formal presentation took place and they were handed the sacred *maro* or royal girdle, the ancient insignia of a royal pedigree claiming descent from the gods. There seemed to have been several of these girdles but the *maro* of the Tamatoa family of Raiatea, the most ancient of the group, was the longest, measuring twenty-one feet in length and six inches in width. It consisted of red and yellow feathers trimmed in alternate patches on a network belt. A new length was added at each coronation, and from variations in the pattern it was possible to read something of the history of the wearer. It was, in fact, an article of very skilled workmanship. In each little hole was set a bunch of *ura* feathers caught into place by a polished needle of human bone. The feathers were made to overlap so that they imitated a bird's plumage. The patterns, mostly in squares, were formed by turning the feathers in different directions. We learn from Teuira Henry that the needle of human bone was never taken out, the girdle was intended to continue for ever. A human victim was sacrificed for the perforating of the belt for each new section and again when the square was finished. Cook describes it as bordered at one end with eight pieces about the size and shape of a horse's shoe, and edged with a fringe of black feathers. Cook also mentions Captain Wallis's pennant, that had been planted on Tahitian soil by Lieutenant Furneaux when he formally claimed the island for his country. As seen in a previous chapter, the pennant had not been allowed to fly for long: it was removed that very evening and immediately attached to the royal girdle. Cook says that parts of it were clearly visible through the feathers that had been stitched on to it. History does not relate whether a further human sacrifice was considered necessary when the British pennant was added, one suspects, however, that it was.

It was this very *maro*, the sacred *maro* of Raiatea, that Pomaré II presented to the Missionary Society after his conversion. Proud of their royal pupil, the society exhibited their pagan spoils in a room set aside for that purpose at their London headquarters. Unfortunately, when the collection was turned over in recent years to the British Museum the famous *maro* was found to be missing. One wonders what happened to it, particularly as very few relics of the Tahitian royal family remain. The natives considered such relics far too sacred to be handled by anyone except members of the royal family, and rather than let them fall into foreign hands they destroyed them themselves.

Superstition also played its part in the general holocaust. An example was the regrettable destruction of heirlooms that lay buried in the royal vault at *Vaitape*, on the island of Bora-Bora. There was said to be a curse on them, and no person outside the royal family could approach the vault without immediately becoming convulsed. In about 1875, owing to political disturbances, the royal bodies were removed from the vault and hidden up in the mountains, but unfortunately, for some reason that is difficult to understand, the beautiful feather cloaks and wreaths were left behind. One presumes that this was a decision made by Pomaré V's niece, the acting Queen of the island. A few months later she sent her retainers back to the spot to shake the dust out of the relics. They never accomplished their mission: no sooner had they approached the sacred objects than they were struck with convulsions. The spell had in no way abated. These facts cannot be discounted as ignorant gossip; several foreign residents on the island bore witness to the validity of the story. Some time passed, then Pomaré V, making a tour of his domains before abdicating, decided to pay Bora-Bora a visit. A family council was held and one of the problems discussed was what should be done about the relics. It was decided that they should be burnt. The Bishop Museum in Honolulu, famous for its collection of Oceania art, arrived too late on the scene to save them.

[Chapter 11]

A Tour of the Two Peninsulas

VENUS HAD been observed on June 3rd. Very early in the morning of June 26th, Cook 'set out in the pinnace accompanied by Mr Banks and one of the natives with an intent to make a circuit of the island in order to examine and draw a sketch of the coast and harbours thereof'. They sailed to the westward, landed at about eight o'clock, and walked the rest of the day, covering some thirty-five miles; the boat being within call all the way. It must have been early in the afternoon when they came to the place where Bougainville's ships, *La Boudeuse* and *L'Etoile* had harboured. At that time Cook believed them to have been Spanish. He had shown a native chief a print of ships' colours, and without hesitating, this man had pointed to the Spanish flag as the one that had been flown. Not until he reached Batavia, on his way home, did he learn his mistake.

It is hard to imagine a more beautiful view than the one from Bougainville's anchorage: a great bay continues to curve down towards the isthmus joining the two peninsulas, where the skyline is broken by Tairapau's mountains jutting out in serrated peaks into the sea. The first time I was there, clouds cut across Pueu's pointed summits and the whole magnificent landscape was washed in a blue haze. A little church now stands adjacent to the place where the Chevalier landed his long boat, its steeple built of lumps of uncut coral and its altar rail inlaid with pearl shells. Most of the churches on the island are built of coral rock which though nearly white when first hewn from the reef, quickly darkens with time so that the churches look almost sooty and venerable beyond their age.

Three miles south of Passe de la Boudeuse is the shallow valley or Faaone. A gentle river leads to a dip in the green-clad mountains over which cascade silver plumes of water. The east coast of Tahiti proper lies open to the wind; much of it falls abruptly into the sea. There is little arable land and consequently the population is sparse. This coast most resembles the Tahiti of the eighteenth century, indeed much of it has remained exactly as Cook knew it.

They camped that night in a friend's shelter on Taravao Bay and in the morning 'found the country to be marshy and flat'. They were on the isthmus of Taravao, a two-mile bare stretch joining the two islands over which the natives used to haul their canoes.

The party found Taiarapu, or Little Tahiti, very fertile and the canoes, ranged along the shore, far superior to any that they had seen before, both in size and craftsmanship. They still are. Boating and walking they came eventually to the Vaitepiha River,' So large,' Cook tells us, 'that we were obliged to ferry over it in a canoe, and our train, which was pretty numerous, to swim.' 'Which they did,' adds Banks, 'with as much facility as a pack of hounds taking to water.' Thus they reached the village of Tautira.

Cook refers to Tautira or Vaitepiha Bay as Ohitepepa. Here he was to anchor for a brief stay on both his second and third voyages. Its great bay walled off with steep mountains towering like pyramids into the distance furnished Hodges with the subject of one of his better landscapes. It was here also that I spent a night in the guest-house of the local chief, a dignified old man with an energetic son who owns a saw-mill where he makes forty-foot canoes that seat ten to twelve people. The canoes are still outrigged but the larger ones now carry detachable out-board motors. There are no roads round the southern extremity of Taiarapu and all transport is either on horseback or by canoe. For this reason the men of the district always win the boat races held in Papeete harbour on the 14th of July. They have more practice with the paddle than other crews, but one wonders how long this will last now that motors are being imported.

Tautira is the nearest approach to be found on the island to a real village. Papeete is Tahiti's town and Tautira its village. A dusty road bordered with hedges of red ginger and great yellow speckled crotons winds up to a cluster of iron-roofed huts; amongst them is a vacant lot where Ori's house used to stand. Ori was the sub-chief with whom Robert Louis Stevenson lodged with his wife, mother and stepson. They had arrived in Papeete via the Marquesas by schooner from San Francisco. Stevenson had fallen ill and it was thought prudent to stop over. It was November 1888, the beginning of the rainy season. 'Ori,' Mrs Stevenson tells us in a letter, 'looks more like a Roman Emperor in bronze than words can express.' Stevenson wrote a good part of *The Master of Ballantrae* in their 'bird cage of a house', and would probably have settled there for good had the climate been more temperate.

Cook and Banks passed the afternoon of the 27th walking; they found the going very rough. One knows what they experienced for I have spent many hours picking my way alternately over slippery coral shoals, and the muddy shore littered with coconut husks and rotting nuts. (Apparently the pigs crack open the nuts by banging them against the rocks with their heads.) The farther one advances down the peninsula the more precipitous the mountains become, sometimes almost pushing one into the sea. At no time is there room for more than a narrow path, reduced from much use to a well-trodden quagmire. The pigs must be farmed out in a semi-wild state, for nobody lives on this part of the coast. 'After having tired ourselves with walking,' writes Cook, 'we took to the boats.' They rowed till dark, 'and then we put into a little creek not far from the S.E. point of the island. Here we found a deserted long house where we spent the night'. But not Banks, who sheltered on board the double canoe of a nobleman who accompanied their progress.

The next day they met a chief who had taken as a prize of war from the defeated 'Queen' Purea, a goose and a turkey-cock which had been given to her by Captain Wallis. The natives appeared to be immensely fond of them. They were both enormously fat and so tame, Banks tells us, that they followed their owners wherever they went.

Both Cook and Banks lavish considerable detail upon the food they sampled. A chief's *poipoi* was, as Cook explains, a kind of pudding made of bread-fruit and plantain mixed with coconut milk and water, 'and beat up together in a half shell to the consistency of a custard'. From similar descriptions, we have some idea of the eating habits of the ancient Tahitians. They ate six times a day, dinner at 11 a.m. and supper at 8 p.m., their other meals being casual collations. Their appetites were prodigious. Banks watched a man down three bread-fruit, two fair-sized fish, fifteen plantains, and about a quart of unbaked custard – all at one sitting. One bread-fruit alone is the equivalent of about six large-sized potatoes. A plantain measures six to seven inches. Forster gives us a similar picture: a very fat chief was lolling on his wooden pillow and before him two servants were preparing his dessert. 'While this was doing, a woman who sat down near him, crammed down his throat by handfuls the remains of a large baked fish, and several bread-fruits.' On being presented to the chief, 'he scarce deigned to look at us, and the few monosyllables which he uttered, were only directed to remind the feeders of their duty, when we attracted their attention'.

The fare was monotonous but judging from the splendid health and the dazzling white teeth of their descendants, clearly adequate. For meat they had pig, fowl and dog. They did not care for the little tree rats, the only other quadruped indigenous to the island. Our explorers, however, were not so fussy. Robert Molyneux, master in the *Endeavour*,

24. Suddenly in front of me stood two hunched-up, wooden figures with heavy pouting lips and great sightless eyes. (*page 115*)

25. The recently restored *marae* of Arahurahu. (*page 115*)

26. The 14th of July celebrations at Papeete.
Members of a female chorus waiting to perform. (*page 127*)

27. The leaf skirts made from the bark of the hibiscus. (*page 128*)

28. A native youth. (*page 116*)

29. A *vahiné*.

31. Bora Bora. The lisping waters of a glass smooth lagoon. (*page 133*)

30. The island of Bora Bora. Dominating the scene is the great Temanu, a monolith of red-brown rock. (*page 133*)

32. It would be hard to find a more impressive or majestic sight than Paopao Bay, Cook's anchorage in Moorea. (*page 135*)

informs us that they shot and snared up to a thousand a day. 'It was not only a pleasant but a profitable amusement, for they are also good eating. The ground swarmed with them and the inhabitants never disturbed them. I have laid in the woods several nights and among other particulars I observed the rats playing about me as indifferent as about a tree.' Parkinson says that 'the gentlemen in the bell tent ate of them and commended them much', having them fried for breakfast.

According to Forster the Tahitians were lazy about fishing, but when they took the trouble, their catch was considerable. They fished without bait, with glittering mother-of-pearl hooks. 'Sometimes they made use of a decoy made of the bodies of cowries and other shells, tied together in the shape of a fish, making a head to it with a small cowrie, the tail being formed of grass ingeniously plaited.' Cook tells us that almost everything that comes out of the sea was eaten; 'conches, mussels and other shell fish which they gather at low water out on the reefs and eat raw with bread-fruit before they come to shore.' Jellyfish, or blubbers as the sailors called them, were another delicacy. 'Being tough,' writes Banks, 'and full of cartileges it was the habit to let them rot before baking them.' They seem to have been particularly popular among the women; 'though,' continues Banks, 'I confess I was not extremely fond of their company after they had eaten of them.'

There were various other farinaceous foods than bread-fruit: sweet potatoes, yams, chestnuts and *taro*, also the roots of different ferns. For fruit they had the *vi*, a bronze-green globe about the size of an orange. The explorers called them apples and the *Endeavour*'s cook used them in tarts and puddings. Pandanus was another fruit, starchy and looking something like a pineapple. There was sugar cane and, of course, the different plantains and *feis*, or wild banana. *Feis* ripen from red, deepening to an orange, almost flame colour, and taste delicious when baked, something like strawberry jam. Banks notes that the plantains were very popular with all the men in the ship 'and with us in the cabin they agreed much better than the bread-fruit which sometimes griped us'.

The fowls must have been very tough, small and stringy as are most chickens in the tropics. Their hogs were only killed on special occasions and baked in earthen ovens. As the Tahitians had no pottery vessels of any kind, their food was either baked or roasted. Hawkesworth says that 'having no vessels in which water could be subjected to the action of fire, they had no more idea that it could be made hot than that it could be made solid'. The potter's wheel and the loom were completely unknown in Polynesia.

'Hogs,' writes Forster, 'are a part of the riches of the Tahitians and would appear to be entirely the property of the chiefs.' Pigs were never so plentiful in the islands as to be a common food. Dogs, on the other hand, were. These were a special breed, kept solely for eating. The race has died out completely and no one quite knows what they looked like. They were small and pretty, says Bougainville and, according to Forster, very stupid; 'the most dull animals imaginable. They do not seem to have the least advantage in point of sagacity over our sheep, which are commonly made the emblems of silliness. In New Zealand where they had the same breed they were fed on fish and in the South Seas on vegetables', a diet that may have dulled their dispositions. It is odd, but no pictorial representation of these dogs exists. They varied a good deal in size, ranging from that of a lap-dog to a large spaniel. Their heads were broad and their snouts pointed, the eyes were very small, ears upright and their rather long and wiry hair of different colours, mostly white or brown. 'They seldom if ever barked but howled sometimes, and were shy of strangers to a degree of aversion.'

Purea offered Cook and his companions a dog to eat and was very surprised when the Englishmen indignantly declined to accept it. 'We refused it,' writes Cook, 'as being an animal we had no use for' – in this capacity, anyway. However, Banks came across 'the thigh of a dog ready dressed', in a basket of fruit he had bought and predictably could not resist tasting it. Cook relented. 'We found that it was meat not to be despised and therefore took Purea's dog and had him immediately dressed by some of the natives. It was the opinion of everyone who tasted it that they had never eaten sweeter meat. . . . Few there were of us but what allowed that the South Sea dog was next to an English lamb in excellency.' Banks and Solander commended it highly, but not Parkinson who found it tasted like coarse beef and had a strong, disagreeable smell. Banks admitted 'that a European dog would probably not eat as well, as these scarce in their lives touch animal food. Coconut kernels, bread-fruit and yams being what their masters can best afford to give them and what induced from custom I suppose they prefer to any kind of food'. But the sailors, although they had endured the salted meat on board and 'had not much prejudice against any species of food', would have no part of them. Probably one would have sided with the sailors, especially as the method of killing these canines was unnecessarily cruel. They held the dog's muzzle down to the pit of its stomach till it was stifled, 'an operation that continued about a quarter of an hour'.

The Tahitians had no salt, using sea-water instead as a sauce. If they lived some distance from the shore, the salt water was kept in sections of bamboo. 'When they eat they always have a cocoanut shell full near them into which they dip everything, especially fish. . . . They may use as much as half a pint of it at one meal.' A strongly flavoured sauce was also made of fermented coconut, beaten up into a buttery paste with salt water.

They ate with their fingers, using leaves as plates and pieces of bamboo to cut meat. Their table manners were not the prettiest. Banks describes a neighbour at table who took first half a bread-fruit, peeled the rind, removed the core with his nails and crammed his mouth as full as possible; then breaking a fish in half (raw or baked), dipped it into salt water and sucked it noisily into his mouth with as much salt water as he could manage. Banks admitted, however, that they quickly learned our manners and after a few lessons 'already held a knife and fork more handily than a Frenchman could learn in a year'.

Cook wondered that women were completely excluded from these meals. 'Nor is it common for any two men to eat together, the better sort hardly ever, and the women never upon any account . . . but always by themselves. What can be the reason of so unusual a custom it is hard to say, especially as they are a people, in every other instance, fond of society and much so of their women. They were often asked the reason, but they never gave any other answer, except that they did it because it was right.' Cook tells us that they used 'all the entreaties we were master of to invite the women to partake of our victuals at our table, but there never was an instant of one of them doing it publicly, but they would often go five or six together into the servants' apartment and there eat very heartily of whatever they could find, nor were they the least disturbed if anyone came in while they were still dining; and it has sometimes happened that when a woman was alone in our company she would eat with us, but always took care that her own people should not know what she had done, so that whatever may be the reason for this custom, it certainly affects their actual manners more than their principles'.

The Tahitians' manners have improved but what they eat is little changed. I have seen them sup up quantities of salt water and they still eat raw fish. My luggage was about to arrive by air freight from Los Angeles, but the TAI official with whom I had to deal was not in his office. I found him instead beyond the edge of the runway, naked, fishing with a circular net, deftly snaring quantities of small, silvery-yellow fish. He flashed his white teeth, at the same time pointing to a shoal just in front of him. 'Très bon,' he said in a thick accent. The net flew out, dropping neatly over the shoal, reducing it to so many arching backs on the runway. At that moment the plane was announced; he donned his uniform and gathered his catch into a small bag. But before doing so he slit one of them up the middle with his thumb, gouging out its entrails, broke off its head, and stuck what remained into his mouth.

Whenever one is invited to a *tamaaraa*, a Tahitian feast, the food is invariably the same: baked pig, baked fish, baked plantain and bread-fruit, and bag pudding. Everything is wrapped up in little parcels of leaves and baked on hot stones covered over with earth. The pork is tender and the fish white and flaky. At first the novelty of the dishes and their preparation fascinates one, but the food very soon palls and becomes almost nauseating, or so I found it. There is too much starch and the meat is too greasy. Everything is soaked in coconut cream, a sweet flavour that eventually is cloying. Nor do the Tahitians understand our taste for hot food. Nearly all their dishes are served lukewarm, or better still, in their eyes, cold. But the present-day traveller is spoilt. For those sailing in the *Endeavour*, these *tamaaraa* must have been repasts of Lucullan splendour.

When we left Cook and Banks they were completing their tour of the peninsula of Taiarapu. The journey had been accomplished mainly by boat, for the hills, rising precipitously from the sea, left no alternative. They felt their way with care through the broken reefs that hugged the shore. It was difficult sailing and Cook was grateful for their native pilot. On the night of June the 28th they had a contretemps with a local chief. 'He complained much of cold and desired a cloak to sleep in. We granted his request as he had behaved so well all day.' Hardly had they gone to bed, Banks having stripped himself 'as was my constant custom . . . sending my clothes into the boat for safe keeping' than they were rudely awakened. Their friend had absconded with his borrowed finery. At pistol point hostages were seized and eventually the cloak was returned.

When next they landed they were once more on the main part of the island at Papeari. 'At this place,' Banks tells us, 'we saw a singular curiosity, a figure of a man made of basket work, rudely made but not ill designed, about seven feet high.' The wicker skeleton was completely covered with feathers, white to represent the skin and black in the parts that were usually covered with tattoo. Cook tells us that horns protruded from the figure's head and it had a cloth draped around its loins, 'under which were proofs of its being intended for the figure of a man'. The image, according to Beaglehole, represented the great hero of Polynesian culture, Manui, and seems to have been the only one of its kind on the island. Further on they came across 'a pyramid about five feet high covered entirely with the pineapple-like fruit of the pandanus, near this stood a stone image of very crude workmanship', the first example of carving they found on the island. The explorers had arrived in a district famous for its *maraes* or temples and what they found amazed them.

They spent the night at Papara which was Purea's territory, and although Purea proved not to be at home, having gone to Matavai to see the distinguished visitors, they found people enough to entertain them, 'and therefore resolved to sleep in her house, a small neat one with open bamboo walls'. The house was near the sea and after settling their things, Banks tells us, they took a walk, making for a point where they had observed some ironwood trees 'from whence we judged that thereabouts would be some *marae*; nor were we disappointed for we no sooner arrived there than we were struck with the sight of a most enormous pile, certainly the masterpiece of Indian architecture on this island'. It was the great *marae* of Mahaiatea seen in its pristine splendour, for Purea had only just finished it a few months previous to her overthrow some time between 1766 and 1768. It had been erected to commemorate the birth of her son. Banks paced out the *ahu* or high altar, a parallelogram measuring 267 by 71 feet rising in eleven stepped tiers, each four feet high. Some of the stones were as large as 3½ by 2½ feet. As there were no quarries in the neighbourhood, they surmised that these must have been brought from a considerable distance. Most of the construction material, however, was rounded coral pebbles 'which from the regularity of their shape seemed to have been wrought'. These also were fairly weighty 'and must have been fished from under the water, where, though it may be found in plenty, lies out a considerable depth, never less than three feet'. Both the blocks and the coral would have had to have been shaped with primitive tools, for iron was unknown at the time of its building. As the Tahitians lacked mortar and cement, it required great care to fit the stones together; the whole undertaking, in fact, must have been a work of incredible labour.

The present remains of the temple give the visitor only a very vague idea of its former impressiveness. A narrow dust road cutting through a copra plantation leads to where the *marae* used to stand. The ironwood trees have vanished and instead a thick clump of *ficus* have taken over, their voracious roots digging into a tumbling pile of rubble. Hunting carefully, pulling aside the heavy leafed branches, one can find a small section of the high altar, a corner which has been partially reassembled. The reddish-black volcanic stones have become even blacker with the years, except where they are stained with light patches of lichen. They are roughly wedge-shaped and are neatly stacked one on top of another, the outer surfaces convex, resembling the segments of a pine cone. The effect is pleasing; primitive, yet at the same time meticulous, almost Japanese in its precision. I have seen similar walls encircling medieval castles in Japan, only the walls of Polynesian *maraes* have not the careful sophistication of the Japanese and are much more modest in scale.

For years this monument suffered no more than the moderate

deterioration of time. Then, in 1865 a Scottish adventurer, William Stuart, planted cotton on the nearby plains, to profit from the high prices paid for that crop during the American Civil War. Needing sheds to store his crops and housing for the imported labour, he first used the paving stones from the enclosure of the great *marae* for building material. Later he decided to construct a bridge over the Taharua River to facilitate the transport of his crops to Papeete for shipping to Europe. Again he attempted to despoil the *marae*, but this time the people of the district rebelled, for although converted to Christianity, they still regarded the monument with great veneration. In the end the French governor persuaded the chiefess of Papara to acquiesce. More than two-thirds of the great altar went into the piers of the bridge, which ironically was washed away within a matter of months after an abnormally long rainy season.

A member of Cook's expedition was guilty of a similar vandalism. Banks describes 'an accident . . . that, notwithstanding all our caution, very near embroiled us with the Indians. A boat was sent ashore with an officer to get ballast for the ship, and not immediately finding stones convenient for our purpose, he began to pull down part of an enclosure where they deposited the bones of their dead. This the Indians violently opposed, and a messenger came down to the tents to acquaint the officers that they would not suffer it'. Banks, hurrying to the place, smoothed things over. In face of such crass stupidity and callousness that needlessly provoked the natives' resentment, is it any wonder that Cook had a reputation of losing his temper?

Teuira Henry notes that all the royal and important ceremonial *maraes* were to be found on prominent points. Those of the nobles were generally situated on the bays, and behind these were those for the general population and women. There were innumerable divinities and sometimes families erected small *maraes* to household gods next to their living quarters. One god, however, was supreme and his name, Taaroa, the creator of all things, was pronounced with respect. No doubt Taaroa was too august to occupy himself with everyday problems, as most of the *maraes* were dedicated to lesser divinities; principal among them, Oro, the god of war and fertility, followed closely in importance by Tane, Tangaroa and Tu. Like those of the Greek Pantheon, the gods all had human characteristics, but it is very difficult to identify them accurately for they changed their attributes freely. Tangaroa appears quite consistently to have been the sun god; but Tane, god of beauty and of masculine strength, who originally represented peace, developed a penchant for war and human flesh and became very bellicose; as did his rival in war, Hiro.

Female divinities were few in number, the most important being

Hina, the goddess of the moon, married to Taaroa. She was supposed to rule over men's physical appetites and, as Forster puts it, 'we may venture to suppose that she was not the chaste Diana of the ancients but rather the Phoenician Astarte'.

Frustrated as he was by the language, Cook complained that he had learned so little about the Tahitians' religious beliefs. Subsequent inquirers have fared little better. From the very beginning the natives have always shown a reluctance to discuss their historic religion, even when baptized; partly from fear of ridicule, and partly, no doubt, from a feeling of veneration for the old gods of their cult. It would have been sacrilegious to have done otherwise.

They seem to have believed in the immortality of the soul, at least in its existence in a separate state. On leaving the body it found its way to a kind of limbo divided into different degrees of happiness, somewhat similar to our heaven and hell. They did not, however, consider them as places of reward or punishment, but rather as a continuation of the social distinctions known to them on earth. Heaven to the Tahitian had a definite geographical location and was known as Rohutu noa noa, or sweet scented Rohutu, and spread invisible to the human eye, in the celestial regions around and above the mountains of Raiatea. The gods also remained intangible, for the natives were not, strictly speaking, idolators; rather they worshipped a divine imminence present sometimes, so they imagined, in a log of wood, sometimes lodged in a rock, or a stone, or temporarily metamorphosed as a white-plumed bird. All white birds were consequently sacred to the gods.

Idols called *ti'i*, or fetchers, did exist but in a limited number and represented familiar spirits of the gods; shapeless little things, with their heads barely detached from the lumps of rock coral in which they were carved. Their stomachs are generally indicated bulging over inadequate haunches while the eyes are either sightless ovals or gouges similar to the sockets in a skull. The arms are summary stick-like scratches that look like the folded legs of a beetle.

These little images were sometimes the servants of sorcerers. The black arts played an important part in the lives of the people and the local sorcerers, like the witch-doctors of Africa, were believed to have great influence over the powers of darkness. It was thought that the *ti'i* carried out the sorcerer's magical commands which were mostly of a malicious nature, concerned generally with getting rid of some unwanted party. The bewitched victim suffered excruciating pains which were ascribed to the rough coral imp who, having worked his way up into his victim through the ground on which he sat or stood, was intent on lacerating and piercing his intestines, causing high fever, palpitations of the heart and foaming at the mouth. If the tortures were not quickly checked by a stronger healing power, the sufferer usually died within a day or two, writhing in agony.

These *ti'i* had special *maraes* built for them and were kept in a small house set on high wooden poles. People approached them with great trepidation and even the magicians went in fear of unwittingly offending them and of being dashed to pieces upon the stone paving of the *marae*. Every so often they would be exposed in a procession, but only after they had been washed and dressed like dolls.

Henry said that people were in constant dread of being victimized by the *ti'i*. As the evil wisher had to have something tangible belonging to the intended victim, a fragment of their clothing, a wreath of flowers, remains of food, nail parings or hair, people were always on their guard against leaving things about. All persons of high rank had special hereditary attendants whose duty it was to burn, bury, or sink in the sea all such *tupu* belonging to them.

The early missionaries were frequent eye-witnesses of the strange workings attributed to these *ti'i* and were deeply impressed. Even when they no longer believed in their old gods the natives still treated them with respect and took every precaution to prevent the *ti'i* from falling into foreign hands, burying them in secret hiding places. Occasionally a stray image is brought to light by somebody working the fields and some of these evil, mischievous-looking little things are today in the Papeete museum. Alongside them, in another case, is an odd tubular basket woven out of sennit about a foot long, with a wooden peg at one end to anchor it to the ground. The curator told me that it contained a *ti'i* but would not allow me to look inside.

One can contribute little towards a more thorough understanding of Tahiti's gods, for they are many and all of them obscure. About the *maraes*, however, one can be more precise. The principal *maraes* served not only for religious ceremonies but also for rituals such as those in preparation for war. It was a place of silence to be approached with humility and respect and, at times, a place of dread where the great drums thudded out their message that a human life was about to be forfeited. When persons approached a *marae*, they gave it a wide berth and lowered their clothes from the shoulders as a sign of respect. Forster notes that even chiefs and their wives were obliged to conform. When a canoe passed along the shore, it withdrew far off as it neared the point on which stood the *marae*; the passengers lowering their clothes and paddling lightly until they had passed the place. It was also a place of sanctuary for fugitives.

The building of a new *marae* was performed with solemn rites and involved a considerable number of men for it was an arduous task. When all the stones had been collected, the ground for the *marae* was cleared and then sprinkled by the priests with sea water to make it holy. Two dedication stones were usually taken from some other *marae*, preferably from the great shrine at Raiatea. A man was slain and placed in a hole dug to receive one stone which was firmly planted on his body. The second was placed at the opposite corner of the new compound, the two being known as the horns of the *marae*. The *marae* consisted of a large enclosed area paved and walled off with an *ahu* or high altar at one end. This was built up in stepped tiers, usually three in number, but sometimes more, and was the most *taboo* part of the *marae*. A sentence of death was passed on anyone who dared to climb it, exceptions being made only for the high priest and the servants of the shrine. As the steps measured anything from four to six feet high, it could not have been easy to ascend the edifice of the gods. The top of the *ahu* was spiked with 'god sticks' on which the gods perched when they descended to earth in the guise of white birds. Upon the paving in front of the *ahu* was a great flat altar for human sacrifice plus several other smaller altars in polished wood of different sizes upon which were heaped more usual offerings such as hogs, fish, vegetables, and coconuts. In the same enclosure were planted carved, ochre-coloured boards that perhaps commemorated important events, such as the death of a chief or a human sacrifice.

Only certain trees were allowed to grow near a *marae*, and these had to be both majestic and high, such as the ironwood tree, which Forster wrongly refers to as a casuarina. He is correct, however, in describing the foliage as weeping 'giving an air of solemnity and pleasing melancholy to the scene'.

The early explorers generally believed the *maraes* to be older than they actually were. Forster found them 'always covered with grasses and ferns and small shrubs'. Describing another Cook wrote that 'it appears to have been built many years, and was in a state of decay, as most of the *maraes* are'. But the *maraes* were only weeded and tidied up before a ceremony, and as they were not in use every day, they merely appeared to be old and neglected.

The consecration ceremony of a *marae* was performed by moonlight and must have been very beautiful. Henry describes it for us. 'The first-born young virgins of the royal families of the kingdom represented their respective districts. They were arrayed in flowing white *tapa* and decked with wreaths and garlands of *tiare* (single gardenia) blossoms, their emblem of purity. Carrying round green coconut leaf baskets of these flowers in their hands, they led a procession formed by the clergy in sacerdotal array. The king wore his royal feather clothes and the chiefs their regal raiment. The procession halted on reaching one side of the *marae*, and then the young virgins walked around it, casting their flowers upon it as high as they could reach and upon the paving close by. The high priest followed, calling upon the gods to fill the place with their presence.'

The priests of the *maraes* were specially picked men. They had to be tall and able bodied and free from blemish; deft of hand and sure footed for the gods would tolerate no awkwardness. As there was no written language and instruction was oral, they had to learn by heart endless prayers and evocations. Even today among the old Tahitian families, men can be found with extraordinary memories who can reel off each other's ancestry going back over a hundred years.

Invocations to be recited at night were taught in the dark, in the moonlight stillness of the hills, or in the woods or by the seashore. The novice learned to read the portents in animals' entrails and to observe the omens and signs in the sky; the fall of meteors, the flight of clouds or the cry of birds – phenomena that had a forcible language in those times.

While meditating and fasting in a completely withdrawn life, the priests often fell into trances. During these spells they wore a strip of sacred cloth round the left arm, as a sign that they must not be disturbed. It was supposed that the priest was then under the influence of spirits and they were thus regarded as oracles. The messages they delivered were usually entirely ambiguous, but they were accompanied by prodigious feats of strength. Henry tells us that Pomaré II and the early missionaries 'testified to having seen priests while possessed in this way thrust hand and arm up to the shoulder, without injury, into the solid ground of hard trodden pathways. They foamed at the mouth, had their eyeballs distorted and their limbs convulsed . . . and uttered hideous shrieks and ejaculations'. While possessed, a priest could ask for whatever he wished and obtain it, even, according to Henry, 'to the wife of the king, as it was a god that was supposed to speak'.

Priests were well paid and lived comfortably. Their vestments were made of bleached *tapa* and consisted of a finely braided scarf worn over the shoulders, and a loin cloth. During the long fasts prescribed for certain ceremonies, when the priests were said to feel their 'intestines filled with emotions', they bound a girdle tightly round their waists to help support them. At all other times their clothes were very scanty. During a night vigil spent praying in the *marae*, the high priest wore only a large cape with a deep fringe flowing from his shoulders. 'It retained no warmth but conveyed cold to the body, producing a sensation of chilled skin or goose flesh which was considered most pleasing to the gods.'

We know the ritual of an important but unidentifiable ceremony where the priest stood at the foot of the altar facing the courtyard. The chiefs and nobles stood at the other end facing the *ahu*. The high chief or *arii nui* had his place marked by a standing stone which he used as a back rest. The multitude remained outside of the courtyard and no women were allowed in. One of these standing stones still exists in Raiatea and not more than six feet away from it the London Missionary Society built a small octagonal church.

It was not until the third voyage that Cook learned about the human sacrifices. They occurred fairly frequently. An *arii nui* would witness at least twelve during his lifetime excluding those made specifically before a war. It was one of the latter that Cook attended.

Tu was struggling to consolidate his rule over the different islands when Moorea revolted. A council of war decided that an expedition should be sent out against it. Towha, a relation of Tu's and the commander-in-chief of the fleet, judged it expedient to offer up a human life to Oro, the god of war, in order to solicit his assistance. The sacrifice was to be performed at the great *marae* at Attahooroo, or Atehuru, on the west coast near the present Paea. Cook, always anxious to learn, asked Tu whether he and some of his party might not accompany him. 'To this he readily consented; and we immediately set out in my boat, with Mr Anderson and Mr Webber; Omai following in a canoe.'

Cook gives a detailed description of the whole ceremony. Omai acted as his interpreter. 'Having had an opportunity of examining the body now offered up; I could observe that it was bloody about the head and face, and a good deal bruised upon the right temple; which marked the manner of his being killed.' Cook gathered, quite correctly, that the choice of the victim was made from among 'low fellows or undesirables'. A pig and a dog were sacrificed at the same time. The pig's entrails were taken out and 'they happened to have a considerable share of those convulsive motions which often appear, in different parts, after an animal is killed'. They were laid down before a priest who inspected them carefully, turning them gently with a stick. The convulsions were considered as a very favourable omen for the expedition.

When Cook was asked his impressions of the ceremony he did not mince matters. 'Besides the cruelty of the bloody custom, I strongly urged the unreasonableness of it. Such a sacrifice,' he argued, 'far from making the god propitious to their nation, as they ignorantly believed, would be the means of drawing down his vengeance; and that, for this very circumstance.' Cook also took upon himself to predict 'that their intended expedition against Moorea would be unsuccessful. This was venturing pretty far upon conjecture; but still, I thought, that there was little danger of being mistaken. For I found that there were three parties in the island, with regard to this war; one extremely violent for it;

another perfectly indifferent about the matter; and the third openly declaring themselves friends of Moorea'.

One part of the *marae* which particularly impressed Cook was 'a heap of stones . . . with a kind of platform at the side. On this are laid the skulls of all the human sacrifices, which are taken up after they have been several months underground'. These details are clearly depicted in Webber's drawing of the subject. Cook, with hat in hand, gestures towards the corpse of the victim. With him are Anderson, his back towards us, also Webber, and Omai dressed in European clothes which he sometimes affected. One presumes that Cook's stern expression is supposed to register his disapproval of the sacrifice rather than disgust at the stench of the dogs and pigs lately offered up. So nauseating was it 'that it kept us at a greater distance than would otherwise have been required of us'.

To the left of the engraving are two priests beating on drums. No festivity was complete without the accompaniment of drums which were made of hollowed logs covered over with shark skin and stretched tight with sennit. Many were two feet in diameter and stood six or eight feet high. The drummers had to mount blocks of wood to play them. The drums shown in Webber's plate were known as the *to'ere* and had a special sound, a high-pitched tone, 'from the appalling sound of which people shrank and fled in terror'.

Cook tells us that the human victims were either war prisoners or taken from the *titi*, the lowest rank in the Tahitian social scale. At times the *manahune*, or middle classes, were also obliged to furnish someone; the choice in this case, however, only falling on men who had made themselves obnoxious to those in power. Once a family had been singled out to provide a sacrificial victim the other males were doomed to follow – women were not considered worthy to be sacrificed to the gods. The victim was always taken unawares and when one was required the sovereign or *arii nui* sent out word to one of the sub-chiefs. Henry explains the procedure: the messenger, who was generally a stern warrior, would go with a club hidden under his clothes and inquire in veiled terms if whom he had been sent for was close by. If the victim happened to be near, the chief would answer with a significant look, and before the man was aware of what was happening, he was felled by a blow on the temple or the back of the neck, care having been taken not to break any bones. It would sometimes happen that the victim was a personal friend of the sub-chief in which case the unfortunate man had a chance to survive. Warned in time by his friend, he could quickly arm himself, and as in the gladiatorial games in ancient Rome he could secure his own emancipation along with that of his family, providing that he slay the warrior who thus became the meat for sacrifice.

There exists a legend to explain the origin of human sacrifice: at one time before the flood, the world was luxuriant and the people were in favour with the gods, then came a great drought followed by excessive heat. The people cried out in their misery 'Taaroa, whose curse is death, is angry; he is consuming us!' The king, moved to pity for his people, told the priests to pray and make offerings to Taaroa that they might regain his favour and obtain rain from heaven to restore the land. No harvests being available, an offering was made of lean pigs, fish and birds' feathers. Alas, it had no effect. Then the king had the idea of making a human sacrifice, saying 'we must humble ourselves before god and tremble with fear'. So the priests slew a man and offered him at the shrine of Taaroa and soon clouds gathered in the sky and rain fell. Thus it was understood that the gods liked human flesh, which was called 'long-legged fish'. It was the custom after this for the king or high priest to decide when such a sacrifice was required, which was seldom until Oro, god of war, came into favour. He, it is feared, required much appeasing.

Some twelve miles to the west of Purea's ruined temple lies the recently restored *marae* of Arahurahu. It could not have been of much importance for it lies a little way inland, up the narrowing confines of a valley, shut in on both sides by hills. It is, however, the only *marae* that remains intact and for that reason is of great interest. I approached it on foot, choosing the golden hours of the late afternoon for my visit. I was quite alone and cannot disguise the fact that I felt vague apprehensions, the nauseating smell of putrid flesh and the thud of drums lingering in the back of my mind. In total silence I picked my way in between the grey, lichen-stained trunks of slender coconut palms. High above glittered their great fronds like burnished metal, and below this again the silvered shields against the rats, shining like slave bracelets. Not a thing stirred, and there were no rats, the only noise being my own breathing. Suddenly, in front of me stood two hunched-up, wooden figures with heavy pouting lips and great sightless eyes, those bulging orbs so typical of Polynesian sculpture; they were the materialization of some nightmare, beings half insect, half man. The figures were not old which proves that artisans still exist capable of gouging out the hard woods of the island's great trees. Nor had they quite forgotten their gods for someone had crowned one of the images with a wreath.

These figures announced the temple limits and beyond them, the other side of the wall, a path led through tall grasses growing among the black boulders imbedded in the ground. A breeze played across their yellowing heads rippling them like the sea, causing them to break gently against the neatly stacked walls surrounding the high altar which bristled with rakishly set 'god sticks'. All was there exactly as Cook had described it, even to the shrouded body of a chief lying in state. Alone and curious I lifted up a corner of the *tapa* to discover a dummy bamboo frame surmounted by a skull.

It was an extraordinarily peaceful place: behind me the green mountains in their clouds, and below, in the far distance, the thundering of the surf. I had no feeling of overawing majesty and certainly the place was not haunted, as the Tahitians believe all *maraes* to be. I felt a slight tingling of the scalp, however, when I heard the crackling of the dense undergrowth nearby, announcing the approach of some living creature. In Africa one would have had the liveliest misgivings; leopard or lion or possibly even elephant, but here it could only be cattle or a man. It was a youth, naked except for a loin cloth and a straw hat wreathed with ferns. He had been up in the mountains gathering sweet potatoes which he carried stowed in two sacks slung from a bamboo pole, balanced over one shoulder. His lithe body glistened with sweat as he came towards me, and he was hissing slightly through clenched teeth from the weight of his load. Approaching, he slid the pole off his shoulder and squatted down on the grass. 'J'ai chaud,' he smiled, wiping his brow with the back of his hand. The country people can seldom speak French, or if they do, it is generally of the crudest form. This boy knew more than most and proved it in between gulps of water from a green-husked coconut which he had slashed open with his hatchet. I asked him if anyone believed in the old gods any more. 'Perhaps,' he parried and shrugged his shoulders. 'And up there,' I pointed, 'are those burial chambers in the face of the rock?' He answered that they were and that some of them still contained bones.

The subject of bones returns us to Cook and Banks on the shore near Purea's house. Ever since the arrival of the *Endeavour* the men on board had been puzzled over Purea's change of status. They realized that something had happened, but it was only here, at Papara, that they learned what it was. 'Our way from her house to the *marae*,' writes Banks, 'lay along the seaside and we observed everywhere under our feet a great number of human bones, chiefly ribs and vertebrae. So singular a sight surprised me much and I inquired the reason.' They were the grizzly remains of the battle fought between Purea's clan and the people from Taiarapu, 'who made a descent on this place four or five months before our arrival'.

The next day, the fifth day of their tour and the last day of June, the men went on foot. 'During the whole day saw little or nothing worth observation,' but it was territory already known to them. It had been in the Punaauia district that they had first witnessed surfing. Banks tells us that 'it was in a place where the shore was not guarded by a reef as is usually the case, consequently a high surf fell upon the shore and a more dreadful one I have not often seen'. Banks insists that the best European swimmers would have been drowned in the monster waves and yet 'in the midst of these breakers ten or twelve Indians were swimming'. One can imagine the scene: the glass-green waves turning over in the sun, breaking into a crashing, tumbling mass of foam that sweeps headlong on to the pebbly beach, lacing the shoreline. The sea edge is smoking with fume from the waves, a mist that sweeps upwards, obscuring the feathery heads of palms growing out from the nearby point. Into these huge, crashing monsters, rising twenty to thirty feet high on the skyline, plunge the young cinnamon-coloured Tahitians, their black hair falling in shiny, black snakes on their square shoulders. They have with them the stern of an old canoe which they use as a board and with this before them they catch the waves in the moment of their breaking and are hurried 'with incredible swiftness almost ashore'. Banks tells us that they stood admiring this very wonderful scene for full half an hour. So engrossed were they in their sport that the young men didn't even come on to the beach to talk to those watching them.

Cook and Banks arrived home in the evening of Saturday, July 1st, having made the circuit of the whole island which they estimated to be something more than ninety miles. They proceeded to the fort where Banks informs us it was raining. Cook was rather pleased with the map he had made. 'Although it cannot be very accurate, yet it will be found sufficient to point out the situation of the different bays and harbours and the figure of the island and I believe is without any material error.'

[Chapter 12]

The Society Islands

THE CHARTING of Tahiti accomplished, there was nothing further to detain Cook. By July 8th, the *Endeavour* was being made ready for sea. 'I had determined,' he wrote, 'to run down to Huahine and Raiatea before we stood to the southward.' This long excursion to the south was the second important task set Cook by the Royal Society. 'When the transit of the Planet Venus shall be finished you are to observe the following instructions': they were secret and ordered the Captain to comb the seas carefully to locate the elusive southern continent, if indeed there was a continent.

This had to wait, however, for some two weeks, as Cook was worried about his food supply. Having heard from Tupia of fertile islands lying only one or two days' sail to the westward, he decided to try to provender there where hogs, fowls and other refreshments abounded in greater quantities than in Tahiti, recently devastated by its civil wars and further impoverished by the livestock consumed or carried off by visiting shipping. The few hogs Cook and Banks had been able to charm or bargain out of the chiefs had hardly been sufficient to give the ship's company more than one, or sometimes two, fresh meals a week. The *Endeavour* had been anchored at Matavai Bay for exactly three months, too long in one district. Cook complained of the men's health; 'the ship's company, what from the constant hard duty they have had at this place and the too free use of women were in a worse state of health than they were on our first arrival.' By this time also 'full half of them had got the venereal disease in which situation I thought they would be ill able to stand the cold weather we might expect to meet with to the southward at this season of the year and therefore I resolved to give them a little time to recover while we ran down to and explored the islands before mentioned'.

On the morning of the 10th two young marines deserted. They had fallen in love with Tahitian maidens whom they had married according to native custom and were determined not to leave. They had taken to the mountains and would not return. 'But at the same time,' Cook explains, 'no one would give us any certain intelligence where they were, upon which a resolution was taken to seize upon as many of the chiefs as we could.' Ten of them were transferred to the ship including Tuteha and Purea to be released when the marines were handed over. It was a tricky situation and could easily have ended as badly as did a similar episode in Hawaii some ten years later. Kidnapping an important chief was, after all, a very drastic measure. At the best one might have expected hard feelings, but as things turned out, apart from a few tears from the women, all was forgiven immediately the marines were restored.

On July 13th, they were ready to sail. 'Notwithstanding the confinement of the day before yesterday which had frightened and effronted them much,' Banks found the ship was crowded with friends. 'Between eleven and twelve we weighed anchor and as soon as the ship was under sail, the Indians on board took their leave and went, with silent sorrow in which there was something very striking and tender: the people in their canoes, on the contrary, seemed to vie with each other in the loudness of their lamentation, which we considered rather an affectation than grief.'

As the ship stood out her guns boomed in salute and slowly the smoke lifted among the sails. The ceremonial canoes, great double boats, carrying the chief and nobles, gathered around, only separating when the *Endeavour* reached the passage in the reefs. A few of the small canoes followed them out through the boiling waters, and the men on the quarterdeck stood waving until they were reduced to mere pencil lines on the horizon.

Cook did not set his course for nearby Moorea as might have been expected – Moorea was to be visited only on the third voyage – but rather for Tetiaroa to the northward, a small island they had seen from the hills above Matavai. It was sighted in the evening, a low, uninhabited island frequented, so Tupiai informed Cook, by fisher people from Tahiti. By the 16th, they had reached Huahine and anchored at Fare, Cook's Owharhe. It differed but little from Tahiti. The inhabitants were fairer in colour and apparently not so addicted to stealing. Banks found very few new plants but observed some insects, among them a species of scorpion which he had not seen before. His meagre success while botanizing put him in a critical mood for he agreed with Cook that 'the people were almost exactly like our late friends', but added that they were 'rather more stupid and lazy'. So lazy that they refused to accompany Banks when he wanted to penetrate inland. 'We should have gone much higher up the hills than we did if we could have persuaded them to accompany us.' They were frightened the fatigue might kill them.

There is little of interest to report on this first visit to Huahine, but Forster, four years later, was very impressed by the number of hogs they were able to obtain from Ori, the *arii* of the island. 'The *Resolution* alone obtained two hundred and nine live hogs, thirty-two dogs, and about fifty fowls, and the *Adventure* had not much less.' Considering the small size of the island compared to Tahiti it was certainly a remarkable haul. Cook graphically describes how these hogs were killed by the islanders. 'It was the work of three men, the hog being placed upon his back, two of them laid a pretty strong stick across his throat and pressed each end with their whole weight, the third man held his hind legs, kept him on his back and plugged up his backside with grass' (perhaps with the idea that it could breathe), 'and in this manner they held him for at least ten minutes before he was quite dead.'

Forster gathered 'a great quantity of bananas, which formed a kind of orchard in our poop', as Banks had done on the first voyage when he found this commodity 'a more useful refreshment' than even the pork. 'What makes it the more acceptable is that our bread is at the present so full of vermin that notwithstanding all possible care I have sometimes had twenty at a time in my mouth, everyone of which tasted as hot as mustard.' Forster, gloating over the number of hogs they had collected, at the same time admits the difficulty of keeping them alive. 'The want of room occasioned the death of several hogs, and the obstinacy of the older ones in refusing to take any sustenance deprived us of the rest of them. But we soon took an effective method of saving our provisions by strewing the meat with salt. By this means it was preserved and remained palatable and juicy without being so unwholesome as the pickled meat we brought from England.'

Cook describes how this was done. The hogs were first cleaned, all veins and blood vessels were emptied of coagulated blood – this being very important for a successful salting – and then the meat was cut up and the bones taken out. While still warm, the meat was hauled to the salters who rubbed it with salt, leaving it to drain overnight on boards pressed under heavy weights. Next morning it was salted again and packed into casks and covered with pickle. Four or five days later it was taken out and examined in case any of it might be tainted. It was then repacked, covered again with pickle, and sealed. Meat preserved in this way in January 1779 was eaten in England on Christmas Day 1780 and found perfectly good.

Raiatea lies about twenty-one miles from Huahine. Leaving Fare at midday the *Endeavour* was in sight of its reefs by evening. Shortening sail, they stood off all night and on the morning of July the 20th the excellent Tupaia showed Cook a large break in the reefs. Within an hour

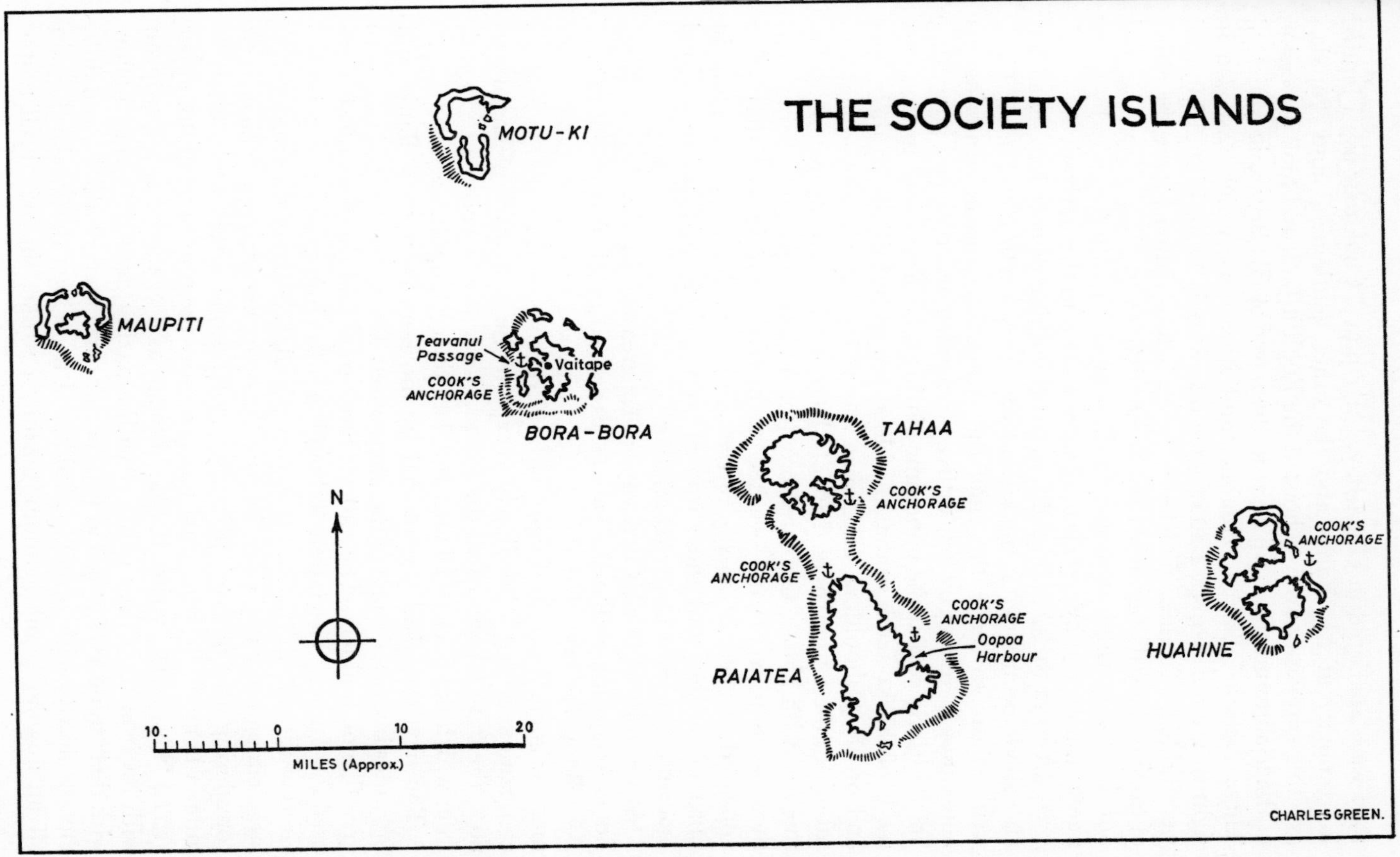

THE SOCIETY ISLANDS

MOTU-KI
MAUPITI
Teavanui Passage
Vaitape
COOK'S ANCHORAGE
BORA-BORA
TAHAA
COOK'S ANCHORAGE
COOK'S ANCHORAGE
COOK'S ANCHORAGE
Oopoa Harbour
RAIATEA
COOK'S ANCHORAGE
HUAHINE
N
10 0 10 20
MILES (Approx.)
CHARLES GREEN.

they were anchored in Opoa Bay. 'At 1 p.m.,' Cook tells us, 'I landed in company of Mr Banks and the other gentlemen,' and Tupaia's greeting ceremony over, 'I hoisted the English Jack and took possession of the island and those adjacent in the name of His Britannic Majesty.' These included Tahaa, Huahine and Bora-Bora which was also in sight to the north-west. Later, when discovered, Motu-iti and Maupiti were added. 'To these six islands, never before visited I gave the name of Society Islands because they lie contiguous to each other.' He did not, however, 'think it proper to distinguish them separately by other names than those by which they were known to the natives'.

Apart from the claiming of the island nothing of note happened but an episode occurring on the second voyage is worth mentioning. Cook went ashore to make the chief the customary present. Entering his house they were met by four or five old women, weeping and lamenting 'most bitterly and at the same time cutting their heads with instruments made of sharks' teeth so that the blood ran plentifully down their faces and on their shoulders, and what was still worse we were obliged to submit to the embraces of these old hags and by that means got all besmeared with blood; this ceremony (for it was merely such) being over, these women went and washed themselves and immediately after appeared as cheerful as any of the company'. Such was the habit in times of sorrow, and these women were merely performing a ritual mourning for some departed relative.

At the time of Cook's first voyage Raiatea was in vassalage to Bora-Bora. According to Banks, Tupaia 'expressed much fear of the men of Bora-Bora. He says that they have conquered this island and will to-morrow come down and fight with us'. Losing no time, Banks and his companions set out immediately to explore the great *marae* of Taputapu-atea, the most famous of all the *maraes*, the centre, according to legend, from which the Society Islands and Tahiti were populated.

The next day, still unmolested by the Bora-Bora men, Banks and Solander inspected some of the boathouses. The natives of Raiatea were great canoe builders. The valley's large trees and the bread-fruit were used for timber. The latter, although not so close grained, was impervious to the salt-worms and thus very popular. Some of the canoes were large enough to carry three hundred people; an amazing achievement considering the natives' primitive tools: stone adzes and chisels of human bone. (The bone used was generally the thin bone of the upper arms.) 'This work,' writes Banks, 'difficult as it would be to a European with his iron tools they perform with amazing dexterity; they hollow with their stone axes as fast at least as our carpenters could do, and dub, though slowly, with prodigious nicety. I have seen them take the skin off an angular plank without missing a stroke, the skin itself scarce one-sixteenth part of an inch in thickness.' Their most difficult task was to bore the holes through which they threaded corded sennit to bind the planks together.

Bora-Bora has always been noted as a land of brave warriors. Its proper name, according to the Tahitian pronunciation, is *Porapora i te hoe manu*, meaning 'canoes with silent oars'; a reference to a night attack its warriors once made on one of the islands when they tied calabashes on to the end of their oars to avoid noise. Looking at the size of Bora-Bora it is remarkable that its people should have even attempted, let alone achieved, the conquest of Raiatea and Tahaa, Raiatea by itself being at least three times larger. Tupaia had not exaggerated his fear of the famous Bora-Bora warriors headed by their chief Opoony, or more correctly Puni; 'the terror', as Banks refers to him, 'of all the other islands'. Puni happily behaved with great civility towards the strangers, and far from attacking the *Endeavour*, he sent Cook a present of three hogs, pieces of cloth, and some fruit. They were brought by his servants who announced that the great chief himself would arrive the next day. The crew was so curious that all hands remained on board awaiting 'the honour of his Excellency's visit'. But the chief sent a delegation of pretty girls in his place; 'to get', as Cook puts it, 'something in return for the present he sent the other day, he not choosing, I suppose, to trust himself on board, or perhaps he thought the persons he sent would succeed better than he should do. Be this as it may, they went away very well satisfied with what they got, although I believe that they were disappointed in some things!' Banks says the girls were handsome and lively, that they stayed all morning, 'and took off all regret for the want of His Majesty's company'. Reading Banks, one wonders if Cook was correct in his suspicion.

When they finally met him, Puni was a great anti-climax. 'We expected to see a young, lively, handsome creature,' writes Banks, 'but how were we disappointed when we were led to an old, decrepit, half-blind man who seemed to have scarce reason enough left to send hogs, much less gallantry enough to send ladies!'

The most interesting thing about Raiatea was that the *arioi* society had its headquarters there. Cook had only a vague idea of the society and its functions, but what little knowledge he and his companions were able to gather shocked them profoundly. As Beaglehole properly observes 'fertility cults had not yet come into general apprehension, and phallic symbolism though obvious enough to the Pacific voyagers was evidence of plain indecency rather than a particular way of looking at the world'. Cook, when he first learned of the *ariois*' existence, mentions it with disapproval, his reaction based on his discovery that the society practised organized infanticide. Defining the *ariois* he tells us 'that more than one half of the better sort of the inhabitants have entered into a resolution of enjoying free liberty in love without being troubled or disturbed by its consequences. They mix and cohabit together with the utmost freedom and the children who are so unfortunate as to be thus begot are smothered at the moment of their birth. Many of these people contract intimacies and live together as man and wife for years in the course of which the children that are born are destroyed. They are so far from concealing it that they rather look upon it as a branch of freedom upon which they value themselves'. At meetings while the men amused themselves with wrestling, boxing and other competitions, the women danced indecent dances, 'in the course of which they give full liberty to their desires but I believe keep up to the appearance of decency'. Had Cook ever seen one of the meetings he would have known that the performers gave frank demonstrations of sexual technique.

Beaglehole makes it quite clear that the *ariois* were a religious association and not merely a band of libertines. Even William Ellis, the missionary, was compelled to admit that 'they were esteemed by the people as a superior order of beings closely attuned to the gods'. Beaglehole writes 'that the *arioi* were a greatly respected society, combining the glamour of the secular stage with their religious functions; licensed satirists as well as, in some ways, children of the temple; highly skilled in mime and dance, with regular apprenticeship and grades of status, their practice of infanticide being perhaps the equivalent, for the dedicated life, of celibacy in more sexually inhibited cultures. One cannot, of course, deny that this practice also had great advantages for the fancy-free.'

The *arioi* in fact, were a religious group of travelling entertainers. The chief priest of Raiatea, which was the centre of their cult, was the principal *arioi* bearing the title of *arioi-maro-ura*, meaning 'comedian of the red girdle'. They claimed that they went back to the mists of time, the first *arioi* having sprung from the union of Oro, the god of fertility, with a maiden of the earth. Oro was thus their patron, but adopted by them not as the fiery god of war, but as a jubilant god of peace. The society, as such, never took part in local wars, and its members were able to pass freely through a war zone and be well received, even in enemy territory. On the one hand they were apostles of free love who worshipped nature and whose dances celebrated its seasons. On the other hand, the *arioi* have been justly appreciated as a civilizing influence. The plays or mimes they performed were generally historical dramas describing the great deeds of departed chiefs, but more popular still were the political sketches and song containing pointed references to current events. As Henry tells us, 'The actors flattered or ridiculed with impunity people and even priests, from the greatest to the least, and they often did much good in thus causing faults to be corrected.'

The society was organized into eight orders through which members rose progressively, each change of grade marked by prescribed ceremonies. Every grade, Danielsson tells us, 'had its own special tattoo mark, and the higher the rank of an *arioi*, the more tattooed he was'.* The highest grade man of the eighth order was tattooed all over his legs from knee to foot and on the arms from the shoulder to finger-tips, with other lines on the body. Ellis says that the members of the lowest grade were the principal actors in all their performances, on them devolved the labour of dancing and performing for the amusement of the spectators. Those who were novices continued a long time in the lower class and were only admitted to the higher orders at the discretion of the leader or grand master.

A man or woman who wished to be received into the society had to go through a probation period, which might be as much as a year. Only well-developed persons of 'comely appearance' were admitted. The novices had also to have a marked aptitude for dancing. They were accepted only on the condition that all offspring born to them should be immediately suffocated at birth. Instant dismissal and disgrace was the punishment for allowing their babies to live. Only the children born in the highest rank were spared on the excuse that they were descendants of the gods.

The justification for infanticide was both social and practical. As members were recruited from all classes and encouraged to live together promiscuously, their children were nearly always offspring of parents of unequal birth and if allowed to live would have weakened the rigid lines dividing the classes. Infanticide was also a practical way of dealing with over-population among a people totally ignorant of birth control. Nor had they the facilities to raise large families, as their life was one of continual travelling from one island to another. Vanity, no doubt, also played its part, for the female members had to think of their appearances.

The missionaries had no words sufficient to describe this black abomination. However, Forster, accompanying Cook on the second voyage, is more moderate and tells us, by way of consolation, that the act was always performed in secret, not even the attendants of the house being present, 'for if it was seen, the murderer must be put to death. This being the case, we may comfort ourselves with the reflection that criminal individuals are not more numerous in the Society Isles than among other people'. It might also be pointed out that the Polynesians

* *Love in the South Seas* by Bengt Danielsson, London, 1956, George Allen & Unwin Ltd.

have always been remarkably fond of children. Adoption was a common practice amongst them and used even as a bond of love and union between relatives and dear friends.

The *ariois* continually wandered among the various islands of the Society group, sometimes in small parties, working their way round a single island, but more often moving in large numbers, several lodges joined together, transported in flotillas of flower-decked canoes. Forster reports having seen a fleet of seventy moving away from Huahine, while Moerenhout heard of one hundred and fifty canoes, each having a band of thirty or forty *ariois* on board.

It must have been an imposing spectacle: the mammoth canoes decorated with coloured pennants that floated out behind them in the wind; the *ariois* themselves all decked out in their festal finery, some wearing breast-plates of ripe yellow plantain leaves shining like golden armour, others hung with garlands of scented flowers and seeds with massed flowers on their heads, their glistening bodies and long hair anointed with fragrant oil. 'On board the largest canoes, nude dancers swayed on raised platforms in time to the dull beating of shark-skin drums. In the stern of the leading canoe stood the grand master with a huge adornment of red feathers on his head, steering the flotilla by signals on his shell trumpet, and at his feet black Polynesian sacrificial swine lay with their feet bound together. From time to time a mighty chorus, as rhythmical as the sea itself, rose to the bright summer sky, and when at last land was sighted all burst into shouts of joy, while the drums beat sensuously, the flutes were played, and the blast of the grand master's shell trumpet, heard above all the rest of the noise, served as overture to the festivities.'*

Crowds of people lined the shore waiting for them. A visit from a party of *ariois* was welcomed by the whole population, and all work was stopped. Any indulgence was permitted, even to the breaking of taboos. The women, for instance, might eat turtle, porpoise and dolphin, sacred fish normally forbidden to them. 'The *ariois*' presence,' Forster says, 'seemed to enliven the whole country, and to inspire all the people with extraordinary cheerfulness. They frequently shifted their garments, made of the best kinds of cloth; they passed their time in luxurious idleness, perfuming their hair, singing and playing the flute and passing from one entertainment to another!' No doubt the entertainment was mainly erotic. In fact, the *arioi* society was closely similar to the Priapus cult of the Greeks and Alexandrians, or the crudely naturalistic worship of a rural Dionysia. Small wonder that the missionaries attacked it with such fervour, for its sexual morality was unusually free, even by Polynesian standards. They recognized the *ariois* as their most serious

* *Love in the South Seas*, op. cit.

competitors, more serious by far than a whole pantheon of formless, bloodthirsty gods.

On their arrival the *ariois* took up residence in a hall specially constructed for them, known as the 'comedians' house'. Here they also gave their entertainments, generally at night by the flickering light of fires and candlenut tapers. A stage was erected at one end on which were placed high stools for the chief *ariois*. The *arii nui* had his seat of honour below among the audience which sat in the building and outside on the grass. The entertainment went on for several days and nights. There were comic pantomimes, sometimes wrestling, or a recital of dramatic poetry; but the dancing was most popular. 'An entertainment so pleasurable,' writes the gentle Miss Henry, 'that even the crickets, it is said, cried with joy.'

There was a variety of dances: the *otea*, a man's dance; and the *hura*, meaning 'impelling', which was only danced by women of rank, the *arii nui*'s principal wife often taking the lead. More ribald were the *timorodee* and the *upa upa* danced to a rapid rhythm where young men and women enacted voluptuous scenes with no other object but to excite the erotic feelings of both participant and spectator. It was not without justification that the missionaries called the Polynesian dancers sexual acrobats. The Tahitians are still extraordinarily fond of dancing and singing, but the experts will tell you that the dances have changed so drastically as to be no longer recognizable. Perhaps so, but something of the old style must remain, for the performances the islanders give on the July 14th celebration at Papeete are still 'impelling'. No people in the world celebrate the fall of the Bastille with more spirit than do the Tahitians. Bottled up all year long by the taboos imposed on them by their adopted religion, they suddenly explode on this historic occasion. Sitting in the *tricouleur*-hung tribune in the Place Maréchal Joffre, one did not have to make a great effort to imagine oneself back in the 'house of the comedians'.

The programme alternates between singing and dancing, the singers all dressed in white, the women in Mother Hubbards or *moumus*, and the men in cotton trousers and shirts. Wreaths of fern sprigged with different flowers crown their black hair, which the women wear long down their backs. A troupe of singers, from forty to a hundred in number, is led by a song master who ranges them in a semicircle facing the tribune where the governor has his box. The women sit in front, cross-legged, while the men half squat behind. Two of the troupe stand behind the men, acting as musical prompters to keep the chorus in key. The song master, generally also the local chief, stands in front, gesticulating and jiggling – a human baton. The performers are possessed by their singing, and women swaying from side to side and the men rocking backwards and forwards with their heads bent to the ground. The delivery is rapid, without pause between songs.

Each dancing team has its own orchestra preceding it, beating on hollow wooden cylinders with sticks, strumming on different-sized drums with their fingers; keeping up a quick, staccato rhythm that stops abruptly for an instant and then starts up again. The effect of the dance greatly depends on the agility of the dancers to time their movements to these sudden halts and starts in the music. The dances are still frankly erotic. So swiftly do the women swing their hips that motion becomes almost static, movement is betrayed only by the swaying of their grass skirts. As in most primitive dances, the shoulders and head remain perfectly still, the arms and the hips marking the rhythm. The men, poised on the balls of their feet with their knees slightly bent, move their legs outward, exposing the flat inner part of the thigh. The women's skirts, belted with cowries, lie just above the pelvis exposing the delicate swell below the waist. The women have beautiful shoulders and slim arms and the men flat, well-marked chests. The cinnamon thighs breaking through the soft falling skirts and kilts are very exciting. The skirts, made from the bark of the hibiscus, are either white or cream, and are belted with looped, braided strands that terminate in tassels.* The dancers carry switches in their hands and wear deep circular collars, like the collars one has seen on the walls of Theban tombs.

The Tahitians have a lively sense of humour and are quick to ridicule. Each troupe has one or two fat members, either male or female, who have been chosen by design. More agile often than their svelte partners, they get terrific applause when they execute a particularly erotic pass. A clown is also generally included in the suite and more often than not parodies the continual flexing of the pelvis, a joke always hugely enjoyed by the crowd. Most of the dances are abstract. Only a few enact a story and these for the most part deal with the appeasement of an angry god by human sacrifice.

As Cook tells us, 'music is little known to them, yet they are very fond of it. They have only two instruments; the flute and the drum, the former is made of hollowed bamboo in which there are several holes; into one of them they blow with one nostril, stopping the other with the thumb of the left hand; the other holes they stop and unstop with their fingers, and by this means produce four notes, of which they have made one tune which serves upon all occasions'. The melodies have altered

* Danielsson tells us that 'the famous grass skirt, which we have come to regard as typical of the South Seas, was generally only worn in Samoa and the low coral island of the Tuamotu, where the soil is too poor for the mulberry tree from whose bark the Polynesian *tapa* was made.'

but the instruments have not changed. Extraordinary drum rhythms throb through the fire-lit nights with the guttural basso of men's voices and the eerie obligato of the nose flute in the background. The music is vibrant and rapid, and strongly melodious. Its repetitive quality makes it seem static and hypnotic. Again and again a certain phase is repeated, is caught up, halted, and then played in another key. The dancers appear to be automatons activated by the vibrations of the drums – its pulse beats thud and ripple through their bodies.

Europe has always been interested in the erotic attractions of Tahiti and a considerable literature exists on the subject. Cook found the women completely amoral. 'Chastity,' he writes, 'is but little valued, especially among the middle classes, if a wife is found guilty of a breach of it, her only punishment is a beating from her husband. The men will very readily offer their young women to strangers, even their own daughters, and think it very strange if you refuse them, but this is done merely for the sake of gain.' Cook is less severe on the second voyage, admitting 'that none but the common women would yield to the embraces of our people, not one of the "gentlemen" were able to obtain such favours from any woman of distinction, though several attempts were made. On the whole, a stranger who visited England might with equal justice draw the character of the women there from those which he might meet with on board ships in one of the naval ports or in the purlieus of Covent Garden.'

Cook was completely detached: whether because he felt he should set an example, or perhaps simply because he did not have time for romantic escapades. Whatever the reason, there is not an instance of his having been involved with a *vahiné*. This certainly was not the case with George Hamilton, a surgeon in the *Pandora*, sent out in 1790 under Edwards to arrest the *Bounty* mutineers. He found the island exactly as Bougainville described it, *Le Mirage Océanien*. 'This may be called the Cytheria of the southern hemisphere, not only for the beauty and elegance of the women, but their being so deeply versed in, and so passionately fond of the Eleusinian mysteries.' He evokes a poetic Arcadia where 'the trees are loaded with the richest fruit', and where 'the carpet of nature is spread with the most odoriferous flowers, and the fair ones ever willing to fill your arms with love'.

Parkinson, the young Quaker naturalist of the first voyage, disapprovingly felt that 'young girls are bred up to lewdness'. Danielsson, who has lived years among the Polynesians and has made a study of the subject, tells us that 'alongside beauty, sexual ability was the quality which the Polynesians valued most highly'. They made no attempt to suppress sexuality in the younger generation. 'They considered that the young people ought to be fully trained as quickly as possible, and took great care that they should obtain expert guidance as soon as they really began to be sexually mature.'* This guidance took the form of practical instruction. Boys and girls would have their first intercourse with an older, experienced person; often an aunt, uncle, or other relative of their parents' generation. 'So uninhibited were they regarding sexual matters that masturbation,' Danielsson says, 'was considered quite a natural thing and parents often urged their children to masturbate when they wanted peace and quiet.'

So candid an approach to sex does not seem to cultivate the sentimental effects to which Europeans attach so much importance. Cook notes that the word 'heart' in our figurative sense was meaningless to the Polynesians to whom the stomach was the seat of affection. 'Yearning of the bowels' they call it. Quite understandably no romantic tradition has flowered in this atmosphere.

Hawkesworth, in editing Cook's first voyage, was conscious that much of the material would shock British public opinion, and as if preparing for their reaction, he asked his readers not to stand in judgement over the gentle South Seas islanders, suggesting that morality, after all, was a matter of social custom. But within a few weeks of publication the Press was in full cry. Critics enthused over the beauties of the country, but it was only too apparent that its inhabitants were nothing better than depraved savages. Banks, the young botanist, was lampooned and accused of being more interested in exotic women than exotic plants, while bawdy couplets dealt roundly with the unfortunate *vahinés*. Hawkesworth, it was said, had handled his sources, namely the journals of Cook and Banks, too freely and had been indiscreet in his descriptions of some of the more erotic Tahitian customs. Such descriptions, as contemporary versifiers were quick to point out, were not calculated to improve the morals of the British nation. The critics, however, seem to have been blessed with convenient memories, for when one considers the state of affairs at home, one is at a loss to understand how the spontaneous behaviour of the friendly Tahitians could possibly be condemned.

In England when a ship of the line anchored in one of the large ports, boatloads of women would come alongside. Each man slipped down the gangway, made his choice, and carried her back to his berth. Sometimes the women would follow the ship by land, if she were ordered to some other home port. 'It was not unusual,' writes Masefield, 'for a monstrous regiment of women to march right across England so that they might join their mates on the other side.'†

* *Love in the South Seas*, op. cit.

† *Sea Life in Nelson's Time* by John Masefield, London, 1905, Methuen & Co.

Women were still being allowed to board ships slightly more than a hundred years ago. In the early 1840's, the captain of a frigate in the West Indies sent ashore for three hundred women so that every man and boy aboard might have a black mistress during their stay in port. During Cook's time the number of loose women in Portsmouth alone was estimated at 20,000.

Today, the yachtsmen and the old beachcombers of Papeete will tell you rather wistfully that there was a time when *vahinés*, bathing on the banks of a river, would call you to join them and thereafter take you home and keep you for as long as you cared to stay. There are few women now by the rivers, and those one finds are washing their household linen; married women of doubtful beauty whose corrugated iron and wooden houses are of no more easy access than those of England and America.

The truth is that the *vahinés* are still there, found now in the bars on the waterfront. Few of them are beautiful, but they are still the uncomplicated children of nature they have always been and will, one imagines, always be willing to sleep with the stranger for the price of a nail – or its modern equivalent which sometimes takes on rather larger proportions, a bicycle or some equally voluminous prize. It must be remembered that for the Polynesians who then knew nothing of metal, a nail represented untold treasure, a wondrous object with which her man could fashion an unbreakable fish hook. But things have not changed so very much, for while the *vahinés* are in fact prostitutes, their calling is not regarded as a crime of so deep a dye as to exclude them from the community in general. The Tahitians' attitude about such things is entirely different from our own. One of the most respected and civilized of Papeete's matrons introduced me one day to her eldest son on the lawn in front of her house in the presence of several people. As casually as if she were saying that he was an architect or a lawyer, she told me, 'he is not my husband's child'.

What of Huahine and Raiatea of the present day? The Society Islands have not altered as much as Tahiti. They are some fifty or sixty years behind the times and not as spectacularly beautiful. I stayed a few days in Raiatea to break my seaplane flight to Bora-Bora. Its principal port is a sad little town boasting only a fly-blown commercial travellers' hotel with its back to a street of modest Chinese shops. Nothing at all remains of the dignity suggested by Cook or of the festive finery of the proud *ariois*. The arrival and departure of the small inter-island steamer is its only animation. I spent my time by the quay watching the loading of the *Benicia*. The passengers stood around, amid baskets of *taro* roots and crates of young pigs; their personal luggage tied up in Japanese fashion in squares of printed cotton. The cotton, specially manufactured for the Pacific trade in Lyon, has bold, colourful patterns of hibiscus or bread-fruit leaves. A woman from one of the outlying districts arrived in an old Chrysler station wagon. A large black hat was planted squarely on her head and a long dress hid her dropsical legs. The dress, and there was a great deal of it, was also black but criss-crossed with bars of deep yellow and within the middle of each square were great bold bunches of blood-red cocoa beans.

The *Benicia* was tied up to the wharf and had her time of departure chalked up on a blackboard attached to her hull. Ten a.m. was the auspicious hour. Having scanned the board a Frenchman, who intended taking his car over, cornered the captain for further information:

'*A quelle heure partez-vous?*' the man asked.

'*A dix heures,*' answered the captain.

'*Vraiment dix heures?*'

'*Mais non,*' answered the captain, the 'non' emphasized in surprise that such a question should be asked.

Cook could not visit Bora-Bora during either the first or the second voyage. He spent all of one day on board the *Endeavour*, standing on and off the reefs barricading its coast and then decided 'to give up our decision of going on shore, especially as it appears to be difficult of access'. The island 'is rendered very remarkable by a high craggy hill, which appears to be almost perpendicular'. It was the great Temanu, or 'Sea of Birds', the remains of a shattered volcano. On the second voyage he writes that he had some thought of visiting the famous island, but that having already procured all the supplies he needed, 'I thought it would be answering no end going there and therefore laid it aside and directed my course to the west'. It was necessity rather than curiosity that finally drew him to the island and obliged him to hunt for the only navigable passage through its shining reefs. He had come to trade for one of the anchors Bougainville had lost in a storm while visiting Tahiti. Having been retrieved by the natives after *La Boudeuse*'s departure, it had been sent as a good-will present to the powerful Puni who, as Cook points out, although not actually dreaded by the Tahitians – their island being almost out of his reach – was nevertheless treated with great respect. 'My desire to get possession of it,' writes Cook, 'did not arise from our being in want of anchors. But having expended all the hatchets, and other tools which we had brought from England, in purchasing refreshments, we were now reduced to the necessity of creating a fresh assortment of trading articles.'

Puni had grown very old and now walked bent almost double, 'an unusual thing in these isles'. The meeting went very well. Cook's presents: a linen-nightgown, a shirt, some gauze handkerchiefs, a looking-glass, some beads and other objects, plus six axes were thought to exceed the value of the anchor. Puni refused to receive them until Cook had seen the article in question. 'I found it to be neither so large nor so perfect, as I expected. It had originally weighed seven hundred pounds, according to the mark that was upon it; but the ring, with part of the shank, and the two palms, were now wanting. . . . Be this as it may, I took the anchor as I found it, and sent him every article of the present that I at first intended.'

This, alas, is all that we hear of Bora-Bora from the captain. 'Having thus completed my negotiations,' he writes, 'I returned on board and hoisting in the boats, made sail from the island to the north.' One would like to have had Banks' or even Forster's impressions of what to my mind is the most beautiful of all the Pacific islands visited by Cook.

It is small and compact. A mountain mass erupting from the centre of an atoll that sometimes encloses and is sometimes enclosed by an incredibly blue sea. One turns and turns about, treading the tortuous contours of the coast and, always above one, dominating the scene is the monolith of red-brown rock, the great Temanu; its flat top against the brilliant cloud-heavy Pacific sky seems man-made. Columned galleries should have been excavated from the perpendicular walls – the fortress palace of some legendary and immortal queen.

I stayed in a small grass hut grown round with young coconut palms, their pale, yellow fronds framing the lisping waters of a glass-smooth lagoon. The sands here, unlike those of Tahiti, are snow-white, which gives luminosity to the sea; a sea which shades from turquoise to lapis lazuli mottled with jade-green, paling again to turquoise towards the reefs. Dawn is soft and pale, with a slight haze lifting off the water. Not a sound is to be heard before the faint rustling of a warm breeze that arrives with the sun's breaking on a pearl-pink horizon.

There would be something sad about the lack of animals on these islands were it not for the teeming life to be found just off their shores. The sea landscape where I stayed is a garden of fan corals spreading out laterally like thorn trees on the Serengeti plains in East Africa. Rippled light plays over them, throwing delicate shadows on the white floor of the lagoon.

The water is crystal clear, and the coral depths seem never to have been disturbed. One floats looking down through glasses, lost in another world; lunar, frightening at times, a Max Ernst landscape. At one moment the coral is pale mauve with touches of lilac, the white coral sand a phosphorescent moon glow. A shoal of iridescent fish, the colour of white opals, pass by, while directly below, tiny electric blue fish refuge in a lump of coral, flickering like tongues of fire as they dart in and out of its protective branches. Continually the landscape changes, also its colours: green slashed with gold or red, then again the nacreous coldness of mother-of-pearl. In the end one is grateful for the hot beach and the burning sun that bleaches and crumbles the bones of that liquid world.

But more beautiful even than these lagoon waters are the reefs proper, a vast world of coral that lies two or three miles off the shore. One paddles out in an outrigger canoe. When it grates on the first rock, one makes it fast, and picks one's way over stepping stones of porites embedded with horseshoe clams. These creatures flaunt mantles of the most extravagant colours: cinnamon, russet, lavender spotted with a dark velvety-blue, and the bright greens and pinks of heraldry. However, the reef itself claims greater attention. The stepping stones grow closer and closer together until one reaches the outer wall, a flat undistinguished battlement, grown over with weeds.

It is wise to go with a native for the first time, for it is lonely and frightening out there. With caution one crosses over to the ocean side where the reef falls sheer down to unfathomable depths. On very calm days you can peer down that wall, which disappears into an indigo blackness, haunted by large finned shadows. But it is seldom calm, and one stands terrified, ankle deep in a cascade of foam, with not a soul in sight, while there in front of you not more than twenty yards away the giant Pacific rollers, sun-shot tons of water, advance without any check. It is only a matter of seconds before one will be swept to instant death. But don't move. Suddenly as if by some miracle the deluge is halted by the reef. In a fury the waves crash on the impregnable, and like fountains flung into the sky, the spray falls shattered and harmless at one's feet, while the broken tide sweeps across the reef to boil over into the lagoon in impotent rage.

These monster waves, though terrifying, are harmless. It takes time to get used to them, but once assured and relaxed, one sees them with a different eye, admiring the beauty of their glass-green concavities in which dolphin, tuna or shark are sometimes silhouetted against the light. I spent hours watching them, marvelling at the sparkle in the air and revelling in the utter wildness of the scene. But one morning I slipped and my leg disappeared down a small crevice. The boy I was with helped me up, warning me to watch my step, but before going on he suggested that I put on my water glasses and look down the hole from which he had extricated me. I had imagined the reef to be a solid mass of rock built up over the centuries inch by inch, the skeleton of myriad marine organisms. I knelt down and plunged my head under the water. Imagine yourself clamped to the dome of St Peter's, looking down through a small aperture. The ledge was but the thinnest crust grown over an immense vertiginous void, a vast cavern shot through with motes of dancing light. Far, far below the white sand floor sloped away into the misty depths while all round fantastic coral towers and turrets lifted towards me.

Here at last was the ideal unspoilt Pacific island. I took one last look at it through the porthole of the plane: jade-green in a peacock sea framed with white foam that hissed past our porthole as we took off, leaving behind us a trench of turquoise.

I say that Bora-Bora is the most beautiful of the islands, but it would be hard to find a more majestic sight than the equally unspoilt Paopao Bay, or Cook's Bay as it is now called, on the island of Moorea, visited by Cook on the third voyage. Passing the island in 1767, Wallis had named it York after the Duke of York and Cook knew it as Eimeo. He was not very complimentary about its women: 'there was not a fine one amongst them', and if they did meet with one better-looking than the rest, 'we were sure, upon inquiry, to find that she had come from some other island'. He was only grateful for the abundant supply of fuel, 'for at Matavai it was impossible to cut any wood there being no tree that did not bear fruit'.

But this is the wrong direction, for it is not from Moorea that Cook sailed in the *Endeavour* when he left the Society Islands, but due south to search for the hypothetical continent. This long excursion is a monument to Cook's thoroughness and determination. The geographers' theory that such a continent existed rested on nothing more than the false idea that dry lands in the two hemispheres would balance one another. Cook himself did not believe it, but he struggled on from 20° to 40° latitude, a 1,500-mile course directed into bad weather.

For days the men in the *Endeavour* sailed through darkening seas, empty days, noting the winds and the waves and the different birds. By September 2nd they reached their farthest point south, where heavy squalls and howling gales decided Cook to change course and 'to stand to the northwards into better weather lest we should receive serious damage to our sails and our rigging as must hinder the further prosecution of the voyage'.

On October 7th they sighted the north island of New Zealand and thus, as far as concerns us, the first voyage was over. For Cook, however, there still remained the coast of New Zealand to be charted and subsequently the 2,000-mile eastern shore of Australia, hitherto quite unknown. In Batavia where they were obliged to stop two and a half months to repair the damages sustained on the Great Barrier Reef, the sickly climate sadly changed the ship's company; Cook lost his surgeon and Tupaia. Worse was to follow. As the *Endeavour* found her way slowly over the Indian Ocean towards the Cape in the wet and unhealthy north-west monsoon, the death roll grew steadily longer. Before half the distance to Cape Town was traversed, twenty-two more were carried off by a murderous sickness, among them the astronomer Green, two more of Banks' staff, two midshipmen, the boatswain and the carpenter. Cook wrote, 'that a man was no sooner taken with the putrid dysentery than he looked upon himself as dead, such was the despondency that reigned among the sick at this time, nor could it be by any means prevented when every man saw that medicine, however skilfully administered, had not the least effect. . . . One man had long tended upon the sick and enjoyed a tolerable good state of health: one morning, coming upon deck he found himself a little griped and immediately began to stamp with his feet and exclaim "I have got the gripes, I have got the gripes, I shall die, I shall die" – in this manner he continued until he threw himself into a fit and was carried off the deck in a manner dead, however he soon recovered and did very well.'

Another incident of such hysteria occurred in a vessel cruising off the west coast of Africa on which yellow fever, or 'black vomit' as it was then called, had just broken out. The mosquito was not yet known to be the cause of various fevers, and when cases of sickness were reported on board in tropical waters, the whole crew were apt to panic believing it both fatal and, worse still, highly contagious. Some doctors having carefully observed the symptoms thought otherwise; such a doctor was Robert McKinnel, the surgeon of this particular ship. Inspecting his men, he felt that something must be done, and done quickly for he saw that their fear was every bit as fatal as the fever. 'He therefore filled a wine glass with the "black vomit" of a patient in the throes of death, drank it jokingly and publicly on the quarter-deck, and continued to walk nonchalantly thereon for two hours lest anyone should suspect that he had taken anything to counteract the effect of this nauseous draught.' He suffered no ill effects and the ruse 'banished their fears and – largely – their fever'.*

On April 15th the *Endeavour* left Table Bay. In May they met with the East India fleet at St Helena, sailing in their company for some three weeks until left behind during a wind that split the *Endeavour*'s top gallant sail. Later a heavy squall sprang her topmast. Their gear was in such a bad state that something gave way every day, and it was not before July 13th that they anchored in the Downs – completing a voyage of nearly three years.

* *A Social History of the Navy* by Michael Lewis, London, 1960, George Allen & Unwin.

[Chapter 13]

The Second Voyage and a Change of Ship

THE RETURN of the *Endeavour* was the cause of much excitement in both the scientific and social worlds. The newspapers were full of it. The Lords of the Admiralty followed by the Royal Society and the King hastened to show their favours. The 'ingenious gentlemen' were summoned to Windsor. Cook, not yet the public figure he was destined to become, retired quietly to Mrs Cook and his unfashionable home at Mile End, where he was 'employed in completing his papers'. However, he was not to be allowed much leisure. On August 14th he had an audience of the King at St James's Palace. Presenting his journal of the voyage 'with some curious maps and charts', he was rewarded with a promotion to Post-Captain and the command of H.M.S. *Scorpion*, an appointment that was simply a 'holding' one, for the Admiralty had other plans for him. The success of his first voyage gave a new impetus to discovery and the immediate thought was to resume it under this heaven-born leader. By autumn of the same year Cook had already been put in command of a second voyage with instructions to hunt out two suitable ships. His harrowing experience on the Great Barrier Reef when the *Endeavour* had nearly been wrecked had proved to him and the Admiralty the advisability of having two ships. Should something happen to one of them, the crew could always transfer to the other.

Cook would willingly have sailed again in the *Endeavour*. As Beaglehole remarks, 'she had proved her worth, but had already been sent to the Falkland Islands as a store ship'.* No one doubted that her design was the type required, and so when Cook went to the London Pool to

* She was sold out of the Navy in 1774 for £645 and for many years was employed as a collier in the North Sea. Next she was reported to have been renamed *La Liberté*, sailing under French colours in American waters, and seems eventually to have fallen into decay while anchored at Newport. A box made from her timbers was presented to James Fennimore Cooper.

make his choice, it is hardly surprising that he selected two similar ships, the *Marquis of Granby* of 462 tons, almost a hundred tons larger than the *Endeavour*, and the *Marquis of Rockingham* of 340 tons. They were both Whitby built, coming from Fishburn, the same dockyards that had produced the *Endeavour*. Cook was put in command of the former and Tobias Fourneaux, who had been second lieutenant with Wallis in the *Dolphin*, was appointed captain of the latter. The ships in the meantime had been renamed the *Drake* and the *Raleigh*. 'Honourable names for vessels of enterprise,' but ones that had to be changed for political reasons; it being felt that Spain, already very touchy about foreign ships sailing in what she considered 'her ocean', might take umbrage at namesakes of her sworn enemies! No records exist to indicate the origin of the names they finally sailed under, but as Beaglehole writes, 'they have taken on for us a sort of classic inevitability' – the *Adventure* and the *Resolution*.

The main object of the voyage was to settle once and for all the much agitated question regarding the existence of a Great Southern Continent. There still remained vast sweeps of the Pacific not yet explored, particularly in the high latitudes adjacent to the South Pole. To traverse these regions Cook decided to reverse the order of all previous circumnavigations, to start his probing from the Cape of Good Hope and from there work eastward. The winter months of the southern hemisphere were to be employed in inter-tropical cruising, his mission in this case being to hunt out the land already encountered by previous Spanish and Dutch navigators, lands very often but vaguely mentioned and certainly not correctly indicated on the maps. Once having located them, he was to survey them by sailing round their coasts, at the same time making inquiries ashore. Quiros's Tierra Austrialia del Espiritu Santo, for instance, claimed by him to be a part of a southern continent, was proved by Cook to be no more than a modest archipelago which he renamed the New Hebrides. In fact, Cook was being sent out on the most elaborate plan of discovery known in the history of navigation. In the three years he was absent he sailed between 60,000 and 70,000 miles, during which time he made numerous major geographical discoveries, one of them being New Caledonia, the largest island in the South Pacific after New Zealand. But ironically, it was what he didn't discover that was to count as his most important contribution. His conclusive proof that there was no Great Southern Continent put our knowledge of the South Pacific on a sound basis. Indeed, the maps of this part of the world still remain essentially as he left them.

The Admiralty had chosen well when they picked this obscure but talented seaman and their confidence in him does them credit. Recognizing his qualities they gave him every chance to develop them. The Admiralty already knew that wherever Cook had gone, 'he had observed, surveyed, sounded, and charted with an exemplary thoroughness'; but the second voyage was going to show them that he was an equally remarkable deep-sea navigator. It is seldom that sailors are both. Instead of mapping coasts and islands, his principal duty was to explore the tempestuous seas bordering on the Pole, searching for this elusive southern land. No gales, no temperatures deterred him and it was only ice in dense masses that finally turned him back. The second voyage was to bring Cook's qualities as a seaman and as an indomitably persevering commander into full view. When one studies his tracks on a chart of the southern hemisphere one is amazed. He loops and crosses over hundreds of miles of empty ocean, feeling his way at the same time through a maze of uncharted islands and reefs and unknown currents, a hazardous form of navigation that worries even the mechanized seaman of our own times. The daylight hours were fairly safe with masthead look-outs scanning the sea for white waters, but the nights must have been very harrowing. At any moment one might hear the dreaded cry of 'Breakers ahead!' From the first voyage Cook already knew the terrors of navigating in reef waters, how suddenly in a sea of an unfathomable depth, mountain-high breakers are heard and seen roaring over a reef not a mile off. 'Between us and destruction,' writes Banks when sailing off the north Queensland coast, 'was only a dismal valley, the breadth of one wave. A reef such as one speaks of here is a thing scarcely known in Europe; it is a wall of coral rock rising almost perpendicularly out of the unfathomable ocean.' But as James King with Cook as lieutenant on the third voyage writes: 'the most dangerous navigation becomes easy, and almost safe under his guidance'.

Banks originally intended to accompany Cook who no doubt welcomed the idea as he had learned a great deal from Banks, learned how to use his eyes. It is evident also from his journal that Banks had a sense of humour and was an amusing companion. But unfortunately for everyone concerned his recently-won celebrity had gone to his head. However, this was not immediately apparent, and to begin with things seemed to be going fairly smoothly. It was said that he was going to invest £10,000 of his own money in the voyage. It began to be less fortunate when he announced to Cook and the Board of Admiralty that he intended to sail with a suite of thirteen, including John Zoffany, the well-known portraitist and genre painter, John and James Miller, the natural history draughtsmen, John Clevely, the marinescapist, a secretary, two horn players, and servants. James Lind, a young physician from Edinburgh, was to come along as doctor and astronomer with a grant from government of £4,000 though 'what discoveries they expected him to make I could not understand', says Cook, as William Wales had already been appointed official astronomer by the Admiralty. Banks had also intended to provide himself with the companionship of a lady who was to join the ship in Madeira. One would be inclined to write this off as idle gossip had not Cook confirmed it in a letter. 'Three days before we arrived a person left the island who went by the name of Burnett. He had been waiting for Mr Banks' arrival about three months. At first he said he came here for the recovery of his health, but afterwards said his intention was to go out with Mr Banks. He was about thirty years of age and rather ordinary than otherwise and employed his time in botanizing. Every part of Mr Burnett's behaviour and every action tended to prove that he was a woman and I have not met with a person that entertains a doubt of a contrary nature.'

'All these gentlemen, except the astronomer,' writes Cook concerning Banks' suite, 'were to embark in the *Resolution* and to have large and separate apartments.' Banks had not even mentioned Zoffany and Lind when the sloop was purchased and 'the addition of these persons entirely altered the plan of accommodations'. It was obviously going to be difficult to find room for them and at the same time to leave space enough for her officers and crew and stowage for the necessary stores and provisions. 'The navy board was prevailed upon, though contrary to the opinion of some of the members, particularly the Comptroller, to alter their former plan which was to leave her in her original state.' The alterations to be made were quite extensive and consisted of raising her upper works about a foot, 'to lay a spardeck upon her from the quarterdeck to the forecastle and to build a round house for my accommodations so that the great cabin might be appointed to the use of Mr Banks alone'. One supposes that Cook had such a high opinion of the ship's design that he believed her capable of supporting the additional superstructure. He certainly was very agreeable to Banks about the whole thing. 'I left a line,' he writes to the young botanist, 'at your house yesterday desiring to know your sentiment concerning a stove for the cabin, it being necessary the officers of Deptford yard should know how to act. If you approve of a green baize floor cloth for the great cabin, I will demand as much cloth from the yard as will make one. As you mean to furnish the cabin well, I think you should have brass locks and hinges to the doors, etc., this, however, will be a private affair of your own, as nothing of this kind is allowed.'

Cook tells us that as the carpenters were working on the different apartments 'many of all ranks visited the ship, ladies as well as gentlemen. Scarcely a day passed on which she was not crowded with strangers who came on board for no other purpose but to see the ship in which Mr Banks was to sail round the world'. Was there a hint of irony in Cook's report? One hardly thinks so for it was not his character. On May 2nd, 'Mr Banks gave an entertainment on board to the Earl of Sandwich, the French Ambassador, Comte de Guines and several other persons of distinction'.

Soon after this the *Resolution* was ordered to proceed to the Downs, under the direction of Mr Cooper, the first lieutenant. Cook had been given leave and was to join the ship later. When he did the news was serious. It was absolutely imperative that the recently added poop should be removed. She was dangerously crank and liable to capsize any moment, exactly as Pallisier, the Comptroller, had predicted. The Navy Board immediately ordered the *Resolution* to their dockyard at Sheerness with orders that she be returned to her original state. According to Cook, Banks, who never seemed to have approved of the ship from the beginning, now 'used all his influence to have her condemned as totally unfit for the service she was going on and to have a forty-gun ship or an East Indiaman fitted out in her place, either of which would have been highly improper for making discoveries in remote parts. I shall not mention the arguments made me by Mr Banks and his friends as many of them were highly absurd and advanced by people who were not judges of the subject, one or two sea officers excepted who, upon this occasion, sacrificed their judgement in support of their friendship, or some other motive. Be this as it may, the clamour was so great that it was thought it would be brought before the House of Commons. The Admiralty and Navy Boards, however, persevered in their resolution of clearing her of all her superfluous works and remained firm in their opinion that after this was done she would answer in every respect better than any ship they could get'.

Cook himself had taken great pains in choosing a ship to replace the *Endeavour* and must have been very upset by the whole business.

The navy yard at Sheerness worked with speed. The *Resolution* had been consigned to them on May 18th. Already by the 20th Cook tells us that he 'found everything in great forwardness' with the poop and spardeck already removed. Cook further ordered that the masts be shortened and that her guns be changed from six- to four-pounders.

'On Sunday the 24th,' he tells us, 'Mr Banks and Dr Solander came down to take a view of the sloop as she was now altered and returned to town again the same evening.' Very shortly after this Banks declared that he had no intention of going on the voyage, 'alleging that the sloop was neither roomy nor convenient enough for his purpose'.

Banks aired his opinions in a regrettable letter addressed to Sandwich. 'When I went down to see the principal ship,' he writes, 'I immediately gave it my opinion that she was very improper for the voyage.'

He argues that returned to her original condition she was vastly over-crowded and so badly ventilated that she was likely to endanger the lives of the men. He argues about the health of the 'people', but not once did Banks ever suggest cutting down his own staff to make room for them. In some of his unpublished papers he even went so far as to criticize the cabin built for Cook, built it may be pointed out so that he and his artists could take over the great cabin – which anyway he claims was far too small for their use. No wonder the ship was crank, he complains, 'when those responsible for the alterations clogged her up with additional improvements of their own, the round house particularly which was no part of my plan'. Where, one wonders, was Cook supposed to go? Banks tells Sandwich that 'he had pledged himself to all Europe, not only to go on the voyage but to take with him as many able artists as the income of my fortune would allow me to pay', intimating that he was going to look very foolish in the eyes of the world when they heard that he was not to embark. The fault was not his, and he felt it his duty to make this point quite clear to the public – in other words he intended writing to the Press.

Banks seems to have forgotten that the expedition was primarily one of geographical exploration and not, as the Navy Board puts it, 'wholly dependent on him and his people with himself as director and commander of the whole'.

One regrets Banks' obstinacy and his newly acquired conceit. His company in Tahiti had proved most enjoyable and the men he had recruited for the second voyage promised even more brilliant results than the first company. One can understand, however, the Navy Board's impatience with his continual complaints. Here was a young landsman, not yet thirty, telling the Admiralty what they ought to do. He certainly was in no position to criticize; indeed the Board 'were surprised in view of his past experiences that he should have remained so ignorant in regards to matters relating to ships'.

Sandwich was also out of patience with his young friend. He warns him that should he be rash enough to write to the Press, the Admiralty would feel obliged to take immediate action 'for it is a heavy charge against this Board to suppose that they mean to send a number of men to sea in an unhealthy ship. I am sure,' writes the First Lord, 'if you will give yourself time to think coolly, you will at once see the impropriety of publishing to the world an opinion of your own. . . .'

There is another letter answering Banks' concern for the 'people' in which Sandwich ruthlessly writes, 'I perceive that your attention extends only to the common man for when conveniences were made for all your suite the officers were stowed as close as herring in a barrel, and yet you never took their distress into your humane consideration.'

And the great cabin which Banks complained was so reduced in size as to make it impossible for working, was in fact larger than the cabin space enjoyed by many an admiral and certainly more commodious than that in the *Endeavour*.

Cook remained remarkably calm and detached and appears not to have borne Banks any ill will, although much of the criticism had been slanted indirectly at himself as being responsible for the choice of the ship and ultimately refusing to consider any change. It speaks well for Cook's character that he remained on good terms with Banks. He writes to him from the Cape of Good Hope giving him an account of the voyage. 'Some cross circumstances which happened at the latter part of the equipment of the *Resolution* created, I have reason to think, a coolness betwixt you and I; but I can by no means think it was sufficient for me to break off all correspondence with a man I am under many obligations to.'

Indeed Cook was to regret Banks' absence even more than we do ourselves. He told Solander as much when he met him on returning from the second voyage. 'He said,' Solander reports to his patron, 'that nothing could have added to the satisfaction he has had in making the tour but having had your company.' Banks also must have regretted his high-handed behaviour, for the tour he took with Solander and two of his artists to Iceland could have been but a poor compensation.

On June 10th, Cook received Lord Sandwich on board the *Resolution* while the First Lord was on a tour of inspection visiting the dockyards in the Admiralty yacht. That same evening Cook posted to London to say good-bye to Mrs Cook and on the way learned that John Reinhold Forster and his son, George, were to embark with him in place of Banks. Banks' outstanding work in the *Endeavour* had set the pattern for all subsequent scientific expeditions and from now on all ships setting out on voyages of discovery were to carry a complement of naturalists and artists.

The new roster included the Forsters as the expedition's naturalists, William Hodges as its painter, and William Wales and William Bayly as its astronomers. All were to sail in the *Resolution* with the exception of Bayly who was posted to the *Adventure*. John Forster and his son George as his assistant were to receive the £4,000 voted by Parliament to Dr Lind, a remarkably generous grant when one compares it to Wales' £400 a year, or Cook's six shillings a day, and a grant that probably helped give John Forster an exaggerated opinion of his own importance. He was not to prove an easy travelling companion, and from the first to the last, as Beaglehole writes, he was an incubus. 'One hesitates, in fact, to lay out his characteristics, lest the portrait should seem simply caricature. Dogmatic, humourless, suspicious, pretentious, contentious, censorious, demanding, rheumatic, he was a problem from any angle. . . . Cook was forced to conclude one interview by turning him out of the cabin, Clerke threatened to put him under arrest, Burr the master's mate knocked him down.' Small wonder he was treated summarily, and mimicked by the crew. There was no love lost on either side, for in a note in George Forster's *Voyage*, the father, speaking through his son, gives his opinion of the crew. 'It will not be improper to acquaint the reader, that we were so situated on board the *Resolution* as to meet with obstacles in all our researches, from those who might have been expected to give us all manner of assistance. It has always been the fate of science and philosophy to incur the contempt of ignorance. . . . Circumstances,' he continues, 'which were known to every person around us, remained impenetrable mysteries to us; and it was assuredly not owing to the good nature of our shipmates, if we have been fortunate enough to obtain even such trifling information as has enabled me to give the true and exact situations of every place in this narrative, and in my chart.'

The picture John Forster gives of Cook is even more aggravating. In his preface to the Berlin edition of an anonymous account of the third voyage he describes him as a 'cross-grained fellow, who sometimes showed a mean disposition and was carried away by hasty temper'. He accuses him of having 'an overbearing attitude which was the result of having his head turned by Lord Sandwich'. Forster then calmly claims that he and his son being his daily companions at table and elsewhere had an excellent effect on him. 'He therefore of necessity acquired through our presence a greater respect and reverence for his own character and good name. Our mode of thought, our principles, and our habits had their effect upon him in the course of time through having them constantly before his notice.'

One sees that Beaglehole was not exaggerating. Forster's own words condemn him. One wonders why such a man was ever chosen in the first place. The answer is that, difficult though he might have been, he was not devoid of charm when he wanted. He was well informed on a variety of subjects and, as the *Voyage* bears out, remarkably observant. It is certainly not a stupid face that stares out at one from Rigaud's portrait; narrow and pale, with high arched eyebrows, heavily-lidded eyes, and a large beaked nose. It is the kind of face that would be noticed but not one that would be found sympathetic.

Father and son were Polish Prussian, descended from a Yorkshire family that had left England on the death of Charles I. George, shown seated in the same painting, looks very German; serious, heavy featured, tending to fat. His short career was to be more successful than that of his debt-ridden parent. On his return from the voyage, after collaborating with his father on a prohibited edition of his journals,* he became professor of natural history at Cassel, moving subsequently to the university at Wilna, later being appointed librarian to the Elector of Mayence. In 1790 he accompanied Alexander von Humboldt on a three months' tour down the Rhine, including Belgium and Holland, afterwards publishing an account of the voyage. He died in his thirty-ninth year of scorbutic fever in Paris. He appears to have been a likeable character, but being only eighteen when he joined his father in the *Resolution*, he was too young to have exercised much influence over his difficult parent.

John Forster was already fifty-seven when Cook met him, quite old to be setting off on such a voyage. He started life in the Church, as a minister in a small town near Danzig but threw aside his clerical duties to devote himself entirely to 'scientific and literary pursuits'. In this new rôle he met Count Orlov who offered him a vague post in St Petersburg. Forster seemed to have been totally incapable of dealing with money as all his life he was in debt, even serving a jail sentence. His Russian venture brought him little pecuniary relief, but it did furnish him with some useful introductions for his projected trip to England in search of prosperity. Once arrived in London, he fared rather better, getting himself known in scientific circles and picking up an F.R.S. George was a great help to his father and learnt English so well that he was soon able to augment the family income by translating odd pamphlets. At seventeen he was already translating Bougainville's *Voyages* for the English edition. With this likely background it is no wonder that when presented to the Forsters, Sandwich should have welcomed them as replacements for Banks and Solander. Apart from John Forster's impossible character and the nuisance he was to prove to Cook, the First Lord was not so wrong in his choice.

Hurriedly – for we are impatient to set off – we must mention the

* The story of this publication is too long to go into in detail here. Briefly, it had been agreed with the Admiralty that Cook should write the account of the voyage and the countries visited, while Forster was to supplement it with a second volume containing his scientific observations; a perfectly fair arrangement, it would seem. Cook carried out his share of the bargain and furnished Forster with a manuscript. The latter, however, proved obstinately insistent in having his own way in everything, with the result that, after submitting two schemes to Lord Sandwich, both extremely unsatisfactory, he was forbidden to write at all. It was decided that Cooks should complete the whole work. To get around this ruling Forster immediately set his son to work on writing a so-called original account of the voyage. His name had not been included in the interdiction from publishing, but George had no journal. His task, therefore, was to produce a book from his father's journal in the fastest time possible. The Forsters' *Voyage* anticipated Cook's edition by some six weeks but fortunately had no deleterious effects, for Cook's version ran into a second printing before the year was out.

remaining supernumeraries included on the voyage. Zoffany's replacement was William Hodges, a young painter of twenty-eight who had studied with Richard Wilson, one of England's foremost landscapists. Of course one regrets Zoffany, for there is a sad lack of accurate and unprejudiced genre paintings dealing with the population of the Pacific. Zoffany, with his talent for exotic conversation pieces, would have been the perfect choice. Hodges, alas, had no talent for the figure, but he was good at landscapes and rapid wash drawings that have an almost Turneresque preoccupation with light. According to Beaglehole he had not been the first choice for the post; 'another young man from Wilson's studio, Thomas Jones . . . had been approached by Mr Stewart in the name of the Dilettanti Society. Jones' parents had refused their consent to his going to Italy, but on this proposal they rapidly changed their mind'. Lord Palmerston, another 'luminary of culture', had suggested Hodges, and on the whole it was a good choice. In any case he was the first professional English landscape painter to visit the South Seas. From the terms of his contract Hodges' pictures were to become the property of the Admiralty, in whose rooms some of them still hang.

Cook and Forster admired Hodges' application and appreciated his talents but tell us nothing of his character. All we have to fall back on are the broad outlines of his career. On his return from the voyage he superintended the engraving of his drawings by Woolett and others for the published account, and the following year had some of his large oil landscapes of the South Pacific accepted by the Royal Academy. Warren Hastings saw them, and admiring his handling of light, invited him to India where he remained about six years. A number of the views he painted there are engraved in aquatint. Back from the East, he then set out for a tour of Europe, including a visit to Russia. His was certainly not a sedentary life, yet in spite of all his travels he found time to contract three marriages. At fifty-one he suddenly retired from his profession, disposed of his pictures by auction, and moved to Dartmouth where he opened a bank, an unsuccessful venture which ruined him. He died shortly afterwards of gout of the stomach, or as gossip would have it, of an overdose of laudanum. His sad end, however, does not concern us here, for he was still a young, enthusiastic painter when he embarked in the *Resolution*. His only problems for the next three years were those set him by the tropical light; those soft shafts of iridescent gold that dappled the tops of trees on a wooded headland, the diffused haze powdered by the surf foaming over the reefs, or the cold green shadows and the blinding whiteness of the icy world that surrounded them in the dangerous waters of the great Antarctic. Hodges was not concerned at all with the flora and fauna, practically all such work on this voyage being carried out by the Forsters.

The two astronomers of the expedition, William Wales who was to sail with Cook and William Bayly with Fourneaux, had not been changed, for owing their appointment to the Board of Longitude, they had never been dependent on Banks. Both men had been carefully picked by Maskelyne, the Astronomer Royal, and as it happened, had both been members of teams chosen to observe the transit of Venus, Wales having been sent by the Royal Society to Hudson Bay while Bayly had taken his readings from Iceland's North Cape. We know very little about Bayly, but Wales is of considerable interest and we shall refer often to his journal. Cook had a high regard for this sympathetic, lively Yorkshireman with a strong north-country dialect and saw to it that he sailed again with him on the last voyage.

Andreas Sparrman was the fourth civilian of the party, but only joined the ship at Cape Town. John Forster met him there and, impressed with the young Swede, a graduate of the University of Upsala, persuaded Cook that he would be a useful addition. Sparrman was not only an able botanist, trained under Linnaeus, but also a qualified physician. At the age of seventeen he had already made his first voyage to India and China as surgeon in a Swedish East Indiaman, and was now, in his twenty-fourth year, in South Africa on behalf of his government, to study Cape flora. Sparrman also published an account of the voyage, the first part of which appeared in an English translation in 1785. Cook rarely mentions the young man in his narrative. On the other hand the latter is responsible for several vivid pictures of his captain. One of them describes an anxious moment in Tahiti when the *Resolution* was in danger of being dashed to pieces on the reefs. Caught by a terrific indraught in one of the passages, Cook was unable to steer his ship clear. Wales tells us that 'she struck so hard that it was with difficulty sometimes that we kept on our legs'. Sparrman reporting on the same episode compliments the sailors on the efficiency with which they carried out their orders, but adds, 'I should have preferred, however, to hear fewer "goddams" from the officers and particularly the captain, who while the danger lasted stamped about the deck and grew hoarse with shouting.' This is quite different from the quiet, self-confident Cook we know, and is the only hint of criticism Sparrman ever makes of his captain whom he admired tremendously. Cook, it is true, did have a hasty temper but what is interesting in this passage is Sparrman's primness, a slight failing, but nothing else one knows about him tells against him.

Saying good-bye to his family on June 21st, Cook, accompanied by

Wales, left London for Sheerness, joined his ship, and dropped down to the Nore. On July 3rd they arrived at Plymouth, having been boarded the day before by Sandwich and Pallissier. The Forsters, waiting at Plymouth, visited Cornwall's tin mines while some shelves were fixed to their cabin, eventually joining the *Resolution* on the 11th. Straight away John Forster complained about his accommodations and offered Cooper, the first lieutenant, a hundred pounds to move out of his cabin. When this offer was refused he tried to force Gilbert, the master, to give up his, threatening to report the matter to the King if he did not oblige. Forster must have regretted these foolish words, for Wales tells us that they were immediately taken up by the crew who repeated them mockingly on every possible occasion. Cook mentions nothing of all this; he had other things to think about.

Finally, at six o'clock in the morning on July 13th, they were ready to sail. The *Adventure* was signalled to weigh anchor and the two ships stood out to sea on their way to Madeira and the Cape.

[Chapter 14]

A World of Ice

THE SHIPS made a sixteen-day run to Madeira, taking a further three months to reach Table Bay. The Forsters proved to be as observant as Banks. With his father peering over his shoulder, George describes blazing lights glowing in a phosphorescent ocean, and the beauty and brightness of the colours which played over a dolphin's metallic flanks as it lay dying on the deck of the ship. Beautiful to look at but rather dry eating. Next comes a sad little story about a swallow that nearly got drowned in a squall. Bedraggled and wet it had perched on the railings of the quarterdeck and was so exhausted that it had allowed George to catch it. 'I dried it and when it was recovered let it fly about the great cabin. Far from repining its confinement, it immediately began to feed upon the flies, which were numerous.' At dinner George opened the window and let it fly out, but it returned in the evening and spent the night roosting somewhere up in the rigging, returning the next day to the cabin. 'Emboldened by the shelter which we offered it, and the little disturbance it suffered from us, the poor little bird now ventured to enter the ship at every port and scuttle which was open; some part of the morning it passed very happily in Mr Wales' cabin; but after having left that it entirely disappeared. It is more than probable,' adds George, 'that it came into the berth of some unfeeling person, who caught it in order to provision a meal for a favourite cat.'

Arriving at Table Bay Hodges painted a view of Cape Town, a sprinkling of white, box-like houses nestling at the foot of the great mountain. It was drawn from the ship and a stormy light strikes the sails of the *Adventure* and the angular walls of the fort lying someways distant across a choppy green-blue sea. When finished it was carefully packed and sent off home to the Admiralty and now hangs at Greenwich. Looking at the canvas one is immediately conscious of the influence of Claude and Wilson, Hodges' master, but the handling of paint is freer, almost impressionistic. Hodges' real concern was clearly atmospherics and the canvas is a naturalistic rendering of the weather conditions enjoyed by the expedition during their stay at the Cape.

They spent three weeks at Cape Town and then sailed due south, a great plunge into unknown seas where storm petrels screeched across their wake and where they saw the mighty albatross, great air king of the lonely South Pacific. Sparrman tells us that they were persuaded to swallow pieces of mutton skin on hooks and hauled aboard on a line like fish.

On December 11th they struck their first real ice, mountains of it, great crystal clear and transparent icebergs shaded a sapphire-blue – high-furrowed walls against which clashed a surge of green breakers. One iceberg measured about two miles in circumference and about sixty feet high and was tenanted by a troop of waddling penguins. Nearby great whales blew sprays of icy sea into the brightness of the sky. Most days the temperature registered 5° below zero and snow lay four inches thick on the decks. Icicles hung from the sails and rigging. The sleeves on the seamen's jackets were so short that they suffered from exposed arms, the fault, Sparrman says, of the contractors who had skimped on the material. Cook set the tailors to work to lengthen them with strips of red baize. Caps of the same stuff were also provided which proved a great comfort to the men. On Christmas Day all the 'people' got very drunk. The rum rations, so bad for the men under the heat of the tropics, had a tonic effect on them here in the Antarctic.

Sparrman, gazing on the mountainous masses of ice surrounding them, threatening possible shipwreck, thinks rather wistfully of his stomach and regrets 'the sherbets missing from the dessert on our table'. Floats of ice, however, were collected by the crew and melted down to augment the water supply. The fact that this source proved to be salt-free saved the ships from turning northward in search of Madagascar or the Cape in order to refill their water casks. The only drawback of the ice water was that it gave the men sore throats. They cured this by pouring a pint of vinegar into the water butts 'and plunging therein a dozen red hot musket balls', a precaution recommended by the surgeon.

One calm day John Forster with Wales left the ship in the jolly-boat to take the temperature of the water and shoot birds. Gradually the fog increased until they could hardly see the length of their own boat, much less the ship. They shouted and let off their muskets but nothing appeared to penetrate the blanketing walls of mist. There was a terrible moment of anxiety when they were faced with the fearful possibility of being parted for ever from the ships. In the end the dinner gong put them out of their agony.

The fog continued and not even the northerly gales dispersed it. To make matters worse they were attended by a constant fall of sleet which froze to the rigging, reducing it to wire, and starching the sails

33. Reinhold and George Forster at Tahiti. Engraved by D. Beyel after J. F. Rigaud. (*page 144*)

34. Floats of ice were collected by the crew and melted down to augment the water supply.
Engraved by B. T. Pouncy after W. Hodges. (*page 150*)

35. An Easter Islander.
On their heads the men wore 'a round fillet adorned with feathers'.
Engraved by F. Bartolozzi after W. Hodges. (*page 157*)

to the hardness of boards. On January 17th 1773 they crossed the Antarctic Circle and reaching 66° latitude found their way blocked by enormous fields of ice. They were the first men to have penetrated so far into the polar circle.

It must have been a great relief when Cook ordered the retreat to the north, but there had been droll moments despite the cold. The ship's sow had farrowed but lost her young on account of the weather. Sparrman remembered that when in China he had bought pig's milk for tea and coffee and mentioned the fact to Cook who immediately gave orders for the bereft mother to be milked. 'But the newly-created milch-cow,' as Sparrman puts it, 'had already proved bad tempered and aggressive, and no one dared to carry out the order.'

By February 1st, the ships had sailed up into 48° latitude. It was still cold and foggy but as the northern limit of pack ice is about 54° latitude, they no longer ran the risk of being seized up and frozen to death. On February 8th, a brisk gale sprang up, accompanied by very hazy weather, thickening into fog, and the two vessels separated. The *Resolution* cruised about, firing her guns and burning flares, but no response was heard. When the weather cleared the *Adventure* had disappeared. 'Our parting,' writes George Forster, 'was almost universally regretted among the crew and none of them ever looked around the ocean without expressing some concern on seeing our ship alone on this vast and unexplored expanse.' Cook, taking it for granted that Fourneaux would make for the rendezvous he had given him in New Zealand, pushed on to the south-east intent on proving, once and for all, that there was no Great Southern Continent. They sailed back down into 60° latitude and slowly edged their way northward towards New Zealand, which they sighted on March 25th.

They had covered a distance of over 10,000 miles from the Cape, thus ending their first cruise in the high southern latitudes. They had been four months and four days without sight of land, the whole course, as the Forsters tell us, being a series of hardships never before experienced. Cook does not dwell on the hardships but he must have been proud of his men.

The *Resolution* anchored in Dusky Bay on the western point of the southern island, a fjord-like place deserted except for the cry of birds and an occasional sight of a native. They stayed there six weeks in order to recuperate from the rigours of the cold, then sailed northward up the coast to Queen Charlotte Sound in Cook Strait where they found the *Adventure*.

Cook intended to make a further plunge south, into the eastern waters of the Antarctic, but this sweep would have to wait on the polar summer. In the meantime he pursued a winter programme exploring an area of this vast ocean, east of New Zealand, never before visited. Reaching 130° longitude and having sighted no land, he sailed due north, narrowly missing Pitcairn Islands, and then west to Tahiti and on to Tonga, or the Friendly Islands, discovered by Tasman in 1642. By November 3rd the *Resolution* was back again in her old anchorage in Queen Charlotte Sound, but alone, for she had parted company with the *Adventure* in a violent gale. They were not to meet again during the voyage. Fourneaux, having no second rendezvous, had little choice but to sail for home. If one looks on the map one will see that Cook had executed a large square, thus exposing further empty spaces, a discovery as important as finding land when mapping an ocean.

Naturally we are to visit the Friendly Islands with Cook, for Tonga is part of our itinerary, but we will wait for his second visit to those islands the following year before joining him. For the moment we are only spectators at these southward probings which eventually will lead us back into the tropics, to Tonga via Easter Island and the Marquesas.

Cook had been 'down', and 'up', and was now turning 'down' again in a giant, irregular zigzag – that was to be the last plunge south. They were to penetrate even farther than they had the previous summer, as far as 70° 10′ latitude, a record not bettered until 1823 by James Weddell in the *Jane of Leith* while on a sealing expedition. They weighed anchor on November 25th. Again the seals, penguins and ice. Again the amusing details that catch one's eye: poor Wales, for instance, who although a bold student of the sky and stars, as Sparrman puts it, disliked experimenting with earthly things. He found it impossible to vary the ship's monotonous fare with the exotic additions enjoyed by the other men, the sea birds were too oily and his stomach turned at the idea of seal flesh basted with sherry. By January the cold was so intense that the moaning winds cut like steel blades and blowing with ever-increasing fury drove monster icebergs down on the ship, threatening her with instant destruction. Huge masses of ice could be seen cracking apart; splintering they fell hurtling with a mighty crash into the black sea. It was even more nightmarish when it was still. One giant iceberg about three miles in circumference and over a hundred feet high suddenly lost its balance and with a gentle sliding movement rolled right over, nearly sucking the ship down with it in the vortex caused by its turning.

It was the end of January when they reached the farthest point south. In front of them stretched an immense field of ice while over it glimmered an unusual snow-white brightness. 'The horizon,' Cook tells us, 'was illuminated by the rays of light which were reflected from the ice to a considerable height. I will not say,' he adds, 'it was impossible anywhere to get farther to the south, but the attempting it would have been a dangerous and rash enterprise and one, I believe, no man in my situation would have thought of.' Later on in the day he tells us that 'since therefore, we could not proceed one inch farther to the south, no other reason need be assigned for my tacking and standing back to the north. I was now well satisfied no continent was to be found in this ocean, but what must lie so far to the south as to be wholly inaccessible on account of ice'.

Cook's mission for the second voyage was over, 'but for me at this time to have quitted the Southern Pacific Ocean, with a good ship, expressly sent out on discoveries, a healthy crew and not in want of either stores or provisions, would have been betraying not only a want of perseverance, but judgement, in supposing the South Pacific Ocean to have been so well explored that nothing remained to be done in it. This, however, was not my opinion; for although I had proved there was no continent there remained nevertheless room for very large islands in places wholly unexamined and many of those which were formerly discovered, are but imperfectly explored and their situation as imperfectly known. I was besides of the opinion that my remaining in this sea some time longer would be productive of improvements to navigation and geography as well as other sciences'.

With these bold words the *Resolution* set her course north-east and by the end of February they were already back again in summer. 'The rapid change to warm latitudes,' writes Sparrman, 'cured catarrhs and the tortures of rheumatism as if by magic.' George Forster tells us that his father who had been 'in exquisite torment' during their southern cruise, suffering from toothache, swollen cheeks and sore throat was also much benefited by the warm weather and was to be seen 'perfectly emaciated', sunning himself on the quarterdeck. The change of climate, however, did not prove so beneficial for Cook who became seriously ill with what he calls 'a bilious colic'. George describes the illness more graphically than does the patient himself. He tells us that Cook was confined to his bed with violent pains. 'He took a purge, but instead of producing the desired effect, it caused violent vomitting, which was assisted immediately by proper emetics. All attempts how-ever to procure a passage through his bowels was ineffectual; his food and medicines were thrown up, and in a few days a most dreadful hiccough appeared, which lasted for upwards of twenty-four hours, with such astonishing violence that his life was entirely despaired of. Opiates and glysters had no effect, till repeated hot baths and plasters of theriaca applied on his stomach, had relaxed his body and intestines. This however, was not effected till he had lain above a week in the most eminent danger.' On the 26th Forster continues 'the captain felt some relief from the medicines which had been administered to him, and during the three following days, recovered so far as to be able to get up sometimes, and take a little soup', made, so Cook tells us, 'from a favourite dog belonging to Mr Forster', the only fresh meat available on board. John Forster, generally so boastful about everything he did, here allows his son to write simply and feelingly. 'By such small help we succeeded in preserving a life upon which the success of the voyage is in a great measure dependent.' The sickness has since been diagnosed as acute infection of the gall-bladder with secondary paralysis of the bowel.

Cook's recovery was slow and when Easter Island was sighted on March 11th he was still weak. He sent two of his lieutenants with a party of men, accompanied by Forster and several more of the 'gentlemen' to examine the country. 'I was not sufficiently recovered from my fit of illness to make one of the party.' He could only potter about the beach with a watering party and 'engage in a pretty brisk trade' with the natives for potatoes. What little he saw seems to have made a very poor impression; there was no safe anchorage, no wood for fuel, and no fresh water worth the taking. 'No nation,' he finishes up, 'will ever contest for the honour of the discovery of Easter Island.'

One is fascinated nevertheless and it is through the eyes of the other members of the expedition that one must see it.

[Chapter 15]

Easter Island

EASTER ISLAND, or Rapa Nui as the natives call it, lies at the extreme eastern point of the Polynesian triangle, about 2,000 miles west of Chile and 1,000 miles east of Pitcairn, the nearest inhabited island. It measures only twenty miles from east to west and seven and a half miles from north to south and has the appearance of a blunted triangle set slantingly in the ocean. The craters of twenty extinct volcanoes pock-mark its rocky slopes grown over with grasses that heave restlessly under a sky pale with heat. There are no real valleys, no rivers or streams and precious little vegetation. Troupes of grazing sheep, recently imported from Chile, move across its lion-coloured hills. All is lava rock and grass, a burnt-out landscape peopled by giant statues.

The first Europeans to land on the island were the Dutch under Admiral Jacob Roggeveen on Easter Day, 1722; whence its name. Next came Don Filipe Gonzales in 1770, and four years later the English, then the ill-fated La Pérouse on a similar lightning visit in 1786.

The Dutch and Spanish left their mark on the island, the former by firing on and killing some natives, the latter by planting crosses on three extinct volcanoes on the northern point of the island. Cook behaved in his usual exemplary manner and left behind only good will to commemorate his visit, as did La Pérouse. The island neither benefited nor suffered very seriously from these contacts with the West, but on Christmas Eve 1862 a flotilla of seven Peruvian slavers anchored off its shore, and enticing the natives on board with bright baubles, absconded with over a thousand of them, killing those who resisted. Among the men carried away to work the fetid guano deposits off the Peruvian coast were the king, his son, and many of the *rongorongo* or wise men, most of whom died of forced labour in unfamiliar living conditions. As elsewhere in Polynesia, the native lore was known to only a few who passed it on from generation to generation. In point of fact the Easter Islanders did have a form of script, a system of pictographs carved on boards and used by the *rongorongo* when reading their religious chants, but the key to this, the only known native writing in Polynesia, died with the wise men. Thus the passing of the *rongorongo* proved fatal to the annals of the island's history, for 'by the time modern investigators arrived, much of it had been lost beyond recall'.*

Peru's piratical behaviour did not go unchallenged. The Bishop of Tahiti managed to procure an order for the slaves' release and return to their island, but by the time the order came through about nine hundred had been carried off by illness. Of the one hundred survivors, eighty-five died on the voyage. In the end only a handful returned alive, and these unfortunates would have been better off dead, for with them they brought smallpox. Within a few months there were little over a hundred people left on the entire island.

It was not until the end of the last century, in 1888, that Easter Island was finally annexed by Chile. Under her authority the native inhabitants were confined to Hanga-roa, a small village that had grown up opposite Cook's anchorage on the south-west corner of the island. They were given 5,000 acres for their own use, while the remainder of the island, some 30,000 acres, was devoted to sheep grazing. The total population of the island now numbers just under nine hundred, not many more people than statues, of which six hundred have been counted.

Cook estimated the population of the island at six or seven hundred souls, while La Pérouse put it at two thousand. Métraux, a French archaeologist, visiting the island in 1840, put the original population at close to four thousand, a figure with which modern authorities tend to agree. It had been difficult for the early voyagers to estimate the correct population, for the women, frightened at the arrival of strangers, had always hidden away in caves. Forster noted that their number was remarkably small in proportion to the men, 'there being not above twelve or fifteen at our first landing and about six or seven when we embarked', and these, the young George remarks, 'were neither reserved nor chaste'. They were not the sort of women to be hidden. 'Their features were mild enough but the large pointed caps they wore gave them the air of possessed wantons.' George was very shocked by the scenes he witnessed. 'Messalinas' he calls the women; 'they were the most lascivious of their sex that had ever been noticed in any country, and shame seemed to be entirely unknown to them; our sailors likewise disclaimed all acquaintance with modesty, for nothing but the shadow of the gigantic monuments screened them from the sun.'

Cook, judging by the natives he saw while trading on the beach, found them a very slender race, nimble and active, well featured with agreeable countenances, 'their faces being thinner than those of other

* Ralph Linton and Paul Wingert, *Arts of the South Seas,* Museum of Modern Art, New York, 1946.

Polynesians'. Both men and women, he remarked, 'had very large holes, or rather slits, in their ears, extended to near three inches in length'. In these they wore bunches of white down or alternately 'some elastic substance rolled up like the spring of a watch, the design of which must be to extend or increase the hole'. These springs were probably sections of sugar cane leaf or a strip of bark. Most of the men were tattooed from head to foot and often all but naked, except for a strip of cloth fastened between the legs by means of a small cord tied round their waist which 'by no means answers the end intended'.

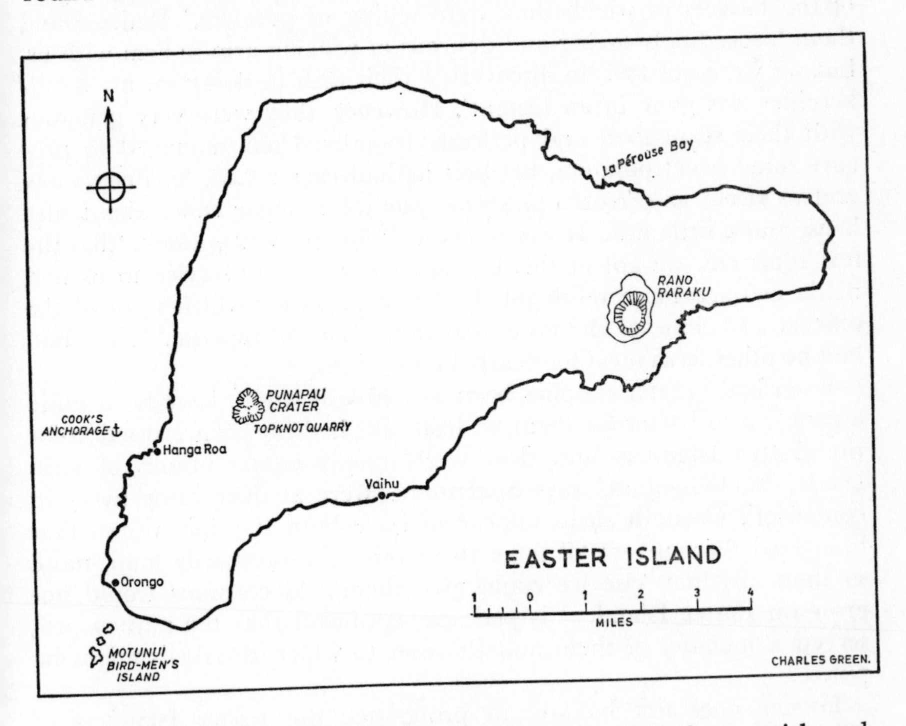

They also smeared their bodies, particularly their faces, with red-brown ochre striped with a chalky white substance. On their heads the men wore 'a round fillet adorned with feathers', or as Forster tells us, bushy caps of brown gulls' quills, almost as large as lawyers' wigs. The women preferred straw bonnets. Hats of one form or another are a necessary protection against the merciless sun, but in addition the Easter Islanders seem to have had a special passion for headgear. Roggeveen, Gonzales, Cook's men, La Pérouse as well as later visitors all report hat-snatching. Duché de Vancy, the artist with La Pérouse in the *Astrolabe*, illustrated a hat thief in action. 'It was with some difficulty,' writes Cook, 'we could keep the hats on our head.' Indeed,

Hodges was unable to retain his. He was sitting on a slight eminence sketching when a native ran up behind him and grabbed it. Wales who was standing beside him at the time tells us that he 'cocked and pointed his musket without thought of anything but firing at him, but when he saw a fellow creature within twenty yards of its muzzle I began to think his life worth more than a hat'.

Cook says that they were not only expert thieves, but 'as trickish in their exchanges as any people we had yet met with'. 'They were fraudulent enough,' reports Sparrman, 'to hide stones in the bottom of the baskets in which they were selling us potatoes.' Wales found them 'exceedingly loving and desirous of walking arm in arm with us, but we were not long in discovering their drift in doing so, my handkerchief was gone in an instant'. However, they were very generous with their scant food and perfectly friendly. Cook managed to procure some sweet potatoes, the best he had ever tasted, 'golden-yellow and as sweet as carrots', plus *taro*, plantains, sugar cane, about fifty hens, and a little fish. 'It was afterwards found,' writes Cook, 'that the few roots etc. we got at this isle proved of infinite service to us and made us once more relish salt beef and pork, for which most of the officers and some of the crew had quite lost all appetite.' They had had no other fresh meat for nearly four months.

Even had greater supplies been available it would have been quite a problem to barter for them, as ironware had no great attraction for the Easter Islanders and they were openly contemptuous of glass beads; 'such baubles,' says Sparrman, 'were at once flung away in contempt'. Coconut shells appear to have been the only things that interested the natives; 'of them they were extraordinarily fond, more so than anything else we could give them'. As coconuts would not grow on Easter Island, it is perhaps significant that the natives preserved a memory of them and the uses to which the shells might be put.

Forster does not hesitate to pronounce the Easter Islanders of Polynesian descent. Their colour, the fact that they tattoo themselves, their use of the mulberry-bark for clothing, the shape and workmanship of their clubs, their mode of eating, all point to the fact that they stem from the west. Only in more recent times has doubt grown up in people's minds about their provenance. How is it possible, it is argued, that so primitive a race as that found by the early explorers could, with only the help of stone adzes, fashion those mysterious giant statues, some of them thirty to forty feet high and weighing up to seventy tons, stone colossi that had to be dragged from a quarry sometimes clear across the island, and hoisted into place on great stone platforms fashioned from gigantic blocks of hard basalt. The working of the platforms provokes the problem further, for the blocks are fitted closely one to another without a visible fault. Even scientists cannot resist the romantic atmosphere that broods over these great monoliths. Various theories have been put forward, even that this tiny spot of barren land lost in the wastes of the Pacific was part of a submerged continent. Thor Heyerdahl, the explorer and archaeologist, has another theory that must be allowed as perfectly plausible. In his book on Easter Island* he reminds us that the forerunners of the Incas had been sailing the Pacific long before the arrival of Columbus. Potsherds found on the Galapagos prove conclusively that they had paid repeated visits to those remote islands over a thousand miles to the north-west of Peru. Why then, Heyerdahl asks, should Easter Island, barely double the distance, not have been included in their expeditions? Heyerdahl maintains that the most carefully worked image platforms, the oldest on the island, are the products of master masons from Peru and argues that no Polynesian could have solved the complicated technique of working giant blocks of stone in so professional a fashion. It was an art practised by the Incas to perfection, and there is little doubt in his mind that they were the original settlers.

Heyerdahl suggests two distinct cultural periods: that of the early monolith workers, followed by a more sophisticated epoch responsible for the elegant, highly stylized sculptures; and then an invasion of a warrior tribe from the west – the Polynesian element on the island – that halted the march of the stone giants across the island. He maintains that this last phase occurred only a few generations before the arrival of the Europeans.

This is only the barest outline of Heyerdahl's hypothesis, which in details is very convincing. Science on the whole, however, rejects his theories and firmly maintains that the Easter Islanders originally emigrated from either the Marquesas or Mangareva farther to the south, sometime between the tenth and thirteenth centuries. Native lore has a similar tradition according to which their ancestors arrived under a chief named Hotu-Matua in two canoes coming from the west.

Forster was equally tempted to theorize; 'It is not in our power to determine by what various accidents a nation so flourishing, could be reduced in number, and degraded to its present indigence.' He suggested a volcanic eruption; 'the devastation which it might make, is alone sufficient to heap a load of miseries on a people confined to so small a space'. But we know geologically that no such eruption took place within an aeon of years. One wonders then, what was the cause, but it is a question that probably can never be answered.

Let us now take a look ourselves at the famous statues, joining the

* *Aku-Aku* by Thor Heyerdahl, London, 1958, George Allen & Unwin Ltd.

party from the ship. They left the beach about nine o'clock in the morning and took a path which led across to the south-east side of the island, accompanied by a crowd of natives, and a middle-aged man armed with a spear who acted as their guide and protector. The country was hard going, barren and dry and thickly strewn with lava rocks hidden in long grasses. Stones had been cleared away to form a path, but so narrow that the men were forced to march in single file. The natives, familiar with the terrain, had a particular technique of placing one foot carefully in front of the other with toes turned inwards and our men, copying them, stumbled along clumsily in their wake.

There may have been trees on the island when the first settlers landed, but it had been completely deforested long before the Europeans arrived. All that was left were some stunted shrubs of the mimosa family, hardly the kind of vegetation to shade a party of foot-weary explorers. The unrestrained sun beat down on the bleak stoniness of the ground with increasing force, reverberating in waves of heat that shimmered above the burnt grasses. The island was cultivated in those days where the soil was deep enough in the rolling downs to support vegetation. Welcoming fields of waving sugar cane and yellow-green bananas spread out over the leeward side of the hills, each tree grown in a hollow carefully dug to collect the rain. There were also *taro* and yams covered over with plucked grass to screen the plants from the sun and preserve what little moisture existed. Cook's men tell us that the bananas were excellent and the sugar cane sweeter than that of Tahiti. The greater part of the liquid on the island seems to have come from these canes, for water was so scarce that the natives were seen to drink from the sea. Ancient stone-lined wells existed but their water smelt strongly of sulphur and was very brackish, covered with a thick green scum. Wales drank from one of them and tells us that the water stank worse than that of Harrogate in Yorkshire. 'Necessity, however, made it go down, and I drank a pretty large draught of it but had not gone one hundred yards before I got eased of it the same way it went down'. Only one fresh water well existed and even this was putrid, 'for the natives had the habit of never going to drink without washing themselves all over as soon as they have done'.

At Vaihu, on the opposite side of the island from the *Resolution*'s anchorage, the expedition came across some long low houses with walls built of reed stalks taken from the crater lake of Rano Raraku and thatched with sugar cane leaves. The doors were so low that they could only be entered on hands and knees and inside it was impossible to stand upright except in the middle. Here the party met the local chief. He saluted them by stretching out his arms with clenched hands which he then lifted over his head and let fall slowly to his sides. He was highly tattooed and his face was painted white. From his shoulders trailed a yellow *tapa* cloak quilted with grass. The Polynesians in general did not sew, but the Easter Islanders were forced to that art by necessity, as the pieces of bark cloth from which such cloaks were made were too small to be used otherwise, the paper-mulberry raised on the island being but a poor, weak variety that attained only a minimum growth. As the island was all but treeless, canoes were assembled in much the same way as the *tapa* cloaks, from bits and pieces of timber, mainly driftwood. They naturally were very unseaworthy.

This chief with his white face was the only man of consequence they met. All the other nobles lay in hiding with the women and children in secret caves. The island was riddled with them, some large caverns, and others what Métraux called subterranean lava tubes. The latter were reached by narrow shafts, built like square chimneys, neatly walled with smooth blocks of stone fitted without mortar and so narrow that they were entered feet first, arms stretched well above the head, and descended by degrees, in wriggles. The last person down rolled a lava block over the opening, a perfect camouflage in the rocky landscape. The natives used these caves in times of trouble, especially during their frequent tribal wars, and each clan had its own secret cave known only to its families.

Forster mentions another type of cave that lay adjacent to their buildings, but he was never allowed into them and supposed that they had some religious significance, and probably contained small carved fetishes connected with ancestor worship. However as the expedition was only on the island for three days, they had little time to gather any concise information on so complex a subject. Nevertheless Cook did guess quite correctly when he thought that 'the stupendous stone statues erected in different places along the coast are certainly no representation of any deity or place of worship; but most probably burial places of certain tribes and families'. When writing this Cook was including the platforms or *ahus* on which the images stood. An *ahu* was a wall built parallel with the sea, measuring up to three hundred feet long and fifteen feet high, buttressed to the landward with a slope of masonry. The images stood on the wall in a single row facing inland. The dead were laid out on the *ahu* and later buried in the vaults under the platform. These were sacred places corresponding to the Tahitian *marae*; indeed *ahu*, as we have seen, was the same term used in Tahiti to designate the high altars of their temples. On Easter Island, however, the *ahus* were the property of the different clans, and the gigantic figures were not national gods but ancestral effigies. Not one of the giants stands in his original place on top of a platform today. The figures familiar to us are the isolated ones deeply embedded in the earth.

These are different from the platform figures and their purpose has never really been satisfactorily explained. Métraux thought that they might have marked boundary lines or the border of some important road.

An *ahu* had from two to fifteen giants standing side by side, the smallest of which weighed about ten tons. The greatest number appears to have been on the north shore, but even in Cook's day they were found in a ruined condition. In one place they saw three *ahu* but only on one were any statues left standing. Forster saw a platform for seven with only four standing, one of which had lost its cap. Wales, measuring one, found it to be sixteen feet high and six feet broad at the shoulders. Each statue, he reports, 'had on its head a large cylindric stone of a red colour worked perfectly round'. Originally every statue had one of these caps or crowns, identified by archaeologists as topknots, stylized after the natives' then current coiffure. The figures were cut from a black-grained, greyish-yellow stone while the topknots were a reddish tinged rock. Both materials are composed of compressed volcanic ash from the craters of two volcanoes, that for the giants themselves from Rano Raraku on the north-east point of the island and that for their topknots from another crater at the opposite end, seven miles away.

A recently excavated statue testifies to the accuracy of the old engravings. These stylized and sophisticated giants, bearing an astonishing resemblance one to another, are unique and have no prototype elsewhere. They are elongated busts terminating in a flat base just where the abdomen ends and the legs begin. The face is slightly upturned and has a protruding forehead, deep-set eyes, and long, pendulous ears.

It is hardly surprising that they have always amazed travellers. How were they quarried and then carried over the hills to different parts of the island? They had to be gouged into existence, wrenched from the very bowels of a volcano, and once freed from their matrix, lowered down the steep walls of the crater. Heyerdahl points out that their size diminishes in a ratio to the distance they had to be transported, which does not lessen our wonder at the remarkable feat. Having reached their destination they had then to be hoisted up on to the *ahu*, and crowned with their red topknots, that weighed from two to ten tons, some of them six feet high and eight feet in diameter, depending on the size of the statue. One thinks of the Egyptians raising their granite colossi and their towering, knife-sharp obelisks. But the Egyptians were a mechanically sophisticated civilization, and these were a handful of people living on a minute island lost in the wastes of the Pacific. Small wonder that the Easter Island giants have become the subject of strange legends. Natives of the island, when asked how their ancestors managed to move these great monoliths, answered that they went of their own accord, 'wriggling'. They knew no more of their actual creation.

The natives, as we have seen, were divided into clans each of which held a definite territory, owning one or more image platforms. It was a regular practice for a victorious clan to overthrow the images of a defeated one. This we know to be definite fact, but why suddenly did the actual production of new images stop? Heyerdahl tells us that more than a hundred recumbent forms still lie in various stages of completion in the quarry, some hardly blocked out, others all but rent from the steep sides of the crater; and still others finished, stand at the foot of the mountain 'like a superannuated army waiting for transportation'. The sculptors' stone chisels were found in the quarries in a manner that indicated that work had suddenly been interrupted and never afterwards resumed. One would like to know the reason. These unexplained mysteries must be unsettling to live with and to deal with the situation the natives had invented another legend, that of an old witch who lived in Rano Raraku at the time when the sculptors made the great figures. Heyerdahl unearthed it and I quote his words: 'It was her magic which breathed life into the stone giants and made them go where they should. But one day the sculptors had eaten a big lobster, and when the witch found the empty shell and realized that none of the contents had been given to her, she was so angry that she made all the walking statues fall flat on their noses, and they have never moved since then.'

Who then were the mysterious sculptors who have disappeared into the dark mists of antiquity? Was Heyerdahl correct in his hypothesis? Had there indeed been two distinct civilizations, one coming from the east to be absorbed eventually by more primitive people arriving from the west?

The tribal wars ended about the middle of the last century. It must have been about 1840 when the last giant was sent toppling from his platform, his red topknot rolling 'like a blood-stained steamroller' down the incline across the burnt grass. The arrival of the Peruvian slaver, some twenty years later, destroyed what hopes we had of learning anything more definite – the secrets of Easter Island were lost for ever in the guano fields with the death of the wise men.

The party from the ship returned exhausted. They had left early in the morning and did not get back until dark, having walked about twenty-five miles, including a climb up one of the volcanoes to view the general coast line. Forster, suffering from his rheumatism, had found it difficult to keep up. A native had taken pity on him and offered his arm for support 'walking on the loose boulders by the side of the path with amazing dexterity; a little boy going before, picking up the stones which obstructed the way'. The party dined in the shade of a huge statue and one wishes that Hodges had made a sketch of the expedition. Forster says that the natives showed them various small images 'made from a wood at present not to be met with upon the island'. They were very impressed with one piece in particular, a woman's hand cut in sandalwood. The fingers were elegantly flexed as if in a dancing position and the nails were abnormally long, a habit they had not observed on the island, but all the women who might have afforded such a luxury were hiding in the caves.

During the afternoon they had come across a surprising sight, a man standing against the skyline with three birds perched on his shoulder. He watched them from some way off but did not approach. The birds were soot-coloured and were called 'noddies' by the naturalists. They did not realize that the mysterious figure was certainly connected with the island's bird cult. The Easter Islanders appear to have been monotheists; a mythological creature with a human body and a bird's head completely unknown elsewhere in Polynesia, was seemingly their only god. They called him Makemake and associated him with the sooty tern, a sea-bird whose eggs and young were an important part of the natives' diet. Each year an elaborate ceremony centred round the eggs of these terns who roost on a rocky islet off the south-west corner of the island. The man to obtain the first eggs became the incarnation of the god until the next mating season. He lived in a special stone house and was subject to numerous taboos. The house was situated in a sacred village known as Orongo, perched in a romantic position on a narrow and precipitous ridge between cliff and crater, overlooking the islet. It is reasonable to suppose that the man standing on the hill had been one of Makemake's acolytes, probably even the 'bird man' of the year, the god's temporary incarnation.

Apart from its mysterious statues, Easter Island was a great disappointment for the men of the *Resolution*. Fifty small chickens and a smart shower of rain that was 'collected by our people from the awning and the sails' were hardly enough fresh provender to revictual the ship. Cook later cites his three days spent there as merely time spent at sea 'for I cannot call it anything else'.

[Chapter 16]

The Marquesas

'THE BREEZES with which we sailed from Easter Island were so gentle,' writes Forster, 'that we were still in sight of it at noon.' The weather was sultry and Cook had a relapse of his former bilious disorder. The difference in temperature must have had something to do with it, the violent heat had come too suddenly. All those who had been on the long excursion across the island had returned with their faces painfully blistered by the sun.

The *Resolution* was heading for the Marquesas. These islands, discovered by Mendaña in 1595, had lain forgotten for nearly two hundred years and Cook wanted to fix their true position, 'erroneously marked,' as he tells us, 'owing to the instruments used in those days'. Alternating between fresh winds and calm, they sailed northward for three weeks towards the Equator, monotonous days varied only by rain-squalls and sun and the changing of the sky. There was no hope even of a passing ship lifting its sails above the far circle of the horizon. It must have seemed a lonely world and often an uncomfortable one full of apprehension. Forster notes that 'we were alarmed to find several people sickening again, particularly complaining of stomach disorders, which are so deadly in hot climate'. The potatoes they had traded at Easter Island were of little help as they proved too starchy for their digestion. 'Nothing therefore remained, but either to return to the loathed diet of salted meat, of which the juices were utterly destroyed by lying in pickle for three years, or to starve on a small quantity of bread, if the stomach could not digest those gross and unprofitable fibres.'

In spite of the physical ordeals there were moments of great beauty when the ocean ran out 'a fine rich blue' under a sky of clouds 'tinged with different hues of green'. On calm mornings the swelling waves were splashed with shoals of leaping fish. Vast and lonely though their world appeared, it was teeming with life. Dolphin, bonito, and shark appeared from time to time and in the sky various birds were at war with the flying fish. Young Forster was interested in birds, and having a real talent for drawing them, he must have spent hours on deck watching the gulls, the boobies and the tropics. The strange frigate-bird must have interested him particularly, those marvellous flyers who soar to stupendous heights and then plunge down in complicated evolutions, snatching at their prey. Sighting a shoal of flying fish driven to frantic leaps from the sea by pursuing bonito, he spirals down out of the sky, and then falls like a rocket to seize a fish in mid-air. But unlike the many similarly adept birds, the frigate-bird is not able to rest on the water, yet he is to be found in mid-ocean, hundreds of miles from land. Beneath his throat is a large distendable pouch. Up and up he flies, his long forked tail expanding and closing continuously, then reaching a certain height, he blows up his pouch which, acting like a balloon, keeps him buoyant as he reposes on outspread pinions in the upper regions of the air. His hollow wing bones also act as air ducts to help support him like a floating feather.

At six a.m. on the morning of April 7th, the first of the Marquesas was sighted, a small islet to the north-west. It was in reality but a large rock now called Fatu Huku. Cook informs us that it was a new discovery and had not been known to Mendaña. 'I named it Hood Island after the young gentleman who first saw it,' the young gentleman being Alexander Hood, age sixteen, a first cousin to the two admirals.

It was hazy and raining when Hiva-oa and Motane hove into sight, great heights of rock lifting above the sea swathed in blackest cloud. As the mist cleared they could distinguish purple-black valleys wedged into the mountains in murky caverns of dank vegetation. These were the strangest, the wildest, and certainly the least typical of all the islands of Oceania. Sailing between the straits dividing Hiva-oa and Tahu-ata, they made down the western shores of Tahu-ata known as Santa Christina in those days. They passed 'several little coves where the white foaming surf tumbles in upon the beaches', and after narrowly escaping destruction from a sudden squall which buffeted them 'with prodigious violence', they hove to in *Madre de Dios* Bay, so named by Mendaña when he anchored there after his run from Peru.

The first canoes to come out to the *Resolution* were manned by natives provided with 'a plentiful supply of stones with which to charge their slings'. Cook also warned his people to be careful, for 'we are not sufficiently acquainted with these men's disposition'. The natives, however, responding to fair treatment, proved friendly enough, though the men in the *Resolution* all felt that given the chance their reactions might have been different.

Everyone on board was struck by the men's looks. Cook found them without exception the finest race of people he had ever seen. Clerke, the second lieutenant, later to become the commander of the *Discovery*

36. The monuments on Easter Island. Engraved by Godefroy after de Vancy, the artist with La Pérouse on the *Astrolab*. (Note a hat thief in action.) (*page 157*)

37. The chief must have cut a very splendid figure.
Engraved by J. Hall after W. Hodges. (*page 170*)

38. A native of Noukahiva showing the intricate Marquesan tattooing.
Forster tells us that the patterns were inked in so close, one to
the other, that they obscured the elegance of the wearer's form.
Plate from A. J. von Krusenstein's
Voyages Around the World 1803–1806. (*page 167*)

39. A sea bird,
an original wash drawing
by George Forster. (*page 165*)

on the third voyage, agreed with Cook and went so far as to find them beautiful. 'Many of them might be placed near the famous models of antiquity, and would not suffer in the comparison,' writes Forster. Sparrman found them lighter complexioned than the majority of the South Sea Islanders. They were the colour, as a Frenchman later put it, of English tea, or better still, the pale terracotta of a Greek vase. Wales is more explicit than anyone and tells us that they were 'exquisitely' proportioned and never corpulent like the Tahitians. 'They go entirely naked except for a strip of cloth which they pass round the waist and then bring forward between the legs.' Quiros, watching a young boy 'with long locks and the face of an angel' was completely overcome by his beauty; 'Never in my life have I felt such a pain as I do now, to think that such a fair creature might be left to go to perdition.'

Few women are described, for as in Easter Island, they were kept out of the way. One enchanting creature, however, did arrive with her child in the train of a chief. Wales describes her as being 'considerably on the wrong side of thirty; but notwithstanding it was in the opinion of most who saw her, one of the most beautiful women that had been seen at any of the islands in these seas'. She was clad from head to foot in *tapa* and very fair, but had some freckles on her nose and cheeks.

Marquesan tattooing was commented upon at length. The middle-aged men were punctured to such an extent as to look almost black. 'Like a coat of mail,' writes Cook. Forster tells us that the patterns were inked in so close, one to the other, that they obscured the elegance of the wearer's form. Only among the youths who were not yet marked 'was it easy to discover beauty singularly striking'. Some of the men were tattooed even on the scalp under the hair, 'and in some cases on the gums, tongue and the head of the penis under the foreskin. Older men or famous warriors frequently had the open spaces between their tattoos filled in until the entire body was coloured a solid bluish-green'.* The ink the natives used for their tattooing came, as in Tahiti, from the soot of the candlenut which is black in itself, but blue upon the flesh, turning copper-green with age.

In later descriptions of the island one gets fascinating glimpses of their dark-patterned faces, of teeth flashing as white as a freshly opened coconut, only the eyes and the teeth being free from embedded indigo ink and gleaming like white clouds in a thunder sky. Occasionally the men had their tattooing done in bands running horizontally across the face, in one particular instance two inches of ink ran across the eyes from ear to ear, covering every inch of lid and eyebrow. From this

* *Arts of The South Seas*, *op. cit.*

seeming bandage the man's eyes gleamed with quick and alert intelligence.

Forster observed that their motifs were all geometric, consisting of a variety of blotches, spirals, bars, checkers, and lines. As in their wood carving, the surfaces to be decorated were often divided into sections, and although the designs within each were different, the sections were balanced to produce an overall pattern. But there seemed to be no set procedure, for one young man Sparrman speaks of, had a tattoo that began in his hair on the right side of his head, and wound in one unbroken line across his forehead, nose, mouth, chin, throat, chest and stomach, ending up on the big toe of his left foot.

The women were only tattooed from the waist down, but nobody seems to have been in a position to admire any virtuosity of the puncturer's needle displayed there.

As with Easter Island the impressions of the Marquesas recorded by the company in the *Resolution* are fragmentary, for they remained only four days in *Madre de Dios* Bay. Apart from the usual scientific observations, Cook's one concern was again the victualling of the ship. The crew were fairly healthy, but stood in need of fresh provisions. They were rather successful with their trading to begin with. The delicious breadfruit were the largest they had seen; the pigs, however, were particularly small, fifty being barely sufficient to give all hands a fresh meal. The absence of barrier reefs and lagoons made fishing arduous and uncertain, but at least there were coconuts, which Sparrman tells us were cut open and a little rum added, 'thus making them more refreshing'. Then suddenly the trafficking was entirely spoiled. Several of the 'young gentlemen' traded a large quantity of red feathers from Tonga, and finding these much more desirable than nails, the natives refused to part with their goods unless more feathers were forthcoming. 'I, nor indeed anyone else had sufficient to supply the demand. Thus,' writes Cook annoyed, 'was the fine prospect we had of getting a plentiful supply of refreshments off these people frustrated.'

George Forster confesses to having been one of the culprits, telling us of the headdress he exchanged for his fiery plumes. We can hardly blame him for his enthusiasm, for the Marquesans' ornaments are very remarkable of their kind. Thanks to men such as Banks, Sparrman, and the Forsters, the cognoscenti of the western world, who had been mainly concerned up to now in unearthing the monuments of antiquity, were beginning to take a genuine interest in the ethnology and the artifacts of the Pacific peoples. A certain interest in 'curiosities' had always existed in the history of taste, but from now on they were to be collected more seriously, regarded as works of art by connoisseurs who could afford to indulge their tastes, such as Sir Ashton Lever who had

FATU-HUKU
(HOOD IS.)

N

HIVA-OA
(DOMINICA)

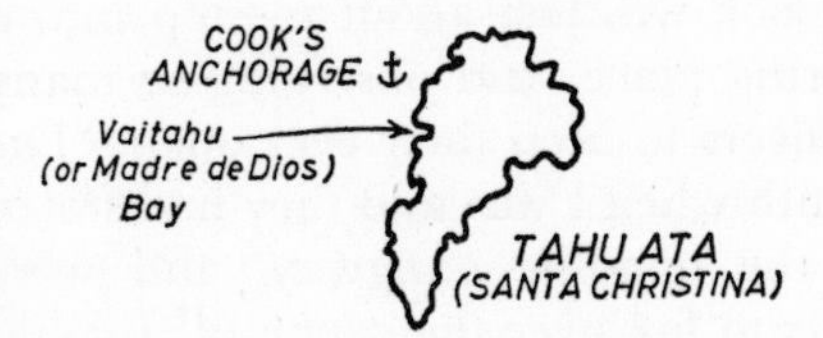
COOK'S
ANCHORAGE
Vaitahu
(or Madre de Dios)
Bay
TAHU ATA
(SANTA CHRISTINA)

MOTANE
(SAN PEDRO)

MARQUESAS
ISLANDS
5 0 5 10 15 20
MILES (Approx.)

FATU HIVA
(MAGDALENA)

CHARLES GREEN.

an extraordinary museum in Leicester House with sixteen rooms filled with such 'curiosities', many of them from Oceania. Cook himself found something to admire in Polynesian carving, and had not the question of supplying been so vital to his crews' well-being, he would no doubt have omitted this note of criticism from his journals. He certainly shared the 'gentlemen's' interest in collecting as is witnessed by the number of exhibits in the ethnographical wing of the British Museum for which he is responsible.

An unfortunate incident occurred on the first day which I tell in Cook's own words for it is typical of his attitude towards the natives. They had anchored and were preparing to warp the ship further into the bay. The *Resolution* was surrounded by canoes and a lively trafficking was in progress, the tea-coloured Marquesans in their meshing of indigo 'mail' exhibiting an aptitude for sharp practice. 'They would frequently keep our goods and make no return, till at last I was obliged to fire a musket ball close past one man who had served us in this manner after which they observed a little more honesty and at length several of them came on board.' Cook was just about to step into a boat to look for a convenient mooring place, and observing so many natives on board, shouted to the officers to keep their eyes open. 'The words were no sooner out of my mouth when I was told they had stolen one of the iron stanchions from the opposite gangway, and were making off with it. I told the officers to fire over the canoe till I could get round in the boat, unluckily for the thief they took better aim than I ever intended and killed him the third shot.' Wales who was watching the scene from the deck tells us that a fellow native (it was the man's son) immediately threw the stanchion overboard and sat bailing out blood, laughing hysterically. Cook went afterwards to the thief's house to try to make amends but the son, hearing their approach, fled. 'I wanted much to have seen him to have made him a present and by other kind treatment have convinced him and the others that it was not from any bad design we had against the nation we had kill'd his father; it would have been to no purpose my leaving anything in the house as it certainly would have been taken away by others . . . especially as I could not sufficiently explain to them my meaning.' The natives, however, seem to have understood Cook's motive and bore the explorers no ill will. The following day they had a visit from the local chief, who, Forster says, seemed to be very good-natured and intelligent, 'a character so prevalent in his countrymen that Mr Hodges who drew his picture could not fail of expressing it'.

The chief must have cut a very splendid figure. He is described as being dressed in a voluminous *tapa* cloak and a turban decorated with a magnificent diadem made out of a flat coir band fixed in the middle with a round mother-of-pearl plaque overlaid by a thin tortoise-shell plate perforated like lace. From the diadem spread a kind of light aureole of feathers, and framing the chief's face, two oval pieces of whitewashed wood stood out hiding his ears. Round his neck hung a gorget of a light cork-like substance on which were glued a quantity of small scarlet beans. These, and the indigo of the tattooing, provided the only contrast in an otherwise predominantly brown and black colour scheme.

Around the man's waist, forearms and ankles were bunches of human hair, plaited and attached to a string. They were judged to be keepsakes, worn in remembrance of his dead relatives, for as Forster notes, everyone affecting hair ornaments showed a certain sentiment regarding them. The natives were willing enough to part with their other possessions, providing they were offered a tempting enough exchange, but not with these locks. They were indeed souvenirs, not of their 'dear ones', but of their enemies, slain and eaten!

As Frederick O'Brien tells us; 'to devour dead relatives, to kill and eat elders, to feast upon slaves and captives, even for mothers to eat their children were religious and tribal rites practised the world over. We have records of these customs coming from the widest areas.'* The Irish, if Strabo is to be credited, thought it good to eat both deceased parents. The Lhopa of Sikkim ate the bride's mother at the wedding feast, while in New Britain human bodies were sold in the markets. The Solomon Islanders fattened their victims like cattle, and the Australian Aborigines ate their fellow-kind as medicine, swallowing kidney fat as we would cod liver oil. In the Marquesas cannibalism was an act of revenge, and since to be cooked and eaten was considered the greatest of all possible insults, the relatives of a person who had been eaten were socially under a cloud until they could capture and eat someone of the offending party. As they lived in innumerable small communities it meant that the feuds between them were unending.

These islands are far from being the tropical paradise pictured by romantic writers on the South Seas. They are inhospitable and extraordinarily rugged with steep, narrow valleys running back to a central core of impassable mountains. The valleys, sealed off as it were from each other by knife-edged ridges, supported from a thousand to several thousand people all divided into clans, the clans of one valley making war on the clans of another. Sometimes, when particularly large, the valleys themselves were divided up into separate parts, the mountain dwellers never knowing the sea, prevented from reaching it by the coastal clansmen, their enemies.

* Frederick O'Brien, *White Shadows in The South Seas*, The Century Co., New York, 1919.

It is from missionaries' diaries and whalers' reports that one learns about the Marquesans' particular form of cannibalism. They found white men's flesh too salty and very tough and could only partake of it when boiled, as opposed to the usual baking in earth ovens. After generations of devouring each other, the islanders had acquired a taste for 'man meat'. The first Catholic fathers had a hard time converting their flock. Among many other things the natives were very puzzled by the communion service. Why, they wanted to know, should they be told not to feed on the flesh of a fellow human when they were urged to eat the body and blood of *Ietu Kirito* himself? It must have been a difficult point to explain.

Cannibalism escaped the notice of Cook and his companions during their short stay but they were remarkably observant of other details. They found the houses haphazardly put together and different from those in Tahiti in that they were raised on great stone platforms, several grouped together, each on its own embankment, facing on to a square assembly place levelled off for dancing. The natives were rather dirty and very slovenly in their eating habits and the manner in which they prepared their meals. Everything was mixed up together and thrown into a large platter or trough, 'out of which,' writes Cook, 'I have seen both men and hogs eat at the same time. I once saw them make a batter of fruit and roots diluted with water in a vessel that was loaded with dirt out of which the hogs had been at that moment eating.' When he expressed his feelings on the subject they laughed at him. Forster, however, defends them on some points, finding them 'particularly cleanly in regards to the *egesta*', not like the Society Islanders, 'who,' scoffs Sparrman, 'scatter it along the paths to the great advantage of the rats'.

Cook and 'the gentlemen' between them managed to collect several good examples of the Marquesan carving, particularly interesting for it attained a technical skill unequalled in Polynesia. They brought home with them intricately carved paddles and several heavy war clubs. These clubs when not being used as lethal weapons served as rests, the club end broadening out into a kind of fan and grooved to accommodate the armpit. One can picture the indigo warriors standing in elegant poses, leaning on their clubs, a silhouette already familiar to one from the Farnese Hercules. Food pounders were smoothed from volcanic rock and laboriously carved, incised 'with rats' teeth, the only material hard enough to cut the stone'.* They were the product of several months' hard work, as were the beautifully cut bowls whose outer surface was covered with complicated rectilinear designs in flat relief. There was a professional class of carvers whose products were much esteemed.

* *Arts of the South Seas, op. cit.*

Looking through his glasses Cook could distinguish 'dwellings or strongholds on the summit of the hills'. Wisely he would not allow anyone up there. What he thought were strongholds were stockaded temples, 'high places' as they were designated by the Marquesans, forbidden heights where dark spirits dwelled and whose only approach, a winding path, was guarded by the demon Po. These trails were taboo and were to be trod only during the dark hours of night by warriors carrying burdens of human flesh. The custom was to erect a gibbet on which living prisoners were hung, a cord being knotted around their hair and passed through their scalps. Their arms were bound behind them and there they swung till the priests sacrificed them as offerings to a deified chief. As with the Easter Islanders their religion was a form of ancestor worship. A deification needed a great number of human sacrifices, 'while additional human victims had to be offered from time to time to maintain the dead chief's powers'.*

But Cook learnt nothing of these secrets in the short time at his disposal. We do, however, have another vivid impression of the explorers before they sail. Sudden squalls rushed down the funnel-like valleys and one such squall caught them returning in the longboat after a day spent ashore. The captain, Sparrman, and the two Forsters had hardly taken their seats when it struck them; 'the boat was flung hither and thither and seemed on the point of being totally wrecked. At one moment,' continues Sparrman, 'we were carried towards the rocks and thought that we were about to be crushed and drowned. It was only the extraordinary address of our oarsmen and their prodigious efforts which finally saved us from the rocks where the waves broke so furiously. My fellow botanists, who were less accustomed to the sea than I, less agile, and still weak from the recent sickness would most certainly have perished. It was, therefore, not remarkable that they should have become paler than any living being upon whom I have ever set eyes'.

Sparrman says that a group of natives were watching their plight from the shore. One can imagine them, blue-black, leaning on their clubs. What, one wonders, were they thinking, or perhaps hoping?

Cook had visited only one of the four islands included in Mendaña's Marquesan group and had added Hood, making the fifth. The Marquesas, in fact, lie in two groups, but the northern group, Nukahiva, was found only in 1791 by Captain Ingraham of Boston, who called the six small islets the Washington Islands. The Marquesas might have passed to America but are now incorporated in French Polynesia. Several attempts to settle the islands have been unsuccessful. The population steadily decreased from about 100,000 at the time of their

* *Arts of the South Seas*, *op. cit.*

discovery to a little over 2,000 in 1956 when the last census was taken. The wild valleys that used to shelter two to three thousand warriors now, at the most, harbour four adults. Unseen the candlenuts put out their violent blooms and vines rampage unchecked over the stone platforms that cluster round what used to be the dance floor of a village.

[Chapter 17]

The Friendly Islands

IN ALL Cook paid three visits to Tonga, or more correctly Tangatapu, meaning Sacred Tonga; two short ones in 1773 and 1774 and a prolonged one from April to July in 1777, during his third and last voyage.

The Tongan group, or Friendly Islands as Cook named them from the extraordinarily courteous and friendly disposition of their inhabitants, lie east of Fiji and south of Samoa, strung out over a distance of about 180 miles north and south with the 20° South latitude running through the centre. There are three main groups, Vava'u to the north, Tongatapu with the most substantial island to the south and Ha'apai with no major island in the middle. Altogether there are over a hundred islands, only thirty-two of which are inhabited. Several are volcanic but for the most part the archipelago consists of low coral islands scarcely rising above sea-level. Seen from far off the vegetation growing on them has the appearance of floating bouquets of green, like lush tufts of jungle that some current has caught up, swirled out and abandoned in mid-ocean.

On his first visit in October 1773 Cook landed at Eau and Tongatapu in the southern group that had not been visited since Tasman discovered them in 1643.

Leaving Raiatea in the Society Islands to return to New Zealand Cook directed his course 'to the west inclining to the south to avoid the tracks of former navigators', hoping at the same time to fall in with Tasman's 'low lying islands much like Holland'. Sparrman tells us that when sailing in new waters they heaved to at night so that 'during the darkness we might not be cheated of the sight of any new island near our trail'.

At sunset on October 1st land was sighted. It was Tasman's Middleburg, or Eau as the Tongans call it, the only inhabited island of the group to boast of a mountain and a stream; all the other islands being entirely devoid of surface running water. No sooner had they approached the land than two canoes put out to meet them, in one of them an old man who was up the side immediately. 'Not a moment's hesitation,'

Wales tells us, 'and there he was, sitting down on the quarterdeck without the least concern.' His companions in the canoe, instead of holding on to the rope and waiting for him, paddled away 'with as much seeming indifference as if they had left him amongst the best known friends in the world'. Presumably Cook had originally intended to go straight on to Tongatapu, the larger of the two islands, but this display of confidence made such a good impression that he decided to anchor here if a convenient place were found. 'This was soon met with, in twenty-five fathoms water about three cables length from the shore, before a small creek.'

Before they actually dropped anchor more canoes came out, recounts Wales, one of them bearing a chief. It was hardly two hundred yards from the ship when it upset. This was in itself of little consequence for the chief left everything to the care of his people and swam to the ship 'without difficulty or ceremony', with so little ceremony, in fact, that he arrived on board quite naked. 'This was the greatest misfortune for we did not recognize his majesty in this trim without his attendants and clothes.' His Majesty, however, was a man of quick perception, and realizing what had happened, saved the situation by issuing some peremptory commands to those of his countrymen who happened to be on board. These were obeyed with such alacrity that it was immediately apparent to whom deference should be shown. Tactful as usual Cook sent down for a large piece of red cloth with which to drape his distinguished guest.

All on board found the island enchanting and indeed it has a particular charm. 'They showed every kind of attention and civility,' writes Clerke which he rightly took 'to be genuine benevolence and goodness of heart, for these people could have no idea of the superiority of our arms, for they never before our arrival amongst them had seen but one European vessel which was that of Abel Tasman.'

In exactly the same place that one wades ashore today Cook was welcomed by 'an immense crowd of men and women no one of which had so much as a stick in their hands'. A gentle grass slope still leads to what is now the village of Ohonua, a scattered collection of houses nestling among trees and joined to one another by sandy paths. The place has an open, cheerful air and one feels that the white wooden bungalows replacing the thatched, woven-sided huts are of very recent date. Eau's civilization is in fact only skin deep, for beyond the first brave display, a little way up the hill, the huts begin again.

Clearing the way the chief conducted Cook and his party to his house; 'which was situated hard by and the most delightful spot – about three hundred yards from the sea, at the head of a fine lawn and under the shade of some shaddock trees'. Forster tells us that the house

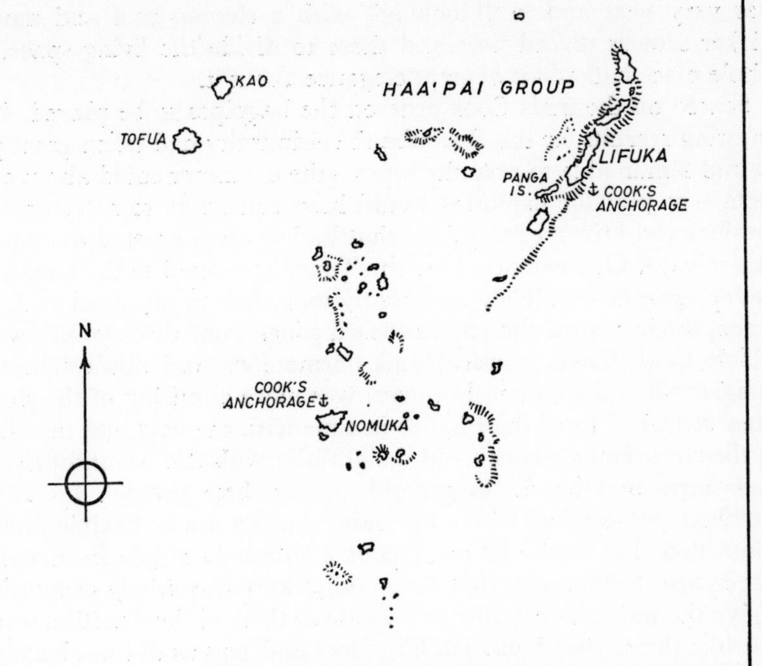

TONGA or FRIENDLY ISLANDS

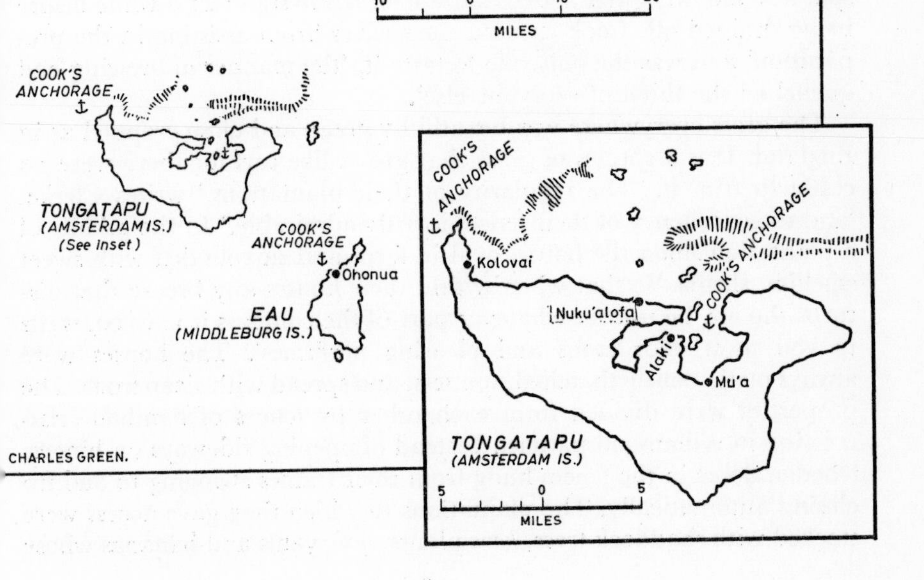

was very neat and 'well-looking', with a sloping roof and movable wicker screens placed here and there to divide the living space. The whole place had an air of great elegance about it.

Seated on the mats Cook ordered the bagpipes to be played. When enlisting recruits for the *Resolution* the Admiralty had taken great pains to find a man able to play the pipes – the drummer could also play the viola – so that the explorers would have some way to reciprocate the musical and miming receptions that had so often greeted them on the first voyage. One wonders how the Tongans reacted to the bagpipes at such close quarters. They apparently took their punishment with good grace, for in return the chief ordered songs from three young women which Cook found 'musical and harmonious and noways harsh or disagreeable'. Sparrman, however, was more admiring of the singers; 'they stretched forth their hands in time with the beat and the charms of their movements concurred delightfully with the beautiful shape of their arms and hands, so general among these people'. I also have watched this dancing where the hand muscles are so flexible and well controlled that waves of movement continually ripple from wrist to finger-tips. Forster says that their bodies were exquisitely proportioned above the waist, 'being fully as delicate as those of the Tahitian women, but like them, they had such large feet and legs as did not harmonise with the rest'.

Kava, the great Tongan drink, was ladled out and handed around, sipped from ingeniously folded banana leaves. Pieces of the root were offered to the gentlemen to chew which when masticated, were then spat into a bowl, water added and the lot left to stand for a while before being drained off. Cook excused themselves 'from assisting in the preparation' and was the only one to taste it, 'the manner of brewing had quenched the thirst of everyone else'.

The grass everywhere was beautifully green and close cropped as in England. It is a species of grass that grows like turf for there were no cattle to trim it. 'The regularity of their plantations,' writes Clerke, 'and the excellency of their fences is truly admirable.' In the middle of a plantation stood the house, oval in form and surrounded with sweet smelling shrubs 'so that when within their houses any breeze that disturbs the air, be it from whatever part of the compass it may be, wafts to you most odoriferous and pleasing perfumes'. The houses were always meticulously thatched, spotless, and spread with clean mats. The properties were divided from each other by fences of bamboo criss-crossing in a diamond pattern. Instead of opening sideways on hinges, wooden doors in the fences hung from their frames swinging to and fro closing automatically. The plantations to which they gave access were stocked with shaddock trees, *kava* plants, *taro*, yams and bananas whose great oil-cloth leaves are very similar in texture and colour to those of the giant *taro*, heart-shaped and ribbed in the manner of the arum family to which they belong. Forster tells us that the fences were overrun with climbers, one of the sky-blue flowering convolvuli. 'I thought I was transported into one of the most fertile plains of Europe,' writes Cook thus evoking for us the poplar-seamed plains of Lombardy or the vine-woven countryside of the Veneto. In point of fact, his description refers to Tongatapu which is entirely flat, but it would have applied equally well to Eau which was far more densely populated then than now. 'Here was not an inch of waste ground, the roads occupied no more space than was absolutely necessary and each fence did not take up above four inches and even this was not wholly lost for in many of them were planted fruit trees and the cloth plant,' the trees serving as posts. 'It was everywhere the same, change of place altered not the scene. Nature, assisted by a little art, nowhere appeared in a more flourishing state than on this isle.' Forster found the Tongan islands far better cultivated than those of Tahiti, but the Tahitians seemed to live more luxuriously. 'We saw but few hogs and fowls here, and that great support of life, the bread-tree, appeared to be very scarce.' The soil was rich enough, but water was scarce. Nowadays artesian wells provide a water supply that is augmented by the rain collected in catchments as it streams off the corrugated iron roofs. In Cook's time there was another ingenious way of collecting it. A groove was cut down the slender trunk of a coconut palm that the trade winds had bent like the arc of a bow and a hollow was scooped out of its swollen base. Trickling down the groove, rain would collect in the bowl prepared for it, but not in sufficient quantities to be of any more practical use than to prepare their *kava*.

Wales says that the roads were as good as those in England. Intersecting the squared plantations at right angles, some of them were sixteen feet broad, 'as even as a bowling green' and planted with rows of palms on either side. 'In these delightful walks,' writes Cook, 'we met numbers of people. Some were travelling down to the ships with their burdens of fruit, others returning back empty, they all gave us the road and either sat down or stood up with their backs against the fences till we had passed.' Forster adds that they always spoke 'in a kind tone when addressed'.

Although 'the gentlemen' had only a day in which to explore the island and so could not penetrate very far, their impressions made me eager to visit it. A government official in Nuku'alofa arranged for me to stay with the resident magistrate of the place in his modest bungalow where one brought one's own bedding and washed in a tin shed across the way. We ate baked *taro*, roots, and tinned corned beef. The same white chickens that Wales described as 'the dunghill kind' pecked at my feet under the table, and small black pigs rootled around the kerosene stove outside that served as the kitchen. Of course there was no electricity on the island.

The night was star-hung and the dawn when it broke spread the colour of raspberry syrup across a lemon sky. Its coming was announced by the clanking of a solitary bell followed by the deep thudding of a Morse-like cadence repeated over and over again on a Tongan drum. On my first morning I walked up the slope behind the magistrate's hut to the church, a wooden shed built on brick supports against the white ant, its doors open to the sea. Standing outside I listened to early prayers. The light was still faint and inside all was tobacco-brown; the benches, the walls, and the cinnamon-coloured heads that I could only distinguish by the whites of their eyes when they moved. The pastor's voice rose to a crescendo of indignant fury, dying down to sibilant whispers, mounting again the next moment, harsh and strident. Hell's fires must surely have been his theme, but one felt that the sermon was not so very far removed from the kind of performance the pastor's ancestors might have staged prior to some punitive expedition.

Harry Terepo, an old Rarotongan from the Cook Islands, guided me on a pony tour of the island, a full day's sight-seeing. Mounted bareback, we climbed the road leading from the village. Four miles out of Ohonua we came to a small Catholic mission of refugee nuns whose entire settlement on one of the outlying islands had been engulfed in a terrible eruption. Conversing across a thick hedge of double-flowering hibiscus, Sister Maria Julia and Sister Marie Angélique told me of their terrible experiences; experiences that recalled the whaling literature of the nineteenth century which is full of references to active volcanoes. One American ship sailed for forty miles through a shower of ashes which the owner had to sweep from the decks.

Beyond the mission the country ran wild under a sky banked with great white clouds. In Cook's day the island had been parcelled out among the chiefs of Tongatapu and worked by tenants or vassals. One can still see traces of cultivation and the sloping land looked like an abandoned park. We rode up a grass-grown road arched over with shaddock trees whose fruit are pale yellow globes as big as a man's head. I tore one open and it tasted delicious.

With the sun came a damp heat noisy with the screeching of parrots. These birds watched our approach and then alarmed at our proximity winged heavily like pheasants over our heads, crashing to rest on a more distant perch, their plumage flashing sapphire-blue, green and red. We had reached a plateau where we waded across a reed-choked marsh and headed across a heath to descend through some woods to the far side of the island. Here under straight and tall trees, which I could not identify, the ground was free of undergrowth but so muddy and slippery that my pony had to pick his way carefully over rotting timber. There was nothing particularly exotic about the scene, but it was somehow different. Looking up, I suddenly realized why: the leaves were all tough and leathery and sun resistant. Their texture precluded all light and it was precisely this sombre darkness that imbued the grove with its tropical atmosphere.

Only ten miles away from Eau is Tongatapu, Tasman's Amsterdam, where as Clerke says there 'are neither hills nor vales, but a fine continual surface, and that, totally covered with trees; so that the prospect is neither more nor less than one complete garden – one of the finest in the world; for all the ground is in a high state of cultivation, and their plantations as regular as any I have ever met with'.

The island is the shape of a medieval shoe with its westernmost point, where Cook first anchored, pulled over like an attenuated toe. The instep is arched in solid land, as is the heel, but the upper part, where Nuku'alofa is situated, is eaten away by salt-water lakes. As shoes go it is that of a giant, but as an island it is on the small side, extending twelve miles from north to south and twenty-five from east to west.

Cook noticed that at the middle of large intersections in the roads there was what he called an *afia-tou-la*, properly a *faitoka*, an artificial mound with a building on it 'like their dwelling houses, with posts and rafters and a covering of palm thatch, the floor being laid with gravel'. The particular mound Cook was describing stood in an open space in a grove of trees where five roads converged, two of them main thoroughfares. Cook was mistaken in thinking it a temple. Instead it was one of several resting places, all situated on a mound with a pleasant view, for important people journeying through the island. The Tongans do not appear to have been a particularly religious people. They had no separate priesthood and the nearest things to temples were large truncated pyramids in which their chiefs were buried. Except for a few small statuettes they had no cult images and their only important religious functions were the funerals of their chiefs and a 'first fruits ceremony' which was essentially a payment of tribute to the king. Cook witnessed both on his third voyage, but does not mention the tombs and remained in general very vague as to their religious practices.

He described the Tongans as light copper in colour with very black hair, except when dyed blue. Both men and women wore it cropped short and brushed upwards, a style they still follow. They also dressed alike, wrapped in a length of *tapa* from the waist to below their knees, a *vala*. Above the waist they were generally naked and anointed with oil. Queen Salote, their present ruler, is very conservative and encourages her people to retain their national costume. Only *tapa* has given way to cotton and shirts and blouses adorn the once anointed torsos. But they still wear a *taovala* bound round the waist over their skirt, a strip of fine matting made from pandanus leaf shredded into strips with a sharp shell and then plaited. Some of the mats are so finely textured that they take months to make, but these are now rare. Cook remarked that these *taovalas* were ragged mats 'that might have served their grandfathers'. Indeed they are heirlooms; the older the *taovala*, the more distinguished the wearer. It is considered bad form to parade in a new one, and they are worn today as formal dress, much the same way as women wear hats in church, or men ties in the city. The Queen and her sons always wear them on official occasions.

The *vala* was formerly gathered around the waist in classical folds but is now a tailor-made product with pockets and pleats over the behind. There is an etiquette that a man's *vala* must fall to about half-way down the calf. The Queen's cousin, a visiting chief from Fiji, explained that in his islands they regarded the Tongans as very old-fashioned for in Fiji the *vala* is a good deal shorter and he laughingly pointed out the difference. With a small clipped moustache he did indeed look much more dashing, the perfect diplomat.

Besides the usual bone and shell ornaments, the natives wore mother-of-pearl and coral drops with added twists of tortoise-shell. Sparrman describes fragile necklaces made of 'small birds' bones or cockles resembling white glass beads'. 'Small wonder,' adds Wales, 'they despise our cheap trumpery.'

Cook writes that 'the same custom of tattooing prevails here as at the other islands, the men are tattooed from the middle of the thigh up to above the hips, even the genitals, I am told, do not escape'. The women, however, had only a slight brushing of the needle on the arms, hands and fingers.

Wales found the women very pretty with regular, soft features, 'but rather too fat to be esteemed beauties anywhere but in Holland'. On the whole 'the gentlemen' found them extraordinarily winsome, but not Cook. 'New faces,' he writes in an unusually cynical vein, 'and new favours add charm to the fair sex which a little acquaintance wears off.' On the first visit before the two ships separated, one good-natured old chief introduced him to a girl 'and gave me to understand that I might retire with her. She was next offered to Captain Fourneaux, but also met with a refusal, though she was neither old nor ugly'. The poor girl must have been quite bewildered. During his second visit to the Ha'apai group the following year a young woman was once more presented to him with the intimation that she was entirely at his

40. Thatched, woven-sided huts on the island of Eau. (*page 176*)

41. The interior of a Tongan hut.
Engraved by J. David after de Sainson, the artist with Dumont d'Urville on the *Astrolab* (1826–9). (*page 177*)

42. Similar construction forms are carried out today.

43. A *taro* plantation on Tongatapu.
'The prospect is neither more nor less than one complete garden.' (*page 181*)

44. The young chief Otago or Ataongo with an amputated finger making the gesture of thanks with a nail. Engraved by J. K. Sherwin after W. Hodges. *(page 184)*

45. The majority of the population are of pure Tongan stock. *(page 183)*

46. The Queen's palace at Nuku-alofa. (*page 189*)

8. Nomuka. Mounting a slight rise in the land
ne comes upon a pool of brackish water. (*page 198*)

47. A view of the royal tombs showing
Queen Lavinia's statue. (*page 190*)

49. Tu'i Malila. (*page 191*)

service. 'Miss who probably had received her instructions wanted by way of handsel* a shirt or a nail', neither of which Cook had with him short of 'giving her the shirt on my own back which I was not in a humour to do'. Cook explained his poverty 'and thought by that means to have come off with flying colours,' but 'I was made to understand I might retire with her on credit'. The chiefess who had appointed herself Cook's mediator in this exchange flew into a rage and abused him roundly, 'sneering in my face, wanting to know what sort of man I was to thus refuse the embraces of so fine a young woman'. The harangue ended in Cook's swiftly retreating to his boat.

It has always been said that Cook never had any connections with 'our fair friends'. John Elliott serving in the *Resolution* records in his memoirs that he often saw them 'jeer and laugh at him, calling him old, and good for nothing'. It may be that Cook felt he had to set a good example, even though no one heeded it, except perhaps Forster senior, who anyhow was too crotchety for such amusements.

The Tongans are by reputation a good-looking race. They are in fact very fine in appearance when young, but later are apt to run to fat. As Tonga is the only important archipelago in the Pacific to have remained independent only six per cent of a population of 60,000 in the island group is of mixed blood. Thus a more or less pure native stock of remarkably uniform looks has been preserved.

Polynesians have always had great regard for physical beauty and perhaps nowhere else was it paid greater due than here where a handsome man was thought to possess divine powers or *mana*. He was groomed for an amorous calling with the care equal to that lavished on an aspirant to an athletic championship. No device that would increase his attraction was overlooked. The dandies that parade in Nuku'alofa's palace square adjacent to the long pier where the copra ships tie up are all that remain of these heroes.

Cook remarked on some other special Tongan customs. Unlike the Tahitians the men and women 'messed together. Nay, I have even seen the men so genteel as to help the ladies first'. One thing that particularly mystified 'the gentlemen' was the number of people with amputated fingers. 'Most of the people on these isles wanted either one or both of the little fingers. We could not learn the cause of this mutilation with any degree of certainty, but judged it to be on account of the death of their parents or some other near relation.' According to Beaglehole, however, amputation was not a sign of mourning but a sacrifice for the recovery of a sick relation of superior rank. Cook also noted that 'everything you give them they apply to their heads by way of thanks, this custom they are taught from infancy. When I

* i.e., the first instalment of payment.

have given things to little children the mother has lifted up the child's hands to its head just as we in England teach a child to pay a compliment by kissing hands'. One of Hodges' better attempts at figure-drawing which Forster judged to express 'the mild character of the whole nation, better than any description' shows a friendly young chief, Otago, or Ataongo, with an amputated finger making this gesture of thanks.

The explorers found only one fault in the Tongans. 'They cannot withstand the temptation of European toys,' Clerke tells us. 'Their finger ends eternally itch to be at work upon some matter that is not their own.' 'They are, however, far less addicted to this vice,' adds Cook, 'than the people of Tahiti, indeed when I consider their whole conduct towards us and the manner in which the few arts they have among them are executed I must also allow them to be in a higher state of civilization.'

Such trouble as they had always occurred down by the landing where the hooligans gathered and where, wrote Wales, 'our people were never alone and unarmed'. One day after wading ashore Wales had his shoes snatched from under his very nose and was left to hobble about on the sharp coral rocks. Patten, the surgeon, suffered an unpleasant experience of the same sort. On stepping into the canoe to return to the ship after a day's duck shooting, he was seized by a band of natives who snatched his gun and most of the day's bag. The astonished Patten clambered on to the nearest high rock to signal the ship for help, but Forster reports that 'seeing that no relief was forthcoming the natives now laid aside all reserve and began to pluck at the unfortunate man's clothes. Patten readily suffered them to snatch his cravat and handkerchief; they also seized his coat and resumed their threatening gestures with such violence that he expected every moment would be his last. He put his hands in all his pockets to search for some instrument, a knife or the like, with which to defend himself, he found nothing but a wretched tooth-pick case; opening it he held it out upon the crowd, who perceiving it hollow, instantly flew back to the distance of two or three yards'. A handsome young woman eventually rescued him, probably a chieftain's daughter, for the ruffians would certainly not have taken notice of an ordinary girl. Forster describes her as having large dark eyes that sparkled with fire and hair that floated around her head and shoulders in soft ebon curls. He concludes that 'her features were more regular than any I had ever seen in these isles, full of sweetness and charm of youth'.

Bayly, the astronomer on board the *Adventure*, reports that the Tongans 'seemed not to have the least compassion for a thief and even rejoiced to see them flogged'. On the third voyage Clerke, by then promoted to Captain of the *Adventure*, put such offenders in the hands of the barber who completely shaved their heads; 'thus,' Cook tells us, 'pointing them out as objects of ridicule to their countrymen'. We learn from another reliable source* that the Tongans considered theft an 'act of meanness rather than a crime; and although some of the chiefs themselves had been known to be guilty of it on board ships, it was nevertheless not approved of'.

Tonga alone among the Polynesian societies did actually have a king whose dynasty could be traced back to the tenth century, but Cook was bewildered by the succession of chiefs presented to him on his three visits, each one in turn claiming to be more important than the last. It was only during his final visit in 1777 that he started to understand the different grades of nobility. He had always understood Ataongo to be a chief but not Tonga's most important man, for Ataongo was not supposed to take food in the presence of two old men, one of whom was so blind that Ataongo cheated by sitting far out of his sight. These old men were known to be of great consequence but were not accepted by Cook as being in supreme command. One evening the officers on shore reported the appearance of a far greater chief than the others, 'no less than the King of the whole island' whom they had found seated in a lane with a few people about him, 'and soon saw that he was a man of some consequence by the extraordinary respect paid to him'. When approaching the people fell flat on their faces and put their heads between his feet, an obeisance called *moemoe*. Cook, properly impressed with the news, landed with his trade bags, 'for my treasures constantly attended me wherever I went'. This meeting took place on Tongatapu where Cook found his 'king' 'seated with so much sullen and stupid gravity that I really took him for an idiot which the people were ready to worship for some superstitious notion. I saluted him and spoke to him, he answered me not, nor did he take the least notice of me or alter a single feature in his countenance, this confirmed my former opinion and I was just going to leave him when one of the natives, an intelligent youth, undertook to undeceive me which he did in such a manner as left me no doubt but that he was the principal man on the island'. Cook presented the seated figure with an axe and a piece of red cloth. Not a word of thanks did he receive in return. The same thing happened the next day when Cook and Fourneaux literally had to dress him when they gave him a shirt, medals and strings of beads. 'All this time he preserved his former gravity, he even did not seem to see or know what we were about, his arms appeared immovable at his side, he did not so much as raise them when we put on his shirt.'

* *An Account of the Natives of the Tonga Islands* by William Mariner, London, 1818. Mariner was an English youth captured by the Tongans in the early part of the nineteenth century.

But on his third voyage when he was anchored at Lefooga or Lifuka, the largest of the islands of the Ha'abai group, Cook's previous notions of the Tongan hierarchy became entirely confused. 'On the sixth [May, 1777] we were visited by a great chief from Tongatapu whose name was Feenou [more commonly spelt Finau]. He was introduced to us as King of all the Friendly Isles . . . a man of about thirty years of age, tall, but thin, and had more of the European features than any I had yet seen here. When the first salutations were over, I asked if he was the king. For, notwithstanding what I had been told, finding he was not the man who I remembered to have been under that character during my former voyage, I began to entertain doubts.' As it happened Finau was a member of the reigning family but certainly not its head. However, he was content to let Cook believe that he was the real king and entertained Cook royally plus, as it turned out, very nearly having him assassinated, but we will return to this again further on.

Some three weeks later, 'about noon, a large sailing canoe came under our stern in which was a person named Futtafaihe or Poulaho, or both', who claimed that he was the real ruler of Tangatapu and all the neighbouring islands. 'It was a matter of surprise to me,' and exasperation, one would have thought, 'to have a stranger introduced under this character, which I had so much reason to believe really belong to another. But they persisted in their account of the supreme dignity of this new visitor; and now, for the first time, they owned to me, that Finau was not the king, but only a subordinate chief, though of great power.' Cook invited Poulaho on board. 'If weight of body could give weight in rank or power, he was certainly the most eminent man in that respect, we had seen; though not very tall, he was very unwieldy, and almost shapeless with corpulence.' Cook was rather impressed with him. 'I found him to be a sedate and sensible man. He viewed the ship with uncommon attention, and asked many pertinent questions; one of which was, what could induce us to visit these islands.' After having inspected the cattle and other novelties, Poulaho was invited down into the cabin. 'To this, some of his attendants objected saying that if he were to accept that invitation, it must happen that people would walk over his head; which could not be permitted.' Cook was willing to have the decks cleared but the king himself 'less scrupulous, in this respect than his attendants, waived all ceremony, and walked down without any stipulation.'

Later they heard of yet another dignitary, even superior to Poulaho but who was old and lived in retirement, 'and thus, would not visit us. Some of the natives even hinted that he was too great a man to confer that honour upon us'. Naturally, Cook's curiosity was aroused and indefatigable as ever he set out to visit this mysterious character.

Chief superseded chief, each one more important than the last. One wants to know which of them in the end could rightfully claim to be king. Cook managed to establish some order in the hierarchy but never understood the different subtleties of their position. Indeed, it took years of inquiry to disentangle the system.

The situation reduced to a simple form can be compared to that found in Japan under the Shogunate when there were two heads of state: the Mikado, the sacred king; and the Shogun, the secular ruler. A similar system had evolved in Tonga. Their sacred king, the Tu'i Tonga, was regarded as the semi-divine representative of the gods, being a direct descendant of the god Tangaloa and a woman of Tonga-tapu. For five hundred years the Tu'i Tongas were supreme rulers, but in the fifteenth century the twenty-fourth of the line, finding the combined weight of sacred and secular functions too much for him, divested himself of the executive powers, making over the burden of temporal government to one of his brothers, the Tu'i Ha'a Takalaua. Some generations later the secular authority was redelegated yet another time to the son of the ruling Tu'i Ha'a Takalaua, who was known as the Tu'i Kanokupolu, a dynasty that eventually eclipsed both its elder branches in power. The Tu'i Tonga, however, carrying office from father to son, remained spiritual leader of Tonga until the thirty-ninth and last one died in 1865. Then the principal chiefs handed the title to the reigning secular king, the great chief Taufaahau Tupou who had assumed the title of King George Tupou I in honour of England's George III when he was baptized by Methodist missionaries in 1831. The present Queen is his great-great-granddaughter.

On his third voyage Cook eventually was able to solve the question of precedence, at least to his satisfaction. The corpulent Poulaho was Tu'i Tonga whom Cook thought of simply as the king, unfamiliar with the further subtleties of his position. Small wonder, for this is still not the end of the complications. There was also a *female* Tu'i Tonga, the eldest daughter of Tu'i Tonga by his principal wife. This princess was known as the Tu'i Tonga Fefine and her rank was even higher than that of her father or her brother. Her traditional mate was a Fijian chief. The Tu'i Tonga Fefine's child, male or female, was known as the Tamaha or 'sacred child' and was regarded by the Tongans as the most exalted being on earth. If this child was a daughter, neither the Tu'i Tonga nor the Tu'i Tonga Fefine could eat in her presence, and when greeting her, had to carry out the *moemoe*.*

One would gather therefore that the inarticulate character whom Cook and Fourneaux dressed in a white shirt on the second voyage was the male Tamaha of the day. Ataongo probably was the son of the Tu'i Kanokupolu, the second temporal king.

* I am indebted to Mr Beaglehole for much of this information.

Cook describes Poulaho's difficulties in receiving the *moemoe*, the obeisance in which the head is lowered to the sole of the ruler's foot. As no one was allowed over his head, 'whenever the Tu'i Tonga walked out, everyone who he meets must sit down till he has passed', as we have seen already. They also were obliged to perform the *moemoe* which, as Cook points out, was very well if the Tu'i Tonga happened to be seated with his foot so placed 'that it can be easily come at'; but it was not so easy if he happened to be walking, 'for he is obliged to stop, and hold up one of his feet behind him, till the person greeting him had performed the ceremony. This, to a heavy, unwieldy man like Poulaho, must be attended with some trouble and pain; and I have, sometimes, seen him make a run, though very unable to get out of the way, or to reach a place where he might conveniently sit down'.

A few years after Cook's final departure the islands underwent a political change. Their traditional complex form of government depended on complete agreement between the different feudal lords and a willingness to accept the inherited right of their kings. Whether contact with the West was responsible for the ensuing civil war is difficult to say, but it would seem more than likely that a taste of a civilization materially superior to their own created a certain amount of discontent and a wish for wider horizons, which to the Tongans meant closer contact with Fiji.

For generations the Tongans had journeyed to the Fiji group, mountainous islands with a plentiful supply of large trees, to procure proper timber for their large sea-going canoes which Clerke describes as being put together 'with such nicety that their seams are as fine as any cabinet work'. A number of Tongans, in fact, were continually employed in building canoes among the windward islands of Fiji. Consequently the Tongans were by reputation the best navigators in the ocean and the Fijian chiefs always used Tongan crews. In turn, the Tongans had great respect for the Fijians, especially in all matters connected with warfare. Young Tongans eager for adventure would engage themselves as mercenaries in the endless Fijian wars, returning to peaceful and conservative Tonga with a zest for fighting and cannibalism and all the other fashionable things learned during their Fiji 'grand tour'.

It was these troubled times that young Mariner wrote about so lucidly in his reminiscences of Tonga, years of savage civil wars which were finally quelled by the wise Taufaahau Tupou who had sense enough to listen to the advice of the Methodist missionaries who arrived on the island in 1822.

King George, as we shall now refer to him, was one of the great figures of Pacific history. He reigned for fifty-two years, from 1845 to

1893, during which time he accomplished a great deal for his country, and adroitly kept his islands free from foreign domination. At home he introduced parliamentary government, established a land system unique in the Pacific under which every male Tongan tax payer is entitled by law to eight and a quarter acres of arable land, and founded a state college independent of the mission. In 1885, the King boldly established a Free Wesleyan Church owing allegiance to no outside religious interest. Previously the Tongans had contributed liberally to the upkeep of their Methodist church, administered by the mission, which in turn remitted a large part of the funds to their headquarters in London or Sydney rather than spending them on the church in Tonga. It had been suggested to the mission authorities that the Tongans be given a measure of independence and a voice in the management and distribution of their church's finances, but the Wesleyans refused at first. By the time a special conference sitting in New Zealand was appointed to visit Tonga, the King had already broken with them.

Behind the King in many of his moves was the remarkable Reverend Shirley Baker, a Methodist missionary who had been appointed head of the Methodist mission in Tonga, but who had evidently decided that politics would be more rewarding than the Church. He had resigned to become instead the Premier of Tonga and for ten years acted as the King's right-hand man.

Robert Louis Stevenson met Baker in Samoa and described him as the only man to have lastingly impressed his name on any nation in the South Seas. Ve'ehala, the keeper of the palace records, let me see a photograph of him taken while still a missionary. It shows him to have been stoutish with a flaccid good-humoured face framed with bushy sideburns and crowned with a large unruly curl, the remains of a fine head of hair. He was undoubtedly a versatile and talented man. At the age of sixty he took his MD, a fact, however, that had not stopped him practising before that. His special interests were leprosy and elephantiasis, the chief scourges of the island and against which we are told he made considerable progress. The Tongan flag, a cross on a field of red representing the blood shed by Christ was, I believe, an idea of Baker's, as were the Tongan arms, crossed swords and three stars representing Tongatapu, Ha'apai and Vava'u. It was also Baker who ordered the material from New Zealand to build the present palace: solid kauri wood posts and boarded walls that were painted white, rust-red corrugated-iron gablings, and scalloped eaves and cornice trimmings. The prefabricated elements were sent down in sections and assembled between 1865 and 1867. A second-storey veranda and the royal chapel were added in 1882. Apart from the palace the only two-storeyed buildings in the town are the rectory and the house Baker built for himself after he became prime minister. The rectory is a handsome building with square, high-ceilinged rooms panelled in varnished wood. False fireplaces ingeniously conceal air-vents.

Nuku'alofa, attaining the majestic height of sixty feet, is the focal point of an otherwise entirely flat country, a distinction that from the very beginning destined this hummock to play an important rôle in the island's history. A redoubtable fortress crowned its summit before King George and his prime minister chose it as the site for the capital, Nuku'alofa, which in Tongan means 'Land of Love'. Indeed, it is a gay little town laid out in a grid of grass-bordered streets lined with frame houses. The mood is vaguely Gothic revival. Picket fences hedge rampageous gardens edged with giant clam shells from the reefs and planted with pawpaw, banana, cannas, and the multi-coloured leafed dracaena. All is white wood and rust-red roofs; Victoriana transplanted to the tropics, a New Zealand-type Victoriana further modified by its subsequent journey across the Pacific. One fervently hopes that the town, unique of its kind, a sympathetic blending of part middle-west and part Cape Cod with more than a hint of the tropics, will escape the usual urban 'improvements'. There is a chance that it may remain unspoiled, for the copra and the banana trade, on which the country depends, is not likely to expand.

A red and white checkered sentry-box dominates the main cross-roads, but it is rarely occupied for there are not enough cars on the island to warrant any kind of strict traffic control. The policemen are smartly turned out in white linen *valas*, truncheon-hung belts, and brass-buttoned jackets. Black sandals and a black felt hat with the brim turned up at one side in Australian fashion complete the uniform. They patrol the precincts of the palace in pairs – not that their offices can be much needed.

Up the way a little from the palace, situated no doubt where the fortress used to be, are the royal tombs. It is forbidden ground but one can see them over the top of a wire fence. Conforming to tradition they are pyramidal in form but capped now with attenuated pedestals from which statues of King George Tupou II and his consort Queen Lavinia, crowned and mantled in white marble, keep vigil over the island ruled by their daughter.

Queen Salote* Tupou came to the throne in 1918 on the death of her father and was crowned in the royal chapel in the palace grounds. She married Prince Tungi, an important noble who was created consort and elected premier to help her rule. He died in 1941 and their two sons Prince Tungi, the elder, named after his father, and Prince Tu'i

* Salote is the Polynesian version of Charlotte, after Queen Charlotte, wife of George III.

Pelehake, took his place. The forty-three-year-old crown prince and premier is an enormous man, intelligent and well informed, a lawyer by training and much travelled. Both the sons are married with numerous children.

They are an endearing family. The dignified Queen, her greying hair brushed up off her forehead, laughs deeply and speaks in a charming voice with no trace of an accent, not even a hint of the harsh 'A' of our antipodes, an idiosyncrasy she might well have as they were all educated in Auckland.

The Queen is conservative and deeply concerned with the traditions of her people. She has succeeded admirably in adapting native customs to the demands of modern constitutional rule. The kingdom, governed by the Queen through a privy council, legislative council and cabinet, enjoys complete self-rule except that the British consular agent acts as adviser to the government in external affairs and finances and has certain juridical powers over British subjects and foreigners.

Wherever one goes in Nuku'alofa there is something fascinating, whether it be the Legislative Assembly's modest hall or the telegraph office in a wood shed run by a handsome boy who confidently counts up the spaced grouping of letters of texts that are perfectly incomprehensible to him. One morning I drove out to see Bishop Blanc at the Monfanga Catholic Mission, a frail little man of ninety with a pointed beard and hands veined like a loofah. On retiring he had planned to return to Toulon but found everything so changed that he couldn't face it. 'The older one gets the more precious become one's memories and I recall my childhood so vividly that I was loath to spoil it.' The Church paid his passage back to Tonga, lodging him at the mission.

The Copra Board near my boarding house was another interesting place where natives from all over the island gather with their crops. Trucks deliver the copra in large sacks which once emptied are rinsed in the sea and spread out to dry in the sun. No amount of washing, however, would rid them of the sweet smell of rancid coconut that permeates everything in the Pacific.

One day at the palace I was introduced to Tu'i Malila, the giant Galapagos tortoise left behind by Captain Cook. He is said to be approximately two hundred and fifty years old and looks it. He is quite blind and carries a much scarred shell, one dent was given him by a kicking horse, another by the wheels of a dray. As he is blind, he had once strayed unseeing into a grass fire in the royal gardens and split his carapace up one side. However, he shows no sign of decline and still topples about after insects and grubs. He was in one of the flower beds when I met him, busy with a large green beetle. He wanders around quite freely and sometimes strays outside the palace grounds, but is so familiar a figure in the community that he is always returned. Doubts have been cast on his authenticity but anyone familiar with the accuracy with which facts have been handed down by word of mouth in Tonga would not question Tu'i Malila's history.

At one time these animals were plentiful in the Galapagos and Seychelles Islands. Ships sailing in the Indian Ocean used to take them on board for fresh meat for the crew, thus severely reducing their numbers. They are now practically extinct. Tu'i Malila has another well-known relation wandering in the grounds of Plantation House, the home of the Governor of St Helena. Jonathan is a good deal younger, but can boast of a fairly advanced age, for he was there at the time of Napoleon's enforced residence.

Tu'i Malila's name when translated means King of Malila. His age has earned him chiefly rank, while 'Malila' was the name of Poulaho's compound at the time he made his début on the island. He is a creature of some importance, for on fête days he rates his own keeper, a fine moustachioed guard who follows him around soliciting your signature in the tortoise's guest book, at the same time giving you to understand that donations are more than welcome. One wonders to what cause one is contributing, for Tu'i Malila must surely be self-supporting. It was not a question I liked to ask, however, at that particular moment.

From a giant tortoise we pass on to another unusual species of animal, flying foxes found in a grove at Kolovai, a small village on the opposite side of the peninsula to Cook's first anchorage. These chattering, furry little animals that are actually a kind of bat also have their own legend according to which they arrived on the island in the canoe of one of Tonga's famed navigator princes – a parting present from a Samoan princess who had lost her heart to him while on his travels. It is said that among this singular gift was an all white specimen. Strangely the flying foxes have never moved from the spot they first roosted in four hundred years ago, and still more striking, an albino appears among them from time to time, a portent to the villagers of an impending death in the royal family. The foxes have always been protected and only members of the royal family may shoot them.

The drive to the village where they live is an attractive road through a lush countryside looking, just as Cook described it, like one continual plantation set with oval huts. Little has changed except that fences are no longer necessary. Arriving at Kolovai one bumps to a stop on the *mala'i* or village green and there right in front of one are the foxes, several hundreds of them, hanging head downwards in bunches from the upper branches of some large trees. Having completely denuded their arboreal habitat and wrapped around with their membranous wings, they look like a monstrous crop of black leather pears. They squeak and fidget through the daylight hours and begin their sorties at dusk, raiding the mango orchards, gnawing at the bananas and descending maraudingly upon the coconuts to bite off the stalks on which the young nuts ripen, to get at the sweet sap.

The Mormon College keep a tame bat, an endearing creature with big round eyes, glazed over in the daytime with blindness. It has pointed black ears, a reddish mask with a wet nose and whiskers, and indeed has something of a fox about it. Its wings which from a distance look leathery are in reality as soft and as heavy as crêpe and have a sheen on them similar to that on the skin of a peach. The brother to whom it belongs enticed it out of its cage on to a stick from whence it transferred itself on to my arm, hooking on to my shirt and at the same time reaching out to lick my bare skin with a tiny pink tongue. There was nothing sinister about him, on the contrary, he appeared very affectionate. Although they are protected, I feel sure that a number find their way into cooking pots in Kolovai.

Even in Cook's day the flying foxes were considered one of the sights to be visited. Sparrman describes them as looking like crows when in flight. 'The gentlemen' could not have understood their special status for they started shooting them, but no remonstrances were forthcoming. Perhaps this was out of consideration for their guests, or perhaps not daring to kill the marauders themselves, the natives were delighted that someone else should do so; for it cannot be doubted that they are something of a pest.

Another of the sights is the assembly of royal tombs at Mu'a, once the capital of the island. For some reason Cook heard nothing about these impressive monuments, great rectangular mounds faced with stone, that mount in steep tiers, and measure as much as thirty-five feet in height. Near to them are villagers' oblong graves of sand with flattened sides. Some are covered with loose coral bleached to the whiteness of chalk and decorated at their corners with floating pennants and white paper flowers. Very often their borders are picked out in beer bottles stuck bottom upwards in the sand. The sun strikes with great effect through the green and brown glass. One supposes that their use is purely decorative and is not intended to indicate the deceased's shortcomings. These graves are contemporary but the royal tombs are said to date from about the twelfth century, as does the Ha'amonga to be found some way farther on lost in a tangle of brush. It is a gateway made of three great monoliths weighing from thirty to forty tons apiece, the smallest block is used as a lintel to cap the sturdy uprights, reminiscent of Stonehenge, but no one has yet been able to explain its significance. Could it have been a symbolical gateway to Pulotu, the Tongan heaven?

Pulotu was imagined to be a large island lost in the mists of distance, lying somewhere to the north-west of Tongatapu. It was the residence of the gods whither the souls of the nobles journeyed after death. According to ancient beliefs, the unfortunate tu'as or peasants had no souls, or if they had them, they dissolved with their bodies at death.

Driving back from the Ha'amonga I took the road skirting the indented north-west coast line, passing Alaki where Cook landed when he returned to the island on his third voyage. He anchored his ships some four miles out in the shelter of a collection of small islands, rowing from there in a longboat to a small inlet cushioned in mangroves. It was low tide when I was there. The foreshore was an exposed flat of dead coral spiked every now and then with fish traps. Some natives, reduced to dwarf figures on the margin of the sea, were shell-fishing. Two boys trotted by on horseback, one mounted behind the other. Their shouts and laughter put to flight a litter of small black pigs that had been rootling in the grass at my feet; their running shadows elongated beyond recognition by the dying sun. For a moment the light became so violent that I had to shade my eyes, but quickly the intensity faded to a gentle glimmering in which emerged a wonderful stillness broken by the regular rat-a-tat beating of women's mallets working *tapa*. Everywhere you go in Tonga you hear this noise and even the oncoming darkness fails to quiet it. At times the rhythmical beats almost compose themselves into a tune. Practised hands, I am told, do sometimes send out messages, tapping them out in different keys as if playing morse on a drum.

I think back on Tonga now to recollect the different things that go to make up my impression of the place. Surely it is the insistent hollow beating of the *tapa* mallets that I hear first, and then the singing. Not an evening passed that I was not attracted by the deep resonance of male voices singing in chorus somewhere nearby. The quality of their voices is quite remarkable; strong, powerful and wonderfully controlled. Their songs are rich and overlaid at times like a Bach chorale. I would wander out into the still, warm night guided by the singing, finding it sometimes in a nobleman's Victorian bungalow and at other times in a simple Tongan hut. I would stand outside in the darkness and listen. Where the houses had no electricity I could only dimly see people squatting on mats, their black curled heads concentrated on their singing.

My most memorable evening was spent with Prince Tu'i Pelehake at a gathering exclusively for Tongans except for myself and one other guest. The Tu'i Pelehakes were a charming couple. The Prince was dressed in a *vala* and a black alpaca jacket with a fountain pen stuck in the breast pocket. He is a large man, not quite attaining the proportions of his brother, but weighing, nevertheless, some twenty stone. It is common for members of chiefly families throughout Polynesia to be large. Princess Melenaite, of a more usual size, wore a dress made from some dark brown batique and a deep shawl. She had a pleasant, open face and like all the rest of the family spoke perfect English.

Their bungalow is situated on the front not far from where I was staying. Like the majority of the better houses it had been shipped out in sections from New Zealand some time in the seventies. The drawing-room is panelled in a dark wood framed with heavy ebony mouldings. Glazed lozenges protruding from the walls take the place of pictures and wooden bosses decorate the ceiling. The furniture is mostly rattan and bamboo. Folding doors lead into a small dining-room which in turn gives on to what one might call a garden room of white boarding crudely stencilled with a pattern of blue vases, red tulips, parrots, and fruit. Two feet from the floor a dark blue dado runs round the room under which were arranged a quantity of carefully folded mats. At the far end a door stood open into the garden.

We were received on a closed-in veranda. Whiskies and sodas were immediately handed around, followed eventually by a buffet dinner prepared by Princess Melenaite and her servants. I remember a delicious dish of *taro* leaves, stuffed with corned beef hash that had been soaked in coconut milk and boiled. There were European cold meats and a pudding of baked bread-fruit cut into small squares covered with sugar and a coconut cream which, when baked and folded in banana leaves, becomes a kind of thick caramel.

Supper was barely over when we heard singing coming from the garden room. My host explained to me that a nobleman from Vava'u was there on his yearly visit and that the entertainment to follow was a form of homage that the chief paid his Prince. This was a particularly musical nobleman who composed songs and always travelled with his own private choir.

We sat in wicker chairs in a small linoleumed alcove off the garden room. The alcove, at a slightly higher level than the garden room, was separated from it by large double french windows that stood open. Prince Tu'i Pelehake took his place on a kind of throne. It was not protocol for him to sit directly in the room where people would be dancing and performing. He urged me, however, to pull my chair up so that I sat right in the window.

The room began to fill up with people entering through the garden door. To acknowledge the presence of royalty, they walked low, looking towards the Prince whom they could not see, and ranged themselves on the matting round the wall. They had not made an actual obeisance but had shown a well-bred deference. When servants approached either the Prince or the Princess they dropped on their knees, leaning forward for a moment before sinking back on their heels.

The singers sat behind a latticed partition on one side of the garden room. We could just see the tops of their heads. The singing was excellent. The harmonies and cadences certainly showed European influence but the songs still retained a strong native flavour.

Every now and then the noble would appear around the screen, a lively little man in his sixties with monkey eyes and a deeply lined face. He would squat down on his heels in front of the Prince wanting to know if everything was all right. Sometimes a man or a woman would get up to dance to the singing. The woman would always gracefully flex her hands. The man, knees bent, feet turned slightly outward would stamp and twist, gesticulating with his arms in a more forceful interpretation.

All the while a girl had been pounding *kava* in the kitchen, kneading it in a large wooden bowl. No entertainment in Tonga is complete without this drink. Tonga is the only island in the Pacific where I actually saw the *kava* growing. It is a handsome plant with coarse-textured, heart-shaped leaves growing on long stalks about six feet high. The roots resemble untidy parsnips and it was the root that the girl was busy bruising in the kitchen in a stone mortar to which she added water as she progressed. When ready it was handed around in coconut shells. It is an opaque liquid, the colour and consistency of tea with a little milk added. It has a slightly stringent, medicinal taste that puckers one's mouth. The little I drank had absolutely no effect on me.

[Chapter 18]

The Unfriendly Islands

TO REACH Nomuka and Lifuka in the Ha'apai group I was obliged to charter a small thirty-five-foot yacht that had been built in New Zealand. Once she must have had a certain elegance but after some seventy years' hard wear she was still seaworthy but slightly down on her beams. Her captain was half Scottish, not that one would have guessed, for his English was monosyllabic and his dark features decidedly native. With him was a young Tongan deck-hand who cut a dashing figure in tight-fitting, very patched blue jeans and a necklace of beans round his neck which at first sight I had taken to be a string of white pearls. When we had arrived at our destination, he got dressed up in a bright red jersey and a large, floppy straw hat, cast off I imagine by one of the missionaries' wives.

Life was simple on board; such cooking as there was was done on a kerosene stove. The fare consisted of *taro* and what fish we caught along the way, generally a species of sweet-eating tuna with silver-blue skin.

We left Nuku'alofa harbour late in the afternoon during one of those hot still evenings with not a breath of wind, chugging into the sunset, sails furled, edging our way forward at seven knots on an underpowered auxiliary engine. Slowly, very slowly, the islands drifted past us, black-green lines drawn against the molten gold sky, mere wedges of vegetation above which exploded the coconut palms like nervous ink splashes thrown up on the horizon. Some of the islands are inhabited and smoke from the natives' fires lay in coils against the yellow sands.

I slept on deck, my mattress wedged in between the companion-hatch and the rails, for in spite of the oily sea, the roll was considerable. A moment before losing consciousness I had the sensation of drifting in space; there just below me within easy reach were the phosphorescents churned up by the prow, an exact replica in another medium of the Milky Way that slanted across the sky above the swaying mast.

Nomuka was sighted at four in the morning. We cut the engine and drifted to the edge of the reef, lying to and waiting for the light before negotiating the passage into the small harbour. Navigation up here is mainly by sight and after sailing in these parts one understands the sailor's love for the open sea. A captain marches the bridge with anxious eyes when approaching Tongan waters where charts are practically useless because the reefs have constantly changed. On to the top of the living reef storms toss up great wedges of coral which can gash the bottom of the stoutest ship. The latest charts published by the Admiralty date from 1939 and these are based mostly on soundings taken in the last century.

Days are not always calm and clear in this part of the Pacific. Indeed on our return to Tongatapu we met some pretty dirty weather, an unexpected squall and lashing rain that cut our visibility. When it cleared we found ourselves not more than two hundred yards away from a bank of huge white rollers. To my inexperienced eye they appeared to be dashing headlong to their destruction on the flatness of the ocean. Only on careful scrutiny does the layman perceive that barely a few feet below the breaking waters lies the tell-tale brown of a submerged reef.

When he visited Nomuka Cook anchored on the opposite side of the island to the present harbour. The whole island, however, is not more than a few miles in extent. An outrigger canoe carried me to the shore where a haphazard collection of unpainted wooden huts forms a village. Mounting a slight rise in the land, one comes upon a pool of brackish water where time-worn trees plunge their gnarled roots into its mirrored surface from which rise veils of miasmic mist slowly evaporating in the sun. Beyond the lake is a lagoon whose salt content is much higher than that of the sea, and where a certain fish, the *Ava*, much prized by the local inhabitants, is caught. On the far side of this lagoon is yet another lake or pond, where both Tasman and Cook watered. No one lives in the vicinity and it runs wild with the usual island undergrowth. Near this pond some of Cook's woodcutters were nearly blinded. James Burney, one of the lieutenants on board the *Discovery*, says that the men gathering fuel for the galley fires were splashed in the eyes by the sap of the trees they were chopping and remained sightless for a whole fortnight.

It is a strange little island, beautiful in its subtle way, but sad, or so it seemed to me. But I was only ashore for part of the morning and possibly this mood was heightened by the fact that the few natives I met were mourning the death of a man who had fallen from his canoe while fishing.

It took us all day to reach Lifuka or Cook's Lefooga, the largest of the Ha'abai group, larger than Nomuka and about half the size of Eau. Islands appeared on the skyline, changed position and slowly

50. Late afternoon on the
Island of Lifuka. (*page 199*)

51. William Mariner in the costume of the Tongan islanders. Engraved by Bragg after Mouchet. (*page 200*)

52. A night dance on the island of Lifuka. The dances were executed with so much skill that the numerous bodies seem to act as if they were one great machine. Engraved by W. Sharp after J. Webber. (*page 202*)

53. A Tongan grave. Very often their borders are picked out in beer bottles stuck bottom upwards in the sand. (*page 193*)

slipped down over the horizon again. We passed close enough to Pangai to see a fat woman with her child and a young man standing by the edge of the sea under some tattered ironwood trees. Beyond them in the distance stood Kao like a giant pyramid rising over three thousand feet directly out of the sea, all the more striking from the contrast it made to the flatness around it. Tofua, another volcanic island, is only half the height of Kao but is interesting for the live volcano that still hisses and steams through the waters that have gathered in its crater. Cook remarked on its flames, and I believe it was steaming the evening I saw it, but cannot be certain for what I saw might very well have been banks of clouds.

There is not much to tell about Lifuka as it is today. I was lodged at the government rest house which provides amenities of sorts. But before undoing my bedding roll I wanted to take a look at my surroundings and a copra truck bumped me out to the south-west point of the island where Cook had anchored. A surprise awaited me *en route* for standing larger than life in a cemetery I found a frock-coated statue of the Reverend Shirley Baker. A watch chain crossed his bulging waistcoat and clumsy lines wrinkled the corners of his eyes which were turned piously skyward. The sculptor whom Baker had chosen duıing his lifetime to cast his likeness remains anonymous, which is perhaps just as well. Poor man, he looked sadly neglected and somewhat incongruous among the clean white coral mounds of the islanders' graves. Towards the end of his premiership Baker found himself at odds with the British Government over the question of a Free Wesleyan Church. Two hundred Methodists, including the King's daughter, had refused to break with the established mission's authorities and Baker had simply exiled them for their lack of co-operation. The British condemned his high-handed behaviour and after a lengthy trial Baker in his turn was banished from Tonga for two years. When he returned, he settled in Lifuka as an Anglican minister, where he died and was buried in the European section of the native cemetery. Alongside him lies his daughter who survived her father by fifty years, a tall lonely figure who barely moved out of the small cluttered house in which she had lived with her father; a fragile recluse dependent in her extreme old age on the bounty of Tonga's Queen.

But these are memories of another age. I was slightly closer to our present interests when talking to an old man in my austere room at the rest house where the capricious flame of a badly trimmed lamp set our shadows dancing over the bare walls. In the morning the old man promised to show me the place where Mariner's ship had been run ashore to be dismantled. As the *Port au Prince* had been carrying a considerable hoard of treasure, the old man assured me that in Mariner's time his ancestors' graves had been heaped with gold and silver coins instead of bleached coral. Furthermore the village where the *Port au Prince* had been beached was called Koula, 'the nearest', he said, 'we Tongans could get to your word "gold" which of course was unknown to us until recently'.

William Mariner was the son of a captain who had served under Cornwallis during the American Revolution. The sea was in his blood and already at the age of fifteen he had engaged himself as captain's clerk on board the *Port au Prince*, a private ship of war with orders at the height of the Napoleonic wars to cruise for prizes in the Atlantic, and if the Atlantic should prove unrewarding, to double Cape Horn and harry enemy shipping in the Pacific. The *Port au Prince* found no ships but did raid the small Spanish town of Ilo in Peru, burning the place to the ground and plundering the church of a rich booty of silver. After that the *Port au Prince* pirated and marauded her way north, later turning to whale-hunting, and the slaughter of sea elephants off the coast of lower California. A leak that had been negligently attended to in Honolulu sprang again no sooner than they had left that harbour, but rather than return it was decided to set course for Sydney via Tahiti. Caught in an adverse current she ended up in the Friendly Islands dropping anchor off the northern end of Lifuka, the very spot where Cook had landed thirty years previously in the *Endeavour*.

It is here that William Mariner and the fate of the *Port au Prince* enter Cook's history. From what happened to them, we learn that while the *Resolution* was anchored at Lifuka, Finau Ulukalala who was pretending to be king of all Tonga was actually only attempting to delay the explorers while a plot to overwhelm and exterminate Cook's company ripened. Cook was completely unaware of his narrow escape, but when the *Port au Prince* appeared, Finau Ulukalala II, who had inherited his father's position as chief of the Ha'apai and Vava'u groups, remembered the coup planned for the *Resolution* and acted more resolutely than his father. The Hawaiian deck-hands taken on board at Honolulu realized what was about to happen and warned the captain who refused to take any notice. A few hours later only three white men remained alive, among them Mariner. Finau II had boarded the ship when she first arrived, and taking a sudden liking to the yellow-haired boy, gave orders that he should be spared. Still not yet sixteen young Will reminded Finau of his favourite son who had died at about the same age, indeed so remarkable was the resemblance that Finau bestowed his son's name on Mariner who thus spent the four years he was on the island in a state of friendly captivity, a chief in his own right with large estates and vassals to work under him. The book he subsequently wrote provides the details of the abortive plot against Cook and still remains one of the important reference works on Tonga.

Cook, as we have seen, met Finau I, or Feenou as he called him, at Nomuka where he was impressed with his energetic bearing and his quick intelligence. Cook had not yet met the Tu'i Tonga or realized that Finau was merely the latter's brother-in-law so for the moment Finau was the great man. He was lavish in sending supplies to the ships, whole pyramids of food were piled up on the beach, not articles of barter but gifts! 'Finau was so fond of associating with us,' writes Cook, 'that he dined on board every day; though, sometimes, he did not partake of our fare.' One evening, 'some of his servants brought a mess which had been dressed for him on shore. It consisted of fish soup and yams. Instead of common water to make the soup, coconut liquor had been made use of, in which the fish had been boiled and stewed; probably in a wooden vessel, with hot stones; and it was carried on board in a plantain leaf. I tasted of the mess and found it so good that I, afterwards, had some fish dressed in the same way. Though my cook succeeded tolerably well, he could produce nothing equal to the dish he imitated.' Cook owns that as no native with the exception of one attendant was allowed to sit at table with Finau or even eat in his presence, he was a very convenient guest, 'for before his arrival, I had, generally, a larger company than I could very well find room for, and my table overflowed with crowds of both sexes'.

As this was during the third voyage when there were two ships to cater for, Cook rapidly exhausted the supplies available on this comparatively modest island and thought to make for his former anchorage on the larger island of Tongatapu. Finau reacted violently to the idea and begged him to alter his plan, 'as if he had some particular interest to promote by diverting me from it. In preference he warmly recommended the island of Lifuka lying to the north-east. There, he assured us, we would be supplied plentifully with every refreshment in the easiest manner and to add weight to his advice, he engaged to attend us thither in person. He carried his point with me; and Lifuka was made the choice of our next station'. Cook was naturally interested to see islands that had never been visited by European ships.

Finau's headquarters were at Lifuka and one suspects that this was part of the plot to murder Cook. Mariner claims that the responsibility lay with the other chiefs who 'envying the rich and splendorous things displayed on the ships' conceived the whole plan, Finau 'only giving consent and advice.... The other chiefs proposed to invite the captain and his officers to a grand *bo-mee* [a night dance by torch light], and at a signal to massacre him, his officers and all the marines. But Finau objected to this, as the darkness of the night would be unfavourable to their operations in taking the two vessels, and proposed rather that it should be done by day, and that they should seize the opportunity of making the attack on the occasion of a grand entertainment which was shortly to be given to him in honour of his arrival. After they were all destroyed, the men who would naturally come in search of him were to be conducted to the farther part of the island under pretence that he was there, and *they* were then to be destroyed in like manner: and thus the two ships, their crews being so weakened, might be taken (as they supposed) with ease. The entertainment was prepared and Captain Cook and several officers being invited were present; it happened, however, a little before the appointed time when the signal was to be given, that most of the chiefs still expressed their opinion that the night-time would have been better than the day, and Finau, finding that the majority were of this opinion, was much vexed and immediately forbade it to be done at all'.

One would charitably like to believe that when it came to the point, Finau found he was only too delighted to have an excuse to call the whole thing off. There might be some truth in this supposition for both the aged Finau and his heir showed great kindness to Mariner, though it must be admitted that both father and son were utterly ruthless if anything stood in the way of their greed and ambition. Anyway, having once decided not to let his guests be butchered, he entertained them magnificently. Cook and his officers had never seen anything to equal it. The afternoon entertainment – the intended scene of their slaughter – consisted of wrestling and boxing. 'What struck us with most surprise was to see a couple of lusty wenches step forth and begin boxing. They seemed to be girls of spirit and would certainly have given each other a good drubbing if two old women had not interposed to part them.' There were about three thousand people at the gathering and about five thousand for the evening dances which were performed in an open space amongst the trees with lights 'at small intervals, placed round the inside of the circle'.

The dances were executed with so much skill, 'that the numerous bodies seem to act as if they were one great machine'. A corps of fifty women appeared, 'garlands of crimson flowers of the China rose upon their heads'. They sang a soft air 'to which responses were made by the chorus in the same tone, all to the accompaniment of drums', large hollow tree trunks from three to four feet long closed at both ends, 'open only by a chink, about three inches broad running almost the whole length'. The chink was turned towards the player 'who beats strongly upon it with two cylindrical pieces of hard wood. They vary the strength and rate of their beating at different parts of the dance; and also change the tones, by beating in the middle or near the end of their drum'. Webber's plate gives an excellent impression of the scene. Cook and his officers with some of the chiefs are to be seen seated in chiaroscuro against the flare torches, while beyond are the dancers, first the male chorus, and the women following later. Cook catches the rhythm for us in his journal, 'the dancers change to a quicker measure, making a half turn by leaping and clapping their hands, and snapping their fingers'. As the pace of the music increased 'their gestures and attitudes were varied with wonderful vigour and dexterity'.

Cook admitted that it was 'the opinion of everyone of us that such a performance would have been met with universal applause on a European stage; and it so far exceeded any attempt we have made to entertain them that they seemed to pique themselves upon the superiority they had over us'. Finau asked Cook to put the marines through their drill – perhaps the decision had not yet been given to postpone the plot. 'As I was desirous to gratify his curiosity, I ordered them all ashore from both ships.' They performed 'various evolutions and fired several volleys' but the military manœuvres were far inferior to the exactness and dexterity of the dancers. They held none of the explorers' musical instruments 'in the least esteem, except the drum; and even that they did not think equal to their own. Our French horns in particular, seemed to be held in great contempt, for neither here nor at any other of the islands would they pay the smallest attention to them'. Cook depreciates the Tongans' obvious pride in their dances and himself is prey to a form of national pride. 'In order to give them a more favourable opinion of English amusement, and to leave their minds fully impressed with the deepest sense of our superior attainments, I directed some fireworks to be got ready.' Some of them did not go off 'but the sky-rockets pleased and astonished them beyond all conception'.

On one of his walks Cook witnessed an extraordinary operation; 'I happened to step into a house where a woman was dressing the eye of a young child who seemed blind; the eyes being much inflamed and a thin film spread over them.' She had actually just removed a cataract with a slender bamboo knife, 'though I entered the house too late to describe exactly how this female oculist employed her tools'.

The Tongans had a rough and impromptu but nevertheless effective approach to medicine for Mariner witnessed a man castrating himself. Elephantiasis of the testicles which one of his friends suffered from badly was a common complaint on the island. Several times he was about to have an operation but when it came to the moment his courage failed him. One day when Mariner was visiting him he was taken with an especially severe spasm 'and he suddenly determined to perform the operation on himself . . . applying a form of tourniquet he opened the scrotum and in a fit of desperation tore the offending article out, falling, not surprisingly, senseless to the ground'.

There were various other cures and treatments, amongst them a particular form of massage where the patient was beaten to sleep. Cook had been watching the dancing, and it being rather late, was persuaded to spend the night ashore, sharing the quarters of the district chief. It was a restless night for Cook was 'considerably disturbed' by the treatment administered to his host. 'Two women sat by him beating briskly on his body and legs, with both fists, as on a drum, till he fell asleep.' When once the person was asleep 'they abate a little in the strength and quickness of the beating; but resume it if they observe any appearance of awakening. In any other country it would be supposed that such a practice would put an end to all sleep; but here it certainly acts as an opiate and is a strong proof of what habit may effect'.

One wonders why Cook never visited the northern province of Vava'u which together with Ha'abai and Tongatapu make up the Tongan archipelago. Always thorough in charting unknown territory, there must have been a reason. It was Finau in this case who must be blamed for the omission. Hearing that the chief intended to make the crossing, Cook had suggested that he join him. 'I thought this a good opportunity to get some knowledge of Vavaoo,' as he called it, 'but he seemed not to approve of the plan; and by way of diverting me from it, told me that there was neither harbour nor anchorage about it. I therefore consented to wait in my present station for his return.' Finau assured Cook that he would be back within a few days and would accompany him to Tongatapu whither Cook intended to return before leaving to replenish his supplies. He lived up to his word and proved very useful for he showed Cook the best anchorage, about three miles up the coast from where Nuku'alofa is now situated.

On this, Cook's last visit to the Friendly Isles, he had an occasion to witness the yearly ceremony of the presentation of the first fruits as well as the celebrations held in honour of the Tu'i Tonga's son's coming of age. They were very impressive but similar to the entertainments witnessed already in Lifuka. There is one last episode, however, that would seem worth while relating before leaving the islands.

Cook had already moved out into the straits opposite his anchorage ready to take advantage of the first favourable wind to get through the narrows. On board was the Tu'i Tonga, invited for his last dinner. Noticing that he seemed to be particularly interested in the plates off which he ate, Cook offered him one, 'either of pewter or of earthenware. He chose the first; and then began to tell us the several uses to which he intended to apply it. Two of them were so extraordinary that

I cannot omit mentioning them. He said that whenever he should have occasion to visit any of the other islands, he would leave this plate behind him at Tongatapu as a sort of representative in his absence that the people might pay the same obeisance they do to himself in person'. A wooden bowl had received such honours prior to the presentation of the plate. The other extraordinary rôle it was destined to play was that of a lie-detector similar to cases one has heard of in Africa. The Tu'i Tonga told Cook that when anything was stolen, 'and the thief could not be found out, the people were all assembled together before him'. A ceremonial washing then took place during which the Tu'i Tonga dipped his hands into the water of the bowl or plate 'after which it was cleaned, and then the whole multitude advanced, one after another, and touched it'. The guilty person touching the bowl died instantly on the spot, 'not by violence, but by the hand of providence'. If anyone refused to touch it, their reluctance was taken as proof of guilt.*

* No trace of this plate can be found, although the present Queen possesses several Cook relics: a bolt of red cloth which is certainly genuine plus two very dubious items, one a ring said to have belonged to Cook, given to the Queen by an unknown admirer in England, and the other a red and white cut-glass decanter also supposed to have been in the great man's possession. Both objects would appear to be some fifty years too late in style to be genuine. The decanter poses no problem for its incongruous date is easy to see. The ring however is not quite so obvious. It is a plain band of some dark metal with a very small diamond set very suspiciously in an indented star-shaped impression surely of Victorian workmanship.

Chapter 19

The New Hebrides

LIBERTIES have been taken with the sequence of events as our last impressions of Tonga are those recorded by Cook on his third voyage. Projections in time have been made in order to shape a more lucid picture of the places involved. We have jumped years and now must regress to re-establish the *Resolution*'s correct route in her course across the Pacific during the second voyage. On July 1st 1777 Cook set sail westward from Nomuka, inclining to the south. By the 15th they were 'in the latitude of Quiros's land', and two days later mountain peaks were seen hovering in an opalescent haze, Quiros's Tierra Austrialia del Espiritu Santo, discovered in 1606 and named Austrialia in honour of Philip III of Spain and Archduke of Austria, and Holy Ghost in pious gratitude. Without further reconnoitring Quiros decided that here, at long last, was the mythical Great Land of the South. His landfall, in reality, was nothing more than the largest and most northern island of the New Hebrides group, but in an access of enthusiasm he loaded his discovery with further sonorous names. The bay in which he anchored became that of St Philip and St James and the river the Jordan. Plans were drawn up for a city to be called the New Jerusalem. It took weeks of continual skirmishes with the natives to bring Quiros out of his apostolic dreams and realize that his projects were ill-founded. Not only was there to be no colony but no treasures either for his king. Disappointed but not yet entirely disillusioned he turned homewards tacking down the coast of New Spain to Acapulco with the holds of his ship quite empty. Nothing more was heard of the Land of the Holy Ghost for over a century. While sailing in these latitudes in 1768, Bougainville discovered several of the adjacent islands which he named the Great Cyclades. He did not attempt to explore the group, nor as Cook explains, did he confirm or refute Quiros's discoveries, 'which is a point I thought well worth clearing up'.

The New Hebrides is a collection of several large and a great number of smaller islands stretching for five hundred miles. On the map the group resembles the letter 'Y' broken into fragments: the left arm containing the largest pieces, Espiritu Santo and Malekula, the crotch

54. Two mortuary heads. The body is moulded in clay upon a core of palm spathes. The head is the actual skull of the deceased overlaid with vegetable paste. (*page 221*)

55. Port Resolution on Tana. (*page 227*)

formed by Efate the administrative centre of the group, the tail consisting of Eromanga, Tana and Aneityum, while the right-hand arm is composed of Epi, Ambrim, Pentecost and Maewo or Aurora. The last two islands were Bougainville's discoveries and so named because, 'I first perceived them with the rising light of dawn on May 22nd which happened to be Whitsunday'. Omba or Ile des Lépreux lies a few miles to the west of Aurora so does not quite fit into the imaginary 'Y' and it was on this stray island that Bougainville landed for a few brief hours.

Cook's first landfall was the mountains of Aurora. He sailed down its western coast zigzagging past Omba, Pentecost and Ambrim to touch at Malekula. Continuing south-west he passed Epi, reconnoitring amongst the small islands to the southward on the way, and swung back past Efate having called in at Eromanga. Finally he anchored in Resolution Bay on the island of Tana, where he remained for over a fortnight to replenish his supply of water and wood. Later Cook passed straight up the whole chain of islands on the western side, that is to say the left-hand side of the 'Y' eventually circumnavigating Espiritu Santo. For many years his was the only chart of the New Hebrides and it compares remarkably well with the maps that superseded it.

Completing his survey of the islands Cook reviews the part Quiros played in discovering Espiritu Santo, mentions also Bougainville's islands but nevertheless Cook claimed the right to re-christen the group. 'We not only ascertained the extent and situation of these islands, but added to them several new ones which were not known before and explored the whole. For the future I shall designate them under the name of the New Hebrides.' One can hardly imagine a less appropriate name for these humid, jungle smothered, monsoon swept, volcano erupting islands. One wonders why Cook who was always so adept at nomenclature chose this misleading evocation of our mist-shrouded Celtic shores? Cook makes no attempt to explain and it is George Forster, recalling the position of the Hebrides in relation to Great Britain, who reveals that as 'this group was the westernmost hitherto known in the South Pacific Ocean Captain Cook named them the New Hebrides'.

A contrary wind had prevented Cook from anchoring at Aurora. On Omba the natives came down fully armed as if to oppose a landing and the *Resolution* passed on to Pentecost. Cook and Wales were too busy with their charts to fret about landing but one can imagine how impatient the rest of the men were, especially 'the scientific gentlemen'. Finally a good anchorage was found off Malekula.

Some of the natives came out in their canoes and two of them were induced to come on board. It was dusk already, so their stay was short.

Their reception had pleased them so much, however, that others came out by moonlight but Cook would not allow them alongside. The next morning the ship was swarming with them. Forster noted that they differed 'from any people that we had hitherto seen', being remarkably slender and small, 'with the flat broad nose and projecting cheek bones of a negro'. Cook found them ugly and ill-proportioned and of a colouring 'between brown and black'. It was his first contact with the Melanesian race, one of Oceania's three great ethnological groups that spread geographically roughly over Fiji, the New Hebrides, New Caledonia, the Solomon Islands, and New Guinea. 'Melanesia' is derived from the Greek for 'black islands' and applies to the Oceanic negroids who stem from a south-east Asiatic aboriginal stock today classified as the pre-Austronesians.

Forster found them very good-humoured and tells us that they chattered away 'pronouncing our words after us with such accuracy that we had reason to admire their quick apprehension. Observing their organs of speech to be so flexible, we tried the most difficult sounds in the European language', even putting them through the 'ruffian sketch', presumably a tongue twister such as 'round the rugged rocks the ragged rascal ran'; all of which they pronounced at first hearing without the least difficulty. 'We presently taught them our numerals, which they repeated rapidly on their fingers: in short what they wanted in personal attraction was amply made up in acuteness and understanding.' Forster called them 'the most intelligent people we had ever met with in the South Seas'.

'They go entirely naked,' writes Wales with obvious enjoyment, 'except for the penis which they wrap up in a very fine fringed case with a string to the end of it by which they tie it up to a sort of belt that goes round their waist.' This cord was bound so tightly 'that it would be fatal to a person unaccustomed from infancy to such an absurd legature', and adds Forster, 'it cuts such a deep notch across the naval, that the belly seemed in a manner double'. Everyone agreed that the penis wrapping 'rather displayed than concealed' and 'produced a much stronger effect of indecency, according to our notion than the total absence of clothing would have done', the more so writes a captain of the Royal Navy in 1850, 'when we noticed that this strange garment has a pocket wherein to depose a pipe, a piece of tobacco or any such article they might obtain by traffic'.

Among the various articles of trade the English had with them were rolls of marbled paper, strange merchandise, but apparently a great success in the New Hebrides. Wales tells us they seized upon it, 'and immediately converted it before our eyes, into a covering for the only part which is covered about them'.

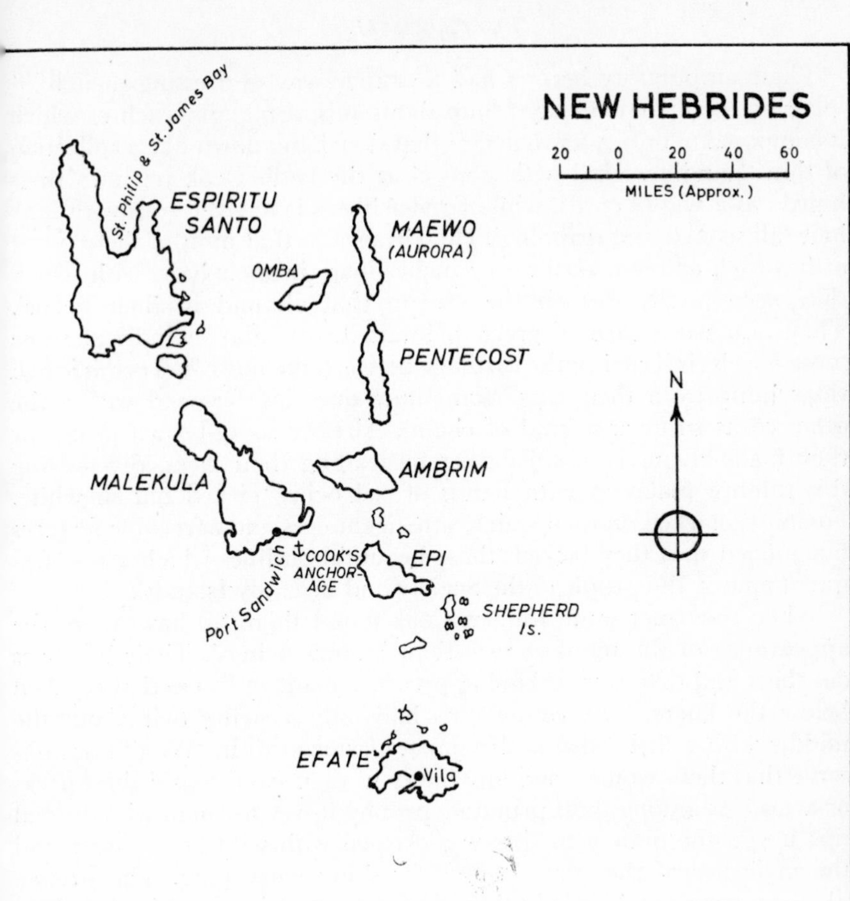
NEW HEBRIDES
20 0 20 40 60
MILES (Approx.)
N
St. Philip & St. James Bay
ESPIRITU SANTO
MAEWO (AURORA)
OMBA
PENTECOST
MALEKULA
AMBRIM
COOK'S ANCHORAGE
EPI
Port Sandwich
SHEPHERD Is.
EFATE
Vila

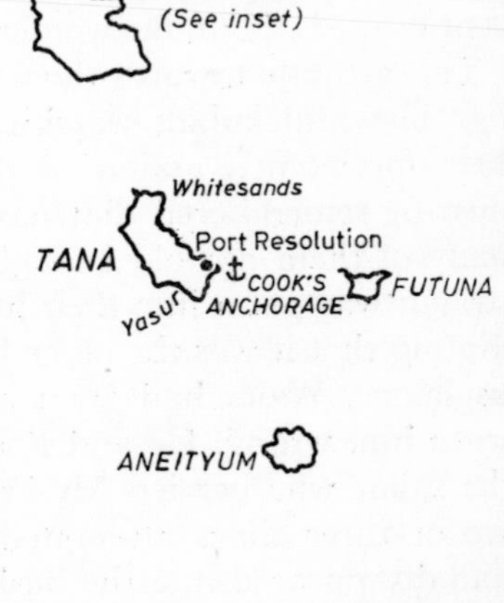
EROMANGA
(See inset)
Whitesands
Port Resolution
TANA
COOK'S ANCHORAGE
FUTUNA
Yasur
ANEITYUM
CHARLES GREEN.

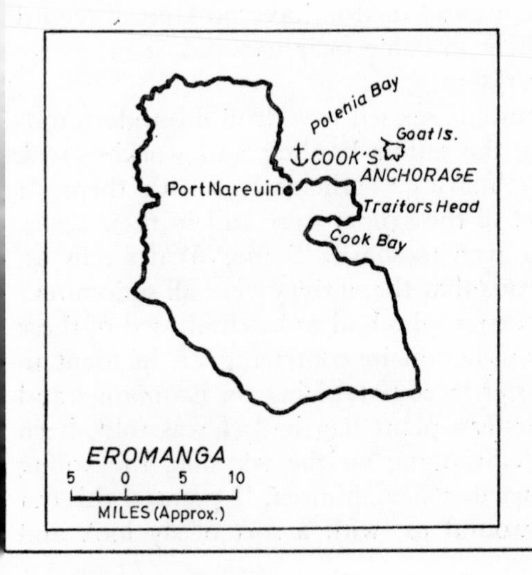
Polenia Bay
Goat Is.
COOK'S ANCHORAGE
Port Nareuin
Traitors Head
Cook Bay
EROMANGA
5 0 5 10
MILES (Approx.)

These ambulatory hermes had a strange way of dressing their hair, 'plaiting it,' Sparrman says, 'into thousands of pigtails, each of which is composed of only a few hairs, so that they hang down like a collection of thin "candle-wicks" with a tassel at the end'. Cook refers to their hairdo as a wig of cords, while Forster likens it to river gods with lank hair 'all soaked and dripping'. He tells us also that most of them 'wear a thin stick or reed, about nine inches long, in their hair, with which they occasionally disturb the vermin that abound in their heads'. They also wore caps of green plantain leaves and cylindrical stone 'nose jewels' inserted in the cartilage between the nostrils. Tortoise-shell rings hung from their ears, 'sometimes one ring fastened within the other so as to form a kind of chain'. Already sooty-brown in colour they made themselves still darker by leading their faces, diversifying this sombre make-up with bands of red ochre picked out in white. Forster remarked on their quick, intelligent eyes and agreeable features but judged that they lacked 'those beautiful outlines which are so frequent among the people of the Society and Friendly Islands'.

When they met some women Cook found them 'to have more the appearance of the monkey race than human beings'. Their hair was cut short and they wore a kind of petticoat made of leaves that reached below the knees. The young girls had only a string tied about the middle with a little wisp of dry grasses fastened to it. 'We did not observe that these women had any finery in their ears, round their necks or arms.' As among most primitive peoples it was the man who dressed up; it was the male arm that was clasped with wild boar's tusks and the male nostril that flared above its shiny ivory plug. The women played a very servile role in the community and were reduced, in fact, to mere beasts of burden. 'The men seemed to have no kind of regard for them, would not permit them to come near us; and as oft as we went towards them, the women ran away.'

This attitude towards the feminine sex led to a droll misunderstanding. The Malekulans watching the sailors hauling and working took them for women and tried to 'ingratiate' themselves with them. It must be remembered that most of the sailors were still in their teens, many of them not old enough even to shave. 'Some,' Wales tells us, 'straightway got it into their heads that the natives were all sodomites.' Hinting that it was the older Forster who had to be disabused of these suspicions, Wales had great satisfaction in contriving an incident to prove him wrong. He and Forster were botanizing on Eromanga and 'the sailor who carried Mr Forster's plant bag had, I was told, been two or three times attempted'. Stopping on the wayside, the young man disappeared into the bushes to relieve himself. 'I pointed this out to the natives who squatted around us, with a sort of sly look and *significant action.*' Immediately two of them jumped up and followed him with great glee, 'but some of our party burst out laughing, calling out that it was a man, on which the others returned, very much abashed'.

What of the natives' disposition? The first impressions could not have been very reassuring as they always appeared armed, and if not openly hostile, were certainly highly suspicious. Cook's landings at Malekula, Eromanga, and Tana taxed everyone's patience and tact and called for a good deal of courage on the Captain's part. The natives on these particular islands had never seen a white man. On Eromanga they were convinced that they were ghosts, and on all the islands Cook says 'they were jealous of our making the least excursion inland or even along the shore of the harbour'. But he sensibly points out that they could not be blamed for their caution; 'it's impossible for them to know our real designs, we enter their ports without their daring to make opposition, we attempt to land in a peaceable manner, if this succeeds it's well, if not we land nevertheless and maintain the footing we thus got by the superiority of our fire arms. In what other light can they then at first look upon us but as invaders of their country; time and some acquaintance with us can only convince them of the mistake.'

That first morning at Malekula there were more natives on board than they could cope with. Cook took some of them into the cabin while the others wandered over the ship even climbing up the shrouds to the masthead. A drawing by Hodges reproduced in the account of the voyage captures the scene but Forster regretted that the engraver thought it necessary to drape the natives.

All was going very well until a boat-keeper refused to allow a native into the pinnace tethered alongside. The islander was fitting an arrow to his bow to shoot the sailor when Cook appeared hurriedly on deck. In fairness to the natives it must be said that his companions were doing their utmost to calm the troublemaker. Cook called out hoping to help but instead the man swung round and pointed his bow at him and was just going to let fly when Cook gave him a peppering of small shot, discharged, Wales tells us, into his face and shoulders. The man just wiped his hand across his face and re-aimed. Again Cook shot at him and this time succeeded in making him drop his bow. Several arrows were shot into the ship and a general confusion among the natives on board followed. The firing of a big four-pounder into the trees accelerated the retreat. Those in the cabin leapt out of the windows while the men nearest the ship jumped out of their canoes and swam ashore. Cook tells us that immediately after the gun was fired they heard drums beating on the shore, 'probably the signal for the country to assemble in arms. After this we took no further notice of them, but suffered them to come and pick up their canoes', while according to Forster, 'we went quietly to breakfast'.

As the *Resolution* badly needed fuel for the galley fires, Cook was resolved to attempt a landing in spite of the fray. Taking two boats, accompanied by his officers and the marines, they made for the shore. It was low tide so they had to wade to the beach. Without a moment's hesitation Cook handed his gun over and stepped into the water and walked towards the natives. There were about a hundred of them fully armed and silently waiting. Wales who was watching through the glasses says that 'when they saw him advance alone without arms, one who seemed to be a principal man amongst them gave his bow and arrows to another and came into the water to meet him, spreading his arms open as if to receive him; and when they met took Cook by the hand and led him on shore'. It took great courage on Cook's part to behave so trustingly and it is small wonder that his men had such immense respect for him. Cook mentions none of these details in his journal.

They procured the wood but little else. A small pig was brought down and presented to Cook. 'This gave us hope,' he writes, 'that a trade would soon be opened for refreshments but we were mistaken, this pig came on some other account, probably as a peace offering, for all that we could say or do did not prevail upon them to bring us above half a dozen coconuts and a small quantity of fresh water.' The natives appeared to be tolerably well provided for themselves so this 'careful economy, stinginess or unconcern' could not be explained until they reached Tana.

The *Resolution* put to sea, 'to take advantage', as Cook puts it, 'of the moonlight nights which now happened'. Supplies or not, the task of exploring and charting an unknown archipelago had to proceed. It must have been hard on the hungry men to watch the deliciously verdant islands slide by. They sailed right up to Ambrim, Paama, Epi and a whole constellation of little islands named the Shepherd Isles by Cook, 'in honour of my worthy friend Dr Shepherd, Professor of Astronomy at Cambridge'. Skirting their shores, they recorded their contours and sailed away again. The close, ill-smelling cabins must have been intolerable and the salt provisions quite loathsome, particularly difficult to stomach in this hot weather when they caused a raging thirst. Every day a net was hung overboard containing the salt meat for dinner, to trail astern in the sea in order to freshen it. 'Sharks,' writes Forster, 'do not offer a very palatable food but they were at all times preferable to what we had, and necessity taught us to relish them.' One huge shark they caught had in his maw 'no less than four young turtles, two large cuttlefish and the feathers and skeleton of a small booby . . . the sailors had no sooner hauled him on deck than everyone drew his knife and in a few moments divided him into small pieces which they hastened to dress and devour. One of the sharks making some resistance on being hauled up was shot dead by our officers who were equally concerned with the rest of their shipmates to prevent his escape'.

John Elliott, a fifteen-year-old midshipman, caught what the men described as two red sea breams which have since been identified as the *Lutianus bohar*, a handsome fish usually weighing from twelve to fifteen pounds but which can grow to a much greater size. He generously presented one of them to the officers' mess and by so doing nearly killed the lot of them. Cook tells us that 'everyone who ate of these fish were seiz'd with violent pains in the head and limbs so as to be unable to stand'. A hog which had been fed on the garbage showed similar symptoms, swelled to a great size, and died in the night. Several dogs, Forster adds, 'having received a share of the entrails and some being fed upon parts of the boiled fish were affected in the same manner; they groaned most pitifully, had violent reaching and could hardly drag their limbs about. A little favourite perroquet from the Friendly Isles which familiarly hopped on to its master's shoulders, having likewise tasted a morsel, died the next day. The only comfort in this misfortune was that our surgeon had dined with the captain this day, and by that means escaped the fate of his messmates'. Cook thought that it must have been the same sort of fish that poisoned the crews of Quiros's ships. The men were sick for days and 'our ships,' writes Forster, 'now perfectly resembled an hospital.' The patients were in a deplorable state, 'they continued to have gripes and acute pains in all their bones, the skin peeled off their swollen and reddened faces and they broke out in a painful rash'. Those who had been less afflicted 'crawled about the decks, emaciated to mere shadows. There was not one lieutenant able to do duty; and as one of the mates and several of the midshipmen were likewise ill, the watches were commanded by the gunner and other mates'.

It must have been a worrying time for Cook. To aggravate matters in this particularly difficult stretch of navigation, they fell in with a series of calms, the ship lying like a log on the water. On another occasion they were caught in a current that all but drove them ashore, sternways. The current was so strong 'that hoisting out our boats would scarcely have availed us anything'.

Then the men caught more of the poisonous fish. 'I wished particularly to draw and describe them,' writes the young Forster, 'in order to enable future navigators to be on their guard.' He did not get a chance, for no sooner landed than they were salted and peppered, and downed by the crew, greedy for anything so long as it was fresh. One would think that their recent experience would have made them more cautious, but the fact that they had boiled a silver spoon in the water with the fish and that it had not turned black was apparently proof enough to the famished sailors that they were good eating, and it was their opinion that the fish were not actually poisonous in themselves but had been feeding on something noxious such as mangrove seeds. *Lutianus bohar* are in fact highly toxic depending on their size. Young ones can sometimes be eaten with complete impunity. Forster was so upset at having the specimen snatched from under his nose that he fails even to describe the fish, which is fancifully pink-bellied and blue-backed and on dying turns bright vermilion.

About ten one morning a fire broke out in the ship. 'Confusion and horror,' writes Forster, 'appeared on all our faces at the bare mention of it.' Cook does not even refer to the incident as it was not very serious. Somebody had carelessly upset a lighted candle on the *tapa* folded away in the store-room causing a good deal of fumes and smoke. 'Our gallant captain,' writes Sparrman, 'had hastened to the quenching of the fire and returned looking pale; and how would it be otherwise for him who had the responsibility for everything?'

More worrying for Cook than the fire was an attempted landing on Eromanga. As was usual the *Resolution* had anchored about half a mile out. Some little way behind rose a precipitous rock, subsequently known as Goat Isle. Before them stretched a wide sweep of coast protected by a great head of land forming a sheltered bay. On the far side of this promontory, which Cook was to christen Traitor's Head, lies a much deeper bay misleadingly bearing his name. Polenia is the bay where he actually anchored and the village of Port Narevin marks the spot where he landed.

Today a crudely built wall of coral rocks separates the huts from the beach. The village, a sympathetic place sheltered by the arched limbs of huge trees, is certainly of a more recent date, for Cook makes no mention of houses. However, it perfectly fits his account of other straggling villages in these islands. The dwellings need no other description than to compare them to the roof of a thatched house that has been taken off the walls and placed on the ground. Some are open at both ends and others partly closed with plaited screens of wild cane. When I visited the place the evening fires had just been lighted and smoke seeped through the tidily constructed walls, drifting up in aromatic coils, filtering through the big trees. Native villages in the Pacific appear to be totally deserted during the day. Only pigs give any indication that the place is inhabited. But as dusk thickens, shadowy forms

56. A New Hebridean showing the strange way the men plaited their hair and striped their faces. Engraved by J. Basire after W. Hodges. (*page* 210)

58. Eromanga today. The beach where Cook attempted his landing. (*page* 214)

57. The landing at Eromanga. Engraved by J. K. Sherwin after W. Hodges. (*page* 215)

59. The poisonous *Lutianus bohar*. (*page* 213)

60. One of the slit gongs. (*page* 221)

detach themselves from the forest, small bands on their way down from the plantations in the hills. The volcanic soil is so rich in the New Hebrides that no manure is used in cultivation. When the soil becomes exhausted they just move on to new land so that in time the plantations lie quite some distance from the village. I climbed up to visit these untidy plots in the jungle. They are cleared by firing with the result that the fields are dotted with half-charred tree trunks in between which have been stuck a collection of edible plants such as banana and *taro* with a small red flowering canna thrown into the confusion every now and then.

This, however, was not Cook's impression of Eromanga for he was never able to land. Taking two boats he had set out at daybreak to investigate the coast. Natives signalling him ashore aroused his suspicion, but he does not explain why. 'The natives,' he says, 'ran along the shore keeping always abreast of the boats and at last directed us to a place, a sandy beach, where I could step out of the boat without wetting a foot. I landed in the face of a great multitude with nothing but a green branch in my hand.' The natives were all armed but seemed civil enough. He made signs for fresh water and food and was given drink from a hollow bamboo and handed some baked yams. His concern was to feed the whole ship not just himself, but the natives did not understand or did not choose to do so. Watching a man he imagined to be their chief, Cook became alarmed. The chief wanted to haul the boats up on to the beach, 'but I gave him to understand that I must first go on board and then I would return – and so stepped into the boat and ordered her to be put off, but they were not for parting with us so soon'. The natives rushed forward letting off a shower of arrows, spears, and stones, superficially wounding two of the crew and grabbing a pair of the oars. 'Our own safety became now the only consideration and yet I was loath to fire upon such a multitude and resolved to make the chief alone fall a victim to his own treachery.' Cook levelled his musket but the piece misfired, 'which made it absolutely necessary for me to give orders to fire'. Narom, the chief, was killed and three other men wounded. 'Happily for these poor people not half our muskets would go off otherwise many more must have fallen.'

Forster complains bitterly about the muskets' constantly misfiring; 'it is remarkable that though the best flints are to be had in England, and though the government allows the highest price for them to the contractors, yet are our troops supplied with the very worst flints by these people, who use every means to amass a fortune at the expense of the public'. He adds that foreigners watching manœuvres in Hyde Park were constantly remarking on the poor quality of the arms.

On first sight this seems to have been nothing more than an attempt to seize the boats, but the reasons for the natives' attacking Cook are nowadays thought to have been connected with their superstitious fears. According to these beliefs the dead were as real to them as the living. Their world was peopled with ancestral ghosts who took a benevolent interest in their welfare or inimical ghosts of some hostile tribe or some foreign influence. A major problem in life, therefore, was to keep safe from evil spirits. They had seen the *Resolution* appear suddenly over the horizon as if from the sky and afterwards her boats coming, it would seem, from the direction of Goat Island, a place of the dead where no one ever ventured. As they approached the Englishmen's white faces could be distinguished, the first the natives had ever seen. How could they be anything but ghosts, and surely malicious ones at that? 'The panic-stricken Eromangans were determined to get rid of their visitors at any cost. If ghosts would have departed for the price of water, well and good, but there was only one small stream at Port Narevin and that was nearly dry.'* So they had to be fought off. Had Cook known that he had been taken for an inimical ghost, he perhaps might not have named the great point separating the two bays Traitor's Head.

Both Forster and Cook comment on the force with which the natives hurled their javelins. They could hit a target at the distance of sixty yards, the barbed head penetrating far into the surface of the hardest wood. They had also watched them practise with their bows when they first landed at Malekula. The bows were very strong and elastic and the arrow sharply pointed with bone which had been coated in poison, a dark gummy substance that the natives maintained was so virulent that the slightest scratch was fatal. The surgeon bandaged a quantity of the stuff into a deep incision in the thigh of a Tahitian dog. The dog limped slightly for a day or two, but otherwise was perfectly all right. The poison was purely psychological. Steeped in the juice of certain herbs and smeared with dirt the arrow heads might conceivably have inflicted tetanus, but no other concrete ill. Cook never realized that the bone of the arrow heads was charmed human bone, which was the really deadly quality of the arrow as far as the natives were concerned. All human relics were thought to be charged with magic and could either be benevolent or malevolent in their influence. To have the very bone of some 'debble-debble' plunged into you was naturally fatal.

* J. C. Beaglehole.

[Chapter 20]

Tana

LEAVING EROMANGA Cook sailed south towards Tana. They had been attracted by a red glow on the horizon which as they approached, proved to be the fires of an active volcano, a low conical hill at the foot of the mountains that piled up towards the south-eastern corner of the island. Every five minutes it erupted sending up a column of heavy smoke, 'like a large tree', describes Forster, 'whose crown gradually spreads as it ascends'. The smoke changed in colour from a yellowish white to dirty reddish grey to brown, depending on the intensity of the fire in its crater. The whole vine-choked countryside was tinged with lurid lights. Not more than a few miles from this perpetual beacon the explorers found an ideal harbour, 'small and snug' and conveniently near to water.

Warped in close to the shore the *Resolution* was made fast with her guns trained on to the beach. It was to be the only anchorage in these islands where they stayed any length of time. Water and fuel were plentiful but Forster grumbled that 'it was very disagreeable to be tantalized with the sight of wholesome vegetables and animal food, with which the natives did not choose to supply us'. Once a train of twenty men wound down from the hills with a load of plantains, yams and *taro* roots hardly sufficient to burden two men. Cook supposed that it had been spaced out like this to make their offerings seem less frugal. He took great care that the natives always had something in return for what they brought, though he noticed that 'whenever we presented a bead, a nail or ribbon to the people they refused to accept it, but desired us to lay it down and then took it up in a leaf'. 'Whether this was owing to some superstitious notion or to a fanciful idea of cleanliness or of civility' remained in doubt to Forster.

Here as at Eromanga Cook and his crew must have been taken for ghosts, probably the spirits of some long dead ancestors, not necesarily malevolent, but ghosts just the same and therefore subject to various taboos. This would explain the short rations, as offerings to ancestors were always small and of inferior quality. The file of men obviously were performing some religious rite and the food they brought represented a token offering, nourishment intended for ethereal beings not live hungry men. The puzzled natives had no precedent for what form of reception, if any, should be given spirits housed in a wooden world shrouded in great white sails. Cook sensed their hesitation or, as he put it, the delicate balance between war and peace, and firmly relieved them of their indecision by giving them no choice in the matter.

No sooner was the *Resolution* laid broadside to the shore than Cook ordered some muskets to be fired over the heads of the waiting crowd, 'to show the multitude on the shore the effect of our weapons without materially hurting any of them'. The crackle of small arms did not have the desired effect. One fellow with great aplomb was so bold as to turn his backside to them, slapping it with his hands like a monkey which, as Forster says, was the usual challenge to fight in the South Seas. 'For this contemptuous behaviour,' writes Sparrman, 'he was sufficiently rewarded, for the lieutenant of marines told me he could not restrain himself from aiming a charge of shot at the proffered target.' Cook immediately followed up with a salvo of four-pounders that went crashing into the woods. This cleared the beach in an instant sending some two hundred frightened natives diving out of their canoes into the water. 'Only a single young man,' writes Forster, 'very well made and of a very open friendly countenance, remained standing in his canoe, without the least marks of surprise or fear, but looking with a mixture of mirth and contempt at his affrighted countrymen.' After this success Cook effected a landing and roped off a small area on the beach for tents and astronomical instruments. The natives were given to understand that it was forbidden territory, which dictum they accepted with perfectly good grace eventually appearing without arms. Whether or not they still regarded Cook as an ancestral spirit is difficult to say.

Some evenings later the youth who had been so brave during the bombardment was persuaded to dine on board. Cook called him Whaagou, while Forster refers to him as Fannokko. 'We had nothing to eat,' Cook said, 'but salt beef and pork. He did but just taste the latter, but ate pretty heartily of yam and drank a glass of wine.' Forster adds that he finished his meal with 'a small portion of pie, made of dried and worm-eaten apples, which seemed to be very agreeable to his palate'. His manners at table were 'extremely becoming and decent, and the only practice which did not appear quite cleanly in our eyes was his making use of a stick, which he wore in his hair instead of a fork with which he occasionally scratched his head. As his hair was dressed in the highest fashion of the country, *à la porc-épic*, greased with oil and paint, our stomachs were so much the more easily offended;

though Fannokko had not the least notion that such an action was reprehensible'.

After dinner Cook walked him round the deck where he thought the dogs were pigs but otherwise 'I did not observe that anything fixed his attention or comment or caused in him the least surprise'. Cook showed another native around 'in the hopes of finding out something he might value and be induced to exchange for refreshments', but again found him indifferent. The only thing that caught this visitor's eye was 'a wooden sand box [for drying ink] which he seemed to admire and turned it two or three times over in his hand'. When the natives admired anything they hissed like geese and snapped their fingers.

They stayed in Tana for nearly three weeks. After about the fourth day Cook reports that 'the people of our neighbourhood are so well reconciled with us that they take no notice of our going shooting in the woods'. He admits, however, that they would have been better pleased had the sailors confined themselves to the immediate vicinity of the shore and whenever they attempted to explore the volcano they were turned back at its approaches by the natives' blowing on shell trumpets.

Every night Yasur shot vast quantities of fire and smoke into the air, every eruption sounding like 'the blowing up of mines'. When it rained the explosions were even louder and when the wind veered in their direction the fine ash turned to what Wales called a 'shower of mire . . . as it was composed of water, sand, earth and some other matter like small particles of asbestos'. Examined under the microscope the asbestos proved to be a conglomerate of minute needle-like crystals, very bothersome to the eyes. Indeed, those exposed to it for any length of time developed a drooping of the upper eyelid, 'the only malady,' according to Sparrman, 'we discovered among these people'.

Once while Sparrman was watching an eruption, an enormous solid mass larger than the longboat was suddenly spewed high into the air and then fell back again into the crater. Yasur still dominates the countryside spewing it with pumice-stone and covering all the plants with so much volcanic ash that one can write one's name in it on the leaves. This continual dusting builds up a rich loam in which the island's vegetation thrives. The sugar canes are larger and juicier and I have seen a yam six feet long. 'Beautiful bind weed,' writes Forster, 'climbed like ivy to the summits of the tallest trees.' The banyians, or *Ficus bengalensis*, are also gigantic with trunks some fifty feet in diameter, spread round with innumerable tap roots like columns plunging earthward, turning each tree into a kind of silvern cathedral. Through this fantastic forest screech innumerable perroquets flashing their bright plumage. The island has changed but little since Cook's day. The sugar plantations, he tells us, were ringed round with great pits four feet deep dug to catch the rats that infest the islands. Forster found some wild nutmeg trees and managed to nurse a sapling home to present to the Queen. Another morning they came across a band of mud hoppers destroying a brood of minute crickets washed out of a crevice in the rock. The mud hopper, *Periophthalmus argentilineatus*, is the paradox of the piscatorial world: a fish that drowns if kept under water and skips over the mud quite as much at home as if swimming. One finds him half submerged clinging to a root breathing through his tail and watching you with his goblin eyes – detached disks which he can move around his head at will, scrutinizing you intently with one ogling globe while with the other hunts his prey.

Reading over the impressions left by Cook and his companions of the New Hebrides, a somewhat blurred picture emerges. The different islands, particularly Tana, appear as places visited in a dream, fascinating but unreal – as unreal perhaps as the Englishmen must have appeared to the Tanese. Why is this? I find it difficult to explain, and indeed my own visit to Tana remains an experience that borders on fantasy – a series of vivid recollections shot with Yasur's fires, picked out in vivid flashes like those sombre gouaches of the Bay of Naples with Vesuvius erupting in the background.

Of all the islands I stayed on I think it is perhaps to Tana that I would best like to return. I even wonder sometimes whether my memory has not played me tricks, whether the whole thing is not a figment of my imagination. Even its name is not real, for it is actually called Ipari. On first landing Cook had pointed to the ground inquiring the name of the island. The natives, thinking he was referring to the earth, replied 'tana', their word for soil and so it has remained ever since.

Cook could learn nothing of these people's religious beliefs or of their social customs as there was no interpreter around to help him. Melanesia anyhow is characterized by an unbelievable profusion of local cultures. Customs change so from one island to another, even on islands within the same group, that Polynesia by contrast appears to be homogeneous in every respect. On Erronan, forty miles to the east of Tana, for instance, the population is predominantly Polynesian while on Embrim and Malekula there is a strong pre-Austronesian strain. Widely varying racial mixtures make for very pronounced local variations in culture. One may generalize to the extent of saying that the New Hebridean religion is a form of animistic ancestor worship and that their societies are meritocracies where position in the tribe depends on achievement rather than birth. The individual progresses from initiation rite to initiation rite attaining a standing commensurate with his capabilities. His grade in the netherworld depending on that reached while living.

In common with the rest of Oceania their art forms tend towards a geometric style. The Melanesian albeit is more concerned than the Polynesian with colour and the human body, especially the head. One sees this in their mortuary images where a body is moulded in clay upon a core of palm spathes. The head is the actual skull of the deceased overlaid with a vegetable paste in which the dead person's features are modelled as faithfully as possible and given a wig of matted spider's webs. The effigies are gaily daubed over with slashes of pattern completely unrelated to the sculptural forms they decorate, in brick-red, black, and white earth pigments, a greenish hue obtained from seaweed, and more recently a Prussian-blue wash from the dye in ordinary laundry bags. With no fixatives, the colours and paste deteriorate very quickly in this climate, but the images are not made with a view to their surviving for long. Once having served their function in the memorial rites, they are stored in the 'men's house' where they remain until they rot away. Other than the museum specimens, very few of them are older than four or five years by which time they are already considered antiques.

Much handsomer than these mortuary images are the effigy statues used in the elaborate rites marking a man's progress from one grade to another. These are carved from the inverted trunks of freshly cut tree-ferns, and are also covered with a thin layer of clay which is then painted. Once the occasion for which they are made is passed, they too are left to perish on the edge of the dance ground. The tropical rains rapidly wash off the outer covering but the tough tree-fern pith survives so that one can find relatively early examples of these figures.

Equally attractive are the trunks of the bread-fruit tree hollowed out to serve as great slit gongs seven or eight feet high. Batteries of them are stood up on the ground in the centre of a ceremonial area. A large pointed head with great eyes squashed into circular disks, an aquiline nose, flaring nostrils, and a receding chin top the gong; a half-moon face rising above a tubular body, for no attempt is made to indicate limbs. Sometimes there is no head at all and then the gongs have a frankly phallic character.

These artifacts are rarely seen outside museums or private collections. Apart from small isolated areas on Embrim and Malekula, only in the interior of south-west New Guinea can one still find old cultures that have not been influenced at all, or only slightly, by the white man. The decrease in the population, which has fallen from 150,000 to 60,000 in the last hundred years, has also limited the production of such objects. People riding through the forest have been known to come upon a thicket of staring ghoulish faces forgotten and rotting in some lost clearing. But this would certainly not befall the casual traveller. The tree-fern figures and slit gongs now command high prices in Europe's auction rooms, and were there any to be found, the local traders would certainly have unearthed them long before this.

The northern islands in the New Hebrides produced most of these images. Tana was never noted for its artifacts, but notwithstanding this the Tanese have always considered their island an important religious centre, telling one that it was the navel of the world, the Garden of Eden having been situated in the burnt-out plains at the foot of Yasur. True to their boast, it is on Tana in fact that a new cult has suddenly sprung up, a travesty of their ancestral beliefs dreamt up by an old man called Nambas. It is a strange story and a last pathetic attempt by the natives to preserve their cultural identity from being completely engulfed by an alien civilization. The cult is nothing but an elaborate make-believe, but already the whole island is under Nambas' sway and the churches nearly empty.

Tana has always been a problem for the missionaries. The first attempt to evangelize the island in 1839 had to be abandoned after the loss of several lives. The white stranger was only accepted late in the century and then hesitantly. Mrs Watt, a missionary's wife writing from Tana in 1885, reported that 'occasionally we hailed a gleam of light, thinking it the dawning of the day: as often have we seen it fade away and the darkness grows more intense'. Their main trouble was an old chief called Nahi-Abba who although opposed to the Gospel himself had nevertheless sent his wife to church which was taken as a hopeful sign, especially as one year being at death's door he had begged for medicines, daily visits and prayers. However, no sooner recovered, his first act in Mrs Watt's words 'was to perform a heathen rite on his son, shunning us in every way and indeed letting us know that we were not wanted. Again he became sick; we again visited and prayed with him, giving him cordials and medicine; once more he was recovered, only to be tenfold more a child of hell than before, and now he has forbidden his wife the church, and is doing all he can to prevent others from attending'. Nahi-Abba's boycott was highly successful and the following year he toured the island in search of a 'sacred man' who could conjure a tidal wave to sweep up the Watts' estuary 'and come down carrying our house out to sea'. Many of the Tanese were so excited that they could not sleep for fear of being washed out of their houses during the night.

Things have not changed so very much. Nambas, the head man at

61. Detail of Tanese cane work. Photograph taken at Robert Cook's trading post. (*page 225*)

62. One of Namba's vermilion crosses with Yasur smoking in the background. (*page 224*)

Sulphur Bay, the largest settlement on the island, carries on where Nahi-Abba left off, only Nambas is more subtle in his campaign to rid the islands of whites. The natives consider it taboo to discuss the movement with strangers, whether out of respect, fear of secretiveness no one can really decide. We know that Frum is the saviour of their cult and that Nambas is his prophet, we even know the saviour's first name which is John. The tenants of the Frum cult are largely materialistic and definitely anti-Christian. '*He* come bring plenty cargo for black man', is the usual answer one gets to any inquiry. One feels that John Frum springs from the memories of the well-fed, well-cared-for American soldier of the last war whose quantities of supplies pouring into the Pacific impressed the natives beyond measure. In Nambas' imagination Frum will one day appear on their island bringing another such reign of plenty. Nambas has been cunning enough not to proclaim himself the central figure of the cult but merely Frum's spokesman, being in daily contact with him by mental telepathy.

Frumism started some time early in the forties. A supernatural being is supposed to have appeared one night to Nambas in the jungle. 'I looked up and he standing in the fork of sacred tree.' Nambas describes him as light coloured but not white. He was dressed in a khaki uniform but the vision was indistinct and only the brass buttons on Frum's tunic shone out clearly. Nearly every night Frum comes to Nambas, either in his tree or in some clearing in the bush. His declarations become more fanciful with each appearance and his predictions are inexhaustible. Among the more spectacular are promises of eternal youth free from illness, that the island will suddenly become flat and twice its size – become again the earthly paradise it had once been and that all whites will be chased away and the people forbidden to attend church. *Kava*, discouraged by the missionaries, has become again the staple drink and old tribal dances have been revived. They dance every Friday now at Sulphur Bay and the thud of drums and the banshee-like wailing of the faithful keep one awake at night. No new prognostication issuing from old Nambas' withered lips is too extravagant to be believed, no edict too preposterous to be obeyed. He has the following of the whole island, some seven thousand souls and, what is more, the resident of Tana responsible to the central government at Vila has officially acknowledged the existence of the Frum movement; probably the wisest move since there appears no use in opposing it. So far no violence has been done to the few whites still living on the island and I cannot say that I was conscious of any animosity.

Some years ago the unquestioning faithful were given orders to clear several acres of bush. When finished Nambas announced that it was intended as a landing strip for Frum's cargo planes that were to appear laden with supplies. There was to be enough food for everybody, prefabricated houses, washing machines, refrigerators, and blondes for the chief men. Further messages came over Nambas' mystic radio, not only were planes to arrive but also giant submarines which people were to watch for from the hill-tops; an order carried out, one presumes, with certain hesitancy, for what if the land suddenly flattened out during the vigil? Coins stamped with a coconut palm will take the place of Australian shillings. Red crosses have been planted throughout the island, each one marking the site of a school where the Tanese will be taught the wisdom of the whites. Occasionally these crosses lack one arm which makes one think of the sinister fetishes of voodooism and its strange rites. Not all the symbols are crosses. Sometimes one finds a small wicker gateway leading nowhere set down haphazardly in a field, a crudely modelled aeroplane, or an effigy that is presumably John Frum in person. These symbols are all painted bright letter-box red, and had just been given a fresh coat when I was there. I am told also that there used to be a large cross planted on the very lip of Yasur's boiling crater, but this has disappeared, probably tumbled into hell's fires by the terrific vibrations.

It is hard to say anything of John Frum himself as Nambas is evasive when questioned on the subject. He cannot surely be white, yet sometimes he is supposed to appear to Nambas dressed as an American sailor. There have been times when Nambas claimed he was a relative of Roosevelt whom the natives conceive to have been royal. 'Him Rusfelt's brother,' he announced. Frum lives either in America or the Argentine; it has never been clearly stated in which. His name seems to be a phonetic deformation of broom, symbolizing the sweeping out of the white man and his religion. On various occasions during the last twenty years Nambas has announced the imminent arrival of Frum and his fleet of white-painted cargo planes. Each time he has been unavoidably detained, the last visit being put off by Frum's surprising activities in the Red Sea where he was cruising in Noah's Ark.

In order to reach Tana I had been obliged to charter the forty-foot cabin cruiser *Trudy* belonging to Keith Cook, a young Australian shell diver. Normally Keith fished five or six tons of green snail and trocus a month for which haul the pearl-shell retailers paid him over £3,000. The beds had been over-fished of late and the authorities at Vila had been obliged to put a three-year restriction on pearling with the result that Keith, in order to keep the *Trudy* running, hired her out as a ferry between the islands.

It took twelve hours to cross the one hundred and sixty miles between

Vila and Tana. According to Keith we enjoyed a remarkably smooth run, though at no point had I been able to stand upright without clutching on to something. On arrival we anchored in a shallow bay appropriately named Whitesands. I was to stay with Keith's brother who runs a trading post on the island and who had agreed to take me to Yasur's crater and then drive me on next morning to Port Resolution where I was to pick up the *Trudy*.

Robert and his wife Eileen, a pretty girl with an Australian mother and a half-Tongan father, were the only white people I saw on the island. They live in a wooden bungalow with thatched outhouses connected by coral paths. Trocus and green snail shells border the flower-beds and in front of the bungalow stretches an apron of lawn overlooking dense jungle. A dentilated screen of pawpaw trees sheltered the wired-in veranda where I slept.

Eileen was dark ivory colour and was expecting a baby, but looked fresh and appetizing in a starched linen bonnet and a green cotton dress with gold hoops in her ears. She gave me a delicious clam soup for lunch, made from large horse-shoe clams whose shells are so large that they could be used as bowls out of which to sup their former occupants. The soup was followed by grated yams mixed with coconut cream and baked in the oven in banana leaves. For pudding we had a delectable food made from a large green fruit called a soursop. It was a noisy meal for there was a young parrot who never stopped screeching. She would fly in from the kitchen, land with a plop on the linoleum floor and skid across it on her feathery rump pursued by an awkward mongrel Alsatian puppy. Over and over she repeated this performance which was clearly a game to her. Every now and then Robert would leave the room in order to attend some dusky customer who had appeared silently in the store that lay on the far side of the kitchen. He must have had an instinct about their presence for we certainly never heard anything. He did a brisk trade in nylon lines and fish hooks, home-baked bread, and cigarettes. Other popular items were tubes of scented oil from Hongkong, brilliantine, mouth organs, and blue jeans made in Japan. Thanks to Nambas there was an enamel basin full of *kava* roots.

Robert drove me to Yasur in a Land-Rover, the only possible transport on the island. The roads are little better than earth tracks, washed out several feet below ground level by the heavy rains. The earth thus exposed in these deep gullies is rich and black, emitting the pungent smell of damp loam, and so porous that Robert could sink a three-foot pole straight into the bank at our side right up to his wrist without the slightest effort. Every now and then where the road strikes a vein of solid clay and lifts out of its gullies we would get wonderful views. Looking down from the crest of a hill one sees a pall of green spreading in a dense network of creepers over the trees, flowing on like an unbroken sea, looping from tree to tree. Immense trees become muffled shapes heaving upward in an agonized attempt to reach air. One almost expects to see the dreadful pall move, pushed outwards by the suffocating branches. But not a thing stirs and the only sound is the gentle booming of green pigeons and the soothing murmur of gurgling streams. One is lulled into a false sense of peace, for silently and irrevocably murder is being committed right in front of one; the lives of the great trees are being slowly choked out of them.

This nightmare scene set the mood for what was to follow, for my memories of Yasur are terrifying. Suddenly turning a corner we came upon the volcano: a grey striated cone rising out of a desolate, ash-strewn plain which generations of soot and hot coals have wasted of all vegetation except isolated clumps of pandanus, whose primitive shape fits well the primeval character of the landscape. The air was hot and heavy with the acrid odour of sulphur. The Land-Rover crunched over the cinder-packed ground as we approached the base of the mountain. It was a surprise to find a circular lake of blue water on the lower slopes of the volcano. For many years this lake was thought to be bottomless until one day some enterprising visitor rolled up his trousers and waded clear across it.

The detonations now were deafening and we had to shout to be heard. Yet, despite the sulphuric fumes and infernal din one's first impression is not one of fear. Yasur is only six hundred feet high, its gentle slopes taper in an almost perfect cone. Its scale is human. One first feels that nature has produced an *objet de vertu*, a collector's piece among volcanoes. Such was my reaction until I started to climb, painfully picking my way over sharp lumps of clinker, attentive to the treacherous footholds. The climb took half an hour. We reached a first rim, dipped down, and then climbed in a veil of warm white smoke another thirty feet to the crater proper. It was difficult to take photographs as the smoke, although white, was heavily laden with black dust. I wondered how it appeared so white. We had nearly reached the rim when there was another terrific, hissing explosion, sending vibrations straight through one. My only reassurance was the knowledge that volcanoes which constantly erupt are considered to be the more restrained type, even at close quarters. I must admit, however, that it took all my courage to get to the top. The rim is no broader than the back of a horse. A great circular cavity three-quarters of a mile in diameter with perfectly perpendicular walls, drops a thousand or more feet straight down to the floor of the crater. It was the height rather than the explosions that affected me more. For a moment I thought I was going to be violently ill. Vertigo is a condition over which one has no control and I had an almost irresistible impulse to plunge madly into the fearful chasm, and fearful is indeed the word. One could see the molten lava gulping to the surface of the vents, six or seven of them, great gaping livid wounds, hissing, gasping, and spluttering in trembling waves of heat. It was terrible to witness a terrific explosion maturing in a torment of molten toil followed, as in a birth, by utter spent exhaustion. One of the molten whirlpools choked itself and then vomited a column of incandescent rocks straight up into the air above our heads. Robert, knowing the winds, had been careful to choose the leeward side of the crater out of harm's way.

Were it not for my ridiculous aversion to heights I would have stayed for hours instead of minutes watching this purgatorial display for there is no denying its horrid beauty. One can understand why the Tanese regarded Yasur as sacred. It was the habitat of Iaranus, lord of the underworld, a Melanesian Hades. For this reason its warrior guardians had warned Cook off with blasts on conch trumpets.

I rejoined the *Trudy* at Port Resolution so named by Cook 'after the ship as she was the first who ever entered it'. He would find his port unusable today, for in 1888 two severe earthquakes so completely altered its depth that even the *Trudy* with her shallow draught had to anchor some way off from the shore. Otherwise it can have changed very little for there still is not a sign of human habitation.

From Tana Cook had sailed north again in order to complete the sounding and charting on the west side of Eromanga and the succeeding islands. No landing was made on Efate, but with his trained eye Cook had spotted a good anchorage, the future harbour of Vila now the principal port for the whole of the New Hebrides. Viewing it through glasses from the ship Wales had found Efate 'one of the most beautiful and desirable islands we have seen in the South Seas'. It is still beautiful, I suppose, as far as nature is concerned, but I doubt very much whether any of the men on board the *Resolution* would appreciate the effects of our colonization. Vila is a ramshackle place of no architectural merit thrown together on a hillside. The inhabitants have tried to give the corrugated iron roofed bungalows, shuttered and ventilated by louvred walls, an air of gaiety by daubing them with daring combination of colours such as bright canary-yellow picked out in orange.

Far more reprehensible than the mediocre cultural influences we have spread over the islands is the shocking rôle we have played in their history. The preliminary contacts with the West were blameless. Following shortly after Cook came Bligh and then the unfortunate La

Pérouse whose two ships, *L'Astrolab* and *La Boussole*, were wrecked on the outer reefs of Vanikoro in the lonely Santa Cruz Islands.*

It is effects of subsequent incursions of whalers, sandalwood traders and 'blackbirders' in search of 'recruits' to man the sugar plantations of Fiji and Queensland, that one would wish to eradicate. For two-thirds of the nineteenth century the 'blackbirders' very nearly depopulated the islands. The sandalwood traders were equally unscrupulous; 'a favourite trick was to capture a chief and hold him hostage until his people ransomed him with sandalwood'.† Then instead of releasing the man, he would be traded to cannibals on another island for more sandalwood. In 1861, bothered by the natives' hostile attitude, one schooner deliberately landed a number of Tana islanders infected with measles on Eromanga, causing death to one-third of the population. Goaded by public opinion France and England agreed in 1887 to establish a naval commission to survey and protect the group and in 1907 an Anglo-French condominium was formed.

Untidy light-brown logs of sandalwood looking like so much driftwood are still piled up on the quay at Port Vila. They would pass completely unnoticed were it not for the delicious scent emanating from it when heated by the sun. At Vila I met Reece Discombe, one of the divers who had located the wreck of the *Astrolab* on the Vanikoro reefs. He now runs a garage where he keeps a sheet of lead stamped with a cross capped with a circle and interlaced with double 'A's', identified by the Brest navy yard as the insignia used by La Pérouse's expedition. It was also in Discombe's office that I saw my first painted heads which he had obtained from a hostile tribe known as the Big Nambas. They live in the mountain fastness of Malekula in palisaded villages that are hardly ever visited and can be entered only by climbing over stiles reached by ladders.

* The fate of this scientific expedition of the first importance, France's answer to Cook's remarkable achievements, was for many years a deep mystery. No survivors were ever found. They were either drowned, eaten or were kept prisoners until they died. Although the French Revolution was at its height when news of La Pérouse's disappearance reached France, the National Assembly sent an expedition commanded by the Chevalier d'Entrecastaux in search of the vanished explorers. The ships were appropriately named *Le Recherche* and *L'Espérance*. As in the case of *L'Astrolab* and *La Boussole* the ships had been fitted out with extra care, and were even supplied with miniature windmills on the quarterdeck to grind wheat for bread. Labillardière, the celebrated naturalist attached to *La Recherche*, wrote an account of the voyage. No trace of La Pérouse was found until 1828, forty years after the wreck, when Captain Peter Dillon sailing for the East India Company, discovered a sword of French manufacture said to come from Vanikoro. A storm prevented Dillon from investigating himself but eventually the French Government appointed another expedition under Captain Dumont d'Urville, which did succeed in clearing up the mystery.

† Douglas L. Oliver, *The Pacific Islands*, Harvard, 1958.

[Chapter 21]

New Caledonia

SAILING southwards from Espiritu Santo they found land almost immediately, an elevated point which Cook named Cape Colnett after the midshipman who first spied it on September 4th.* The *Resolution* found a clear passage in the reefs and by the 5th lay at anchor just below the north-east point of the largest island in the South Pacific after New Zealand and one that had never before been visited.

At the passage, they were met by double canoes supporting heavy platforms on which fires were burning in stone hearths. The canoes had inverted lateen-type sails made from matting, and immediately it was noticed that they were not guided by paddles, but that one man stood at the stern sculling with a large oar. 'We resembled a man-of-war,' Wales writes, 'with a large fleet of merchantmen under convoy.' The natives were solidly built, tall, and generally well proportioned. 'I should take them to be a race between the people of Tana and the Friendly Isles or between the Tanese and the New Zealanders,' writes Cook. They were Melanesians, of course, but 'spoke a language quite new to us. They were totally naked to the penis which like the Tanese they wrapped up in leaves. They do not tie it up to the belt as at Tana, but suffer it to hang down, nor do they untie it when they want to make water, but piss through all and when done shake off what drops may hang to the coat'. Sparrman and Forster observed some of these wrappers that were so long 'that the extremity is fastened to a string round the neck'. Clerke gleefully tells us that they cared not a farthing 'for any article of dress that would not, in some form, be made to contribute to the decorating of their favourite part. I gave one of them a stocking which he deliberately pulled on there. I then gave him a

* James Colnett, twenty-two at the time, was a 'clever and sober boy' who was to have an interesting career pioneering the fur trade in the American north-west, an occupation which took him to the Far East and particularly to Japan, still an unknown country to Europeans in those days. Promoted to Captain at forty-four, he spent the last few years of his life transporting convicts to Sydney, a less enviable pastime, no doubt, than sailing into Nagasaki harbour, but not without its adventures. Trained and seasoned by voyaging with the famous Captain, many of Cook's young men went on to distinguished naval careers.

string of beads, with it he tied up the stocking. I then presented him with a medal which he immediately hung to it – in short let that noble part be well decorated and fine, they're perfectly happy and totally indifferent about the state of all the rest of the body'. Young George, anticipating that the general public would be shocked at the New Caledonians' manner of arranging themselves, defended them by citing our own cod piece; 'the fashionable dresses and suits of armour which were worn in the fifteenth and sixteenth century at every European court would, at present, be looked upon as the most indecent that can possibly be contrived; and yet who will choose to assert that there was less modesty in the world at that age than in this?'

In spite of Clerke's dictum, the natives also wore black cylindrical caps. These, writes Cook, 'seem to be a great ornament among them and we thought betokened warriors or men of note. . . . It could thus be said,' he adds with humour, 'that they only ornamented or clothed the head and the tail.' The men generally clipped their hair short, in a style 'the gentlemen' referred to as 'mopp heads', over which fitted the cylindrical hat, resembling, says Forster, 'the cap of an hussar'. They were woven out of pandanus and dyed black with bunches of long black cock's feathers at the top. The men generally tied their cord slings round their hats, letting them hang down like tassels, while in their ears clattered a number of tortoise-shell rings. All in all the New Caledonians must have cut rather dashing figures.

Women, as we know, played a very subordinate role in Melanesian society and were kept well in the background. They were judged to be rather ugly and wore black or straw-coloured bunched skirts of pandanus leaves low down on the hips, standing out like 'thatch all round the body'. According to Cook 'they were made at least six or eight inches thick but not one inch longer than necessary for the use they seemed to be designed for'. They looked, in fact, like a ballerina's *tutu*. In common with the women of Tana he found them 'far more chaste than their sisters of Easter Island. I never heard that one of our people obtained the least favour from any one of them; I have been told that the ladies here would frequently divert themselves by going a little aside with our gentlemen as if they meant to grant them the last favour and then ran away laughing at them. Whether this was chastity or coquetry I shall not pretend to determine, nor is it material since the consequences were the same'.

On landing, the explorers met the handsome young chief of the district, Teabooma, who made a welcoming speech and let them water in the vicinity 'at a fine stream about a third of a mile from the sea-shore where it ran into a little creek and mixed with the salt water. It was necessary to have a boat in the creek to float the casks down to

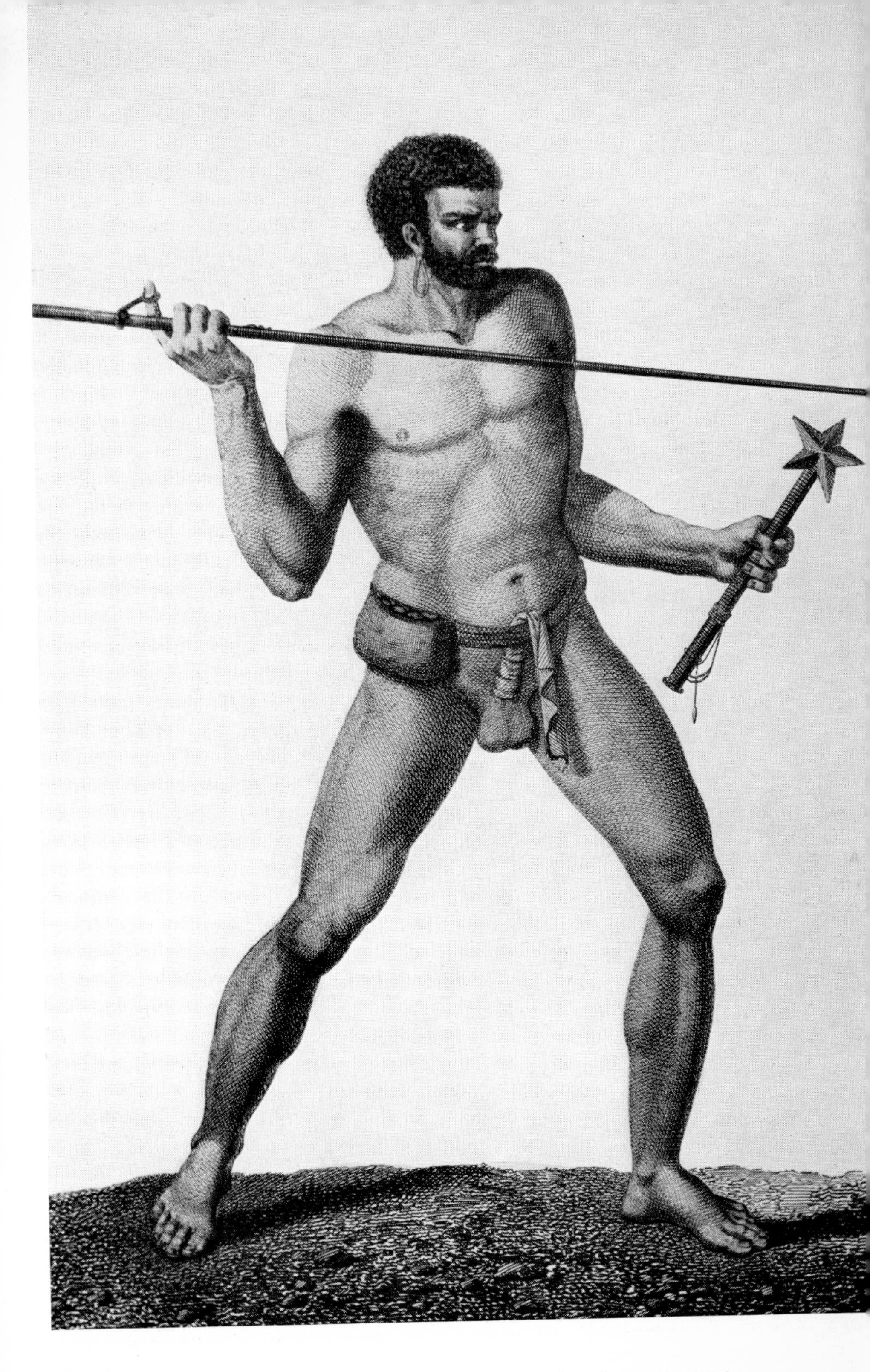

63. A New Caledonian native. 'They were totally naked to the penis which like the Tanese they wrap up in leaves.' From the atlas of Labillardière's *Relation du Voyage à la Recherche de La Pérouse*.
Engraved by Copia after Piron. (*page 229*)

64. The New Caledonian hats
were woven out of
pandanus and dyed black.
Engraved by Record after Chapman.
(*page 230*)

65. The rare and strange kagou or *Rhinochetus jubatus*. (*page 236*)

66. The much discussed *pin colonnaire* or *Araucaria cooki*, photograph taken on the Isle of Pines. (*page 237*)

67. Basalt-rock pillars in Staffa from Pennant's *Tour in Scotland*. Engraved by P. Mazell after John Frederick Miller. (*page 238*)

the beach over which they were rolled and then taken into the launch'.

Right away Cook realized 'that we were to expect nothing from these people but the privilege of visiting their country undisturbed for it was easy to see that they had little else but good nature to spare us. In this they exceeded all the nations we had yet met with, and although it did not fill our bellies it left our minds at ease'.

Accompanied by native guides a party climbed the north-eastern arms of the two ranges cradling the Diahot, the largest river in New Caledonia. Cook saw 'that it seems not to be a country able to support many inhabitants; nature has been less bountiful to it than any other tropical island we know in this sea'. 'Indeed,' adds Wales, 'the soil of the whole country seems sterile, being a dry sandy mould that produces no underwood, but is everywhere covered with a long dry grass and trees chiefly of one sort, whose bark is very white and hangs in rags. The leaves, which are long, narrow and few in number are of a very pale, dead green.' Sparrman remarks that no bushes or shrubs grow beneath these trees, 'so that a company of cavalry could comfortably pass between them'. Forster added that 'the earth in many places consists of a shining red glimmer, and large pieces of quartz'. All agreed on the poverty of the country. From their vantage point they could see the hills roll away, 'without a single habitation upon them', the plain they had crossed being similarly destitute. Eastward the coast was swamped and cushioned with mangroves, an ungrateful kind of vegetation as anyone who has visited the Pacific knows. It was a lonely desolate landscape and reminded Forster of Easter Island.

The white-barked trees mentioned above were Linnaeus's *Melaleuce leucadendron*, one of the eucalyptus family. Later French colonists, who named New Caledonia *La Grande Terre*, called this tree Niaouli, using it as a symbol of their island. Girl children born in New Caledonia are also often christened Niaouli. Towards the end of the nineteenth century a chemist in Noumea discovered that it contained a particular oil, which he named gomenol, whose pungent odour is supposed to purify the air and render the island particularly salubrious. The tree looks like a cross between an olive and a eucalyptus. A thin white trunk twists up, separating into branches which are bunched at the end with curving, smoky-green leaves. Corot would certainly have been inspired by it. Given enough water they can become as majestic as an oak but seldom attain larger proportions than our silver birch. The settlers on the island have a saying: *Qui dit 'terre à niaouli', dit terre qui ne vaut rien* – and that is just about it. For mile upon mile the country rolls out thinly wooded with these white-trunked trees. Round their black roots grow long grasses, yellow except where they are parted by the winds to reveal a tender green. Useless grasses, as Cook remarks, for people who have no cattle to graze them.

The land is not all bleak. There are parts that are almost as tropically luxuriant as the other Melanesian islands. 'In the valleys,' writes Forster, 'and on some parts of the plains are to be found a variety of shrubberies, bind-weeds, gay flowers and tufted shade trees.' Cook reports that 'the plains along the coast, on the side we lay, appeared from the hills to great advantage. Winding streams water their slopes while lesser streams conveyed by art fed the different plantations'. Necessity made the natives skilled cultivators, for neither the coconut nor the bread-fruit will thrive in their thin mineral-veined soil. On the steep hills, terraced like the sides of an Aztec pyramid, they raised *taro*, keeping the roots moist by a system of irrigation that brought water over considerable distances in frail gutters of bamboo.

New Caledonia slants diagonally from north to south-east, a long narrow island 248 miles from top to toe and only thirty miles across. It is divided along its length by rugged mountain ranges over 5,000 feet high which are in turn slashed across by deep valleys interspersed with occasional plateaux. Landing in the Balade district, that is to say the north-east section, Cook saw the most fertile part of the island, for it is the eastern slopes and valleys that receive a full measure of rain from the prevailing easterly winds.

It was September, a period of unsettled weather on the island, a time of year when great blue and mauve cloud shadows lie like bruises across the pleated mountains. Mists veil the distances and there are moments when it is hard to believe oneself in the Pacific. Indeed, one sometimes longs for a respite from the rubbery leaved foliage of the torrid zones, a vegetation interminably spiked with the clattering, shiny fronds of the coconut; one wonders if this sudden change of landscape did not attract Cook and his men in the same way. Might it not have been out of gratitude, in an impulsive moment of relief, that he named it New Caledonia? Although to our knowledge he had never been there, he must have known Scotland by instinct, for there certainly are parts of New Caledonia that resemble it, especially when the hills roll away in mauves and greys and soft greens. Whatever the reason, the name was more aptly chosen than the one picked for the last group of islands he christened.

The *Resolution* remained at Balade for one short week. Again one is astonished at the amount of material gathered by Cook and his men, it is not only a question of the amount they absorbed, but also the accuracy with which they noted it.

They describe the native huts, rounded in the shape of thatched hives, which were scattered everywhere, sometimes standing alone, sometimes in small communities of three or four. Unlike all the other archipelagos where they are either oblong or square, New Caledonian huts are conical. Forster tells us that the houses were generally grouped under very lofty trees 'of which the branches were so closely entwined that the sky was scarcely visible through the foliage'. One can visualize the natives living in a perpetual gloom on the hard-trodden earth, for no grass will grow under the *ficus*. It is surprising that they should have built their houses out of the sun, for according to Cook, the New Caledonians appeared susceptible to cold and were always huddled

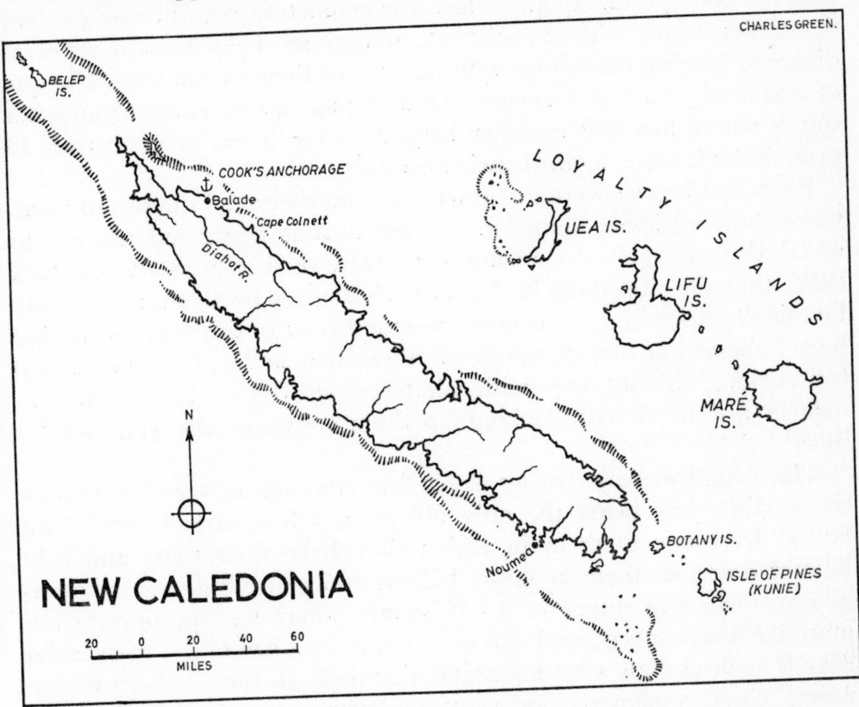

round fires even when in their canoes. Their huts were never without a fire 'and as there was no vent for the smoke but by the door, the whole house was not only smoky but hot too, insomuch that we who are not used to such smoky holes could hardly endure to be in them a moment'. He admits that 'smoky houses may be necessary to keep out the mosquitoes which are pretty numerous here'. Cook commented also upon the spires that pointed their roofs, high carved poles 'generally ornamented with either carving or shells, or both'. Not being able to converse with the natives, he could not discover their true significance. They are, or rather were, for one does not find them any longer, family insignias; or if carved with a face, ancestor symbols. Like all

Melanesians the New Caledonians worshipped their ancestors. The faces skewered on to such poles were highly stylized; squashed between two medallions on the head and below on the chin, the face burst sideways into angular patterns. A very poor engraving by Hodges gives one no idea of the decorative value of similarly carved door jambs. Nearly every house had these heavy convex posts about five feet high and eighteen inches wide. The top of each panel had a broad rectangular face with a beak nose, flared nostrils, a slit mouth and lozenge eyes, generally painted black. The red-painted body beneath, for one must take it as such, is an equally schematic geometric pattern. The painted decorations vary with the district; sometimes a design is a series of diagonal herring bones representing ribs, or then a complex arabesque of diamonds, stars or lozenges. These jambs again represent ancestor spirits whose function is either to protect the house or conversely to protect the inmates against their ancestors.

Bows and arrows were unknown. Instead they used slings and hardwood clubs, curiously shaped in a variety of stars, knobs and mushrooms which the crew collected in numbers. 'The reader,' writes Cook, 'will think that the ship must be full of such articles by this time. He will be mistaken, for nothing is more common than to give away what has been collected at one island for anything new at another, even if it is less curious, this together with what is destroyed on board after the owners are tired with looking at them prevents any considerable increase.'

'Household utensils,' writes Cook, 'are confined to very few articles, the earthen jars being the only objects worth noting. Every family has at least one of them in which they bake their roots and fish.' Forster describes them as large, bellied and clumsily shaped. Pottery in any form was unknown in Polynesia where an appropriate raw material was wanting, and was only found in a few of the Melanesian islands such as New Caledonia and then only in the northern district where Cook anchored. For want of fire-proof utensils boiling was practically an unknown method of cooking in the Pacific. In Hawaii they practised only a primitive form of it where red-hot stones were dropped into their bowls of food. However, even the New Caledonians preferred to use their pots as ovens to bake their vegetables, as do all the other Oceanic people. They did not have to bury their victuals under hot stones and earth as elsewhere but stuffed 'their pots full of dry grasses and green leaves in which they had wrapped up a few small yams'. Forster also saw them on the beach fill pots with shells 'by which means they roasted the fish'. Cook notes that 'their chief subsistence must be in roots and fish and the bark of a tree'. Clerke tells us that the natives were 'very busy at low water when they always get an abundance of shell fish'. Crustacea must also have been included in their diet for I have seen the carapace of an enormous langouste measuring all of four feet. Sparrman thought that they ate their fish rotten, much the same way, he says, as the Scandinavians ferment Baltic herring or as we hang game. The bark of the tree which they roasted and were continually chewing was the *Hibiscus esculentus*, better known as okra, the pod of which forms a favourite ingredient in Creole cooking for thickening soups. Cook found it sweetish and insipid but tells us 'that it was liked by some of our people'.

Cannibalism constantly preoccupied the explorers. A party from the *Resolution* were chatting one evening around the fire when suddenly, as Sparrman narrates, 'the natives started to talk shrilly between themselves, at the same time regarding the foreigners with amazement'. The cause was discovered to be a beef-bone which someone had begun to gnaw for his evening meal. 'It had given the Indians the horrible suspicion that it was the bone of some human, especially as the Caledonians, in spite of repeated tours between decks to view the cattle could not get it through their heads that they were used as provender.'

It is strange that the natives should have been so surprised, for they were certainly cannibals themselves. Patten, the ship's surgeon, says that some of the islanders pinched and examined his plump and fleshy arms exclaiming on them with admiration and greed.

Labillardière, visiting the island with d'Entrecasteaux eighteen years later, bears out this fact and tells us that the natives gnawed away happily in front of several Frenchmen at the grisly remains of some young person's pelvis. Another time they chewed on a roasted arm to which part of the skin still adhered. They even supplied Labillardière with details regarding their 'horrible meals'. The man who gave the death stroke received the genitals as his portion while women were not considered worth eating.*

The New Caledonians were very short of food when the French were there. A combination of bad droughts and interminable tribal wars had laid waste the *taro* fields and they were starving. They traded their weapons for anything the French could give them, 'with one hand reaching out for worm eaten biscuits, while with the other they pointed to their thin, pinched-in stomachs which they dragged still further in with their muscles to indicate hunger and arouse pity'. In such times well-cooked spiders were considered a great delicacy, the same long-legged spiders that one sees on the beaches round Noumea dancing on great elastic cartwheels bellied out by the wind. Lumps of earth were also cut up and chewed to mitigate the aching pangs of hunger.

* *Relation du Voyage à la Recherche de La Pérouse* by Jacques Labillardière, Jansen, Paris, 1800.

However, the natives had been devouring their own kind for generations before the drought. It must therefore remain a mystery why the men on the beach that night exclaimed over one of Cook's crew gnawing away at what they thought was a human relic. Cook was concerned over their 'monstrous' diet and out of kindness tried to stock the island with hogs, hoping thus to influence their feeding habits. But when presented with a couple of pigs, the New Caledonians, Forster tells us, 'expressed so much dislike and dread of them that they made signs to us to take them back. It must be allowed,' he adds, 'these swine are far from being well looking quadrupeds and those who have never seen such an animal cannot be supposed to like them at first sight'. Cook had wanted to give them to Teabooma who had already accepted a pair of dogs and might also have taken care of the pigs. But Teabooma had completely disappeared, and it was impossible to find anyone else to take an interest in them. Cook pathetically tried to peddle his vociferous cargo to some tribal elders; 'our guide conducted us to a house where in were seated in a circle eight or ten middle aged men to whom I and my pigs were introduced and with great courtesy I was desired to sit down, when I began to expostulate on the merits of the two pigs, showing them the distinction of their sex, telling them how many young ones the female would have at one time. In short I multiplied them to some hundred in a trice, my only view being to enhance the value of the present that they might take the more care of them, and I had reason to think I in some measure succeeded'. But Cook was mistaken, for Captain John Erskin wrote some eighty years later that 'the few domestic animals left at Balade by Captain Cook seemed to have been destroyed soon after his departure'.* Those that are to be found on the island today are descended from stock imported by French missionaries.

'Our Caledonia' as Sparrman proudly refers to the island, proved a rich hunting ground for the naturalists. They found an unidentified passion-flower which excited Forster because 'all its species formerly known to the learned world were confined to America'. The land birds were not numerous but they discovered 'a kind of crow, its feathers tinged with blue', probably a cuckoo-shrike. They never came across the rare and strange kagu bird, *Rhinochetus jubatus*, now all but extinct and found only in the wilder parts of southern New Caledonia. It is about the size of a large chicken but looks a good deal larger on account of its aigret-crowned head which is out of proportion to the rest of its body. Its strong beak, eyes and legs are red, while the feathers are speckled grey and white except for its wings which are barred in brown

* *Journal of a Cruise among the Islands of The Western Pacific* by John Muncy, London, 1853.

and black. Like the almost mythical dodo of Mauritius it cannot fly and uses its wings only to hurry itself along the ground. Fortunately the curator of Noumea's museum has a tame kagu caged in his garden. It is a lively nervous bird that runs very quickly, flapping its convict-striped wings and yapping at the same time like a puppy. It produces one egg at each cover which it lays in a nest of twigs hidden away in dense shrub.

While anchored at Balade the *Resolution*'s butcher, Simon Monk, fell down the fore hatchway and died. 'A man much esteemed in the ship,' says Clerke, 'and beloved alike by both his comrades and superiors'. 'A rare enough occurrence,' adds Sparrman.

It had been Cook's intention to circumnavigate the whole island but sailing north from Balade he found that a reef ran for a hundred miles beyond the extreme point of the island. Another reef projects in a similar manner beyond the western shore, thus forming two long antennae between which cluster a group of small islands now known as the Belep. Cook was nervous; 'we were already carried far out of sight of land and there was no knowing how much further we might be carried before we found the ends of the shoals'. A sudden gale or a calm might prove fatal in such waters. 'These considerations together with the risk we must run in exploring a sea strewn with shoals and where no anchorage without them is to be found, induced me to abandon the design of proceeding round the NW and to ply up to the SE in which direction I knew there was a clear sea.' It was thus the work of d'Entrecasteaux in 1792 to explore and chart the side of the island that Cook felt obliged to leave unseen.

Having left Balade on the 13th they had already turned south by the 15th. On the 16th they struck one of those calms that Cook so dreaded and were left to the mercy of a swell that was pushing them 'directly upon the reef hardly one league's distance'. They sounded with a two-hundred fathom line but found no bottom so there was no hope of anchoring. 'I ordered the pinnace and cutter to be hoisted out and sent ahead to tow, but they were of little use against so large a swell.' In the end they were saved by a current into which they had unsuspectingly drifted. The next day they passed by Balade again and reached the southernmost tip of the island on the 23rd. On two small islands off the coast they saw 'an elevation like a tower'. Then several more appeared on different parts of the coast, 'so numerous,' writes Cook, 'that they looked not unlike the masts of a fleet of ships – not that anyone thought they were such'. It was their first sight of the *pin colonnaire* or *Araucaria cooki*, a species of pine that grows nowhere else in the world.

'Various were the opinions and conjectures about them,' writes

Cook, and although he himself never had any doubts that they were a singular sort of tree, wagers were made as to what they could actually be. The Forsters had quite different ideas. John Forster positively asserted that they were columns of basalt similar to those found at Skye or Staffa or the famous Giant's Causeway on the northern coast of County Antrim, clusters of irregular hexagons caused by the rapid cooling of lava flows where they enter the sea. It was a very sensible explanation, considering that they were in a volcanic belt and that these 'castellated masses' viewed through the glasses had a somewhat columnar appearance; especially as trees of such colossal height 'could not reasonably have been anticipated on an island where all the vegetation was fairly low'. Feelings were very divided on the subject and were decidedly inclined to asperity. Wales was markedly out of temper with old Forster. 'I have often been struck with surprise,' he scoffs, 'at the excellency of this gentleman's eyes and glasses or the imperfection of my own. He has seen oranges or lemons growing on a tree at three miles distance.' John Forster, who had got on everyone's nerves for so long, was not to get off lightly when his companions were able to catch him out on his own ground, even if their irony was confined to paper. Forster himself gives a very mild version of the whole story and Cook does not overplay Forster's mistake, but the tension it caused is revealed in Sparrman's journal published some twenty years after the voyage in which he felt obliged to stand up for his old patron; 'those who had neither seen nor perhaps read of basalt columns, which Mr Forster surmised them to be, should not have judged this notion as "extravagant", especially as the critics themselves had scarcely any idea on the subject, nor ventured any suggestion'. One can discern Forster's bitter relations with the crew from a passage in his son's account of their New Caledonian adventures that relates how one of the surgeon's mates had collected 'a prodigious variety of new and curious shells . . . but the meanest and most unreasonable envy taught him to conceal these discoveries from us, though he was utterly incapable of making use of them for the benefit of science. . . . It is certain that the traveller who visits the ruins of Egypt and Palestine cannot experience greater mortification from the ignorant selfishness of Bedouins and other Arabs, than fell to our lot. . . . If there had not been a few individuals of a more liberal way of thinking, whose disinterested love for the sciences comforted us from time to time, we should in all probability have fallen victims to that malevolence, which even the positive commands of Captain Cook were sometimes insufficient to keep within bounds'.

The *Araucaria columnaris* had been sighted on the 22nd. For the next seven days the *Resolution* tacked in and out of a labyrinth of reefs and rocks, probably amongst the ablest feats of navigation ever accomplished. Cook was trying to round the southern point of La Grande Terre and finding his way blocked by a continuous barrier of coral, he sailed on past 'an islet somewhat larger than the rest whose skirts are wholly covered with the trees so often mentioned on which account it obtained the name *Isle of Pines*'. Continuing southward the *Resolution* cut to the west and tried to sail up the island's opposite shore but found herself completely embroiled. Every few minutes men at the mastheads called out 'breakers ahead'. 'We hauled up several points, still "breakers ahead"; in fact we found we had been running into a net of breakers and no way out, but as we had come in, which was now right in the wind's eye'. Cook tells us in what is strong language for him that they 'spent the night under the terrible apprehension of every moment falling on some of the many dangers which surrounded us'. I have seen the spot he speaks of and can only add that his fears were certainly not ill founded.

To reach the Isle of Pines I chartered a small single-engine plane. Sitting in front with the pilot, the President of Noumea's Aero Club, I had enjoyed a bird's-eye view of the waters encountered by Cook. Seen from the air one is doubly conscious of the dangers. It is an area that measures roughly twenty-nine miles by forty miles, and counting only summarily, I noted at least three score islets and shoals spread between the mainland and the Isle of Pines. In the clear morning sun the sea shaded from sapphire-blue to aquamarine to brilliant turquoise. Every shallow was ringed around with foaming traces of surf. All very well from my vantage point but how dreadful the sudden paling of the sea must have been to the men on the lookout from the mastheads of an eighteenth-century ship.

'I was now almost tired of the coast,' writes Cook, 'where I could not longer explore but at the risk of losing the ship and ruining the whole voyage.' He was determined nevertheless not to leave the islands 'till I was satisfied what sort of trees those were which had been the subject of our speculation. Everyone,' he says, 'were now satisfied that they were trees, except our philosophers who still maintained they were stone pillars.'

The Isle of Pines lacked an anchorage, but they were eventually able to make land in a small islet midway between there and La Grande Terre, Cook christened it Botany Isle 'because it contained in so small a space a flora of near thirty species'.

The famous *Araucaria* were packed one against the other, unnaturally straight and very high. Cook describes their branches as shooting out 'in the same manner as all the pine kind, with the difference that they are vastly smaller and shorter, so that the knots become nothing when the tree is worked for use, and what is most extraordinary in them is, the larger the tree the shorter and smaller are the branches, this is what led our philosophers into the extravagant notion of their being natural pillars of stone'. Seen from a distance against the skyline they look like giant asphodels. Green tufts grow at the end of each branch in the same way the starlike flowers of the asphodel cluster airy and light around the central stem.

Cook's carpenter 'who is a mast-maker as well as a shipwright', was of the opinion that the *Araucaria* would make excellent masts. The wood is white, closer grained than the fir, and seemingly tougher. Cook was delighted: 'if I except New Zealand, I know of no island in the South Pacific Ocean where a ship could supply herself with a mast or yard, were she ever so much distressed for the want of one. Thus far the discovery may be both useful and valuable'.

On their last evening in New Caledonia's waters Forster reported 'a ball of fire to the north-west in size and splendour resembling the sun, though somewhat paler'. It appeared with a hissing sound and soon burst leaving behind it a few shining sparks 'among which the largest, oblong in shape, sped from our view, followed by a bluish, flaming streak'.

From New Caledonia Cook set course for New Zealand and Queen Charlotte Sound. Summer was approaching and he wanted to refit before standing south once more in a last effort to locate the supposed continent.

Ten days out at sea they discovered an uninhabited island, 'we were undoubtedly the first who ever set foot upon it'. Cook named it Norfolk Island after the Duchess of Norfolk but gave no explanation why the Howard family particularly deserved to be commemorated in the Pacific.

On Norfolk Island they found another variety of pine which they christened *Araucaria excelsa*. It is similar to the preceding one and for some reason it is this rather than the much more singular tree of New Caledonia that one finds in amateurs' collections. The island also produced an abundance of small cabbage palms so called because the tender shoots form a compact bud, or heart, which is edible. Forster said it tasted more like almond than cabbage and they dressed it as a salad with oil and vinegar. This and roast dolphin which tasted rather like beef provided the most agreeable meal they had had for quite some time.

The *Resolution* left Queen Charlotte Sound on November 11th and by the end of December had passed Cape Horn. Should an undiscovered continent exist it could only be in the high latitudes south of Cape Horn. Dipping down to 58° and 59° South latitude Cook met such bad weather that he had to keep throwing the ship into the wind to shake the snow out of her sails. In the course of this cruise he rediscovered a large island which he named Southern Georgia and some days later he sighted The South Sandwich Lands, but there was no continent. By the end of March 1775 he was anchored in Table Bay, having solved a problem that had been tormenting geographers for years.

On arriving at the Cape Cook received a copy of Hawkesworth's edition of the *Endeavour*'s voyage, an amalgam of Cook's journal and Banks' diary written in the first person and purporting to come from Cook's hand. Cook must have been surprised at many of his supposed impressions, among them Banks' criticisms of St Helena which caused Cook some awkward moments two weeks later when dining with the Governor and his lady, the sprightly Mrs Skottowe. Banks had taken against St Helena and described it in his diary in highly unflattering terms, criticisms that Hawkesworth had attributed to Cook: the town was ill-built, the church and market building almost in ruins, all the labour was performed by slaves, poor creatures who were treated like pack animals for 'there wasn't a cart or a wheelbarrow on the whole island'. Although Hawkesworth had fortunately cut much of Banks' text, such gross misinterpretations were retained plus Banks' open regret that St Helena was not in the hands of the Dutch who would 'infallibly have turned it into a paradise'. Small wonder that Mrs Skottowe called the Captain to account, 'displaying to advantage', says Forster, 'her witty and satirical talents probably troubling the naval officers more than many an ocean storm'.

Cook was mortified but there was little else for him to do 'than lay the blame on the absent philosophers whose papers had been consulted'. The island was apparently abounding in wheelbarrows and carts, 'some of which', Forster adds, 'seemed to be studiously placed before Captain Cook's lodging every day'.

Leaving St Helena on May 21st they had crossed the Line by June 11th. After calling in at the Azores, they anchored at Spithead in the last days of July, 'having been absent from England,' writes Cook, 'three years and eighteen days, in which time I lost but four men and one only by sickness'. A record unprecedented in the annals of British naval history.

Cook had sailed between 60,000 and 70,000 miles in his second circumnavigation of the globe. No previous navigator had remained so long at sea, sailed so far, or brought back such extensive and accurate knowledge. It was a remarkable achievement.

[Chapter 22]

The Sandwich Islands

Cook returned on the last days of July, six weeks after the declaration of war with America. In spite of deep anxiety over international affairs the newspapers gave a full and more or less accurate report of the voyage. Cook's reputation was steadily growing. One paper predicted that as a 'reward for the discoveries he has made in his last voyage in the South Seas', he would be made an Admiral of the Blue to command the fleet due to depart in the spring to chastise the 'insurgents'. Admiral he was not to be, but the much harassed king found time to grant him an audience during which he presented him with his commission as Post-Captain. A few days later, acting on advice from the Admiralty, Cook applied for the position of Captain at Greenwich Hospital with the understanding that if his services were required elsewhere he would be permitted to resign. With this appointment came a small salary, a house, and certain living allowances. No doubt he was grateful for the office, but it was not one he accepted with any enthusiasm. 'A few months ago,' he writes to his old employer at Whitby, 'the whole southern hemisphere was hardly enough for me, now I am going to be confined within the narrow limits of Greenwich Hospital, which are far too small for an active mind like mine. I must confess it is a fine retreat, and a pretty income, but whether I can bring myself to like ease and retirement time will tell.' He needn't have worried for by July of the following year he was already at sea, his mission to hunt out the North-West Passage which it was still hoped existed. Indeed, it is more than probable that Cook never took up residence in Greenwich. He hardly would have had the time as he was fully occupied already in preparing his journal for the press, the only account of the three voyages he edited himself. Besides the journals there were also the papers he was preparing for the Royal Society, one on the tides of the Pacific, the other dealing with the methods he used in preventing scurvy. On the strength of these he was elected a Fellow, a great distinction for a man of his upbringing. The paper on scurvy won him the much esteemed Coply Gold Medal, awarded to Mrs Cook after he had sailed.

Cabot in 1497 had been the first to sail in search of a north-west passage across the top of the world from the Pacific to the Atlantic. It was obvious that if such a passage could be effected, voyages to the Far East would be much shorter and consequently more profitable than the tedious circuit of the Cape. A series of other enterprising adventurers followed Cabot but with no greater success. Discouraged by these failures no further attempt had been made since the middle of the seventeenth century, but the renewed interest in exploration brought the subject to the Admiralty's mind again. They felt they could not send Cook out so soon after his return and were looking about for another man to lead the expedition. Cook solved their problem by volunteering for the command without being actually asked. It happened at a dinner given by Lord Sandwich when the conversation turned to the North Pacific. In all his searchings for the Continent Pacifica Cook had kept below the Equator. Now the virgin ocean above it was being subtly offered him over the dinner table. On hearing the details he is said to have jumped up declaring he would go. To further incite him, if any persuasion were necessary, a reward of £20,000 voted some thirty years back was still offered to the man who succeeded.

By February 1776 Cook had once more received his commission to command the *Resolution*, this time accompanied by the *Discovery*, a vessel very similar to the *Adventure*. Charles Clerke, a master's mate in the *Endeavour* and second lieutenant in the *Resolution*, was made commander of the *Discovery*. Under Cook as first lieutenant was John Gore who had sailed with Wallis in the *Dolphin*; James Burney who sailed as lieutenant with Fourneaux in the *Adventure* was Gore's counterpart under Clerke. They were in fact a well-seasoned lot. The number of civilians was reduced to a minimum. 'From the Admiralty's point of view they had proved difficult. Banks had quarrelled with the Navy Board, and Cook's relations with the Forsters were anything but pleasant. On this occasion, therefore, a naturalist was chosen within the service. William Anderson, surgeon's mate in the *Resolution*, became in fact if not in name the expedition's naturalist and William Ellis, his assistant, acted as a natural-history draughtsman.'* Both men were under thirty. James King, an extraordinarily intelligent young man of twenty-six, was appointed astronomer in the *Resolution*, serving simultaneously as second lieutenant. Bailey, who was with the *Adventure* on the previous voyage, was made astronomer in the *Discovery*. Cook himself qualified by this time as a cartographer, astronomer, and naturalist which reduced the need for civilian experts.

King was the son of a Lancashire clergyman and his younger

* *European Vision and the South Pacific* by Bernard Smith, Oxford, The Clarendon Press, 1960.

brother eventually became Bishop of Rochester. He had enrolled in the Navy at the age of twelve under the patronage of a kinsman captain, serving first in African waters and later under Captain Palliser in Newfoundland where he must have had some acquaintance with Cook. By twenty-one he was already lieutenant. He then seems to have felt himself in need of additional education not to be had serving in a ship at sea and we next hear of him in Paris 'devoting himself principally to scientific study', presumably astronomy. On his return he settled at Oxford to be with his brother, the future bishop, who was then a Fellow of Corpus Christi College. Here he met Dr Thomas Hornsby, a Fellow of the Royal Society and the first Radcliffe astronomer, who recommended him for Cook's third voyage. Cook took a great liking to the slight, blond-haired young man who always proved so quick and efficient – tactful too, for it was generally King who was delegated to cope with delicate situations arising between themselves and the natives. The Hawaiians, in fact, regarded him as Cook's son and Cook never bothered to correct their error. On Clerke's death in August 1775 King succeeded to the command of the *Discovery* and it was King also who assisted in preparing Cook's journal for the press, writing the conclusion that forms the third volume. He died of consumption in Nice at the age of thirty-four.

The one man who did not have a double rôle was the expedition's artist, the twenty-four-year-old John Webber, the son of a Swiss sculptor settled in England. Employed by the Admiralty Hodges was busy completing the paintings and drawings brought back from the second voyage, so he could not be sent out again. One cannot regret the change. Hodges was good at large romantic landscapes in oil worked up from notes and sketches and managed admirably to render the beautiful Tahitian light, the iridescence that hovered over bursting waves on the reefs, or the cold light reflected by icebergs in the Antarctic; but his figures are hopeless and his well-known 'landings' in the New Hebrides quite ridiculous. They no more evoke the atmosphere than would an Angelica Kauffmann group of elegantly clad muses that one finds posturing round the curved sides of Mr Hepplewhite's satinwood furniture. Hodges employed other painters to execute his full-length figures (Cipriani in the case of the voyage), but this does not lessen the absurdity of his *Landing at Middleburg* nor of his trumped-up view of the Isle of Pines, which, anyhow, must have been taken through the glasses and would have been much better not produced at all.

Webber at least could draw, and although not so expert as Hodges with light, was accurate and painstaking, the ideal artist for a scientific expedition. As Cook writes, 'Mr Webber was pitched upon, and engaged to embark with me, for the express purpose of supplying the

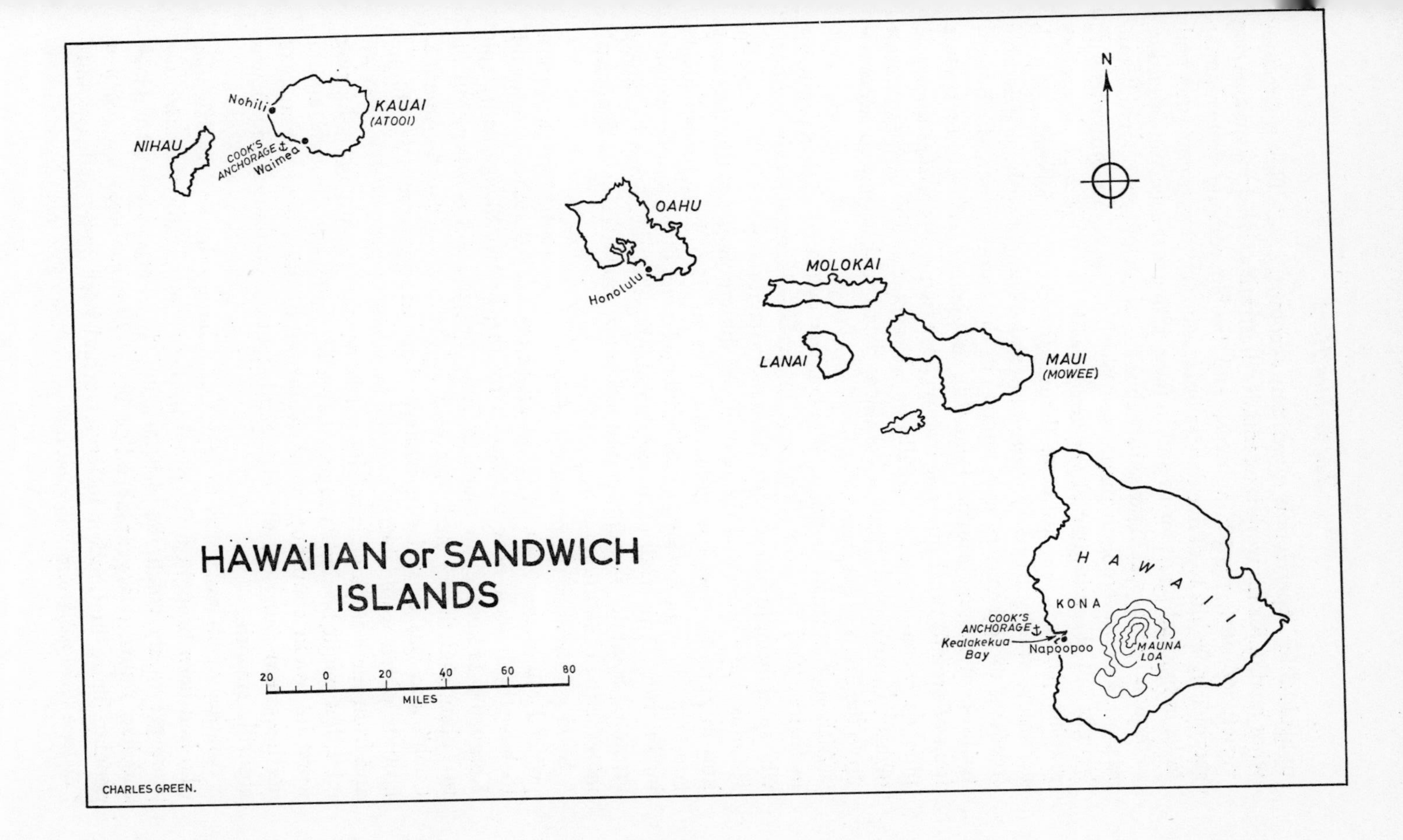
HAWAIIAN or SANDWICH ISLANDS
N
NIHAU
Nohili
KAUAI
(ATOOI)
COOK'S ANCHORAGE
Waimea
OAHU
Honolulu
MOLOKAI
LANAI
MAUI
(MOWEE)
HAWAII
KONA
COOK'S ANCHORAGE
Kealakekua Bay
Napoopoo
MAUNA LOA
20
0
20
40
60
80
MILES
CHARLES GREEN.

unavoidable imperfection of written accounts. . . .' This is precisely what he did, for his work is essentially illustrative. He drew an amazing variety of sites, plants, animals, and people ranging from human sacrifice in Tahiti to native dances in Hawaii. 'He drew vegetation both in its individual plant forms and in mass with great care and attention, as though he was seeking to satisfy the critical eye of professional botanists. . . . Few watercolour painters of Webber's day,' Mr Smith tells us, 'sought out the minutiae of vegetation with the same zeal. The topographic painters, for instance, though they rendered buildings with accuracy, usually treated foregrounds and distances with considerable freedom, to add variety and interest to the composition. Much eighteenth-century topographical painting uses foliage as a setting to some item of architectural interest. But Webber frequently makes an exotic plant: a cocoa-nut, a bread-fruit, or a banana tree the central interest of his painting, and renders botanical detail with care and accuracy up to the limits of his frame.'*

Although born in London, Webber was educated and brought up in Switzerland by a maiden aunt in Berne. A painter called Aberli who specialized in picturesque views of Switzerland was his first master. He must have been well thought of, for the municipal authorities sent him to Paris to complete his training. From there he returned to his family in London, working for a builder who employed him in decorating interiors. A portrait of his brother exhibited in the Royal Academy attracted Solander's attention and led to his appointment as draughtsman for the expedition.

So much then for the personnel of the voyage. Cook's orders were to proceed round the Cape of Good Hope to look for some islands said to have been seen near Mauritius by the Breton navigator Joseph Kerguelen-Trémarec, to touch at New Zealand if necessary, sail on to Tahiti, and thence make his way up the coast of North America. Cook's aim was to strike its western shore at approximately the 45° latitude which would bring him off the coast of present-day Oregon, and from there to move carefully north, nosing into any likely-looking inlet that might be the Passage. At best he would get through, and at worst he would contribute some realistic indentations to the map of north-western America, the eighteenth-century outline of which was absurdly smooth.

Another of his tasks was to take Omai home, the Society Islander who had been brought to England by Fourneaux in the *Adventure* two years previously when the *Adventure* had been separated from Cook and had returned a year ahead of the *Resolution*. Omai had been a popular figure in London society. He had been presented at Court

* *European Vision and the South Pacific*, op. cit.

68. James King.
(*page 243*)

69. John Webber.
(*page 244*)

71. The Hawaiian nobles wore close fitting helmets; 'impossible not to liken to the crested helmets of the Greeks'. Engraved by J. K. Sherwin after J. Webber. (*page 252*)

70. Portrait of Omai by Sir Joshua Reynolds showing him in the flowing *tapa* robes of a Tahitian nobleman. (*page 247*)

72. A typical Hawaiian house, looking somewhat like a haystack. (*page 261*)

73. The isle of Kauai. The tumble of lava rocks
on the beach at Waimea where Cook landed. (*page 253*)

'amidst a brilliant circle of the first nobility'; and he sat for portraits by Reynolds, Dance, and Hodges. Sir Joshua depicted him in the flowing *tapa* robes of a Tahitian nobleman which he had no right to affect, being of humble origin and not a *teuteu* or hereditary attendant upon the king as he pretended. He was much too dark and his features too flat to belong to even the upper classes much less the ruling hierarchy. Forster regretted that he had not been consulted in choosing a native 'to carry home', for he assures us that he would have selected a much finer representative of Polynesian culture, both physically and mentally. True Omai's nose was a little too flat and his colour darker than it should have been, but he had charming manners and even Forster conceded that he was warm-hearted and very appreciative. He had adapted astonishingly well to England and we hear of him doing the rounds dressed in the conventional attire of the times, 'reddish-brown coat, white waistcoat, breeches and sword'. Solander reports having dined with him at the Duke of Gloucester's when the Duchess gave him her pocket handkerchief 'which he promptly received with thanks, and observing her name marked upon it he took an opportunity when she looked at him to kiss it'. He cut such an elegant figure that Dr Johnson sitting behind Omai and Lord Mulgrave (better known as Constantine Phipps, commander of an expedition to the North Pole) at Vauxhall Gardens 'was afraid to speak to either lest I should mistake one for the other'. Fanny Burney, whose brother sailed with Cook on the second and third voyages, met Omai after he had been presented at Court and was very impressed. 'He had on a suit of Manchester velvet, lined with white satin, a bag, lace ruffles, and a very handsome sword which the king had given to him. He is very tall, and very well made, much darker than I expected to see him and of a pleasing countenance . . . he seems to shame education, for his manners are so extremely graceful and he is so polite, attentive and easy that you would have thought he came from some foreign court. You will think that I speak in a high style; but I assure you there is but one opinion of him.'

Miss Burney was not exaggerating. He played chess with 'amazing proficiency' and bathed at Scarborough looking like 'a specimen of pale moving mahogany – highly varnished' by the insipid waves through which he thrashed supporting young blades who wished to be taught how to swim. Having overcome his fear of firearms, he shot grouse at Mulgrave in Yorkshire, 'but since he could never be induced to recognize the distinction between wild fowl and the cocks and hens of the barn yards, it was mostly the latter which fell to his gun'. Journeying in Banks' ponderous coach, a natural historian's laboratory on wheels, he enjoyed his excursion in the country enormously, his pleasure marred only by an irate bull which he called a 'man-cow' and wasps which he called 'soldier-birds'.*

One is surprised that no one tried to convert Omai to Christianity and perhaps Forster is right when he accused him of frivolity. Knowing he was returning to Tahiti, he might have made some effort to acquaint himself with the useful products of our civilization such as agricultural implements or carpentering tools. In addition to a perfectly inappropriate and very extensive wardrobe, his baggage on departure consisted of a barrel organ, various electrical machines, and a suit of armour; possessions chosen with an eye to dazzling his countrymen, or as Cook puts it, 'of attaining to a distinguished superiority amongst them'. In that poor Omai failed miserably. Jealous no doubt of his travels and resenting his trying to assume a rank to which he had no right, they practically ostracized him. We have a pathetic glimpse of him shortly after his return: dressed in his armour and mounted on the stage of a double canoe, he had himself paddled slowly along the shore of Matavai Bay, a display Cook tells us, that fell very flat. His countrymen had already seen armour 'and there were others who had taken such a dislike to Omai by now that whatever he did, however singular, they would have ignored him'.

During May Cook sat for a portrait by Sir Nathaniel Dance. He is shown sitting on the edge of his chair with his right hand – the one that bore a scar and not shown in the painting – resting on an indistinct chart, his forefinger pointing to the top of the sheet at Bering Strait where it was hoped that the Passage might lie.

By June the ship had sailed for the Nore, and on the 24th at six o'clock in the morning, Cook and Omai set out together from London to board an Admiralty yacht at Chatham which would convey them to the *Resolution* at Sheerness. Cook noted that Omai found it difficult to refrain from tears, 'but the instant the conversation turned to his own islands his eyes began to sparkle with joy'.

The *Resolution* stood out of Plymouth Sound on the evening of July 12th. The crew took it to be a good omen that this was the anniversary of the day they had begun the second voyage. Clerke was detained in London and the *Discovery* was to join them at a later date.

August saw the *Resolution* anchored in the Canaries and the Cape Verde Islands. The weather, Cook tells us, was hot and sultry with some rain, and how aptly he turns his phrases; 'a dull whiteness prevailed in the sky, that seems a medium between fog and clouds'. Years at sea with 'philosophers', however difficult, had taught him to use his eyes and had sharpened his perception. He remained modest

* *Random Records* by George Colman, London, 1825.

nevertheless about his style and in trying to describe some island, he insists that his 'very imperfect account is written more with a view of assisting my own memory than to give information to others. I am neither a botanist nor a naturalist; and have no words to describe the productions of nature, either in the one branch of knowledge or the other'. But contemporary critics reviewing the second voyage thought otherwise. They admired his 'manly style' and his 'good sense and penetration', a great deal of 'which does not fall within the lines of his profession: so that we shall not hesitate to place the author in the foremost rank of navigators who have written their own memoirs'.

Still discussing these tropical regions Cook says that they 'seldom enjoy that clear atmosphere observable where variable winds blow; nor does the sun shine with such brightness. This circumstance, however, seems an advantage; for otherwise perhaps the rays of the sun being uninterrupted would render the heat quite insupportable. The nights are nevertheless often clear and serene'. We can imagine Cook writing this seated at a small table in the shade of a green awning stretched over the stern. There exists a letter describing such a scene. The haze he speaks about was not protection enough, however, for the decks of the *Resolution* whose badly caulked seams opened in the hot weather 'so wide that they admitted the rain as it fell. There was hardly a man that could lie dry in his bed; and the officers in the gun-room were all driven out of their cabins, by the water that came through the sides'.

The Equator was crossed on April 1st and they reached Table Bay seventeen days later. The King had stocked the *Resolution* with some horses, goats, sheep, rabbits and chickens, 'with the benevolent view of conveying some permanent benefit to the inhabitants of Tahiti, and of the other islands in the Pacific Ocean'. At his own expense Cook added to their number. To house this menagerie Omai had to vacate his cabin, which he did with good grace. 'Nothing is now wanting,' Cook writes home in a letter, 'but a few females of our own species to make the *Resolution* a complete Ark.' Leaving the Cape a very strong gale followed by a mountainous sea 'made the ship roll and tumble exceedingly, and gave us a great deal of trouble to preserve the cattle'. Cook lost several goats and a considerable number of sheep.

Six days out from the Cape 'they passed through several spots of water of a reddish colour. Some of this was taken up and it was found to abound with a small animal, which the microscope discovered to be like a cray-fish'. A succession of empty days followed as the wind strained at their crowded sails carrying them in a south-easterly direction across the Indian Ocean towards fog-bound seas inhabited by penguins and divers and laced over with rock-weed. They fell in with the several small islands discovered already by Kerguelen, and the day before Christmas reached the bleak, mountainous island that the Breton explorer had christened Rendezvous, 'though,' writes Cook, 'I know nothing that could rendez-vous at it, but fowls of the air; for it is certainly inaccessible to every other animal'.

'Mr Anderson, my surgeon, who had made natural history a part of his studies, lost no opportunity during the short time we lay in Christmas Harbour of searching the country in every direction.' 'Perhaps no place,' he tells us, 'hitherto discovered in either hemisphere, under the same parallel of latitude, affords so scanty a field for the naturalist as this barren spot.' Even the coarse grasses were scarcely worth cutting for the animals. Anderson described a sort of saxifrage 'which grows in large spreading tufts, to a considerable way up the hills'. It grew on 'a kind of rotten turf, into which one sinks a foot or two at every step. This turf dried might, in case of necessity, serve for fuel and is the only thing we met with here that could possibly be applied to this use'. They also found water and a kind of cabbage which they ate raw, finding it somewhat similar to the New Zealand scurvy-grass in flavour. It acquired a rank flavour when boiled; 'which, however, some of our people did not perceive, and esteemed it good'.

By the end of January, the *Resolution* and the *Discovery* were off Tasmania, or rather Van Diemen's Land as it was still called. By the middle of February they were anchored at Queen Charlotte Sound. As we know already, the following year was spent among the islands of the South Pacific, during which time Omai was deposited at Huahine in the Society group. The crew built him a wooden cabin in which to house his valuable possessions. When they parted Omai controlled himself manfully in his adieus to all the crew but broke down completely before Cook. King who rowed him back to the shore in the skiff reported that he wept the whole way. No one knows his fate. He had been dead several years already when Bligh reached Tahiti in 1788.

Various odd details emerge at about this time regarding the life of the expedition. Burney informs us that each ship published a weekly paper and exchanged them whenever possible. He tells us that Cook was a constant reader, but not a contributor. It is to be regretted that no copies survive. Cockroaches which at first were a nuisance had now become a real pest. Nothing they did to rid themselves of them had any effect. According to Anderson there were two kinds, the *Blatta orientalis* and the *germanica*. The *Resolution* had always abounded with the *orientalis* but the *germanica* made their appearance only after leaving New Zealand. They increased at so alarming a rate that they even got amongst the rigging and when a sail was unfurled thousands fell on to the deck. Any food left exposed for a moment was riddled like a honeycomb. They proved particularly destructive to the naturalist's stuffed birds, and even worse, were uncommonly fond of the ink on the labels attached to the different specimens, causing bewildering confusion. Their brothers, the *orientalis*, came out only at night, but in such numbers that the noise they made crawling about the cabins kept everyone awake.

Cook left the Society Islands on December 8th and stood to the northward, embarked now on the principal object of the voyage. 'Before I sailed,' he writes, 'I lost no opportunity of inquiring of the inhabitants, if there were any islands in the north or north-west direction from them; but I did not find that they knew of any.' The Line was crossed on the 23rd and two days later they sighted an atoll, one of those low islands so common in this ocean, 'lying coiled,' as Robert Louis Stevenson describes them, 'like a serpent, tail to mouth in the outrageous ocean'. Cook decided to try catching some turtles as 'it seemed to be a likely place to meet with them'. He had guessed quite correctly. They spent the night on shore turning them on the white sands, bagging between forty and fifty. It so happened that an eclipse of the sun was due on the 30th and Cook had the telescope sent ashore to facilitate observation. In the end clouds interfered with the viewing but they were content at the continued success of their turtling expeditions. During one of these forays two of the sailors got lost. It was a matter of surprise to everyone how they managed it for the whole island was not more than three miles across. 'Nor,' writes Cook, 'was there ought to obstruct their view; for the country was quite flat with but few shrubs scattered upon it.' One would have thought that the ship's masts would have guided them. However, adds Cook, 'considering how strange a set of beings the generality of seamen are, when on shore, instead of being surprised that these two men should thus lose their way, it is rather to be wondered at that no more of the party were missing'. They were lost for nearly twenty-four hours. One of the men killed a turtle and drank its blood to quench his thirst, 'the other poor fellow proving too squeamish suffered far greater distress'. Having nearly lost two of his men Cook decided to plant some coconuts and yams and some melon seeds in the hopes that they would propagate and 'thus furnish nourishment for any future traveller emerging on the scene, though I doubt he would be able to prolong existence for more than a short space of time'. To commemorate the date of their visit Cook christened the atoll Christmas Island.

Their next landfall was Hawaii, named by Cook the Sandwich Islands in honour of the First Lord of the Admiralty. Land was seen at daybreak and soon afterwards another island appeared to the north. They had fallen in with the western islands of the Hawaiian group. Had the ships veered north-east towards their initial landfall they would have sailed right into what is now Pearl Harbor, but the direction of the wind made it difficult to approach Oahu so Cook held straight north for Kauai or Atooi as he called it. This was to be their first encounter with a Polynesian people who had never known Europeans before or ever dreamed of their existence. It was an exciting event. Sounding their way carefully as usual, they came to anchor off the village of Waimea. During the time they were anchored there Cook went ashore three times. 'In the course of my several voyages,' he writes, 'I have never before met with the natives of any place so much astonished as these people were. The very instant I landed,' he tells us, 'the collected body of natives all fell flat upon their faces.' It is difficult to know at precisely which point, whether during their first short stay or whether on their return ten months later, the Hawaiians decided that Cook was one of their gods. But this is a question that must be taken up later. Even if he was not immediately considered a divinity, the natives understood him to be a great chief, and in their eyes there was little difference.

For the moment we are only concerned with the explorers' first impressions. They noted the natives' striking features, their nut-brown colouring and their general resemblance to the Tahitians; 'the language of both places may be said to be almost, word for word, the same'. Again they remarked on the natives' propensity to pilfer 'innate in most of the people we have visited in this ocean'. Unlike the Tahitians these people lived in villages but they resembled them 'in the slovenly state of their religious places'. Only the oracle towers, wooden-framed obelisks four feet square and about twenty feet high covered with a thin, light grey cloth, were well maintained. The people of importance all wore magnificent feathered cloaks worked with 'the most beautiful red and yellow feathers, so closely fixed that the surface might be compared to the thickest and richest velvet' and close-fitting helmets, 'impossible not to liken to the crested helmets of the Greeks'. Cook met with no chiefs on this first encounter but Clerke received a visit from one on board the *Discovery*, a handsome youth, magnificently regal, clothed from head to foot and accompanied by a young woman supposed to be his wife. 'He came off in a double canoe; and like the King of the Friendly Islands paid no regard to the small canoes that happened to lie in his way, but ran against, or over them, without endeavouring in the least to avoid them.' It was impossible anyway for his people to avoid him as they had to prostrate themselves flat in their canoes as he approached. 'His attendants helped him into the ship, and placed him on the gang-way. Their care of him did not cease there; for they stood around him, holding each other by the hands; nor would they suffer any to come near him but Captain Clerke himself.' They exchanged presents and Clerke received a large wooden bowl supported by two figures, similar no doubt to the lively and expert piece of sculpture in the British Museum.

The formation of the land was unlike any island they had visited. The hills were high in the centre but sloped gently to the sea. Cook admired these green undulations so unlike the 'delightful borders of Tahiti' and the 'luxuriant plains of Tongatapu'. The appraising eye of a man born to the land found the Kauian slopes 'capable of improvement'. His observation was shrewdly correct. Today Kauai is known as the Garden Island.

No village exists any longer where the ships anchored, and the place where they watered, described by Cook as a pond, is now a small river estuary silted up with grey sand. The foreshore is a tumble of black lava rocks bearded over with jade green weeds kept constantly shined by a brown sea breaking in from the cerulean deep. The waterfront is quite deserted and untidy with driftwood, great twisted trunks of trees shooting off branch-like roots. Small, greyish-black crabs dart across the sand in between the rocks so rapidly that they appear not to be touching the ground at all but flying. At the approach of danger they turn in a flash, their stalk eyes trained on the intruder, and dash for the sea without a break in their leap. Their turns, of a precision only equalled in perfectly executed choreography, are a joy to watch. Far in the background are the mountains and tilting up to them the slopes that Cook prophetically found 'capable of improvement', patched now with fields of pineapple, blue-green fields tinged with rust, or then soft green if planted with cane.

On the margin of the sea, tumbling over a tidal bank grow tough-leaved convolvuli, their roots plunged into tightly packed sticks of coral that crunch like schoolroom chalk as one treads on them. A little way inland a more fragile member of the same family opens its blue and white flowers to the brightness of the morning. If one penetrates farther along the banks of the river one comes upon the remains of a Russian fort built during the early part of the last century. It would seem that they had hoped to acquire a base in Hawaii to further their interests in the Pacific fur trade. These crumbling bastions of reddish-brown lava rock represent their broken dreams, for the attempt was frustrated by the determined Hawaiians. The ruins now lie quite forgotten encircling an emptiness of tired grass, the red dust in which it struggles for existence patterned by the imprints of hundreds of small birds. On the far side of the tumbled walls someone has set up an apiary, a collection of twenty neglected wooden hives, humming in the still heat. Everything about the place is improbable and it is hard to picture it as it must have been in Cook's days.

Kauai is off the visitors' track but it is nevertheless a lovely island. Geologists will tell you that it was the first of the Hawaiian group to rise in an explosion of molten rock from the ocean bottom. It is the most weathered of the larger islands and its rocky peaks are eroded into strange shapes. The skyline at Wailua resembles the form of a sleeping giant while another mountain has an enormous hole thrust through it, so the legend goes, by a giant's spear. The natives will tell you that giant shadows often cross the dappled landscape, and in the half light of dusk or early dawn a phantom giant still strides across the sand flats of Nohili, spear in hand, clad in a feather helmet and a long feather cloak.

Beautiful also is Waialeale, the island's central mountain, rising nearly a mile into the clouds, sheltering in its crevices tremendous ferns of such size as to startle even the prepared botanist.

Cook, summarizing his first visit to the Sandwich group, marvels at the vast area colonized by one people; 'how shall we account for this nation having spread itself in so many detached islands, so widely disjointed from each other, in every quarter of the Pacific Ocean! We find it, from New Zealand, in the south, as far as the Sandwich Islands to the north! And, in another direction, from Easter Island to the Hebrides! That is, over an extent of sixty degrees of latitude'. The actual distance from Hawaii in the north to New Zealand in the south is 5,000 miles; and from Tonga in the west to Easter Island in the east, nearly 4,500 miles, a vast area known as the Polynesian triangle; perhaps not the most numerous but certainly the most extensive nation upon earth.

It was once thought that a Spanish navigator had touched at Hawaii in the sixteenth century, but this is now generally discredited. Cook also rejected the theory; 'had the Sandwich Islands been discovered at an earlier period, by the Spaniards, there is little doubt that they would have taken advantage of so excellent a situation, and would have made use of Kauai, or some other of the islands, as a refreshing place for the ships that sail annually from Acapulco for Manila. They lie almost midway between the first place and Guam, one of the Ladrones (Marianne Islands) which is at present their only port in traversing this vast ocean'.

Cook was fully aware of the Hawaiian Islands' strategic significance and their future consequence to European navigation. No geographer or cartographer had ever guessed that there would be a great archipelago between the northern and southern routes of the ancient galleons. Although he failed to find a northern passage Cook rejoiced 'to enrich our voyage with a discovery which, though the last, seemed in many respects to be the most important that had hitherto been made by Europeans throughout the extent of the Pacific Ocean'.

The entry is dated January 17th 1779 and was fated to be the last one written by Cook in his own hand. He was killed almost exactly a month later before he had had time to sort out his notes. We now turn to the young James King for what remains to be told.

[Chapter 23]

Kealakekua Bay

On leaving Kauai the ships sailed towards the coast of New Albion as Sir Francis Drake had christened the west coast of North America. They first sighted land off Cape Blanco on Oregon's shores which struck Cook as having an 'uncomfortable appearance', although he allowed that it might make an agreeable summer prospect. Hugging the coast the ships zigzagged up Canada's western seaboard, rounded the Alaska Peninsula, and plunged into the Bering Sea, eventually penetrating the straits leading to Icy Cape in the Arctic. 'We sailed to such a height of north latitude,' Cook informs us, 'as to demonstrate the impracticability of a passage in that hemisphere.' Anyhow further progress was out of the question as ice seized up the sea from continent to continent.

They had travelled well over 3,000 miles in under six months, surveying all the way. The men had suffered the hardships usually encountered in the Arctic such as ice hanging from their hair, from their noses, and even from their finger-ends when they were exposed to the air. Hot food froze at the table before it could be eaten. They saw a prodigious number of walruses which made good eating provided they were cooked right away, but became rancid and fishy if kept for any length of time. Poor William Anderson, the surgeon and naturalist of the *Resolution*, who had been 'lingering under a consumption for more than twelve months' died before reaching the straits. Cook named an island after this 'sensible young man and agreeable companion'. The next day 'I removed Mr Law, the surgeon of the *Discovery* into the *Resolution* and appointed Mr Samuel, the surgeon's first mate of the *Resolution* to be the surgeon of the *Discovery*.'

Just a month before his death, Anderson confided to his great friend Burney that he and Clerke, whose health was also declining, had decided to petition Cook to leave them behind in Kauai. 'Being a doctor Anderson realized the consequences of a prolonged encounter with a frozen climate but unfortunately owing to the fact that Clerke's papers and accounts were not in order, the execution of the plan was deferred and finally abandoned.'* Cook presumably knew nothing of it as he never mentioned any such request.

After reaching Icy Cape and realizing that he could penetrate no farther, Cook decided to winter in the Sandwich Islands and to resume his exploring from there in the spring, for he fully intended to make another attempt to find the North-West Passage.

They reached Maui or Mowee as Cook calls it on November 26th. No landing was made but the ships traded while making their way leisurely down the eastern shore line. Hawaii or Owahee was sighted on the evening of the 30th and they were surprised to see its mountains capped in snow.

A lowering sky loaded with heavy clouds and rain came with the New Year. First squalls and contrary winds and then calms and adverse currents prevented Cook from landing. For almost six weeks he was obliged to stand off from the land. The inhabitants of the small villages they sailed by came out in their canoes 'thronging the ships with hogs and women'. It was not possible, Cook tells us, to keep the latter from coming on board 'and no women, I ever met with, were less reserved'.

The Hawaiians seemed to know all about the ships' previous visit to Kauai earlier in the year and everywhere they were greeted with joy, as if being fêted.

The island of Hawaii is one huge lava bed, built up from a succession of lava flows and it is only in their crevices, now valleys, that patches of rich soil are to be found. The coasts are deep plunging cliffs piled up with fragments of black rock, behind which the ground rises gradually for about two and a half miles, sloping up into the clouds. Everywhere one walks there are loose burnt hunks of lava, tumbled every way, hard and unyielding and painful to the feet. One wonders how the natives managed in their primitive sandals made of twisted coconut fibres which they strapped on only when the going was particularly rough. Cook complained of the lack of vegetables and then remarked on the dismal aspect of the country. 'Indeed from its appearance it did not seem capable of affording them. Marks of it having been laid waste by explosions of a volcano, everywhere presented themselves; and though we had as yet seen nothing like one on the island, the devastation that it had made in this neighbourhood was visible to the naked eye.'

Day after day the boats were sent out to look for a suitable harbour. Finally at daybreak on the 16th William Bligh, ship's master in the *Resolution*, discovered a safe anchorage on the west side of the island. Canoes now began to arrive from all parts 'so that before 10 o'clock

* *My Friend the Admiral*, by G. E. Manwaring, George Routledge, London, 1931.

there were not fewer than a thousand about the two ships'. By eleven the next morning they were safely anchored in Karakakoo Bay, or more correctly Kealakekua Bay, riding about a quarter of a mile from the shore. Cook tells us that he had never before seen so many people assembled at one place. 'Besides those who would come off to us in canoes, all the shore of the bay was covered with spectators and many hundreds were swimming around the ships like shoals of fish.' There must have been some three thousand. Quite by accident the ships had anchored off the capital of the island, the residence of the great chief Kalaniopuu. It was no surprise to the natives. Indeed the ships had been expected, for unwittingly Cook was acting out a rôle in Hawaiian mythology. The Hawaiians firmly believed him to be the reincarnation of one of their demi-gods, the beloved Lono.

In a former age, so the story goes, a god-king, one Orono or Lono by name, had left Hawaii from Kealakekua Bay, promising one day to return in a floating island with trees. He had been remembered first as a legend and then, with the passage of time, had been deified, becoming Lono-i-ka-makahiki, the god who presided over the *makahiki* season; a period of four months beginning in October or November for paying taxes which were settled with the produce of the land. He was thus the deity of the New Year, a kind god, the opposite to the ferocious Ku, Hawaii's bloodthirsty god of war. Lono was the god of rain, of growing crops. His symbol was the clouds, and on earth one of his manifestations was a long pole with a strip of white *tapa* attached to it. The *makahiki* god, thus adorned, was carried all round the island stopping at the boundary of each district to receive the taxes.

On each of his visits Cook appeared during the *makahiki* season. It is therefore hardly surprising that his ships were taken for Lono's floating islands of trees and the sails his *tapa*-hung banners. The way also in which Cook's squadron had sailed leisurely along the coasts of the various islands was more than a little suggestive of the progress of the god around the island during the *makahiki* festival. Small wonder that the Hawaiians saw in Cook the embodiment of their beloved Lono. Later when the missionaries and whalers had settled on the island and his death was discussed, the Hawaiians, although regretting the episode, blamed Cook for having consented to his deification by the priests. He was a Christian, they argued, and did wrong to enter their places of worship and accept gifts offered before idols and eat food dedicated to them. His death, they felt, was the retribution of their gods. But indeed, poor Cook was never aware of the singular distinction meted out to him. Hawaii, like Tahiti and the Friendly Islands was governed by a ruling class that enjoyed every possible privilege, and the respect with which he was treated was that due, he thought, to a great chief and a mortal, not a god. One certainly cannot blame him, anyhow, for submitting to this extraordinary display of favours which made for a very agreeable relationship between the natives and the British. Only at moments and then only very vaguely does King ever intimate that perhaps the adulation went too far, that they suspected that the showers of presents, the crowd's enthusiasm, and the religious ceremonies were more than just respect due to a great chieftain. Some of the officers might have noticed that the warrior chiefs were not quite as wondrously deferential as were the priests and the populace, but it could only have been a brief shadow cast over an otherwise sunny and cheerful atmosphere of friendliness and good will.

It is from this moment on that James King takes over the narrative. The change in style, however, is not so abrupt as might be expected, for Cook exerted a strong influence over his young entourage, and reading King, one is all the time conscious of the Captain's presence. It must be remembered also that everything was discussed over the dinner-table and therefore it is reasonable to suppose that a good deal of the time it was Cook's own reactions that King records. Clerke, usually an excellent source of information, was too ill to take part in the expeditions on shore. There is a wash drawing of him by John Taylor, made just before he sailed, showing his thin, sensitive face set on narrow sloping shoulders. It needs little effort of imagination to visualize the sick man who at times had to be helped to his feet and escorted to the companion-way where he walked slowly down the stairs leaning heavily upon the guard-rail. He anyhow burnt all his papers before he died and thus King and Burney are our chief sources of reference, also David Samuel who published a full account of Cook's death. Samuel, it will be remembered, had been surgeon's mate to the *Resolution* and had later been promoted surgeon in the *Discovery* after Anderson's death; an emphatic little Welshman with a determined chin and a tilted nose, a well-known figure in the Welsh literary circle in London who ended his days as a surgeon to British prisoners of war at Versailles.

Owing to its remote position in the Polynesian triangle Hawaii was the last of the island groups to be settled. Series of migrations from central Polynesia, that is to say Tahiti, began arriving about the fifth century. A fairly continuous contact was kept up until the end of the twelfth century. After that all ties seem to have been broken off, which explains the numerous superficial differences between the two groups. The basic type of Polynesian culture has already been described when dealing with Tahiti, so we needn't go into all the details.

The group consists of some twenty islands, eight of which are inhabited. Each small island was ruled by a *moi*, a paramount chief. If the island was large, it was divided among several *moi*. These chiefs, drawn from amongst the *ariis* or nobles, were believed to be descended from the gods. There were degrees of sacredness amongst them, the highest of them all being so venerated that when taken prisoner of war he was generally starved to death since only an equal could lay hands on him. Thus the whole population was divided by the same rigid class distinctions that were to be found in Tahiti and Tongatapu, an hereditary nobility and an hereditary proletariat and great pains were taken to maintain the division between these two classes. King tells us that the power of the chiefs was absolute and that the public were continually prostrating themselves in front of them. However, he never witnessed any acts of cruelty or injustice, although he admits that 'they exercised their power over one another in the most haughty and impressive manner'.

At the period of Cook's visit the Hawaiian group was divided into four kingdoms. The island of Hawaii, the largest of the group, under the rule of Kalaniopuu who also had holdings in Maui, was the most important. Indeed, the ageing chief was away fighting in Maui at the time of Cook's arrival, and returned only later to pay the ships a state visit. Kalaniopuu, like Tu in Tahiti, visualized uniting all the islands of the group under one rule, an ambition that was finally realized by his nephew Kamehameha who became the great Kamehameha I, the founder of a dynasty that continued governing in direct descent until 1893 when a bloodless revolution established a republic that transferred its sovereignty to the United States in 1898. In 1959 Hawaii was admitted into the union as its fiftieth state.

We know that Cook's first impressions of Hawaii were not overflattering, and King echoes his opinion when describing the Kona coast where they were anchored; 'it presents a prospect of the most horrid and dreary kind'. Everywhere the ground was covered with cinders and scoured with lava courses that had flowed not many ages back from the gentle slopes of Mauna Loa. The explorers came to the conclusion that in spite of its snow cap the great mountain rising above them must be an active volcano. All was not desolation, however, for 'notwithstanding the dismal aspect of this part of the island, there are many villages scattered over it'. Fearing this might appear contradictory King explains that 'the islanders have no cattle and consequently have no use for pasturage and prefer land that lies convenient for fishing'. He tells us also that amidst the crevices and lava flows there are patches of rich loam suitable for the cultivation of yams, plantains, and *taro*. In places the rocks had been cleared away 'to about the depth of three feet and upward; which labour, great as it is, the fertility of the soil amply repays'. These improvised fields were enclosed by stone fences and 'are interspersed with groves of coconut and bread fruit which flourish with great luxuriance'.

The villages were large and unfortified, the houses built very close together and joined one to another by winding paths. There was no prescribed size for the houses. Some were small and others were up to fifty feet long. They were gabled on both ends, windowless, and carefully thatched with *pili* which gave them the appearance of haystacks. The dark interiors were tidy and clean, the floors strewn with grass overlaid with very finely woven mats. Very often the steeply pitched roofs were covered with ripening gourds which the Hawaiians cultivated for a variety of domestic purposes. Some of them grew to enormous size, capable of containing from ten to twelve gallons of liquid. Others were bandaged to give them special forms, while others were netted over with coir so that the gourds bulged through the meshing as they grew, hardening to a series of globular protrusions. They were twisted and tortured into such a variety of shapes that they looked like a collection of Venetian glass.

Kealalekua Bay is about a mile deep, a perfect crescent flanked by two low promontories thrusting out into the sea. From point to point it measures roughly a mile and a half. On the flat and barren northern point Kalaniopuu had his residence. Another village known as Kakooa nestles at the opposite end in a grove of coconut palms. Between them runs a high rocky cliff, inaccessible from the sea, that shielded the ships from the north wind. King tells us that 'the shore, all round the bay, is covered with a black coral rock, which makes the landing very dangerous in rough weather, except the village of Kakaooa, where there is a fine sandy beach with a *marae* at one extremity and a small well of fresh water at the other'. The bay is exactly as Webber shows it in his engraving. The *marae* or rather the platform on which it stood still exists and the village, if one can call it that, is now known as Napoopoo. No trace remains, however, of the royal domain on the northern point.

My own impressions of the bay coincide with King's. It is half an hour's drive from Kona over a road that swings across Mauna Loa's great bulging flank, the largest single mountain mass on earth, rising to nearly 14,000 feet above sea-level. The last eruption occurred in 1950. The writhing lava flows that fingered down towards the coast in brown whorls and ridges are now netted over with vines. For centuries the mountain has sent its molten rivers over the land leaving solidified blocks of grey and purple among the forests of giant ferns. Much of the island is a moonscape, a lunar vision that the white man's machines have been able to coax into prodigal fertility. My way was lined with coffee plantations above which, hidden in the clouds, lurked Mauna Loa's flat snow-capped crater, an eerie desolation haunted by the goddess Pele, the keeper of volcanoes, dressed in her shiny robes with strange glass-like hair. The natives say that when there is an eruption the lava gets blown with the wind, whipped up into the cold air and spun out into tiny glassy strands – Pele's hair.

From these heights a narrow road winds down to the famous bay. It is exactly as one expected it, precise in every detail from the high wall of cliffs to the long gentle curve of the shoreline. There are changes, of course, but they are superficial. The coconut palms have nearly all disappeared and some Friesian cows were browsing on a tangle of herbage growing adjacent to the grey beach. Where the well once stood is a marshy patch and the place is deserted except for a few tumbledown huts belonging to Japanese-Hawaiian fisherfolk. Only one native made his appearance on my first visit. He was selling shell souvenirs and trinkets made of 'weed-seeds' in a stall set up below the black volcanic walls of the *heiau* as temples are called in Hawaii. I wondered if he ever had any clients but decided it was probably the weather that was keeping the people away. The sky was leaden-grey with rifts of pale light that promised weak flashes of sun. For a brief moment it broke over the white shaft erected in Cook's memory at the far end of the bay. However, the weather is not often overcast on the coast. One shower after another can fall inland while there is fine weather and a clear sky on the shore. The coast people call the rain 'liquid sunshine', and their island the 'rainbow land'.

It was a glorious day when Cook finally dropped anchor in the bay, all blue and gold in the sparkle of the sun with the whiteness of the rain-washed sails shining above them against the dazzling sky. 'As soon as the inhabitants perceived our intention of anchoring, they came off from the shore in astonishing numbers. The sides, the decks and rigging of both ships were soon completely covered with them.' The crowd on the *Discovery* was so dense that it looked as if she were going to keel over. Orders had to be given to clear the decks whereupon the natives plunged from great height into the ocean. They were remarkable swimmers and took to the water, diving off their canoes, with the slightest encouragement. When writing about Maui, 'where the surf was so high that they could not land in their canoes,' Cook tells us that he often saw nursing mothers with infants at their breasts 'leap overboard and swim to the shore, through a sea that looked dreadful'. There were special beaches for surfing and their skill in handling their boards amazed the Englishmen. They would ride the boards in on gigantic waves and just as they were about to break, slip off at the last moment. King tells us that he often saw the board

74. Mauno Loa's great bubbling crater. Engraved by W. Finden after E. Howard. (*page 260*)

75. Kealakekua Bay showing a section of the *heiau* on its high wall. Kalaniopuu's village lies at the far end of the bay beyond the ships and is hardly visible in the plate.
Engraved by W. Byrne after J. Webber. (*page 260*)

76. Surfing. 'They rode in on gigantic waves.' (*page 262*)

dashed to pieces on the rocks at the very moment the man quitted it.*

Kalaniopuu being away, a man called Pareea deputized for him in welcoming Cook. With him was another chief, Kaneena. 'Both these men,' King tells us, 'were of strong and well-proportioned bodies and of countenances remarkably pleasing.' Kaneena, 'one of the finest men I ever saw, about six foot tall, with regular expressive features and lively, dark eyes', was drawn by Webber. They were very authoritative, almost despotic with their people. One man slow to obey an order to quit the ship, was just picked up by Kaneena and flung into the sea.

Following the chiefs' visit another dignitary came on board, Koah or Pu'ou, the high priest of Lono. He had once been a distinguished warrior but was now 'a little old man of an emaciated figure; his eyes exceedingly sore and red, and his body covered with a white leprous scurf, the effects of an immoderate use of *kava*. . . .' He approached Captain Cook with great veneration and threw a piece of red cloth over his shoulders. A small pig was also offered up. This ceremony was often to be repeated during their stay. King admits that it smacked of religious adoration but never for a moment did any of them suppose that their captain was identified with one of the Hawaiian gods.

Cook spent his first evening ashore in the company of King and Bayly the astronomer. They landed on the beach adjoining the village and were met by four priests carrying long wands tipped with tufts of dog hair. 'They marched before us pronouncing with a loud voice a short sentence, in which we could only distinguish the word *Orono*. The crowd which had been collecting on the shore retired at our approach; and not a person was to be seen, except a few lying prostrate on the ground.' *Orono* was, of course, Lono. King tells us that Cook always went by this name in Hawaii but says that they could never learn its precise meaning.

The party headed for the *heiau* situated on a high platform and fenced around by a wooden railing decorated with grinning human skulls, victims of past sacrifices. In the centre of the temple area stood a ruinous old building and at the far end an oracle tower. Two wooden

* Surfing and sledging were the favourite sports on the island. The sledging tracks of beaten earth and grass sloped for over a mile down to the beaches. A competitor would throw himself on to the sledge and career down the track, racing an opponent who had chosen an equally distant wave. The sledge rider mounted at the moment the surfer caught his giant wave, both racing to a finish on the black volcanic sands. One would have thought that the surf rider won every time, but apparently not. William Ellis, the missionary who had watched the Hawaiians sledging, assures us that the force with which they flung themselves on to the sledges carried them at great speed. But much practice and skill were needed to keep an even balance. The Historical Society had just restored the royal slide at Kona when I was there.

images with violently distorted faces greeted the visitor at the entrance while twelve more of them stood in semicircular formation round the high altar which was a wooden platform piled with the usual putrid offerings. The images were cut in the round from the trunk of a large tree and tapered to a peg-like pedestal by which they were stuck into the ground. Among the hard volcanic rocks the pegs seldom sunk all the way to the base of the image, thus they were considerably higher than the impression had from the few that have survived where the peg support has been cut off below the foot. The great grimacing heads, disproportionately large for their bodies, are all the same, with elliptical eyes curving downwards to a fine point, figure-eight mouths, protruding tongues, and elongated ears. Strictly speaking these images were not supposed to represent gods, only guardians.* The actual manifestation of divinity rested in small unpretentious objects, shapeless things, as King describes them, without form, wrapped round with red cloth.

The Hawaiians preserved the religion which their ancestors had brought from central Polynesia. Although their names had changed with the dialect, the gods were the same as those in Tahiti. Tu, for instance, became Ku, the god of war; and Tane became Kane; and Tangaroa, Kanaloa. The chieftains had a whole pantheon of minor gods of their own.

The unique features of the Hawaiian temples were the oracle towers. Most drawings and engravings show them to be hollow inside, but the drawings must have been made when the towers were not in use, for when ceremonies were performed temporary floors were inserted, each with a particular use. Offerings were placed on the lowest; the high priest and his attendant performed certain rituals on the second; and the third was sacrosanct, reserved for the king or high priest, where the god took possession of his servant and spoke through him of coming events.

It was dark by the time Cook arrived at the ramp leading up to the temple. Flare torches sent flickering shadows dancing over the top of the trees, quickening the leering masks of the images. From the village below came the heavy thudding of drums, and above their vibrant rhythm wailed the dirge of the temple attendants. A tall young priest with a long beard waited for the party at the entrance. He chanted a welcome in a weird, high-pitched voice and led them in. The priests were scantily clad in a breech cloth that passed between their thighs, their black hair scraped back and piled in a ridge down the middle of

* 'In spite of the great number of images mentioned by early visitors very few examples have survived. For once this was not due to the zeal of Christian missionaries but to the natives themselves who destroyed the temples and their contents.' *Arts of The South Seas*, Ralph Linton and Paul S. Wingert in collaboration with Rene D'Harnoncourt, The Museum of Modern Art, New York.

their heads. Cook was led to the altar and made to sit under the offering platter held aloft on four tall poles – a baldaquin reeking of putrescence. No sooner was he installed than Pu'ou, the high priest, reached up and took the carcass of a pig lying on a pile of sodden vegetable matter and held it out to Cook before letting it drop to the ground in a scattering of maggots. He then took him by the hand and led him to the oracle tower 'which they began to climb together, not without the risk of falling'. King describes his captain as swathed around with red cloth 'and with difficulty keeping his hold amongst the pieces of rotten scaffolding'. Trapped in this awkward position he was obliged to listen to a long dirge intoned in turns by Pu'ou and the young bearded priest. Further ceremonies followed including a ritual feeding with freshly roasted hog. Pu'ou and the young priest pulled the flesh to pieces and put it into their guests' mouths. King said he had no great objection to being fed by the young priest 'who was very cleanly in his person; but Captain Cook, who was served by Pu'ou, recollecting the putrid hog, could not swallow a morsel; and his reluctance, as may be supposed, was not diminished when the old man, according to his own mode of civility, had chewed it for him'.

Needless to say they were completely puzzled as to the meaning of the various ceremonies but as King points out, at least it indicated a great respect on the part of the natives. The explorers were happy to leave it at that and pass no comment on what they might well have damned as heathenish mumbo jumbo. It is admirable, after all, that the Englishmen should have suffered the rituals without protest or ridicule and it plainly indicates that the bigoted reactions of a later age had not yet affected man's reasoning.

Everywhere Cook went during the time he was anchored in Kealakekua Bay he was attended by a priest from the temple who went before him giving notice that Lono had landed and ordering the people to prostrate themselves. 'The same person also constantly accompanied him on the water, standing in the bow of the boat, with a wand in his hand.' At his approach the natives in their canoes immediately left off paddling and lay down on their faces till he had passed.

Quite frequently minor chiefs would ask to be presented to Cook or Lono, as they called him. On meeting him they always 'presented a hog with evident marks of fear in their countenances'. Every day a supply of hogs and vegetables would be sent to the ships, canoe loads of provisions, far more than they needed. Never was anything asked in return. They enjoyed this prodigality for a week and then suddenly no canoes were allowed to come near the ships. They were worried for they could not understand what had happened until it was learned that the bay had been put under taboo on account of Kalaniopuu's return.

On the afternoon of his arrival he paid an unofficial visit with his wife and children to the *Resolution* and the following morning appeared again in state. Three large double canoes were seen to set off from the shore; the first, with a sail, carried the king and his nobles; the second was loaded with religious images and priests, while the third was full of gifts. They must have presented a fine spectacle, the nobles and the king resplendent in their feathered helmets and shining capes glimmering in the sun like polished gold rimmed with fire.

The images, also uniquely Hawaiian, were made of feathers fixed to a wickerwork base moulded in human form, and were as terrifying as their wooden counterparts. They had large staring black and white eyes of mother-of-pearl and a protruding black peg for the pupil. They were red, with yellow crests and black eyebrows. A double row of dogs' fangs gaped from their mouths.

King does not mention them but attendants at Kalaniopuu's side probably carried *kahilis* or royal feather standards. The first official record we have of them dates from the beginning of the nineteenth century but it is very probable that they were used prior to this. Eye-witnesses describe the lofty noddings of these great cylinders of grey and white feathers fixed at the end of long poles made up of alternating rings of tortoise-shell and human bone. Certainly they must have added considerable dignity to the groups whose distinction they proclaimed. When not in use the cylinders were removed from the poles and carefully preserved in storage gourds.

Everyone on board thought that the chief intended to visit the *Resolution*, but after circling the ships the canoes headed again for the shore towards the spot where Cook had struck his tents. As soon as Cook realized what was happening he called his boat and followed them, arriving at almost the same time as the chief and his cortège. Elaborate salutations were performed on the sand and then Cook conducted Kalaniopuu into the tent. They had scarcely been seated 'when the king rose up, and in a very graceful manner threw over the captain's shoulders the cloak he himself wore, put a feathered helmet upon his head and a curious fan in his hand. He also spread at his feet five or six other cloaks, all exceedingly beautiful and of the greatest value'. Cook and the King then exchanged names and pledged eternal friendship. In short, the meeting was a great success.

These feather cloaks were very rare and were worn only by men of the highest rank. The length of the cloak depended on the rank of the wearer, some of them reaching no lower than the waist, others trailing on the ground. King tells us that they were only worn on very special occasions, one of them being the ceremony we have just described and later on 'by some chiefs who were seen among the crowd on shore when Captain Cook was killed; and afterwards when they brought us his bones'.

The most famous of all the capes was the great yellow one belonging to Kamehameha I. It was made of bright feathers and reached from his shoulders to the ground. It was sent to George IV as a present and for some time was to be seen among the other cloaks at Windsor Castle, but unfortunately has since disappeared. It bore two spear holes received in battle the first time the King wore it. It was also the last cloak to be made and the only one known without a pattern.

These cloaks were made by overlapping the feathers like fish scales. Hundreds of birds had to be caught to provide feathers for a single cloak. It has been estimated that Kamahameha's cloak required half a million golden feathers of the rare *mamo*, the *Drepanis pacifica*, or at least eighty thousand birds. They of course took months, sometimes years, to make and it upsets one to learn that one of them was used as a sleigh rug by a family in Boston.

King remarked that though extremely beautiful the birds on the island were not very varied. The ones he describes all belong to the *Trochilidae* or humming bird family that feed principally on nectar siphoned up through long curved beaks.

The feathers were collected during the moulting season by a guild of feather gatherers who camped in the mountains. Black feathers came from the *o'o* or *Acrulocerus nobilis*; the red, from the *i'iwi* or *Vestiaria coccinea*; and the yellow, from the *mamo* or *Drepanis pacifica*. The bird-catchers snared their victims with lime and nets and let them go again once the necessary feathers from the tail and under the wings had been plucked. The unfortunate *i'iwi*, however, was the only exception. As it was entirely red, it would never have survived plucking and therefore had to be killed. The birds were thus more or less protected, but in spite of this both the *mamo* and the *o'o* have become extinct, probably because of changed forest conditions or the introduction of bird diseases.

Returning now to Cook's meeting with Kalaniopuu, King tells us that he was surprised to see in him 'the same infirm and emaciated old man that came on board the *Resolution* when we were off the north-east side of Maui; and we soon discovered amongst his attendants most of the persons who at that time had remained with us all night. Of this number were two younger sons of the king, the eldest of whom was sixteen years of age and his nephew Maiha-maiha' or more correctly Kamehameha. At first they had some difficulty in recognizing the favourite, 'his hair being plastered over with a dirty brown paste', which did not flatter him since it framed 'the most savage face I ever beheld'. But, adds King, 'it by no means seemed an emblem of his disposition which was good natured and humorous, although his manner showed somewhat of an overbearing spirit and he seemed to be the principal director in the interview'.

King tells us nothing about Kalaniopuu and what little there is to learn about him we gather from John Papi I, a contemporary and a nobleman who tells us that in his old age the king greatly enjoyed the *hula*. 'He would come forth and stand before the dancers and with outstretched hands would tell the drummers to liven up the tempo. "More excitement! More excitement!" he shouted. People who did not recognize Kalaniopuu complained that he spoiled the show, grumbling at an interfering old man.'

As to Kamehameha, he must have been about twenty-five* at the time of Cook's visit and was, as King says, fierce-looking but handsome with a good figure and a lively intelligent mind. He was later to prove an able statesman and of the great chiefs was the first to appreciate the advantages to be gained from friendly relations with foreigners without weakening his own power. During the latter part of his reign he had several foreigners in his service as advisers.

In general the explorers found the Hawaiians a more robust people than the Tahitians and the women less delicately limbed. Cook thought that they resembled more the Maoris. Their physiques had perhaps improved over the centuries in this ideal sub-tropical climate where the extremes of temperature lie between 71° and 78°. Apart from their size they differed little from their ancestors, their dress was more or less similar except that they wore less of it. They also tattooed themselves, but generally in squares and lines, and then only on the hands and near the groin although some of the early engravings show a more extensive treatment. The women tattooed their tongues as a sign of mourning and were very fond of feather necklaces or *leis*. King tells us that 'the ladies never think themselves dressed without one or two of them round their necks, and those who can afford it wear many'. The chiefs had a special insignia of rank, a hook-shaped ornament called a *lei palaoa*, made originally from the tooth of a sperm-whale and suspended from two coils of braided human hair.

They wore *tapa* of a fineness seen nowhere but in Hawaii, like gauze and dyed unusual colours such as pink, yellow, pale blue, and a fragile almond-green obtained from one of the arbutilons and not used in any other part of Oceania. Thicker kinds of *tapa*, King tells us, were 'painted in a variety of patterns with a regularity of design that bespoke infinite taste and fancy. The exactness with which the most intricate patterns are continued is the more surprising when one considers that they have

* He died in 1819.

no stamps and the whole is done by eye with pieces of bamboo dipped in paint'.* Cook was also struck by their quality and already in Maui reported that 'one would suppose that they had borrowed their patterns from some mercerer's shop in which the most elegant productions of China and Europe are collected'.

Their mats were also exceptionally fine, patterned with squares and rhomboids and then splashed with red and green spots. 'In this article of manufacture,' King writes enthusiastically, 'they excel the whole world.' The closest woven of all were made from a variety of sedge from the island of Nihau. It is unfortunate that these fine pandanus mats are no longer made, but the Bishop Museum has a collection of them, some of the better ones of which came from burial caves. One such mat in the museum is so fine that Kamehameha I wore it as a cloak.

The Hawaiians wore gourd masks for helmets. They were large bulbous affairs covering the head and most of the face with various shaped holes cut in them for the eyes and the nose. The gourds were the same tawny colour as the men who wore them and along the top were stuck small green twigs, like a mane, which at a distance must have had the appearance of elegantly waving plumes. From the lower part hung narrow strips of white *tapa* like a beard. King remarks that they only saw these masks worn twice and both times by a number of people together in a canoe who came alongside the ship, 'laughing and drolling with an air of masquerade'. A much later reference to them indicates that they were worn by men working for the priests as Ogpu or dreaded secret police. According to this source† these were the men who brought in the human sacrifices as they were needed in the temple.

Cook's meeting with Kalaniopuu had a most favourable effect: from this moment on the Hawaiians and the sailors fraternized completely unarmed. The officers from both ships went daily up country in small parties or even singly and frequently remained out the whole night. They were never able to penetrate further than twenty miles on account of the roughness of the terrain. One party who tried to climb the great Mauna Loa had a hard time of it. The paths cut through the dense undergrowth were very narrow and continually they found their way blocked by enormous fallen trees over which they had to climb. The second night out there was no water and they were obliged to drink from a wine-red puddle in the bottom of an unfinished canoe. During the night they nearly froze and the next day the going was

* King is wrong here, for the Hawaiians did possess wooden stamps, though they often executed their designs free hand.

† *The Return of Lono* by O. A. Bushnell, Boston, Little, Brown & Co., 1956.

even worse; a great lava flow lay across their path, its gaping fissures slippery with moss which made them stumble. They threw stones down several of the chinks and listened with alarm to the distant clatter of their fall. At this point the native guides refused to go on, an ultimatum that probably saved all their lives.

For the ten days that the ships had been anchored in the bay everything had been going very well. Then, by degrees, imperceptible to the explorers, the situation began to deteriorate. Episode followed episode. There seemed to be an inevitability about the way things happened, almost as if the fates had decreed the end. The following events must be seen in retrospect for the explorers were still unaware of the rôle they were playing and never realized, even after Cook's death, the motivation of the crime – at least to us a crime but hardly to be judged so from the natives' point of view.

The first cloud must have been the death of William Watman, a gunner. He was an old man and King says much respected on account of his attachment to Cook. He had been with Cook on this second voyage and was to have accompanied him in his appointment at Greenwich. He had apparently suffered several strokes and finally one, more severe than the rest, carried him off. There was no reason for Cook to conceal his death and hearing of it Kalaniopuu requested that the man should be buried at the foot of the *marae* walls. Cook gratefully conceded, himself reading the burial service. The solemn rites no doubt impressed the natives but what perhaps impressed them more was the fact that their guests were not immortal. There is no evidence to go on and it is only in the light of subsequent events that one supposes this to be the moment when a certain resistance took seed. The warrior nobles, less amenable to the influence of the priests and jealous of their own authority, might easily have resented this much fêted stranger in their midst. The two ships had been a terrific drain on the island, provisions had been poured into them with lavish prodigality. What if, in the end, after great sacrifices to themselves, Lono's return had been nothing but an act of wishful thinking on the part of the priests? It is the vaguest shadow but one that must be taken into consideration just the same.

King admits that Kalaniopuu and his chiefs 'had, for some days past, been very inquisitive about our departure'. They were obviously nervous about the question of supplies. Cook, anyhow, had already set their date of sailing and preparations were in hand.

Among their needs was fuel. 'The ships being in great want of it,' writes King, 'the Captain desired me to treat with the priests for the purchase of the rail that surrounded the top of the *marae*. I must confess, I had at first some doubts about the decency of this proposal and was apprehensive that even the bare mention of it might be considered by them as a piece of shocking impiety. In this, however, I found myself mistaken. Not the smallest surprise was expressed at the application and the wood was readily given even without stipulating for anything in return. Whilst the sailors were taking it away I observed one of them carrying off a carved image; and, on further inquiry, I found that they had conveyed to the boats the whole semi-circle. Though this was done in the presence of the natives who had not shown any mark of resentment at it but had even assisted them in their removal. I thought it proper to speak to Pu'ou on the subject; who appeared very indifferent about the matter and only desired that we would restore the centre image.'

Even this strange act of vandalism, so unlike Cook's general behaviour, had no immediate repercussion. The day before their departure Kalaniopuu invited Cook to the place where he resided and King says they were 'astonished at the value and magnitude of their presents which far exceeded everything of the kind we had seen either at the Friendly or Society Islands'.

On the morning of February 4th the ships drew up anchor and sailed out of the bay followed by a great number of canoes.

Cook intended to finish surveying Hawaii and map the other islands before proceeding once more to the north, but as ill luck would have it the ships were caught in a gale that blew so violently that the fore and main topsails were split. They plunged all night in a merciless sea and at daybreak on the 8th discovered that the *Resolution*'s foremast had given way under the strain. Cook was undecided whether he should sail on and risk finding a harbour on one of the islands to the leeward where the repairs could be made or return to Kealakekua Bay, impoverished already as far as provisions were concerned, and where he knew that he had already outstayed his welcome. It was decided in the end that they should return, a decision that was to cost the Captain his life.

[Chapter 24]

The Fatal Morning

HOW DIFFERENT the ships' return from their first arrival; no crowds, no welcoming natives on the beach. Everything was silent. Here and there a canoe stole close along the shore. They soon found out the reason; Kalaniopuu was absent and had left the bay under taboo. The priests, however, received them with as much friendliness as before and the *heiau* was turned over to them as a place of repairs for the damaged mast.

Hearing of their return Kalaniopuu hurried back and removed the taboo but the natives' dispositions had changed. The officer commanding a watering party reported trouble with some chiefs who had ordered off the natives helping the sailors roll the casks down to the beach. Thefts followed and the capturing of a canoe in reprisal caused a scuffle on the beach in which a chief was knocked down. Cook was annoyed at what had happened, afraid that this kind of behaviour would oblige him to use some violent measures. King tells us that armed guards were posted that night at the *heiau*, 'their former confidence in the natives being much abated'.

During the night of February 13th the *Discovery*'s cutter was dragged off silently from the buoy where it had been swamped to protect it from the sun. Cook had to take strong measures as the cutter could not possibly be replaced and was too serious a loss to be taken lightly. King reminds us that it had been the usual practice 'whenever anything of consequence was lost at any of the islands in this ocean to get the king or some of the principal chiefs on board and keep them as hostages till it was restored. This method which had been always attended with success our Captain meant to pursue on the present occasion'. Cook also gave orders that any canoe attempting to leave the bay should be stopped. In case he could not recover the cutter peaceably, these were to be seized and destroyed. The stolen boat belonged to the *Discovery* and not the *Resolution* and Cook, according to Burney, wanted Clerke to go 'and exact retributions from the king', but Clerke's health forced him to excuse himself, obliging Cook to undertake the job, thus adding to the extraordinarily unfortunate sequence of events.

While King was posted to Napoopoo to quiet the priests at the *heiau* and guard that end of the bay, Cook himself was to land with a small armed force to procure Kalaniopuu.

Cook left the *Resolution* in a pinnace at about seven o'clock with Molesworth Philips, the lieutenant of marines, and nine of his men, accompanied by a launch under the command of John Williamson.

The fairest account of the actual tragedy is thought to be that of Samwell, the surgeon of the *Discovery*. King's account of course is the official one based on Molesworth Philips' report. Philips was on the spot, while Samwell with Clerke only watched through a telescope from the decks of their ship lying about a quarter of a mile off the shore. They must anyhow all have gone over the events together countless times and Samwell's is the most vivid.

Cook landed with his marines at the upper end of Kalaniopuu's village, 'the natives immediately flocked round as usual and showed him the customary marks of respect by prostrating themselves before him. There were no signs of hostility or much alarm among them. Captain Cook, however, did not seem willing to trust to appearances; but was particularly attentive to the disposition of the marines and to have them keep clear of the crowd. He first inquired for the king's sons, two youths who were very much attached to him and generally his companions on board. Messengers being sent for them, they soon came to him and informed him that their father was asleep at a house not far from them; he accompanied them thither and took the marines along with them. As he passed along the natives everywhere prostrated themselves before him and seemed to have lost no part of that respect they had always shown to his person'. Two chiefs had joined the procession and helped keep the crowds at bay. 'Being ignorant of his intention in coming on shore they frequently asked him if he wanted any hogs or other provisions; he told them that he did not and that his business was to see the king. When he arrived at the house he ordered some of the natives to go in and inform Kalaniopuu that he waited without to speak to him. They came out two or three times and instead of returning any answer from the king presented some pieces of red cloth to him which made Captain Cook suspect that he was not in the house; he therefore desired the lieutenant of marines to go in.' This must have seemed rather high-handed behaviour to the chiefs and the people crowded outside, but nothing was said. 'The lieutenant found the old man just awakened from sleep and seemingly alarmed at the message; but he came out without any hesitation. Captain Cook took him by the hand and in a friendly manner asked him to go on board to which he readily consented.'

It was quite obvious that the village of Kaawaloa had heard nothing as yet of the loss of the cutter, in other words Kalaniopuu had had nothing to do with the theft. 'Captain Cook expressed himself a little surprised, saying that as the inhabitants appeared innocent of stealing the cutter he should not violate them but that he must get the king on board.'

Kalaniopuu's behaviour showed that he had perfect confidence in Cook and was entirely friendly whether he believed in the Lono theory or not. But the crowd was distinctly nervous and obviously mistrusted Cook's intentions towards their chief. No word was spoken but the natives 'were observed arming themselves with long spears, clubs and daggers and putting on thick mats which they use as armour'. At this moment a man came running up the beach waving his arms and shouting. 'It is war,' he cried, 'it is war, they have killed a chief!' One of the *Discovery*'s guard boats had fired at a canoe attempting to leave the bay and killed a man.

Given this latest development one might have supposed that Cook would have given up all thought of persuading Kalaniopuu into the pinnace, but he still held the old man by the hand and was just approaching the water's edge when the king's favourite wife flung her arms around Kalaniopuu's neck, entreating him not to go, wailing that he would surely be killed. Several of the chiefs joined in forcing him to sit down, insisting that he stay where he was. The crowd were now openly hostile. Philips was attacked by one of the chiefs who tried to stab him, but Philips warded off the blow with the butt of his musket. Before he could stab again Cook had fired at the native and killed him. Immediately a general attack began with a shower of stones. The marines and boatmen retaliated by a discharge of musketry. 'The islanders,' King tells us, 'contrary to the expectation of everyone stood the fire with great firmness and before the marines had time to reload they broke in upon them with dreadful shouts and yells. What followed was a scene of the utmost horror and confusion.' As no more is heard of them, it is supposed that Kalaniopuu and his sons had withdrawn as the confusion began, leaving a crowd of his relations, attendants and chiefs on the scene.

King, isolated at the other end of the bay, hearing all the firing and aware of the bustle, must have been suffering agonies of suspense. 'Where a life so dear and valuable was concerned, it was impossible not to be alarmed. But, besides this, I knew that a long and uninterrupted course of success in his transactions with the natives of these seas had given the Captain a degree of confidence that I was always fearful might, at some unlucky moment, get him too much off his guard.'

According to King, Cook was last seen distinctly standing at the water's edge calling out to the boats to cease firing and to pull in. 'If it be true, as some of those who were present have imagined, that the marines and boat-men had fired without his orders and that he was desirous of preventing any further bloodshed, it is not improbable that his humanity on this occasion proved fatal to him. For it was remarked that whilst he faced the natives none of them had offered him any violence but that having turned about to give his orders to the boats he was stabbed in the back and fell with his face into the water.'

Let us turn now to Samwell who actually saw his death through the glasses. Four of the marines had been killed and the rest, some of them badly wounded, floundered out to the pinnace which Roberts had brought in as close to the shore as possible without grounding it, and managed to clamber on board. It was at this moment, says Samwell, that Williamson 'in command of the launch, instead of pulling in to the assistance of Captain Cook, withdrew his boat farther off'. Williamson's claim that he had mistaken the signal probably cost Captain Cook his life. 'The business of saving the marines out of the water in consequence of that fell altogether upon the pinnace; which thereby became so much crowded that the crew were in a great measure prevented from using firearms or giving what assistance they otherwise might have done to Captain Cook; so that he seems, at the most critical point of time, to have wanted the assistance of both boats owing to the removal of the launch.' It was said afterwards that the men in Williamson's boat, maddened at their inaction, tried to move close in to shore but that Williamson threatened to shoot the first man who fired a shot.

Sir Maurice Holmes in his introduction to Samwell's narrative mercilessly writes that 'the upshot of all the evidence is that though it is not possible to assert that resolute action on Williamson's part would have saved the Captain's life, his complete inaction sealed his fate. . . . In seeking a reason for his extraordinary conduct apart from his puerile excuse that he misunderstood a signal it is not necessary to look beyond anxiety to save his own skin. After the battle of Camperdown Williamson, who commanded the *Agincourt*, was court-martialled for "disaffection, cowardice, disobedience to signals and not having done his duty in rendering all assistance possible". He was found guilty on the third and fourth counts and sentenced to be "placed at the bottom of the list of Post-Captains and be rendered incapable of ever serving on board of any of His Majesty's ships".'*

Disconnected events had fallen together with disastrous results; first Clerke's ill health, then the news of a chief's having been killed arriving just as Cook was about to embark, and now Williamson's – to put it in its most favourable light – cowardly irresolution.

Samwell says Cook now stood alone on the sloping rocks; 'he was

* *Captain Cook and Hawaii*, David Magee, San Francisco, 1962.

observed making for the pinnace, holding his left hand against the back of his head to guard it from the stones and carrying his musket under the other arm. A native was seen following him but with caution and timidity; for he stopped once or twice as if undetermined to proceed. At last he advanced upon him unawares and, with a large club, or common stake, gave him a blow on the back of the head and then precipitously retreated'. Burney here interrupts to say that being no swimmer and stunned by the blow, Cook turned towards the shore instead of trying to make for deeper water. Samwell simply tells us that Cook fell on his hand and one knee and dropped his musket; 'as he was rising and before he could recover his feet another native stabbed him in the back of the neck. He then fell into a bit of water about knee-deep where others crowded upon him and endeavoured to keep him under; but struggling very strongly with them he got his head up and casting his look towards the pinnace seemed to solicit assistance. Though the boat was not above five or six yards distance from him, yet from the crowded and confused state of the crew it seems it was not in their power to save him. The natives got him under again but in deeper water: he was, however, able to get his head up once more and being almost spent in the struggle he naturally turned to the rock and was endeavouring to support himself by it when a savage gave him a blow with a club and he was seen alive no more. They hauled him up lifeless on the rocks where they seemed to take a savage pleasure in using every barbarity to his dead body, snatching the daggers out of each other's hands to have the horrid satisfaction of piercing the fallen victim of their barbarous rage'.

The fatal accident happened at eight o'clock in the morning, about an hour after Cook had landed. Samwell says that the native who first stabbed him was called Nooah, whom he had met with Kalaniopuu. 'I was induced to take particular notice of him, more from his personal appearance than any other consideration, though he was of high rank and a near relation of the king: he was stout and tall, with a fierce look and demeanour and one who united in his figure the two qualities of strength and agility in a greater degree than I ever remember to have seen before in any other man. His age might be about thirty and by the white scurf on his skin and his sore eyes he appeared to be a hard drinker of *kava*.'

When the boats pulled away from the beach, the *Resolution*'s big guns which only then could come into play opened up on the howling crowd, eventually dispersing it. King tells us that a small boat manned by four or five young midshipmen started out to pick up the bodies left behind on the beach, but as their ammunition was nearly spent and as they were so small a force, they returned to the ship leaving their dead in the possession of the islanders. Samwell finds this disgraceful and affirms that at that moment they could easily have been gathered in, but given the circumstances, it would seem almost impossible for the midshipmen to have acted otherwise.

One can imagine the men's feelings when they finally realized that they had lost their commander. It must have taken some time for the dreadful news to be fully appreciated. Samwell does not even try to describe their reactions. No man, he tells us, was ever more beloved or admired by his people. King, probably Cook's favourite, was completely stunned; 'how shall I attempt to paint the horror with which we were struck and the universal dejection and dismay which followed so dreadful and unexpected a calamity'. For so long, he says, they had felt secure in his skill and consoled in their hardships by his tenderness and humanity. King attempts to philosophize, arguing that 'his death as far as regards himself cannot be reckoned premature since he lived to finish the great work for which he seems to have been designed'. Indeed, his Hawaiian slayers may perhaps have dealt him a merciful blow, for he might have found England and Greenwich Hospital intolerably confined after the vast spaces of the Pacific. But these thoughts were cold comfort for those left behind.

Order and some plan of procedure had now to be established for the two ships. In spite of his condition Clerke was forced by seniority to take over command and removed accordingly to the *Resolution*, appointing Lieutenant Gore to captain the *Discovery*. A meeting was then held and it was decided that they must demand the restoration of the cutter and the return of Cook's body and that 'some vigorous steps should be taken in case the demand of them was not immediately complied with'.

It was to take a week of patient negotiation to recover Cook's remains. The cutter they were never to retrieve 'for she had been broken up for the nails she contained'.

Much against the opinion of some it was happily decided that pacific measures were to be adopted rather than any active hostility. King writes that 'it was justly urged that the mischief was done and irreparable', besides which 'the natives had a strong claim to our regard on account of their former friendship and kindness; and the more especially as the late melancholy accident did not appear to have arisen from any premeditated design'. Kalaniopuu was also exonerated. 'His ignorance of the theft, his readiness to accompany Captain Cook on board and his having actually sent his two sons into the boat must free him from the smallest degree of suspicion.' As to the conduct of his women and the chiefs 'this might easily be accounted for from the apprehensions occasioned by the armed force with which Captain Cook came on shore and the hostile preparations in the bay'. To these motives of humanity others of a prudential nature were added; 'that we were in want of water and other refreshments: that our foremast would require six or eight days of work before it could be stepped: that the spring was advancing apace; and that the speedy prosecution of our next northern expedition ought now to be our sole object: that therefore to engage in a vindictive contest with the inhabitants might not only lay us under the imputation of unnecessary cruelty but would occasion an unavoidable delay in the equipment of the ships.'

The Hawaiians, of course, failed to understand their visitors' behaviour. Hourly expecting some fearful retribution, they prepared accordingly. They had already attacked the men working on the repairs at the *heiau*, but King with reinforcements from the ships had managed to beat them off and assisted by some of the priests had made a truce during which the articles on shore were got off.

All night fires flickered and shell trumpets sounded in the villages above the face of the cliff. Reinforcements were seen marching over the hills, 'while a prodigious concourse of natives still kept possession of the shore'. Kalaniopuu had apparently retired to a cave in the mountains where he remained, having his food let down to him by cords. King tells us that their lenient behaviour gave the natives a very poor opinion of their courage; 'for they could have but little notion of the motives of humanity that directed it'. Some of the natives were brazen enough to paddle out in their canoes within pistol shot of the ships and 'insult us by various marks of contempt or defiance'. It was with great difficulty that the officers restrained the sailors from firing at them. One man had the audacity to parade about wearing Captain Cook's hat, at the same time flinging stones at the ships. This was more than the men could bear. Clerke allowed them to fire the great guns 'which boomed out towards the shore expressing their impotent rage'. He also promised the crew that if they met with any trouble the next day at the watering-place 'they should be left at liberty to chastise them'. Incidents did occur and King, on duty somewhere else, was not there to restrain the men who in retribution fired the whole village including the houses of the priests who had always remained their friends. Grisly trophies were brought back to the ships.

There had always been women on board the ships and the morning of Cook's death had been no exception. But strangely they had remained. King says they never offered to leave 'nor discovered the smallest apprehension either for themselves or their friends ashore. So entirely unconcerned did they appear that some of them who were on deck when the village was in flames seemed to admire the sight and frequently cried out that it was very fine'.

77. A Hawaiian temple image.
'The great grimacing heads are all the same.' (*page 264*)

78. The Hawaiians were tattooed but generally in squares and lines and generally on the hands and near the groin. Plate 85 in 'Voyage autour du Monde' by Louis Claude Desauler de Freycinet, Paris, 1825, drawn by Jacques Arago. (*page 268*)

79. Head of a Hawaiian feather god and thought to be the image Kamehameha I carried around with him and the one to which he prayed as he died.
(*page 266*)

80. Hawaiian warriors wearing their gourd helmets.
Engraved by C. G. Rignion after J. Webber. (*page 269*)

81. The Hawaiian ladies are very fond of feather necklaces.
Engraved by J. K. Sherwin after J. Webber. (*page 268*)

82. The rare *mamo* or *Drepanis pacifica*. Plate from *The Birds of The Sandwich Islands* by Scott Wilson. (*page 267*)

83. A copper plaque indicating the approximate spot where he fell. (*page 281*)

84. It would seem that I was fated never to see Kealakekua Bay under a blue sky, always these lurid, dramatic lighting effects. (*page 280*)

The night following the fire happened to be particularly dark and at about eight a canoe was heard paddling towards the *Resolution*. In it were two priests who, crying out that they were friends, came alongside and clambering on board, presented Clerke with a small bundle containing, they informed the Captain, all that remained of Captain Cook's body. The rest had been cut up and burned, all except for the head and the bones which were in the possession of Kalaniopuu and the other chiefs. What they saw now had been given to Pu'ou and this he had sent out surreptitiously as a proof of his friendship. The Englishmen did not understand at the time, but this form of dismemberment was the usual procedure when an important chief died. Cook's body, according to Hawaiian custom, had been treated with the greatest respect and honour.

Anxious days followed with skirmishes between watering parties sent ashore under cover of the ships' guns and the natives. After a series of unfortunate episodes the Hawaiians seem to have understood 'that it was not the want of ability to punish them which had made us tolerate their provocation'. On the evening of the 18th a chief came bearing presents from Kalaniopuu, suing for peace. The presents were received but the chief was made to understand that until Captain Cook's remains had been restored no peace could be granted.

Early in the morning of the 20th 'we saw a great number of people descending the hill which is over the beach'. They wound slowly down preceded by two drummers and, depositing their offerings on the sand, retired. Soon afterwards Kalaniopuu's emissary appeared in a long plumed cloak 'bearing something with great solemnity in his hand; and having placed himself on a rock made signs for a boat to be sent him'.

Presuming the chief's offering to be Cook's remains Captain Clerke went himself in the pinnace to receive them. The royal emissary came forward carrying his burden covered over with a spotted cloak of black and white feathers. Refusing to hand it over, he stepped into the pinnace, motioning to Captain Clerke that he would accompany him as far as the *Resolution*. Once arrived he could not be persuaded to come on board, probably choosing, as King writes, not to be present when the bundle was opened.

It must have been a harrowing moment for those on board. Unwinding folds of fine white *tapa* they found Captain Cook's hands, 'so well known from a remarkable scar on one of them'. Then worse; there was the head, but scalped and mercifully not recognizable. Arms and legs followed but the feet were missing. All showed marks of having been in a fire, except the hands which had the flesh left upon them and were cut in several places 'and crammed with salt, apparently with an intention of preserving them'. They were informed that the lower jaw and the feet had been divided between different chiefs and that Kalaniopuu was making every effort to recover them. They appeared shortly afterwards, brought on board by the King's son along with Captain Cook's shoes and some other trifles that belonged to him.

As King words it: 'nothing now remained, but to perform the last offices to our great and unfortunate commander'. Clerke asked Kalaniopuu's emissary to taboo the bay and running the colours half staff up waited on the setting of the sun. Ten-minute guns boomed out, puffs of white against the metallic sky as the coffin slid into the fiery waters of the bay.

'What our feelings were on this occasion,' writes King, 'I leave the world to conceive; those who were present know that it is not in my power to express them.'

On the evening of the 22nd the chief who had brought Cook's remains rowed out to the *Resolution* and Clerke asked him to lift the taboo. 'The ships were soon surrounded with canoes and many of the chiefs came on board, expressing great sorrow at what had happened and their satisfaction at our reconciliation. Several of our friends who did not visit us sent presents of large hogs and other provisions.' They were never to see Kalaniopuu again.

'About eight in the evening we dismissed all the natives.' Affectionate farewells were exchanged and immediately they weighed anchor and stood out of the bay. 'The natives were collected on the shore in great number; and as we passed along, received our last farewell with every mark of affection and good will.' The closing scene speaks very well for both the Hawaiians and the British.

A whitewashed obelisk now stands at the far end of the bay in memory of the great circumnavigator. It can be reached from land only by a rugged four-mile trek down the side of the cliff so I had made arrangements to approach by water. A young Filippino named Juan was to meet me at the Napoopoo jetty and paddle me across.

It was to be yet another overcast morning. It would seem that I was fated never to see Kealakekua Bay under a blue sky, but always with these lurid and dramatic lighting effects. Leaden clouds lay in bands parallel to the horizon, casting grey shadows on the flat sea. Far beyond, between the clouds and the distant hills, cumuli had gathered like static wadding modelled by a sulphuric sun.

Of course, Juan was not at the landing. We eventually found his house, a tumbledown shack perched on stilts over an eruption of volcanic rock. We called him and he appeared through a curtain of creepers trailing over his roof, not young at all but a toothless old man in his late sixties. Yes, he knew about the boat. Another short drive over crunching cinder and we came to a cove in which he kept his outrigged canoe. It had a small outboard motor attached to it and was painted bright orange. The waters were oily and heaving as we spanked our way noisily over to the monument, the sea-birds screeching mournfully as they wheeled, white specks against the towering cliffs.

The monument stands on a platform guarded by chains looped between gun-barrel posts topped with cannon balls. An inscription informs us that it was erected in 1874 by the Australian Commonwealth. Undaunted by the chains, cows were browsing at the foot of the obelisk. Some way from here is a square copper plaque fixed to the rocks, indicating the approximate spot where he fell. It was high tide when I first arrived and the letters danced through about a foot of water; 'near this spot Captain James Cook was killed February 14th, 1779'. I thought also of the twenty-five Hawaiians who had died defending – so they believed – their chief.

A family of Hawaiians had chosen this spot for a day's outing. In the meantime the weather had cleared and the men, quite naked except for rubber fins and goggles, were out spear fishing while a fat woman in trousers and a straw hat, probably their mother, stood on one of the rocks hopefully casting, the flick of her nylon line like a strand of Pele's glassy hair against the blueness of the morning.

The well-known 'deaths' and various engravings illustrating the attack certainly do not prepare one for the actual spot. In Zoffany's dramatic rendering Cook agonizes on the ground in the position of the Ludovisi gladiator; his assassins appearing as Greek or Roman warriors rendered by Poussin or David rather than the well-modelled but thickset Hawaiians. His rocks are too high and the topography altogether incorrect. Even Webber's canvas is not accurate for he shows us a milling crowd extending indefinitely into the distance. Palms there might have been in his day but certainly not in the quantity he shows them. The real place is much smaller in scale, less theatrical, and more poignant for its simplicity; or so I found it.

When he was in Kauai the previous year Cook ironically described the type of dagger with which he was later slain. Contemporary accounts would have us believe that it was made of iron, but it was wooden; 'a sort of weapon,' Cook writes, 'which we had never seen before . . . about a foot and a half long, sharpened at one or both ends, and secured to the hand by a string. Its use is to stab in close fight, and it seems well adapted to the purpose.'

I had just returned from Kauai and was having tea one day with a well-known local character in Honolulu. While sitting on the lawn in front of her house looking out over Diamond Head and talking about her collection of Oceania, she casually asked me if I had seen the Cook dagger in the Bishop Museum. I had not. There were three known daggers, she told me, one of which she possessed but unfortunately did not keep at her Honolulu house. Annoyed at having missed the museum's specimen I returned the next morning, having made an appointment with Mr Bryan, the curator. 'Captain Cook's daggers,' he laughed, 'are as numerous as locks of Charles I's hair. Besides, there is no evidence whatever for believing any one dagger to have been the fatal instrument.' He offered, however, to show me the kind of weapon he believed was used. The reserve in the basement was stacked high with accoutrements of war, among them some forty daggers on the Hawaiian shelf; lengths of smoothly polished wood with pointed ends like a large peg. Twisted coir hung in a loop from a small hole drilled in the top, forming a noose through which the warriors would pass their wrists – exactly as Cook had described it.

The *Resolution* and the *Discovery* had been at sea now for nearly four years and were in very poor condition. Their rigging had rotted and both ships leaked considerably. The new commander was a dying man. Normally a ship in such circumstances would have set course for home but these were sailors trained by Cook. They had such respect for their dead captain that it never entered their heads not to carry out his original intentions. Cook, in fact, was still in command.

The ships stayed in the Sandwich group until the middle of March, mapping the remainder of the islands, and then sailed for Petropavlousk, better known as the harbour of St Peter and St Paul, in Avacha Bay, Kamehata, where preparations were to be made for the summer voyage north.

They again passed through Bering Strait, but there was no question of finding a passage for everywhere they were blocked by deep masses of ice. It was considered futile to make any further effort and Captain Clerke, who was by this time a living skeleton, at last abandoned the struggle. They repassed Bering Strait and on August 22nd Clerke died.

In the afternoon of the 24th the *Resolution* with her ensign half staff up-anchored once more in the harbour of St Peter and St Paul and was followed soon after by the *Discovery*. By December 1st they were off the Macoa Roads where they first heard that war had broken out with France and Spain and that the conflict with the American Colonies continued; 'which,' writes Burney, 'gave us some apprehension of being captured in our progress homeward'. They did not know that the respective governments with which England was at war had, out of respect for Cook, issued orders for their free passage. Benjamin Franklin signed the pass for the North American States.

Finally, the ships came to anchor off Yarmouth on September 30th, arriving at Deptford on October 6th.

Thus ended the most extraordinary series of voyages ever likely to be undertaken by one man, a man who surely must be counted the most illustrious navigator of any age. No previous explorer had remained at sea for such long periods or brought back so much accurate knowledge from so vast an area. The expeditions had been both difficult and dangerous, and yet not once in his journals does Cook play the hero. Modestly, in simple direct language, he notes the facts and lets his readers draw their own conclusions.

Lord Sandwich tells us that the King shed tears on hearing of his death. It would seem almost certain that Cook would have received a knighthood. A grateful government awarded Mrs Cook a pension and allowed her a share in the proceeds of the journals. The family was also granted a coat of arms, said to be the last ever bestowed in recognition of service. It shows a sphere revolving on an azure shield between the two polar stars; Cook's tracks traced thereon in red lines. The crest was an arm bowed in the uniform of a Captain of the Royal Navy, the hand holding the Union Jack encircled by a wreath of palms and laurels. Cannons, flags and oak leaves rounded out the composition through which was threaded a ribbon bearing his motto: *Nil intentatem relinquit.*